ASIAN STUDIES ASSOCIATION OF AUSTRALIA
Southeast Asia Publications Series

NO. 13
INDONESIA: THE RISE OF CAPITAL

ASIAN STUDIES ASSOCIATION OF AUSTRALIA
Southeast Asia Publications Series

EDITORIAL COMMITTEE

INDONESIA: THE RISE OF CAPITAL

RICHARD ROBISON

A publication of the
Asian Studies Association of Australia

First published in 1986
Allen & Unwin Pty Ltd
8 Napier Street, North Sydney, NSW 2060, Australia

Allen & Unwin (New Zealand) Ltd
60 Cambridge Terrace, Wellington

Allen & Unwin (Publishers) Ltd
18 Park Lane, Hemel Hempstead, Herts HP2 4TE, England

Allen & Unwin Inc.
8 Winchester Place, Winchester, Mass, 01890, USA

National Library of Australia
Cataloguing in Publication entry:

Robison, Richard, 1943–
  Indonesia.

  Bibliography.
  Includes index.
  ISBN 0 04 909024 0.

  1. Capitalism – Indonesia – History – 20th century. 2
Capital – Indonesia. 3. Military government –
Indonesia – Economic aspects. 4. Indonesia – Economic
conditions – 1945–   . 5 Indonesia – History –
1945   . I. Asian Studies Association of Australia.
II. Title (Series: Southeast Asian publications
series; no.13).

330.9598'03

Printed in Singapore
Typeset in the Philippines by Vera-Reyes, Inc.

For Jude

Preface

THE most important revolutionary force at work in the Third World today is not communism or socialism but capitalism. This does not mean that Third World societies are in the process of reproducing the historical experiences of English or American capitalism, replete with the political paraphernalia of bourgeois democracy. Neither does it mean that Third World societies are irrevocably destined for a 'deformed' and dependent variety of capitalism imposed by their relative position in a world economic system.

While there are clearly features common to the process of capitalist development in all Third World countries, the value of 'Third World' as an analytical category is limited when we consider that it groups together countries as diverse as Singapore and Mauritania, Brazil and Bangladesh, Malaysia and El Salvador. In some countries, the capitalist impulse is so weak it barely creates a ripple on the surface of feudal society, whereas others are highly industrialised with developed classes of free wage labour and capitalist. Consequently it is most fruitful to study capitalist revolution within specific historical and social contexts.

The particular form which capitalist revolution takes is conditioned by a complex variety of factors, including the nature of the pre-colonial social structure, the impact of colonialism upon society and economy, the formation and disintegration of classes under colonial rule, the nature of political conflict in the post-colonial period, the country's relationship to the international economy and the extent of its natural resources.

One factor which has proven crucial in determining the nature of capitalist economic and political systems has been the process by which a capitalist class emerges. Bourgeois democracy in England, for example, was the political outcome of a process of capitalist revolution under the political leadership of a powerful domestic bourgeoisie. Fascism and other varieties of authoritarian rule have emerged where the bourgeoisie played a weaker political role. In the Third World the general pattern has been for the state to assume political leadership of the capitalist revolution given the relative weakness of the domestic capitalist class. The bourgeoisie has generally developed within the framework of state-led capitalism in which political ascendancy lies with the officials of the state itself. One of the more interesting questions relating to social and political change in the Third World is whether these state-led capitalist societies constitute a new and enduring historical model or an interlude. Will they be entrenched and refined as capitalism is extended and deepened or will they give way to bourgeois rule as the capitalist class develops?

There have been few studies which focus either directly or indirectly upon development of a capitalist class in Indonesia. This has largely been because the theoretical framework within which most scholars have worked does not include 'capitalism' or 'class' as significant analytical categories. Rather, such scholars have seen change as a process of evolutionary transition from 'tradition' to 'modernity' in which the forces of modernity ('pragmatic' and 'secular', 'rational' and 'legal') wrestle with forces which represent the cultural vestiges of ancient Java: at once charismatic and patrimonial.[1]

For those who have seen class as of some significance, the capitalist class in Indonesia has evoked little real interest except for expressions of regret at its weakness and its maltreatment at the hands of bureaucrats, political parties and the military.[2] Schmitt more or less abandoned hope for the prospect of capitalist revolution and the rise of a capitalist class and looked to a populist form of state capitalism to constitute the driving force of industrialisation and economic growth.[3] There are several very good reasons why this approach was taken. First, most commentators sought a nascent capitalist class among the ranks of indigenous, predominantly Muslim, petty capitalists who were the traders and petty commodity producers of Java and Sumatra,[4] a class which was in fact in decline.

Second, during the 1950s and 1960s one could indeed be forgiven for regarding the emergence of a significant capitalist class as a remote possibility. It took almost two decades after independence for real political and class power to begin to crystallise in the vacuum left by the Dutch. The capitalist revolution in post-colonial Indonesia has become the dominating social and economic force only since the early 1970s.

A third reason is the continuing political dominance of the military which has given the impression of a regime floating above a social vacuum. Without a bourgeois party able to exercise recognisable authority over the apparatus of the state, how could one conceive of a capitalist class of significance? This puzzle led political analysts to such formulations as the 'bureaucratic polity' or the 'technocratic' state which will be dealt with in Chapter 4. Rule by the military or a party of politico-bureaucrats has even puzzled those who have seen class as the basis of social structure and analysis. Such terms as 'Bonapartism', 'bureaucrat bourgeoisie' and 'state class'[5] have been developed to explain the apparent divorce of political and class power.

Finally, little significance has been attached to the capitalist class in Indonesia because observers have tended to define that class in terms of its weakest element, the indigenous capitalists. Foreign and Chinese capitalists have been regarded as being outsiders and therefore, somehow, neither part of a capitalist class in Indonesia or part of the general relationship between state and capital.

Radical scholarship on Indonesia since the mid-1960s has
been very heavily influenced by dependency theory, dividing
the capitalist class in Third World societies into multinational
corporate capital which syphons surplus on behalf of the
metropoles and a weak comprador domestic capitalist class
which facilitates this process. The compradors, however,
are too weak to establish leadership of the capitalist revolution or to determine its nature. Power is therefore vested in
the hands of generals and technocrats who are in turn little
more than the handmaidens of international capital.[6]

In contrast to these interpretations, it is the intention of
this study to demonstrate that a domestic capitalist class and
state-owned capital have been crucial factors in shaping
contemporary Indonesian history. Conflicts between elements of capital, domestic and foreign, indigenous and
Chinese, merchant and industrial, have been a central feature of Indonesian politics for almost eighty years. Perhaps
the primary occupation of the Indonesian state since 1949 has
been to provide the conditions for capital accumulation, and
to intervene in disputes between the different and competing
elements of capital. The very autonomy of the state and its
officials is closely related to the way in which the capitalist
class developed in Indonesia and to the dominance of its
foreign and Chinese elements. More recently, the relationship between state bureaucrats and private capital has developed a complexity and closeness that suggests the formation
of a new social base for state power. Essentially, then, this is
a history of the development of a capitalist class in Indonesia
(focusing on larger corporate elements rather than declining
petty capital), the way in which the state has been involved in
its development and in the general process of capital accumulation and the way in which the very nature of state
power has been shaped by capital.

THE study stretches back into the colonial period because the
social, political and economic legacy of colonialism is crucial

to the post-colonial development of capitalism. We might speculate how different Indonesian capitalism would have been had the Spanish ruled instead of the Dutch and created a colonial economy based on the hacienda and dominated nationally by a consolidated powerful landowning class. Some attention is also given to the period 1949–65 because the state, then under military domination, emerged out of the post-colonial vacuum to establish itself as the central actor in the process of capitalist revolution, politically autonomous of class-based parties.

Chapter 4 is somewhat of a pause in the history because I felt it necessary at this point to try and clarify some of the theoretical confusions about the relationship between state and capital in New Order Indonesia. Chapters 5 and 6 look at the politics of state policy relating to general development strategy and the place of the various elements of capital within this strategy, particularly domestic and international capital.

Chapters 7 to 10 examine the development of the various elements of domestic capital. I have chosen to distinguish here between state-owned, military-owned and private capital. Perhaps the sub-division of private capital into Chinese-owned (Chapter 9) and indigenous-owned (Chapter 10) requires some explanation. Just as the conflict between domestic and foreign capital, state and private capital, has been crucial in shaping Indonesian capitalism, so has conflict between Chinese and indigenous capital. There are important differences in the historical development of the Chinese and indigenous elements of the capitalist class, even though this is further confused by the existence of distinct sub-categories within both. The political relationship of the state with Chinese capital is different from that with indigenous capital. Official legislation to constrain Chinese capital has been a constant feature of Indonesian economic history.

In Chapter 11, I look at some of the factors impinging upon the development of Indonesian capitalism in the 1980s which suggest that some significant changes may be taking place in the relationship between the various elements of capital — and between state and capital.

Finally, I should like to point out that the capitalist revolution in Indonesia is a drawn-out process which has been under way for well over a century. If we define capitalism as a system of production and exchange characterised by specific class structures rather than simply a system of exchange, then it is apparent that the capitalist revolution in Indonesia is uneven and fluctuating. For a significant proportion of Indonesia's rural population the impingement of capitalism is real enough, but has not yet extended down into the realms of production to transform peasants into proletariat and capitalist. Nevertheless, it is capitalism which constitutes the most dynamic social, economic and political force at work in Indonesia today, rapidly and remorselessly uprooting and reshaping the lives of its people. It is within the development of capitalism that we may also find a key to the understanding of political power in contemporary Indonesia because it is within the growing interaction between politico-bureaucrat and capitalist that the genesis of a new ruling class is to be found.

In the writing of this book I was greatly assisted by a large number of people, both directly in terms of discussion of the substance and indirectly in terms of encouragement and hospitality. In particular I would like to thank all those Indonesian colleagues and friends who extended their hospitality and who were patient and thoughtful in explaining the intricacies of the Indonesian political economy. In Australia I would like to thank Bill O'Malley for his friendship and for sharing his room while I was writing part of the manuscript at ANU. Jennifer Brewster and Tony Reid did a meticulous editing job on a rather chaotic manuscript while Jan Bide, Joyce Aavramides, Cynthia Baker and Irene Finlay of Murdoch University all contributed to transforming my byzantine copy into a first class typescript. Murdoch University has given the outside study and research leave necessary for me

PREFACE   xiii

to get the bulk of the writing done and my colleagues at
Murdoch University have provided an environment stimu-
lating for research.

Perth   RICHARD ROBISON

August 1985

1. For a more extensive examination of this question see, R. Robison,
   'Culture, Politics, and Economy in the Political History of the New
   Order', *Indonesia* 31 (1981).
2. For example, L. Castles, 'Socialism and Private Business: The Latest
   Phase', *BIES* 1 (June 1965).
3. H. Schmitt, 'Foreign Capital and Social Conflict in Indonesia', *Econ-
   omic Development & Cultural Change* 10, 3 (1962).
4. Perhaps the focus upon indigenous petty capital was initiated by C.
   Geertz in his, *Peddlers & Princes: Social Change & Economic
   Modernization in Two Indonesian Towns* (Chicago, 1963). A further
   important work in this direction was L. Castles, *Religion, Politics and
   Economic Behaviour in Java: the Kudus Cigarette Industry* (New
   Haven, 1967).
5. The notion of the bureaucratic bourgeoisie is developed by I. G. Shivji,
   Class Struggles in Tanzania (London, 1976). For Bonapartism, see F.
   H. Cardoso, 'Associated Dependent Development: Theoretical &
   Practical Implications', in A. Stepan (ed.), *Authoritarian Brazil* (New
   Haven, 1973). For the notion of a state class, see C. Meillassoux, 'A
   Class Analysis of the Bureaucratic Process in Mali,' *Journal of Devel-
   opment Studies* 6, 2 (1970).
6. R. Mortimer, 'Indonesia: Growth or Development', in R. Mortimer
   (ed.), *Showcase State* (Sydney, 1973).

Contents

Tables

Abbreviations and Glossary

ABRI   Angkatan Bersenjata Republik Indonesia (Indonesian Armed Forces).

Aspri   Asisten Pribadi (Personal Assistant). Referring to the group of generals who were personal assistants to President Suharto to 1974 and who constituted a *de facto* inner cabinet.

AWSJ   *Asian Wall Street Journal*

Bamunas   Badan Musjawarah Pengusaha Nasional. State-sponsored National Council of Businessmen in the Sukarno period.

Banpres   Bantuan Presiden (Presidential Assistance). Development funds controlled by the President.

Bakin   Badan Kordinasi Inteligen (Intelligence Co-ordinating Board) — the major state intelligence body.

Bappenas   Badan Perencanaan Pembangunan Nasional (National Development Planning Board).

BE   Bonus Ekspor. Referring to export bonus certificates issued in the late 1960s to importers and exporters.

bengkok	land traditionally provided to officials in lieu of salary.
Berdikari	Berdiri diatas kaki sendiri (to stand on your own feet). (a) A policy of economic self-sufficiency begun by President Sukarno in the Guided Economy period. (b) A state-owned company which took over the confiscated assets of several private trading companies in 1966. The trading arm of Bulog (see below).
BIES	*Bulletin of Indonesian Economic Studies*
Bimas	Bimbingan Massal. Agricultural extension programme providing credit for farmers for packages of inputs (fertilisers, pesticides and high-yielding seed varieties) for increased rural production.
BIN	Bank Industri Negara
BKPM	Badan Kordinasi Penanaman Modal (Capital Investment Coordinating Board).
BNI	Bank Negara Indonesia
BNPT	Berita Negara Tambahan Perseroan Terbatas (Company registration supplement to the Government Gazette).
Bulog	Badan Urusan Logistik Nasional (National Logistics Board). Responsible for purchase and price stabilisation of basic commodities, especially rice.
bureaucrat-capitalist	A term originally used by the PKI in the 1950s to identify officials with control over state capital and corporations. The term has since been widened beyond state managers of capital to include state officials who use state power to build private corporate groups.

CSIS — Centre for Strategic and International Studies

CTC — Central Trading Company

cukong — A name given to major Chinese businessmen, particularly those in collaboration with leading figures in the state bureaucracy or military.

DPR — Dewan Perwakilan Rakyat (House of People's Representatives) — the Indonesian parliament.

DSP — Daftar Skala Prioritas (Investment Priority Scales).

EOI — Export-oriented industrialisation.

FEER — *Far Eastern Economic Review*

Finek — The Finance and Economic Sections of the military commands.

Gapindo — Gabungan Pembelian Importir Indonesia (Indonesian Importers Association).

Garpri — Gabungan Persatuan Pabrik Rokok Indonesia (Congress of Indonesian Cigarette Manufacturers Associations).

GKBI — Gabungan Koperasi Batik Indonesia (Association of Indonesian Batik Co-operatives).

Golkar — Golongan Karya. State political party under the New Order.

GPS — Gabungan Perusahaan Sejenis (Federation of Homogenous Enterprises).

Guided Democracy — Political system of the period 1960–65 in which the focal point of political power shifted to the President, and parliament was transformed into a nominated body of representatives of 'functional' groups.

Guided Economy	Economic policy in the period 1959–65 which emphasised state direction of the economy, state ownership of capital and economic self sufficiency.
Hankam	Departemen Pertahanan dan Keamanan (Department of Defence and Security).
Hipmi	Himpunan Pengusaha Muda Indonesia (Young Businessmens Association of Indonesia).
HPH	Hak Pengusaha Hutan (Forestry Exploitation Concession).
IBRD	International Bank for Reconstruction and Development — the World Bank
ICN	*Indonesian Commercial Newsletter*
IGGI	Inter-Governmental Group on Indonesia.
Ikini	(National Importers Association).
IMF	International Monetary Fund
Inkopad	Induk Koperasi Angkatan Darat (Army Central Co-operative Board).
Inpres	Instruksi Presiden (Presidential Instruction). Programme for providing finance for infrastructural works at the local level.
IPKI	Ikatan Pendukung Kemerdekaan Indonesia (League of Upholders of Indonesian Freedom).
Ir.	Ingenieur (Engineer, a Dutch academic title).
ISC	Indonesian Service Company.
ISI	Import-substituting industrialization.
ISS	*Indonesian Sociological Studies*
JCA	*Journal of Contemporary Asia*

Kadin	Kamar Dagang dan Industri (Chamber of Trade and Industry).
KAMI	Kesatuan Aksi Mahasiswa Indonesia (Indonesian Students Action Front).
Kapni	Kesatuan Aksi Pengusaha Nasional Indonesia (Indonesian National Businessmens Action Front).
Kensi	Kongres Ekonomi Nasional Seluruh Indonesia (All-Indonesian National Economic Congress).
Keppres	Keputusan Presiden (Presidential Decree)
KIK	Kredit Investasi Kecil. A credit programme providing fixed capital for small and medium scale enterprises.
KMKP	Kredit Moral Kerja Permanen. A credit programme to provide working capital for small and medium scale enterprises.
KNIP	Komite Nasional Indonesia Pusat (Indonesian Central National Committee).
KNPI	Komite Nasional Pemuda Indonesia (Indonesian National Youth Committee).
Kodam	Komando Daerah Militer (Regional Military Command).
Kodim	Komando Distrik Militer (District Military Command).
Kopkamtib	Komando Operasi Pemulihan Keamanan dan Ketertiban (Operations Command to Restore Order and Security).
Kosgoro	Koperasi Serba Usaha Gotong Royong (Mutual Aid All-Purpose Co-operative).
Kostrad	Komando Cadangan Strategis Angkatan Darat (Army Strategic Reserve Command).

KOTI	Komando Operasi Tertinggi (Supreme Operations Command).
kretek	clove cigarette.
LBH	Lembaga Bantuan Hukum (Legal Aid Office).
LNG	Liquified natural gas.
LP3ES	Lembaga Penelitian, Pendidikan dan Penerangan Ekonomi dan Sosial (Institute for Economic and Social Research, Education and Information).
Malari	Malapetaka Januari (January Disaster). Specifically applied to the riots of 15 January 1974 in Jakarta.
Masyumi	Majelis Syuro Muslimin Indonesia (Council of Indonesian Muslim Associations). Modernist Muslim party banned in 1960.
New Order	The Suharto era, 1965 to the present.
NU	Nahdatul Ulama (Muslim Teachers Party).
OPS	Organisasi Perusahaan Sejenis (Organisation of Homogeneous Enterprises).
Opsus	Operasi Khusus (Special Operations)
PD	President Director (of corporation).
PDI	Partai Demokrasi Indonesia (Indonesian Democracy Party). Amalgamation of non-Muslim parties.
Pekuneg	Team Penertiban Keuangan Negara (Team to Regularise State Finances).
pengusaha	businessman/businesswoman
Peperti	Penguasa Perang Tertinggi (Supreme War Authority).
Perabri	Persatuan Purnawirawan ABRI (Union of Retired ABRI Personnel).

peranakan	Indonesian Chinese of mixed ancestry, Indonesia-born.
Pertamina	State-owned oil company.
PKI	Partai Komunis Indonesia (Indonesian Communist Party).
PMA	Foreign Capital Investment Law of January 1967.
PMDN	Domestic Capital Investment Law of July 1968.
P.N.	Perusahaan Negara (State Corporation)
PNI	Partai Nasionalis Indonesia (Indonesian Nationalist Party).
politico-bureaucrat	Individual whose base of power reflects the integration of political power and bureaucratic authority.
PPP	Partai Persatuan Pembangunan (United Development Party). Amalgamation of Muslim parties.
pribumi	indigenous Indonesian.
PSI	Partai Sosialis Indonesia (Indonesian Socialist Party).
P.T.	Perseroan Terbatas (Limited Company).
Pusri	State-owned fertiliser company.
Repelita	Rencana Pembangunan Lima Tahun (Five Year Development Plan). There have been three of these; Repelita I, 1969/70–1973/74, Repelita II, 1974/75–1978/79, Repelita III, 1979/80–1983/84. The current plan is Repelita IV, 1984/85–1988/89.
7th Assistant	The Officer responsible for the financial aspects of the military commands.

TUB   Tri Usaha Bhakti, the business group of the
               army central command.

USPRT   Translations of the Jakarta Press by the Un-
               ited States Embassy's Press Review Transla-
               tion Unit.

YDP   Yayasan Dharma Putra, the business group of
               the Army Strategic Reserve, Kostrad.

Soksi   Swadiri Organisasi Karya Sosialis Indonesia
               (Indonesian Socialist Workers Organisation).

STC   State Trading Corporation.

totok   pure Chinese, China-born Chinese.

PART I

The Historical Context

State and Capital to 1965

1
The Colonial Origins of Indonesian Capitalism

ONE of the most persistent themes developed by economic historians of Dutch colonialism in Indonesia has been that the penetration of capitalism failed to generate an indigenous capitalist economy or an indigenous bourgeoisie. One interpretation, that of Boeke,[1] argues that the capitalist and non-capitalist sectors existed within mutually impervious capsules, constituting a dual economy. Capitalist enterprise which entered Indonesia in the late nineteenth and early twentieth centuries was, according to Boeke, so highly developed that it provided no point of access for a weakly developed indigenous merchant class.

Clifford Geertz argued that the development of agricultural production on state plantations in the mid-nineteenth century entrenched pre-capitalist social structures in Javanese villages, retarding the development of private land-ownership and indigenous entrepreneurship.[2] Further, he argued that the development of Indonesian industrial capitalism was severely retarded by the drain of economic surplus generated within the plantation sector from Indonesia to Holland where it provided the capital for industrial investment.[3] Other writers, such as Onghokham and Sutherland,[4] develop the theme that traditional politico-bureaucratic authority was simultaneously entrenched and integrated into the colonial system with the emergence of the state plantations.

Such approaches imply that the capitalist mode of production may actually entrench, and even depend upon, the continuing existence of pre-capitalist modes for an indefinite period of time.[5] The question whether different modes of production remain insulated and interact or whether one must become dominant has of course long been a central focus of theoretical debate on the nature of social and economic transformation in the Third World in general. Frank[6] and the dependency theorists categorically reject the concept of dualism on the grounds that inclusion in a world capitalist system of exchange renders all elements of a society capitalist. Marxist critics take issue with Frank, arguing that capitalism is defined by relations of production, not by systems of exchange.[7] Consequently, they argue, different modes may co-exist, but not permanently. Capitalism will eventually assert its dominance, although the process may be a fitful, long-term and uneven one involving nothing less than a social revolution, destroying old class structures and political and ideological superstructures and laying down the material base for the emergence of capitalist society.[8]

It is precisely this corrosive and creative revolutionary process which was at work in Indonesia over the 300 years of Dutch colonial rule. Partly because of the relative weakness of Dutch capitalism itself, the process of capitalist revolution in colonial Indonesia was limited. Village subsistence production continued to co-exist with the modern plantation sector, and elements of pre-capitalist political authority operated side by side with the Dutch colonial administration right up until the end of the colonial period. By the end of the colonial era, the Indonesian bourgeoisie was still relatively weakly developed and concentrated in the sector of trade. Its weakness was magnified by the fact that its most important element, the Chinese merchants, were not able to assume a position of legitimate, public, social or political leadership.

Nevertheless, Dutch colonialism did result in fundamental

changes to the pre-capitalist economic and social structures of the Indies which have provided a framework for the intensification of the capitalist revolution in the post-colonial period. Trade and plantation agriculture brought a money economy, wage labour and relatively generalised commodity production. To a large extent, the state became separated from the process of production, while relationships between producers and owners of the means of production became less reliant on political coercion and increasingly economic in nature. A weak class of landowners was consolidated, and a pervasive class of merchants and moneylenders flowed into every pore of the colonial economy.

THE COLONIAL FRAMEWORK

Initially the Dutch were simply one group of traders among Chinese, Gujeratis, Portuguese, Arabs and others — who bought cheap in the Indies and sold dear in other markets. In the 200 years from the beginning of the seventeenth century, the Dutch, organised as the Dutch East India Company (VOC), expanded its control over local rulers by means of military conquest, political alliances and financial arrangements, forcing local rulers to hand over produce, to grant domestic trade monopolies and to yield traditional political rights to land, labour and produce.

Until well into the nineteenth century the forms and relations of production at the grassroots level remained unchanged, with the Dutch merely superimposing themselves upon an existing system of peasant production in which the surplus was extracted by means of political coercion. Under pre-colonial political systems, villagers in the major rice-producing regions were required to provide labour to the rulers and to yield some 40% of village lands (in effect its produce) as tax/rent to the state. For the producers, little changed with the arrival of the Dutch because the VOC simply established its primacy in this existing system of forced labour and forced crop delivery.[9]

This pre-capitalist, mercantile system reached its height in the period 1830–70 in Java, the most heavily populated rice-producing area in the Indies, with the introduction of the cultivation system. The Dutch government (which had replaced the VOC in 1800 and re-established its rule after the British interregnum from 1812 to 1818) established a more sophisticated and co-ordinated refinement of the system of forced crop deliveries. Villagers were forced to allocate 20% of village lands to production of specified commercial crops for delivery to the state and to provide sixty-six days of labour per year to work on these state plantations. This system was organised and supervised by an increasingly regularised apparatus of Dutch and Javanese officials who drew both salaries and commissions.[10] Much of lowland Java was operated as a virtual state sugar plantation, and the value of sugar exports from the Indies in 1840 constituted 77.4% of the total value of exports and remained at 62% as late as 1880.[11]

Beginning in the mid-nineteenth century, the mercantile nature of the colonial economic presence was transformed into an increasingly capitalist enterprise. As a result of the growing strength of the Dutch industrial and financial bourgeoisie, investment in capitalist agriculture involving leasing of land, clearing, planting, building mills and hiring wage labour was now possible. To secure an entry for private capital, the Dutch bourgeoisie first had to dismantle the state mercantile monopoly.[12]

During the latter part of the nineteenth century the colonial state progressively withdrew from direct involvement in the supervision of production and the operation of trade monopolies, to establish the general political and economic conditions for the expansion of private Dutch and other Western capital in Indonesia including an increasingly regularised and complex infrastructure and the provision of fiscal and welfare policy.[13]

The new corporate plantation sector required the drafting of new land legislation in 1870 and 1875 which facilitated long-term leases over 'unused' land (*erfpacht* - up to seventy-five years) and shorter-term leases over village lands (up to twenty-one years). The extent of plantation lands was considerable, and the incursion of estate planting into village land normally used for rice had a significant effect upon village economic structures, particularly in Java. By 1930 the area of land in plantation agriculture was as follows:

TABLE 1.1
AREA OF PLANTATION AGRICULTURE IN 1930
(ha. '000, granted)

	Private Estates	Erfpacht	Held from Native States	Rented from Cultivators	Total
Java	502	680	70	204	1 475
Outer Provinces	2	1 071	1 250		2 324
Total	504	1 751	1 320	204	3 799

Source: Furnivall 1944. p. 312.

Between 1870 and 1949 several important developments occurred in the structure of the corporate plantation sector, the first of which was the increase in the scale of enterprise and the replacement of individual planters by banks and large trading houses as the demands for increased capital investment and vertical economic organisation became heavier. These large trading, banking and planting conglomerates, variously known as the 'big five' or the 'big eight', assumed a dominant role in the Indies economy from the late nineteenth century.[14]

Sugar and coffee, the two big money-earners in the 1800s, began to decline in importance relative to production of petroleum and rubber.[15] Investment in the plantation sector moved from Java to the other islands, and there occurred a significant movement of non-Dutch capital into plantation investment, particularly rubber on Sumatra.[16]

Perhaps the most significant change in the structure of the colonial economy was the disastrous impact of the Depression upon the sugar industry. In 1929, 180 mills produced

3 million tons of sugar and employed 60 000 permanent
hands and over 700 000 temporaries. By 1933, only forty-five
mills worked, and they produced just over half a million
tons.[17] The industry never recovered from this blow, and
with the dismantling of the colonial state apparatus after
1945 the private sugar industry was deprived of the power
required to enforce the complex and onerous land appropria-
tions upon which sugar cultivation, especially in Java, was
based.

Sugar was not the only plantation crop to suffer from the
Depression. In 1933 average export prices were 30% of the
1923–27 average. The amount earned by export sales in 1935
was 25% of that in 1925.[18] In both the rubber and sugar
industries the colonial government negotiated international
pricing and production agreements to maintain prices. In the
case of rubber these were achieved at the cost of significant
reductions in production, the bulk of which were borne by
indigenous small-holders.[19]

Tin and petroleum had become important export earners
by the early twentieth century but manufactures continued to
be imported or produced locally on a small-scale household
basis until the 1930s. Dutch manufacturing investment in
Indonesia to this time had been overwhelmingly concentrated in the processing of agricultural products.[20] With the
reduced export earnings resulting from the crash in prices for
exports, the capacity of the Indies economy to import manufactures was reduced. In addition, European manufacturers,
the traditional suppliers of Indies imports, faced stiff competition from cheap Japanese manufactured imports, both in
the basic cotton cloth used in the textile industry and also in a
wide variety of consumer goods.[21] In 1933 the Dutch passed
a 'Crisis Act' for discriminatory tariff protection against these
imports, but Western manufacturers also established import
substitution industries in Indonesia during the 1920s and
1930s.

British and American capital was concentrated in plantation estates, in petroleum and in large manufacturing ven-

tures including the General Motors assembly plant, Goodyear Tyre and Rubber, British-American Tobacco, Unilever soap and oils, a cement plant at Padang and breweries in both Jakarta and Surabaya. By 1940 the value of industrial produce was f430 million compared to f252 million for mining products and f593 million for estate produce. Domestic investors (mainly Dutch and Chinese) continued to ignore manufacture, with only f27 million private capital investment in manufacture in 1940 out of a total of f1431. Estate infrastructure and petroleum investment still dominated in this category.[22]

Of the gross value of industrial production in the 1930s, 40% was located in the large-scale mechanised sector, 35% in small industry and 25% in cottage industry.[23] The small industry and cottage sector was dominated by Chinese and indigenous capital, but it was the large-scale sector which generated the growth in industrial production. Between 1929 and 1939 f25 million was invested in industries capitalised at over f10 000, of which 15.5% was Dutch, 23.5% originating in Indonesia but mainly Chinese or Dutch, and 61% British, American or other foreign.[24] So already in the 1930s there was emerging a pattern of large-scale, non-Dutch, foreign investment in manufacture.

We may therefore categorise the stages of development of the colonial economy of the Netherlands Indies as follows:

(a)　The seventeenth and eighteenth centuries: spreading political hegemony of the VOC; tightening control of trade monopoly and forced delivery of crops. This was essentially a period of mercantile activity in which the VOC utilised existing political structures to appropriate the surplus of a pre-capitalist mode of production.

(b)　The early to mid-nineteenth century: the Dutch state moved directly into supervision of the production and appropriation process, concentrating the colonial economy upon the production of sugar and coffee in Java.

(c) The late nineteenth century to the 1930 Depression: a period characterised by private corporate plantation production in which the focus shifted from sugar and coffee to rubber and tobacco, and from Java to the Outer Islands. It was also a period in which the state moved from direct involvement in production and appropriation to provision of economic and administrative infrastructure for private capital.

(d) The 1930s: a period characterised by the dramatic decline of the estate sector, especially Javanese sugar (and least of all Sumatran rubber) and the growth of investment in petroleum, tin and medium and large-scale manufacture. It was a period also characterised by the increasing importance of non-Dutch foreign capital.

Quite clearly the Dutch left an economy dominated by Dutch corporate and financial capital. It was an economy still predicated upon the import of manufactures (despite the flurry of import-substitution industrial investment in the 1930s) and the export of primary products (oil, tin, rubber, tobacco). Domestic class structures bore the imprint of this particular colonial framework, and the focus of the remainder of this chapter will be upon the origins of a domestic capitalist class as it developed within this colonial environment.

THE DEVELOPMENT OF AN AGRARIAN BOURGEOISIE

The dominant element of the capitalist class operating in the rural economy of colonial Indonesia was the large Dutch, British and American estate corporations and associated trading and banking institutions. A second element was that of the predominantly Chinese merchant bourgeoisie which developed along with the intrusion of the money economy and commercial agriculture, collecting agricultural produce,

wholesaling and retailing imported commodities, providing
rural credit networks and establishing small manufacturing
enterprises which processed agricultural products. However,
under Dutch colonialism, landownership, land rents or profits
from commercial and/or capitalist farming did not provide a
significant base for capital accumulation and the development of a politically cohesive landowning class comparable
to the *principales* of the Philippines and the landlords of
South Vietnam.[25] There has been no pattern of large landowning families emerging from the countryside of Java or
Sumatra to dominate politics or business at the national level
either during the colonial period or since independence.

It is important to explain the failure of an agrarian landowning bourgeoisie in terms of the specific nature of Dutch
colonialism and the structure of pre-colonial social forma-
tions, especially on Java, the most populous rice-producing
region and the locus of political power. Three major factors
emerge:

(a) The relative weakness of the institution of private
    property in pre-colonial society and the dominance of
    politically secured but alienable rights to use land or
    to appropriate produce and labour.
(b) The continuing importance, under colonial rule, of
    the state in economic activity and the persistence of
    political appropriation as the basis for accumulation.
(c) The use of state power to establish foreign corporate
    capital as the dominant element in the agrarian com-
    mercial economy from the late nineteenth century
    onwards when capitalist production established its
    dominance.

The Failure of a Landowning Bourgeoisie

One of the most crucial developments in the colonial period
was the failure of the Javanese *priyayi*[26] to transform their
traditional rights of appropriation over land, labour and

produce into rights of private ownership on a large scale.
Why did the *priyayi* ignore the possibilities of securing formal ownership over land and directly entering production of
commercial crops? Part of the answer lies in the nature of
economic and political relationships in the pre-colonial Javanese kingdoms. Whereas the institution of private, inherit-
able ownership of land was the basis of the power of the
European feudal aristocracy, the Javanese nobility based
their power upon access to rights to labour and produce
allocated by the king in the form of appanage benefices. Now
it is true that appanage benefices (*lungguh*) tended to become hereditary and that in the regions close to the capital
(*nagaragung*) the nobility sometimes assumed a proprietory
relationship to land and lived upon their benefice lands much
like feudal lords. However, many benefice holders in the
nagaragung remained within the court, appointing officials
(*bekel*) to collect their tribute from the 'appanages'. Beyond
the *nagaragung*, the outlying land, the *mancanegara*, was
administered by officials (*bupati*) appointed by the chief
minister of the king and required to administer the collection
of taxes. This was done through a network of officials appointed by the *bupati* and rewarded with rights to labour and
produce from specified lands (*bengkok*). The most important
of these was the village headman (*lurah*). Again there was a
tendency for the offices of *bupati* and *lurah* to become
hereditary.[27] While the differences between feudalism and
the pre-colonial Javanese social formation are not as clear
cut as might appear on the surface, it is nevertheless apparent that private and hereditary land ownership was not as
clearly institutionalised in Java as it was in Europe.

The essence of this difference lies in the fact that appanage
benefices and official position were granted and terminated
by the king and were never widely institutionalised as a legal
right. The continuing centrality of the king as the personal
dispenser of benefices, and in turn of the nobles and higher
officials as dispensers of lesser benefices, gave politics a
special character of personalised hierarchial relationships.

Networks of political loyalties focused around personal attachment to individual leaders and dispensers of benefices whose political fortunes decided the fate of a host of clients.[28]

The difference was also emphasised by the fact that abundant land and a small population gave the peasants a decided advantage over officials and landowners, forcing the *priyayi* to concentrate on the control of labour rather than land. As Onghokham points out:

> Mataram's land locked character and absence of money economy strengthened another feature, controlling men was more important than owning land. This was reflected in the ideology of *kawulagusti* or in today's terms of patron and client. With land relatively abundant and population scarce, one's leadership over men became the basis of political, military and, more importantly economic power rather than the possession of land itself.[29]

VOC rule in the seventeenth and eighteenth centuries brought the produce of the Indies onto the world market, but although some private land grants were given, land under VOC control was leased by Dutch or Chinese agents or administered by *priyayi* officials as an exercise in the collection of forced crop deliveries and in the supervision of compulsory labour. Far from introducing capitalist relations of production, the VOC reinforced the existing mode of accumulation through the exercise of political power and shored up the authority of the *priyayi*.

The period 1800 to 1830 appears to have been a watershed for the *priyayi*. Under Raffles, and later as a result of the land grants of 1830, several regents were given significant grants of land, and Onghokham notes that regents in the *pasisir* (North Coast of Java) and in the western *mancanegara* enjoyed large incomes from the cultivation of rice and sugar.[30] It would appear, however, that until late in the nineteenth century production still depended upon the political claims of the regent/landowners to labour and land rather than upon economic relationships involving rent or wage labour. The

majority of regents rejected the 1830 offer of grants of land in
favour of a combination of salaries, a percentage commission
on crops cultivated for the Dutch and traditional tributary
rights over the peasantry. By doing so, the *priyayi* chose the
state rather than private landholdings as the basis of their
economic and political position. Consequently they were to
develop as a class of politico-bureaucrats rather than as a
class of large landowners.

Although in retrospect their decision may appear ques-
tionable, at the time substantial incomes were still afforded
by the salary/commission/tribute combination, and Onghokham reports that *bupati* of Madiun were able to maintain
standards of living as grand as those of the landowning
regents of North Java.[31] Opportunities were also given to
both *priyayi* and local officials to secure the best land as
bengkok in the course of the redefinition of village boundaries which accompanied the cultivation system.[32] Economic
activities were conceived in terms of the financial and political costs of maintaining a household rather than capital
accumulation and expanded reproduction. The exercise of
state power remained the most effective means of securing
wealth in early nineteenth century Indonesia.[33] Most important were the political benefits of choosing to act as the
political and administrative agents of the Dutch. The social
and political position of the *priyayi* came to be guaranteed by
the Dutch colonial government. In particular, the Dutch
recognised the office of chief *bupati* (regent) as hereditary,
giving such officials greater security than they had hitherto
enjoyed.

From 1830 onwards, the *priyayi* were progressively integrated into the machinery of the colonial state and divested
of their traditional rights of tribute from the peasantry. This
process was accelerated as the function of the state began to
change from that of enforcing crop deliveries and corvée
service to that of providing the conditions of existence (infrastructure and general policy) for the Dutch bourgeoisie. In
1868, cultivation percentages for *priyayi* ceased and officials

of the colonial state were placed on a fully salaried basis.

By the end of the colonial period, the *priyayi* were essentially officials in the service of the Dutch colonial administration. Only in isolated cases had they transformed their traditional rights to land, labour and produce into private land title and commercial agricultural production. They had become colonial officials rather than capitalist farmers.

Nevertheless, within the villages the development of classes took place rapidly with the onset of the corporate plantation system. From 1875 onwards, the tension between communal and private landownership in Java was gradually being resolved in favour of the latter, with the introduction of legislation providing for the conversion of 'native possession' into private ownership.[34] In West Sumatra, Schrieke[35] also drew attention to the breakdown in communal control over land and the gradual conversion to private ownership which followed the introduction of money taxation and the abandonment of compulsory coffee cultivation in 1908 and the ending of the rice export embargo in 1912.

By the 1920s, it was clear that the corporate plantation economy and the attendant development of the money economy was creating a concentration of economic power in villages, increasing debt, landlessness and wage labour. Wertheim cites evidence which shows landless peasants, coolies, poor peasants/semi-proletarians constituting 65% of the village population of a sample survey in Java and 51% of a sample survey in West Sumatra. Among those who did own land, a small minority controlled the bulk of holdings. Here Wertheim cites the results of an investigation of land ownership in West Java which revealed that 82% of total land area was owned by 13% of family heads while the remaining 87% of family heads owned either no land or less than one hectare.[36]

Geertz noted that around the sugar mills of Modjokuto there developed:

. . . something of a large landholders class made up of village chiefs and other well to do peasants. Both groups had a tendency to be members of the purist Moslem element of the rural population . . . These large landholders, in addition to being labour hirers and harvest contractors, were commonly moneylenders as well, though they most often made loans in the form of consumer goods — sugar, rice, textiles — at increasingly exhorbitant interest rates. With factory credit or personal savings some of them bought agricultural equipment . . . that they resold, lent or rented to small peasants or their tenants, and a few traded in the dry land cash crops that were coming increasingly to be cultivated at this time, selling them to the town Chinese.[37]

However, the development of classes based upon owner-ship or control of land does not necessarily mean the trans-formation of rural society into capitalist farmers and rural proletariat. In fact this impulse has been relatively weak in the Indonesian case. A primary reason for this was the dominance of the corporate plantation in commercial crop production. As Geertz argued, this did not lead to a general proletarianisation of the rural masses:

By attempting to control the processes of production all the way down to the raw-material level, the plantations hindered the devel-opment of a class of independent agricultural entrepreneurs with a predominatly developmental rather than a circular flow orientation [i.e. expanded reproduction rather than simple reproduction]. By keeping their labour force maximally seasonal and their wages low and by preventing Javanese mobility upwards through the ranks of their organization, the plantations encouraged the formation of a very large partial proletariat composed of worker-peasants who were neither wholly on the pre-capitalist nor wholly on the capitalist side of the dual economy but who moved uneasily back and forth between the two in response to the movement of sugar prices.[38]

Where Indonesians directly undertook commercial pro-duction of major export crops, they generally did so as small-holder producers. In Java, however, the growing pro-duction of small-holder sugar was severely retarded by a law prohibiting commercial mills from purchasing freehold cane.

Despite this, small-holder sugar production processed by Javanese mills for local consumption doubled in the years before the Depression.[39] However, the collapse of sugar in 1930 devastated sugar small-holders and by 1940 only 0.2% of the planted area in Java was cultivated by small-holders.[40] Rubber small-holders in Sumatra were more successful, producing 300 000 tons in 1934, as compared to 220 000 tons produced by estates that year. The International Rubber Restriction agreement cut this production to 145 000 tons while reducing estate rubber marginally to 205 000 tons. This was partly achieved by taxes which reduced the price of small-holder rubber to 5-20c per kilo compared with 30-62c per kilo for estate rubber.[41]

The Chinese had been active in plantation production up to 1870, but with the entry of the big Dutch trading corporations and culture banks after 1870 and the impact of the Depression only six Chinese sugar plantations survived, five of them belonging to the Oei Tiong Ham concern of Semarang. Indonesian estate agriculture was limited to only two estates of significance, both operated by a business trust of the Mangkunegoro royal family in Solo founded in 1917 and managed by Europeans.[42]

As for the Javanese, landowners generally leased land to tenants rather than using wage labour for production and were thereby rentiers rather than capitalists. Many of the landowners were holders of *bengkok*, which meant that it was political power and influence rather than capital which was the basis of ownership.

Until 1930 the income of many of the larger Javanese landowners was derived from renting land to the mills, and in fact the mills quite often financed the purchase of village land by village officials or mill employees.[43] However, the growth of this landowning class received a check in 1930 with the collapse of the sugar economy in Java and the severe depression in the other commercial export crops. Money, previously circulated in the villages through small-holder income, wages earned on plantations and rental income, now dried up. Sugar mills moved to revoke 21-year leases with villages and landlords, who, as mentioned above, were often also the debtors of the mills. To some extent the concentrations of land ownership built up were broken down.

Following independence there has been a continuing trend towards concentration of landholding and the consolidation of a landlord class. Often military and civilian officials have moved into this sector with capital accumulated outside the commercial world. However, the countryside has not been transformed by capitalist farming. Instead, the tendency has been to combine production of agriculture for the market with an intensification of sharecropping practices.[44]

With the introduction of the Green Revolution, rural credit programmes and increased state expenditure on rural construction projects under the New Order, we are beginning to see increased public and private capitalisation of agriculture. Wage labour, contract harvesting and the use of padi tractors are all becoming more common.[45] But there remain few signs of a significant capitalist class emerging upon the basis of capitalist investment in agriculture. The basis of an Indonesian agrarian bourgeoisie has not been constituted by ownership of land and production of commercial crops as much as by the control of trade in agricultural products. It is to the development of an agrarian trading bourgeoisie that we must look if we are to understand the real basis of the post-colonial Indonesian bourgeoisie.

The Agrarian Merchant Bourgeoisie

The gradual development of the money economy, wage labour and commodity production in the nineteenth century led to the rapid expansion of a class of traders collecting rural produce, distributing commodities and providing credit.

The bulk of these merchants, especially in Java, were Chinese. Before the VOC established its political and mercantile hegemony over Java, both Chinese and Javanese were active in trade. The Javanese were more seriously

damaged than the Chinese by the Dutch seizure of control of
international trade, because the most important of the Javanese traders were merchant princes whose mercantile activities relied heavily upon the exercise of political power to
enforce tolls and taxes on trade and to control sources of
supply and trade routes.[46] The decline of these Javanese
merchant princes in the seventeenth century left only a
residue of small-scale indigenous traders who spread into the
agrarian hinterland of Java.

Chinese merchants fared better under the VOC, which
used them as an intermediary economic force in the process
of mercantile extraction. There were obviously advantages in
using non-indigenous people as collectors and operators of
monopolies: their insulation from the local population made
them politically vulnerable and dependent. However, Chinese trading groups also impressed the Dutch with their
degree of economic organisation and efficiency, and their
dedication to the process of accumulation.[47] Indeed, the
Chinese trading family was a resilient institution situated
within a wider clan/kinship-based economic association which
was an exclusive and mutually supportive network of supply,
credit and distribution. The VOC not only left the bulk of
rural trade to the Chinese but leased them various monopolies, including road tolls, bazaar fees, salt collection and sale,
slaughter fees and customs duty. The most significant of
these was tax farming, a complex institution, at the one time
both mercantile and feudal in nature. Chinese also leased
appanage benefices from the VOC or even indigenous benefice holders, and, using the feudal powers attached to the
benefice, forced labour and produce from the peasantry for
sale on the market.[48]

Tax farming was quite extensive. Furnivall noted that in
1796, 1 143 out of 8 535 villages belonging to the VOC were
leased to Chinese. By the end of the eighteenth century:

. . . in the Company's lands on the north-coast of Java alone,
1 134 villages (out of a total of about 16 000 for all Java) were

leased to the Chinese. Not only villages, but three entire districts
had been leased by it to the Chinese, who thereby held about the
same position as the regents did elsewhere.[49]

With the demise of the VOC, Chinese tax farming and
operation of tax monopolies ceased, but were replaced during the nineteenth century with the operation of pawnshops,
gambling dens and the opium monopoly.[50] However, the
decline of state control of production and export of commercial crops and the emergence of private capitalist production
in the latter part of the nineteenth century meant that Chinese economic activity became quite firmly focused upon
wholesale and retail import, collection of produce and moneylending. Trade and moneylending had always been a central
part of Chinese economic activity, but the development of
the money economy stimulated by wages and rents from
estates and the introduction of money tax and the ending of
state control of trade greatly increased the opportunities for
merchant capital.

Because of the domination of production and export of
estate crops by Dutch and other foreign corporations,[51] the
Chinese expanded into areas which fed off this activity:
retailing, credit and distribution. It became common for
independent peasant proprietors in need of money for taxes
or consumption to borrow at high rates of interest from
Chinese merchants, often pledging the next crop. The resulting widespread peasant indebtedness facilitated Chinese control of the market and agricultural prices in this
sector of agricultural production.[52] The growing small-holder
sector was also controlled by predominantly Chinese middlemen who provided credit, collected produce and retailed
commodities.[53]

Although the Chinese had established dominance over
domestic trade and distribution networks by the end of the
colonial period, their position was more fragile than appeared. The Chinese firm did not have the capital, technology or large-scale corporate structure of Dutch firms. As is

characteristic of family-based merchant capitalist enterprise, their firms tended to decline with the death of the founder, so that despite Chinese economic dominance in general, we are not confronted with specific Chinese firms which dominated trade and credit networks over several generations. This limited the potential for concentration and organisation of political and economic power.

What then of indigenous penetration of the agrarian trading sector? Those surviving *pasisir* traders who had spread through Java exerted only a weak and fragmented commercial influence through the VOC period and much of the nineteenth century. However, the stimulation of the money economy late in the century by rents, wages, money taxes and small-holder production saw a surge in the activity of small-scale Javanese rural traders. This appeared to be connected with the development of private land ownership, involving social and economic interaction between indigenous merchant and landowning classes and the cross-flow of investment from land to trade and vice versa.[54] With the removal of travel and residence restrictions on the Chinese between 1910 and 1926, Javanese trading dominance within the villages was eroded and a period of economic and political struggle between indigenous and Chinese merchant capital ensued. The collapse of the sugar plantations in the wake of the Depression removed the central prop of the Javanese landowning/trading classes. While it must be assumed that the economic collapse had a similar impact on Chinese traders, Geertz reports that the Depression nevertheless heralded the end of a short period of vigorous competition and resistance by indigenous traders and the assertion of Chinese dominance in trade in the villages and towns of which his study was illustrative.[55]

Indigenous traders developed more vigorously in Sumatra than in Java. During the latter part of the eighteenth century and the early decades of the nineteenth century, local Minangkabau merchants developed a flourishing trade in gambier, coffee and textiles. This led to conflicts with both local rulers and the Dutch because the Minangkabau traders, in seeking free markets on the east coast of Sumatra, were attempting to break the monopolies of the Dutch and the local political authority of the Minangkabau nobility. This economic conflict was a significant element in the Padri wars, which ended in the military victory of the Dutch and the Minangkabau nobility over the merchants in the late 1830s.[56] Despite efforts to contain the emergence of a domestic petty trading bourgeoisie, a cohesive merchant class persisted in Sumatra and re-emerged in the early years of the twentieth century with the growth of small-holder export production of rice and rubber following the lifting of Dutch political controls on indigenous commercial crop production and export in 1908 and 1912.[57]

Sumatrans were to become dominant among indigenous traders. Beginning from small-scale and local trade in rice, rubber, pepper and other cash crops in Sumatra and Sulawesi, they spread to urban Java, generally as pedlars, food-stall holders and small retailers and traders. West Sumatrans, in particular, are still prominent in the petty merchant sector in Jakarta. A few of these were able to expand beyond the petty trade sector into import and export at the national and international level. From trade in agricultural commodities, they penetrated the Chinese import networks, mainly in the import of cotton and cloth for the Javanese weaving and printing industry. For some of these traders, a final step in the 1950s took them into import and distribution of foreign manufactures and directly into manufacture. The most significant of these Sumatran family trading firms to expand in the 1950s were those of Djohan Soetan Soelaman and Djohor Soetan Perpatih, Rahman Tamin, Agoes Dasaad and Haji Abdul Ghany Aziz. All of these business groups, which will be examined in later chapters, emerged from trading companies founded in Sumatra in the 1920s and 1930s.

TRADE AND MANUFACTURE

Manufacture in the colonial period may generally be divided into three sectors: household petty commodity production, small-scale and largely non-mechanised manufacture, and large-scale, mechanised factory production using free wage labour. In broad terms the first category was dominated by indigenous producers, the second by Chinese and the third by foreign capital.

Until the 1930s, it was the general case that manufactured products were either imported from overseas or manufactured within Indonesia on the basis of petty commodity production or in small workshops or factories. Weaving, spinning, batik work, furniture making and *kretek* cigarette manufacture were primarily carried out by household producers who obtained raw materials from merchants and handed back the finished or partly finished products. In return they received a commission on work done. Under this system, control of the industry lay not with the thousands of part-time household producers but with the merchants who imported and supplied the raw materials. These merchants (*bakul*) received between 50% and 70% of income in specific industries, maintaining their control through credit networks and paternal social and political relationships with the peasant/worker producers.[58]

To expand production, the *bakul* simply imported more raw material and employed more household producers. The intense economic and political struggles which took place within the batik and *kretek* industries in particular did not involve increased productivity and mechanisation but were struggles between rival trading groups for control of the import of raw materials. However, in the era of capitalist production when capital investment and free wage labour made relative (rather than absolute) surplus product the key to economic growth, household production and the *bakul* system were soon to be bypassed.

Indigenous merchants, particularly in the batik industry in

Central Java, successfully formed trade co-operatives which drove out Chinese interlopers in the 1920s and 1930s by purchasing direct from the importers and cutting out the predominantly Chinese middlemen.[59] However, survival was determined not so much by control of trade networks as by the investment of capital in production. In all industries, the pattern was repeated: larger mechanised factories controlled by foreign capital, partially mechanised medium and small-scale factories owned by Chinese, while indigenous producers found it difficult to expand beyond petty commodity production and trade. Where they attempted to compete with the Chinese in mechanised small and medium-scale factory production, they were usually swamped by the superior capital and organisational resources of the latter.

A prime example of this was the textile industry, where quotas on the import of Japanese cloth stimulated domestic production in the 1930s. The number of mills increased from nineteen in 1930 to 1 123 in 1937 and the number with more than 250 looms increased from nil to sixteen. Indigenous merchants in Majalaya and other West Javanese mill towns previously engaged as middlemen in petty commodity production began to move into factory production under the umbrella of producer and trade co-operatives, and even began to invest in mechanised looms.[60] Wertheim reports that:

In 1935 and later years, in the Regency of Bandung, many Indonesian traders and landowners invested money in the weaving industry. It was only later, when this industry had demonstrated its vitality, that foreigners, the Chinese included, began to show an interest. And although the danger arose here, too, that the small Indonesian entrepreneurs would become dependent upon foreign middlemen, in this field they managed to retain a high degree of independence and a much larger share of the invested capital than in other middle class occupations right up to the outbreak of the Second World War.[61]

However, occasional success in bypassing Chinese middlemen did not prevent indigenous manufacturers from becoming an increasingly insignificant element in textile production. Ultimately the problem was not one of exchange but of production. Sutter noted that:

Although 412 weaving licenses were held by Indonesians at the end of 1939 compared to 122 by Chinese . . . the latter had forty per cent of the production capacity and were rapidly buying up the licenses issued to the Indonesians.[62]

The expansion of the machine loom sector was largely in the hands of the Dutch and Chinese, while indigenous textile manufacturing was typically constituted by small factories using handlooms, as the following table demonstrates.

TABLE 1.2

OWNERSHIP OF MILLS AND LOOMS IN THE TEXTILE INDUSTRY
IN 1942

(per cent of total)

	Mills	Mechanised Looms	Hand Looms
European	1.5	39.5	2
Arab	10.0	22.0	28
Chinese	16.0	31.5	35
Indigenous	72.5	7.0	35

Source: Sutter 1959, p. 42, citing Achsien speech, 5 June, Ichtisar Parleman (1952), p. 609.

Nevertheless a few indigenous operators did establish a substantial base in the textile industry. West Javanese tended to form producer co-operatives, but two Sumatrans, Haji Sjamsoeddin and Agoes Dasaad, individually owned large and relatively mechanised mills.

As mentioned earlier, the indigenous merchants in the batik industry successfully fought off Chinese intrusion into the industry by forming buyers co-operatives. However, while there was a movement of production away from the household system to small factory production, no large-scale mechanisation of the industry occurred. In fact it was not until the 1970s that large capital investment in mechanised printing of batik occurred.

In the *kretek* industry there also occurred a pattern of movement from household production to factory production, and in the four years between 1929 and 1933 the percentage of *kretek* workers who were factory wage labourers increased from 10% to 36%.[63] Indigenous manufacturers were able to perform strongly in this industry in the inter-war years, and one producer, Nitisemito, opened a factory in Kudus which reportedly employed 10 000 workers.[64] Nevertheless, the Chinese by the mid-1930s had established a dominant position in large-scale factory production of *kretek* (although the two biggest factories, for Western cigarettes, were foreign owned), while the indigenous producers either remained small-scale operators or collapsed back into this sector.[65]

Chinese proved able to move into factory production, in particular into medium-scale mechanical production, in a whole variety of industries including beverages, foodstuffs and processing of agricultural products. Unlike the indigenous merchants, they were able to accumulate the capital necessary for the leap from petty commodity to capitalist production. Various reasons have been put forward to explain the failure of the indigenous merchants and the success of the Chinese. Castles found that indigenous *kretek* producers had a poor record of capital accumulation which he attributed partly to cultural characteristics. He found a tendency to consume rather than reinvest profits and a tendency for the family-based firms to be plagued with disputes over inheritance, resulting in a rapid rise and fall of firms over a period of one or two generations.[66] However, the Chinese suffered from these same problems. A major difference was the structural entrenchment of Chinese merchant capital within the framework of Dutch colonialism in tax farming, pawn shops, and wholesaling, which provided a long-term basis for accumulation and economic organisation. The enduring umbrella of Chinese merchant capital was the class, kinship and ethnic business associations/networks which provided an exclusive and mutually supportive trade and credit framework within which individual family-based firms operated. Not only did Chinese merchants have a much larger capital base, but they had the structure to sustain the accumulation process. With the entry of *totok* or *singkeh* (new immigrant) Chinese in the late nineteenth century, leading sectors of this network of credit and trade were expanded beyond Indonesia to operate on a regional basis.

Most importantly, leading elements of the Chinese business community, primarily the *totok*, were able to use their networks of credit, collection, import, wholesale and retail distribution to entrench capital investment in the production process. Where the indigenous producers sought to resist by securing control of raw material imports, as in the case of the batik industry, they merely secured a temporary reprieve for merchant capital and commodity production. They did not complete the other half of the equation, the accumulation of capital and the transition to industrial capitalism.

POLITICS AND THE FORMATION OF THE INDONESIAN BOURGEOISIE

The indigenous merchant bourgeoisie and petty bourgeoisie remained, with few exceptions, locked into commodity production and small-scale trade which, while persistent, was rapidly being overtaken by medium and large-scale capitalist production. Consequently, attempts by indigenous merchants and commodity producers to organise politically in defence of their interests failed because these attempts constituted political action in defence of declining forces and relations of production. This was an effort, not by a rising bourgeoisie to sweep away feudal restraints, but by declining merchant capitalists to halt the development of more advanced forms of capitalist production and to struggle against competitors with superior capital resources.

The resistence of the indigenous merchants took place at the point where their traditional areas of economic activity were breached. This meant that they did not confront the Dutch, who operated in the large-scale estate, import and manufacturing sector, but instead confronted the Chinese merchants and manufacturers who moved into agrarian trade, trade and manufacture of textiles, batik, *kretek*, foodstuffs, beverages and furniture, and into the transport sector. Immediately after the easing of restrictions on Chinese travel and residence between 1904 and 1911, indigenous merchants formed the Sarekat Dagang Islam (1909) which became the Sarekat Islam (1912). Leading figures included Haji Samanhoedi, a Javanese merchant and batik manufacturer from Solo and a Muslim religious leader, and Raden Mas Tirtoadisoerjo and Omar Said Tjokroaminoto, Javanese aristocrats involved in commerce.[67] The movement provided a basis for boycotts against Chinese merchants, and for co-operative action by indigenous merchants, and was associated with several outbursts of violence against the Chinese throughout Central Java.[68]

In its early years the Sarekat Islam was dominated by a devout Muslim leadership closely associated with the indigenous merchant community. The interests of the indigenous merchants were apparent in its programme, which announced the intention of promoting commerce among Indonesians and of giving mutual support to members who encountered economic difficulties.[69] However, the Muslim merchant bourgeoisie lost control of the Sarekat Islam after 1918. At the village level, the mass wing degenerated into a vague religious and occasionally millenarian movement controlled by village *kiyayi* (Muslim religious leaders) who were antagonistic towards the modernist reformism of the Muslim merchants. At the national level, the majority of the Sarekat Islam was captured by the communist/trade union wing, causing a split in 1922 which left only a rump of the original Muslim merchant bourgeoisie. From the 1920s onwards, the nationalist movement was secured by secular organisations with little specific commitment to the economic interests of the indigenous merchant bourgeoisie and commodity producers or the devout, reformist brand of Islam that was associated with them.

Neither, however, were the Chinese capitalists able to establish themselves as a national bourgeoisie in its full dimension, or as a ruling class. They remained primarily merchant in nature and family-based in structure and, despite control over domestic trade and credit networks, were certainly in no immediate position to challenge foreign capital for dominance in the large-scale capitalist sector. Chinese capital was split between the *peranakan* (local-born), who were more fully culturally integrated and tended to operate in small-scale trade, money lending and agricultural processing, and the *totok*, who were more culturally exclusive and more succesful in penetrating the capitalist manufacturing sector. Additionally, clan and kinship structures obstructed the development of national economic and political cohesion.

Most importantly, the Chinese were not generally accepted by the bulk of Indonesians as having a legitimate public political role, and, as we have mentioned, they were subject to periodic demonstrations of hostility, particularly from the Muslim merchant bourgeoisie.[70] This situation placed very real limitations upon their potential for collusion with a post-colonial state, so necessary for the generation of a national bourgeoisie.

The dominant element of the capitalist class in Indonesia at the end of the colonial period was Dutch, and even here the corporate capital of the trading houses and cultivation banks was tied to a declining estate economy. Dutch capital was proving unable to provide the capital basis for a restructuring of Indonesian capitalism around resource development and industrial production. Already in the 1920s and 1930s, American, British, Japanese and European capital had established firm foot-holds. The penetration of capitalism had eroded the old class and political structures of Indonesia but had not yet produced well-defined class forces of bourgeoisie and proletariat. Instead there existed an agricultural society which had been transformed by commodity production but where landlord-tenant social relations of production rather than capitalist relations had been generated. Similarly, the domestic bourgeoisie remained primarily a merchant bourgeoisie torn by serious political, social and economic conflicts between indigenous and Chinese sections. The partial development of capitalist social and economic structures and the weakness of the domestic bourgeoisie left a social vacuum in the Indonesian capitalist political economy. Such a vacuum meant that the state would occupy a strategic and relatively autonomous position, at least in the immediate post-colonial period.

The search for a nascent national bourgeoisie amongst the ranks of Muslim merchants and petty commodity producers is based upon the tenuous assumption that small-scale trade and commodity production will provide a basis for accumulation enabling the merchant bourgeoisie to transcend the gap between petty merchant and industrial capitalist production. As it has transpired, accumulation, in the historical context of a global capitalist economy dominated by large-scale transnational corporate capital, has not been the painstaking, incremental process of accumulation by merchants and petty commodity producers, but has been underpinned by capacity to gain access to the power of the state and to existing capital and corporate structures.

1. J. H. Boeke, *Economics and Economic Policies of Dual Societies* (Haarlem, 1951).

2. C. Geertz, *Agricultural Involution* (Berkeley, 1970). This work has led to a significant debate. See: R. E. Elson, *The Cultivation System and "Agricultural Involution"* (Melbourne, 1978); G. R. Knight, Capitalism, Commodities and the Transformation of Java (Brisbane 1980).

3. Geertz 1970, Chapter 6.

4. Onghokham, The Residency of Madiun: Priyayi and Peasant in the Nineteenth Century (Ph.D. thesis, Yale University, 1975); H. Sutherland, *The Making of a Bureaucratic Elite* (Singapore, 1979).

5. The concept of dual economies and dual societies wherein the 'lesser' or dominated mode of production is resistent to but gradually infiltrated by the dominant element, is used by both structural functionalists and Marxists. Within the Marxist school the concept of articulation (i.e. that capitalism props up and uses pre-capitalist structures) is most clearly developed by the French structuralist anthropologists including Rey and Meillassoux. See H.

Wolpe (ed.), *The Articulation of Modes of Production* (London, 1980). See also E. Laclau, 'Feudalism and Capitalism in Latin America', *New Left Review* 67 (1971). In the last decade the question of articulation of modes of production has become most complex — one of the interesting developments has been the concept of a specific colonial mode of production. The best short discussion of these is to be found in A. Brewer, *Marxist Theories of Imperialism* (London, 1980), Chapters 4, 11.

6. A. G. Frank, 'Sociology of Development and Underdevelopment of Sociology', in J. Cockcroft et al (eds), *Dependence and Underdevelopment* (New York, 1972).

7. R. Brenner, 'The Origins of Capitalist Development: A Critique of Neo-Smithian Marxism', *New Left Review* 104 (1977).

8. For an overview of this position see Brewer 1980, Chapters 1 & 2.

9. The gradual erosion of the political power of local rulers to extract the peasant surplus is treated in a wide variety of general histories of colonial Indonesia, but for close analysis of the process at the ground level see Onghokham 1975, and S. J. Siddique, Relics of the Past? A Sociological Study of the Sultanate of Cirebon, West Java (M. A. thesis, Bielefeld, 1977).

10. Onghokham 1975, pp. 130–8. The gradual separation of local bureaucracies and rulers from their traditional rights to tribute and their incorporation into a salaried colonial administration in the twentieth century will be treated later in the chapter.

11. W. O'Malley, Indonesia in the Great Depression: A Study of East Sumatra and Jogjakarta in the 1930s (Ph.D. thesis, Cornell University, 1977), p. 23.

12. The colonial government had tried to develop privately owned sugar mills in the early years of the cultivation system, but found it difficult to attract private investors. By the 1860s and 1870s capital was strong enough to move out of trade and into production. Furnivall noted that: 'A leading Chinaman was warned that he could not expect to succeed his father as Chinese captain unless he accepted a contract to become a sugar miller; after vainly offering 5 000 for a substitute he had to comply and within a few years was one of the wealthiest men in Java'. J. Furnivall, *Netherlands India: A Study of Plural Economy* (Cambridge, 1944), p. 143. (It must be noted that labour for these mills was often compulsory.)

13. These activities included the building of ports, railways and roads, establishment of a department of agriculture, trade and industry, government research facilities, state-credit banks and pawnshops, provision of land leasing legislation and negotiation of international commodity pricing and production agreements. See Furnivall 1944, p. 265.

14. R. Anspach, The Problem of a Plural Economy and its Effects on Indonesia's Economic Structure: A Study in Economic Policy (Ph.D. thesis, University of California, Berkeley, 1963), pp. 51–5. O'Malley (1977, pp. 114, 115) specifically looks at this process in relation to the tobacco industry and the emergence of the Deli Maatschappij.

15. By 1913 coffee and sugar combined accounted for only 25% of export value compared with 50% in 1900. O'Malley (1977, p. 23) provides the following comparative statistics of the value of exports (in millions of guilders):

Year	Rubber	Sugar	Petroleum	Coffee	Tobacco	Total Exports
1928	281	376	150	81	96	1 577
1930	173	254	190	36	59	1 157
1932	34	99	99	35	47	541
1934	89	46	100	23	37	487
1936	88	34	98	16	38	538
1938	135	45	164	14	39	658
1940	332	53	175	8	38	882

16. Agricultural Capital (f.mil.) in the Three Culture Areas, 1929

Nationality	Culture Area			Total	Total invested in	
	Java	East Sumatra	South Sumatra		Sugar	Other Crops
Dutch	1 118.0	360.7	57.2	1 535.9	779.6	756.3
British	142.0	124.7	11.2	277.9	10.1	267.8
Franco-Belg.	35.9	72.5	3.2	111.6	–	111.6
U.S.A	–	53.0	–	53.0	–	53.0
Japanese	5.9	131.7	–	19.6	3.7	15.9
German	5.7	8.1	4.0	17.8	–	17.8
Swiss	–	4.4	0.7	5.1	–	5.1
Italian	2.1	–		0.1	–	2.1
Others, known and unknown	22.3	4.9	13.8	41.0	–	41.0
Total	1 332.4	642.2	90.4	2 065.0	793.5	1 271.5
% of foreign (non-Dutch) capital	16.1	44.1	36.8	25.7	1.7	40.5

Source: Furnivall 1944, p. 311.

17. Furnivall 1944, pp. 317, 436.

18. O'Malley 1977, p. 62.

19. In 1934 the export of native rubber was fixed at 71.5 tons for every 100 tons of estate rubber. This quota turned out to be only 50% of potential native output (Anspach 1963).

20. J. Sutter, *Indonesianisasi, Politics in a Changing Economy, 1940–1955* (Ithaca, 1959).

21. Furnivall 1944, pp. 429–40. The Japanese not only imported these commodities at a cheaper price but established distribution networks which, in some cases, began to compete effectively with the Chinese.

22. Sutter 1959, pp. 54–8, 78, 108.

23. Ibid., p. 59.

24. Ibid., pp. 58–9.

25. The dominance of landowning families in the new export promotion joint venture industries is outlined by W. Pomeroy, *An American Made Tragedy* (New York, 1964). For a general overview of the development of the *principale* class see: M. McLennan, 'Land and Tenancy in the Central Luzon Plain', *Philippine Studies* (1969).

The importance of the landlord class in the colonial economy of Vietnam is treated by E. Wolf, *Peasant Wars of the Twentieth Century* (London, 1971), Chapter 4; and in D. G. Porter, Imperialism and Social Structure in Twentieth Century Vietnam (Ph.D. thesis, Cornell University, 1976).

26. The *priyayi* were the nobility and administrative literati of the agrarian kingdoms of Java. In the Madiun regency of eastern Java, for example, Onghokham (1975, p. 281) estimated the *priyayi* to comprise 0.3% of the population — or 350 families. Other social categories, counted in families, were: 1 500 village headmen; 1 100 religious leaders; 5 000 merchants (mostly Chinese); 2 000 artisans; 111 000 peasants.

27. For the social and economic basis of *priyayi* power see: Onghokham 1975; B. Schrieke, 'Ruler and Realm in Early Java' and 'The Native Rulers' in his *Indonesian Sociological Studies* (hereafter *ISS*), Vols. 2 & 1, resp. (The Hague, 1957 & 1955).

28. Onghokham (1975, p. 18) notes that the execution of a prominent rebel might mean the execution of 5 000 families, so closely were bonds of loyalty considered to bind individuals to a leader.

29. Ibid., pp. 339–40.

30. Ibid., p. 139.

31. Ibid., p. 140.

32. Ibid., p. 192.

33. O'Malley (1977, pp. 109, 111) notes that in East Sumatra the local rulers did not directly undertake commercial production but were content to draw income in rents from the Dutch estate companies.

34. Some figures on development of private land ownership are given in Furnivall 1944, p. 319.

35. B. Schrieke, 'Communism on the West Coast of Sumatra', in *ISS* (1955), pp. 95–109.

36. W. Wertheim, *Indonesian Society in Transition* (The Hague, 1959), pp. 112, 113.

37. C. Geertz, *The Social History of an Indonesian Town* (Greenwood, Conn., 1975, pp. 40–41.

38. Ibid., p. 46.

39. Ibid., pp. 49, 50.

40. Sutter 1959, p. 15.

41. G. Kahin, *Nationalism and Revolution in Indonesia* (Ithaca, 1952), pp. 22, 23.

42. Sutter 1959, p. 15.

43. Geertz 1975, pp. 36, 40, 49.

44. F. Husken, 'Landlords, Sharecroppers and Agricultural Labourers; Changing Labour Relations in Rural Java', *JCA* 9, 2 (1979).

45. Works on changes in the agricultural sector include: W. Collier, 'Tebasan System, High Yielding Varieties and Rural Change', *Prisma* 1 (1975) and 'Food Problems, Unemployment and The Green Revolution in Java', *Prisma* 9 (1978); J. Hinkson, 'Rural Development and Class Contradiction in Java', *JCA* 5, 3 (1975); Boedhisantoso, *Rice Harvesting in the Krawang Region in Relation to High Yielding Varieties* (Melbourne, 1975); A. Arun, A. Booth, R. Sundrum, 'Labour Absorption in Indonesian Agriculture', *BIES* 17, 1 (1981).

46. J. C. van Leur, *Indonesian Trade and Society: Essays in Indonesian Social and Economic History* (The Hague, 1956), pp. 109, 116; B Schrieke, 'Shifts in Political and Economic Power in the Sixteenth and Seventeenth Centuries', in *ISS* (1955), pp. 27, 28.

47. Anspach 1963, p. 79; Furnivall 1944, p. 46.

48. Anspach 1963, pp. 78–81; Kahin 1952, pp. 9, 12.

49. Furnivall 1944, p. 46.

50. Ibid., pp. 213, 357, 412, 413. Furnivall reported that in 1900 the bulk of Chinese wealth came from pawnshops, opium and usury. The Dutch attempted to end Chinese control over pawnshops and rural credit in general in the early years of the twentieth century by making pawnshops a state monopoly and by establishing rural credit banks. This move was encompassed with the new 'Ethical Policy' and was designed to halt spreading indebtedness amongst rural producers and local indigenous officials.

51. Sutter 1959, p. 15. Apart from the estates and trading companies of the Oei Tiong Ham concern, the bulk of Chinese estates were held by absentee landlords; they produced rice and other crops and constituted a small portion of the shrinking residue of privately held estate lands (Furnivall 1944, p. 168).

52. Furnivall 1944, p. 93; Anspach 1963, p. 16; Kahin 1952, p. 22; Boeke 1951, p. 44.

53. Sutter 1959, pp. 242–56.
An excellent article on the Chinese in the small-holder rubber industry is: K. Thomas and J. Panglaykim, 'The Chinese in the South Sumatran Rubber Industry: A Case Study in Economic Nationalism', in J. Mackie (ed.), *The Chinese in Indonesia* (Melbourne, 1976).

54. Geertz and Castles present a picture of Javanese merchants as constituting a small and rather isolated social element in rural Javanese towns, attached to modernist Islam and linked with larger landowners in the district. In some cases landowners used capital accumulated from rents to establish themselves in trade and, likewise, traders purchased land. Geertz 1965; Castles 1967.

55. Geertz 1965, p. 59.

56. C. Dobbin, 'Economic Change in Minangkabau as a Factor in the Rise of the Padri Movement, 1784–1830', *Indonesia* 23 (1977).

57. B. Schrieke, 'Communism on the West Coast of Sumatra', in *ISS* (1966), pp. 98–109.

58. P. Sitsen, *Industrial Development of the Netherlands Indies* (New York, 1942), p. 25.

59. Sutter 1959, pp. 45–8.

60. Ibid., p. 43.

61. Wertheim 1959, p. 111.

62. Sutter 1959, p. 43.

63. Castles 1967, p. 37.

64. Sutter 1959, p. 48.

65.   Kretek Enterprises in Central & East Java
                    by Nationality of Operators, 1933/34

Size	Central Java			1933 Total	(1934 Total)	East Java			1934 Total
	Indonesian	Chinese	Arab			Indonesian	Chinese	Arab	
Large	8	6	1	15	17	1	14	–	15
Medium	18	29	1	48	55	1	27	–	28
Small	524	272	3	799	575	237	165	4	406
Total	550	307	5	862	(647)	239	206	4	449

Source: Ong, *Chineezen in Nederlandsch-Indie*, p. 158. From Sutter 1959, p. 50.

66. Castles 1967, pp. 58–66.

67. Kahin 1952, p. 67.

68. Castles 1967, p. 63.

69. Kahin 1952, p. 58. The emergence of the Sarekat Islam and the Muslim merchant bourgeoisie and petty bourgeoisie political interests is treated in R. van Niel, *The Emergence of the Modern Indonesian Elite* (The Hague, 1960).

70. These demonstrations have also become an intermittent feature of the post-colonial period. See: J. Mackie, 'Anti-Chinese Outbreaks in Indonesia, 1959–1968', in Mackie (ed.) 1976. Positions of any significant authority within the political or state apparatus of post-colonial Indonesia have not been available to Chinese. This is not to deny that many Chinese have been powerful or influential, but such power and influence is developed outside public office, as advisors or financiers. I will develop this aspect of Chinese-indigenous political relationships in later chapters.

2
The Failure of Domestic Private Capital: 1949–1957

THE period 1949 to 1965 is the period in which the Dutch colonial economy was dismantled and new socio-economic and political forces gathered themselves within Indonesia. To a certain extent the decline of the import/export, estate-based economy had begun in the 1930s, but a further and decisive blow to these structures was the loss by the Dutch of state power to maintain and enforce the legal, political and fiscal framework of the colonial economy and Dutch economic supremacy. At the same time the power of the state was reconstituted by political forces within Indonesia and used at various times to modify or confront the colonial economic structures and the Dutch and Chinese bourgeoisie which dominated them, and at the same time to protect and subsidise various elements of domestic capital, both state and private.

This was not a cohesive and systematic process. The influence of the domestic indigenous bourgeoisie was, for example, sporadic and generally ineffective, symptomatic of the vacuum of socio-economic power in which the new state was to operate. Nevertheless, from 1949 to 1957, disengagement from the colonial economy was sought by a strategy of facilitating gradual domestic capital formation within existing structures. By 1957, however, it had become clear that private domestic capital was unable to provide the basis for capital formation and the leaders of the new republic began to turn towards state capital.

THE POLITICS OF ECONOMIC POLICY-MAKING

In the years between the formal establishment of independence in 1949 and Sukarno's appointment of a working cabinet under Djuanda in 1958, formal political power in the new republic lay in the hands of a series of parliamentary cabinets which reflected to varying degrees the fluctuating influence and interests of the major political parties. None of these parties could be said to represent or constitute the specific interests of any class in a cohesive way. This was largely because the pre-capitalist structures of social class and political power had been eroded by the money economy, commodity production and the colonial state without being replaced by well-defined or politically organised classes of landlords, wage labourers or capitalists. The new political leaders operated in a social vacuum for the first decade of independence, and political struggle tended to be confined to a small elite in Jakarta. In this decade, politics clearly enjoyed a substantial degree of autonomy.[1]

Nevertheless all the major parties had committed themselves, in the years before 1949, to broad programmes of economic nationalism. In general this meant an end to 'imperialism', a transfer of economic power to Indonesian nationals and the replacement of a colonial economy based upon the export of estate crops by a more industrialised and self-sufficient economy structured around domestic markets. The Communist party, PKI, stressed state ownership; elements within the Nationalist party, PNI, envisaged cooperatives playing a dominant role; while Masyumi and the other Islamic parties were more sympathetic to private capital provided it was in Indonesian hands. However, even the Masyumi, which drew much of its support from the Muslim merchant bourgeoisie, expressed opposition to 'free-fight

liberalism' and saw co-operatives and central planning playing a crucial role in a future national Indonesian economy.[2]

Nevertheless, the various coalition governments from 1949
to 1959 did not make a blanket expropriation of Dutch
capital because, when it came to the point, Indonesia
possessed neither the capital nor the political resources to
maintain or replace the colonial economic structure. No
party had either the political power or the administrative
machinery to establish a coherent set of policy directions or
organise or plan production and capital formation. Nor was
there a domestic capitalist class able to provide anything
substantially more than petty trading and commodity production.

The Masyumi, which dominated the Natsir and Sukiman
cabinets and was a partner in the Wilopo cabinet, moved
cautiously against foreign capital for three basic reasons:
first, it argued that the Indonesian economy was dependent
upon an inflow of foreign capital; second, it felt that foreign
capital could be controlled by government regulation; and
third, it saw no purpose in nationalisation where foreign
capital could not be replaced by national enterprise able to
maintain the same levels of productivity and efficiency. Masyumi's leading spokesman on economic affairs, Sjafruddin
Prawiranegara, was arguing by 1952 that government intervention should only occur where private enterprise no
longer served general social interests and that foreign capital
investment should remain a crucial component of the Indonesian economy until a national productive capacity based
upon the formation of national capital could be achieved.
Masyumi took the view that the most appropriate strategy
for cultivating a domestic capitalist class was to provide state
assistance to the existing indigenous merchant bourgeoisie
and petty bourgeoisie, allowing development to begin from
the bottom upwards.[3]

A similar approach was taken by those elements of the
PNI which gained power in the early cabinets. Hatta's concept of an economy based upon co-operatives was never

seriously pursued by any government, and the party officially adopted the position that private capital should assume a role in the creation of a national economy under state protection and with state subsidy.[4] At the same time, the PNI substantially modified its approach to the question of industrialisation. Like nationalisation, industrialisation was not to grow within the existing import/export framework. In 1952, Wilopo (PNI Prime Minister, April 1952–June 1953) stated that: 'Industrialisation would take place . . . where it appeared more profitable than continuing the import of a commodity. Such industrialisation would succeed within a reasonable time only if Indonesians worked together with capital and experts from abroad'.[5]

The softening of the approach to private capital also partly reflected the growing connections between political parties and powerful families with business interests, as well as the temporary ascendancy of political planners holding a 'gradualist' approach to the question of economic development. The economic approach of these earlier cabinets, formulated by such men as Wilopo (PNI), Sumitro (Socialist party — PSI) and Sjafruddin (Masyumi), represented the beginning of one of the two orthodoxies in Indonesian economic policy-making. This orthodoxy, and the so-called technocrats who have been its practitioners,[6] is committed to neo-classical growth economics, to the importance of foreign capital investment and market forces. It is cautious of state subsidy and protection of particular economic groups. However, the economic structures inherited from the Dutch placed the state in a naturally strategic position primarily because only the state possessed the financial and political resources to modify the economic dominance of the foreign and Chinese bourgeoisie. In political terms too, the desire of the technocrats to minimise the economic role of the state was opposed not only by socialist and economic nationalist forces but by various economic and political groups which were able to benefit from the appropriation of state resources and state economic power.

STATE CAPITAL TO 1957

For the most part, in Glassburner's words, 'The task, then, which the Government faced in 1950 was to stabilise and expand an economy that was (a) foreign-dominated and (b) privately owned'.[7] Nevertheless, the tension between contending political forces and their interests, objectives and strategies produced a piecemeal and half-hearted attempt to transfer parts of the economy to national ownership. The burden of economic nationalisation, such as it was, fell upon the state, not only because of residues of socialist sentiment and the demands of the PKI, the left PNI and some PSI elements that the state should play a crucial economic role, but also because national private capital, both indigenous and Chinese, was too weakly developed to play the major role. This was especially so in large-scale sectors of economic activity, particularly in manufacture and infrastructure.

In the period 1949–57 the Indonesian state moved into four sectors of economic activity. A most crucial move was to secure control of the central banking apparatus by taking over the Java Bank and reconstituting it as the Bank of Indonesia. Allied to this was the establishment of two state finance banks: Bank Industri Negara (BIN) which financed industrial projects, and the Bank Negara Indonesia (BNI) which was a foreign-exchange bank and financed importers.

The state also secured a range of existing public utilities including pawnshops, some agricultural estates, post telegraph and telephone services, electricity, ports, coalmines and railways. A third move was into industry, where state corporations, financed by BIN, established themselves in cement production, textiles, automobile assembly, glass and bottle manufacture and hardboard.

Finally, the state attempted to break the Dutch control of the import-export trade, by establishing the Central Trading Company in 1948 to export Indonesian agricultural products, and Usindo in 1956 to export the products of BIN-financed factories and import raw materials for their use.[8]

However, the development of state enterprises did not represent a concerted move towards socialisation, or indeed even nationalisation, of the economy. Some profitable enterprises were taken over, including the Java Bank, on the grounds that state control of such crucial sectors was a minimum requirement for the creation of a national industrial economy. But the intervention of the state in the economy, to 1956, was heavily influenced by the idea that the state would provide the infrastructure for the development of a domestic capitalist class, operate enterprises that were necessary but beyond the capacity of national capital, and directly finance and protect a national (and by national was generally meant indigenous) bourgeoisie.

Dr. Sumitro's Economic Urgency Programme epitomised this approach. Commenced in 1951, it provided the BIN with Rp160 million to finance industrial projects to be operated by subsidiary corporations with the long-term objective of handing over the capitalised and operating enterprises to co-operatives, private owners or joint state-private ownership. A wide variety of enterprises including rubber re-milling, cement, textile and printing plants were planned and some actually established, but the state had to retain ownership and management in most cases because private domestic capitalists were either unable to mobilise the capital to enter into partnership or found more lucrative opportunities elsewhere.[9]

In addition to the Central Trading Company (CTC), BNI and BIN established an auto assembly plant, Indonesian Service Company (ISC), purchased the General Motors auto assembly plant at Tanjung Priok, and established the state shipping company, P.T. Pelni. BNI and BIN credits (together with those of a range of smaller government finance institutions) were also provided for individual indigenous enterprises. By 1956 such credit totalled Rp665 million. BNI concentrated on providing foreign-exchange credit for indigenous importers and allocated Rp117 million to the Indonesian Importers Association, Gapindo, much

of which was never repaid.[10] The government also gave
generous credit assistance to indigenous banking, including
Rp35 million to Rachmat Mulyomiseno's Indonesian Banking
Corporation.[11]

STATE POLICY AND INDIGENOUS CAPITAL

The state provided not only credit but protection for indigenous business against both foreign and Chinese competition.
In rice milling, the government restricted membership of the
boards of milling companies to Indonesian citizens, which
excluded most Chinese. Similar protection was granted in
other fields, including stevedoring and bus transportation.[12]
In the import sector, the state attempted to foster indigenous
importers between 1950 and 1956 by reserving licences under
the Benteng programme.

Despite the concerted attempt by the state to build an
indigenous bourgeoisie, the growth of this class was not
impressive. By 1956 it was clear that indigenous capitalists
had not made inroads into Chinese economic dominance, a
large percentage of government-financed indigenous enterprises were failing, and government credit was being misused
on a large scale.

Despite strong government support for national banks, by
the end of 1956 forty-two indigenous national banks accounted for only 11% of domestic credit outstanding and
many of these banks were dependent upon continuing government finance rather than strong performance in the market
place. Where the government had attempted to establish
co-operative credit in the countryside, Anspach reports that:
' . . . indigenous rural credit institutions failed to reduce
materially the Chinese hold on village credit'.[13]

In the agricultural sector, 70% of the estates on Java and
Sumatra were back in foreign hands by 1953, the government
being reluctant to interfere too much with a sector so vital to
foreign-exchange earnings. BIN took over several large es-

tates but, with a lack of potential indigenous partners, was forced to operate them as state subsidiaries.[14] Indeed it was Chinese rather than indigenous private investors who stepped into the gap created by the ending of colonial rule. Whereas in 1929 they owned none of the estates on Java, in 1952 they owned 19%.[15]

Indigenous small-holder production of crops, particularly rubber and sugar, increased substantially in the 1950s, but the state was anxious to extend indigenous ownership into the processing, collection and export of these crops. Concerted moves to break Chinese monopolies in the collection and export of rubber and copra and in the milling of sugar and rubber re-milling met with little success. In the case of rice milling, the government proved unwilling to enforce Regulation No. 42 of 1954, restricting licences (in effect) to indigenous citizens because of the potential damage to such a crucial industry. Licences continued to be issued to Chinese, and by 1955 Sutter reports that only a fraction of the Chinese mills had passed into indigenous hands.[16] The attempt by the state-owned Yayasan Kopra (Copra Foundation) to direct exports through 'national' traders encountered difficulties, not only because the appointed 'national' traders were unable to operate the export trade and were forced to deal through Chinese exporters, but because the position of producers deteriorated when the Yayasan replaced Chinese traders as purchasers of the crop. In 1956, the Yayasan Kopra was disbanded.[17]

In manufacture, the Economic Urgency Programmes were abandoned in 1956, because the state itself was unable to mobilise capital for many of the industrial projects proposed and because it was found to be impossible to attract indigenous partners with sufficient capital resources to participate. In the crucial textile sector, for example, the ownership of capital in the weaving industry in the Bandung districts (the centre of the industry) in the late 1950s was estimated as follows:[18]

Alien enterprises using Alien capital	Rp90 mill
National enterprises using all or part Alien capital	Rp26 mill
National enterprises using "warga negara' (Indonesian Chinese) capital	Rp24 mill
National enterprises using indigenous capital	Rp 5 mill

Domestic Capital in the Import Sector: the Benteng Programme

Probably the most concerted efforts to generate an indigenous domestic capitalist class were in the sector of import under the auspices of the Benteng programme.

Benteng was implemented first in the period of the Natsir cabinet (September 1950–March 1951) as a component of the Urgency Plan, but was most enthusiastically prosecuted by Iskaq Tjokrohadisoerjo, Minister of Economic Affairs in the Ali Sastroamidjojo cabinet (August 1953–November 1954). Benteng was intended to secure indigenous dominance in the import sector, which appeared to be most responsive to state direction through controls over the allocation of import licences and which would be most easily penetrated by indigenous bourgeoisie because of the limited amounts of capital and corporate resources required in comparison to manufacture. It was hoped that the import sector would constitute a base for accumulation which would sustain the expansion of indigenous capital into other sectors.

The initial Benteng programme, announced in April 1950, reserved certain categories of goods for indigenous importers and made provision for credit to be available through BNI for those eligible to participate. Qualifications for entry were, on the surface, quite stringent. Each beneficiary had to be a new Indonesian importer, operating a legally constituted corporation or partnership with a working capital of at least Rp100 000, an office and several employees with previous business experience. Seventy per cent of the capital was to be provided by indigenous citizens. Until 1955, Chinese were treated as aliens and were not eligible for inclusion in the programme.[19]

As the programme progressed it became apparent that few recipients of import licences were established indigenous importers but tended instead to be individuals associated with powerful figures in the bureaucracy or the parties who controlled allocation of licences and credit. More disturbing, it also became apparent that the majority of Benteng firms were not using the licences for importing but were simply selling them to genuine importers, mostly Chinese, and often failing to repay BNI credit. What was being consolidated was not an indigenous merchant bourgeoisie but a group of licence brokers and political fixers.

The government was well aware of the problem and took steps to eliminate the brokers. Screening in mid-1953 cut the number of Benteng importers from 7 000 to 3 500. Such measures had a short-term impact. In August 1954, the Central Office of Imports estimated that 90% of registered national importers were not bona fide, and this was confirmed in a screening ordered in 1955 by Economic Affairs Minister, Roosseno. Benteng's most enthusiastic supporter, Economic Affairs Minister Iskaq, acknowledged that licences were freely sold at 200% to 250% of their nominal value.

Despite these problems the government persisted with Benteng for several years, and in fact during the period 1952–55 the categories of imports reserved for Benteng importers and the amount of credit available increased while prepayment requirements were reduced. The numbers of indigenous importers increased from 100 in 1949 to 250 in 1950, 751 in 1972 and 7 000 in mid-1953. The percentage of total government foreign-exchange credit made available to Benteng importers rose from 37% in 1952–53 to 76.2% in late 1954.

By the mid-1950s, however, the sharp decline in Indonesian foreign-exchange reserves after the end of the Korean war boom brought pressures to reduce imports. A few indigenous importing companies did participate successfully in Benteng, and these will be examined later in the chapter, but for the most part, small indigenous traders were at a disadvantage not only because they had few political connections but because they did not possess the capital resources to make large prepayments on imports and were increasingly dependent on state-financed bank credits which were seldom repaid and which governments were increasingly reluctant to provide.

Political pressures to end state subsidy of indigenous capital came from two sources. The PSI, Masyumi and moderate PNI groups argued for a return to a more market-oriented economy where, it was envisaged, production and exchange would be carried out by the most efficient capitalists, even though this would slow down the process of economic nationalisation. On the other hand, those who saw economic nationalism as a priority — the left wing of the PNI, the PKI and Sukarno — placed little faith in the capacity of indigenous capitalists to act as the instrument of a nationalist economic revolution. Instead, they came increasingly to the conclusion that the state itself must assume the burden of creating a national economy.

In 1956, the cabinet of Burhanuddin Harahap (August 1955–March 1956) extended Benteng privileges to all Indonesian citizens regardless of ethnic origin and introduced an auction system for import licences. Finally, in 1957, under the Djuanda cabinet, Benteng was ended.

THE NATURE OF THE STATE-CAPITAL RELATIONSHIP

What then were the social and political consequences of the programmes of state protection and subsidy of national and indigenous capital? First, it became clear that the Chinese-owned capital was so integral to the structure of Indonesian capitalism that, short of a radical, socialist transformation of the economy, it would continue to constitute the dominant element of domestic investment. Second, indigenous capitalists proved generally unable to expand beyond petty trade and petty commodity production. Third, the resources of private domestic capital, including Chinese, were insufficient to replace foreign capital, particularly in large-scale industrial and mining enterprise. Consequently, the state itself was forced to begin to assume the central role of financing, owning and managing investment in these sectors.

State power, however, existed at two levels: a level where public policy (fiscal, monetary and legal) established general relationships between 'state' and 'capital', and a level where relationships were conducted between the officials of the state and individual capitalists on the basis of the private appropriation of state power and resources by its own officials. It was this 'patrimonial' aspect of state power that was to prove significant in determining which individual enterprises prospered and which declined within the context of general state policy.

Control over the allocation of state credit, licences, monopolies, contracts and other concessions was to become an object of struggle between state managers who wished to use them as tools in regularised economic strategies, and politico-bureaucratic factions which sought to use the authority of the state apparatus to secure sources of income for their political and personal needs and establish a basis for accumulation by their political/business clients. In the 1950s, political parties were able to establish hegemony over economically strategic offices within government authorities and departments, such as the Department of Trade, BIN and BNI, which carried the authority to allocate credit and various concessions. Licences, credit and other concessions were then be channelled to companies directly owned by the party, or to companies owned by relatives or political associates, or could be sold for cash or used to establish an

economic partnership between political parties, individual
politico-bureaucrats and individual business groups, often
Chinese.[20]

State power exercised in this manner is both patrimonial
and mercantile. It is patrimonial because individuals and
political factions personally appropriate elements of the state
apparatus and the authority of state office, thereby blurring
the distinction between political power and bureaucratic
authority. The apparatus of the state becomes the possession
of the political power-holders. It is mercantile in the sense
that revenue or 'tribute' is raised by the state by means of the
creation and sale of trading monopolies and general political
control of access to state finance, contracts and licences.

Nevertheless the mechanisms of patronage did provide the
basis for the emergence and consolidation of a group of
indigenous capitalists and established a series of politico-
economic alliances which constituted a potential basis for a
powerful national and indigenous bourgeoisie.

There was of course no absolute reason why a domestic
indigenous capitalist class could not be generated by
politico-bureaucrats through provision of state credit and
trading monopolies. In fact, the use of politically secured
economic privileges proved to be the path to capital accumulation rather than spontaneous transformation from a base of
traditional small-scale trade and commodity production. Indeed, bureaucratic capitalism, or capital owned by the
officials of state and party bureaucracies, became a major
feature of private capital ownership in Indonesia.

Political Parties and Business

The PNI established the largest of these politico-economic
empires. Its corporate interests were centred upon the holding company Yayasan Marhaen and the Bank Umum Nasional. The business groups of the parties relied upon
influence within the state banks and financial institutions as
well as their own private banks, because of the importance of

access to credit and foreign exchange in circumstances where importing was the most lucrative economic activity. In 1952 the PNI established Bank Umum Nasional (BUN) with the deputy chairman of the PNI, Soerwirjo, as president, Dr. Ong Eng Kie as vice-president and Iskaq as chairman of the board. With the formation of the PNI-dominated Ali cabinet in 1953, Ong and Iskaq were appointed Minister of Finance and Minister of Economic Affairs respectively. At the same time Soerwirjo resigned from Bank Umum Nasional to take up an appointment with BIN, and PNI members Abdul Karim and Hadiono Kusomo secured the offices of president and vice-president of BNI to replace the previous PSI incumbent.

Such a complex network of interlocking offices of authority certainly assisted the development of the Bank Umum Nasional. During their ministries, Iskaq and Ong ordered several government instrumentalities to deposit funds in the Bank Umum Nasional. In late 1953, Yayasan Persediaan Perindustrian (which at one time held a monopoly on the import of cloves and cambrics) was ordered to deposit Rp6 million and the Yayasan Administrasi dan Organisasi was ordered to transfer Rp4 million. In March 1953, Ong ordered Rp20 million to be transferred from BNI to Bank Umum Nasional.

The PNI banking network was also connected with the national importer's association, Ikini, a co-operative holding import licences on behalf of Benteng importers unable to afford prepayments and operated as a funnel for BNI import credits. Under the chairmanship of PNI party chairman Moh. Tabrani, Ikini became a central terminal for allocation of state bank credit and licences for Benteng importers. To the dismay of opponents of Benteng and, no doubt, of businessmen with no PNI patronage, members of Ikini were able to continue to attract loans despite poor records of repayment.[21]

Individual PNI members also undertook business ventures, usually with Chinese partners. Using either capital accumulated in their period of party or government office or their capacity to attract licences, contracts and concessions, twenty-eight of the forty-seven members of the PNI faction in parliament had business interests.[22] Prominent among PNI businessmen was Herling Laoh, a former cabinet minister who established the construction companies N.V. Birokarpi, N.V. Perintis and N.V. Paka, the last two as joint ventures with the government. Moh. Tabrani, former minister, party chairman, chairman of Ikini and director of Bank Umum Nasional, went into partnership with Chinese interests in N.V. Indonesian Bottlers (Coca Cola franchise holders) and N.V. Indos Knitting Factory.[23]

The business community quickly assumed a position of vital importance to the party as a source of revenue. In 1952, the PNI Election Funds Committee estimated that Rp1 million was to be raised from 100 PNI businessmen, each of whom was expected to give Rp10 000. An additional Rp63 285 400 was to be raised from other than PNI businessmen or from special levies on the PNI clients for specific party favours.[24] Further fund raising involved the allocation of special import licences outside Benteng such as those which secured privileges for PNI-associated companies: N.V. Suez in the import of cambrics and P.T. Interkertas in the import of paper.[25]

Other parties established similar business structures including banks, holding companies and trading companies, which were ready-made vehicles for the channelling of import licences, foreign-exchange credits and other concessions appropriated by the parties from the state. For example, Bank Banten was closely associated with Masyumi, whilst Bank Niaga and the Zoro Corporation were associated with the PSI.[26]

PRIVATE INDIGENOUS BUSINESS GROUPS

Apart from the political brokers, the 'brief case' entrepreneurs and business groups operated directly by the parties for purposes of revenue raising and accumulation of economic power, there emerged several private indigenous business groups which benefited from access to state-bank credit, state-allocated import licences and government contracts, taking advantage of preferential credit and licensing policies towards indigenous capital and specific politico-economic alliances with the parties. Some of these concentrated on import and distribution of commodities which involved assembly processes and sole distributorships.

The new businessmen included both established traders mainly from Sumatra and party officials or their political associates. The most prominent were:

Rahman Tamin;	Sidi Tando;
Wahab Affan;	Fritz Eman;
Omar Tusin;	Moh. Tabrani;
Pardede;	Hashim Ning;
R. Rudjito;	Djohan & Djohor;
Agoes Dasaad;	Soetan Sjahsam;
Haji Sjamsoeddin;	R. Mardanus;
Usman Zahiruddin;	Eddy Kowara;
Herling Laoh;	R.M. Kusmuljono;
Soedarpo Sastrosatomo;	GKBI (Association of
Ir. Sosrohadikoesoemo;	Indonesian Batik
H.A. Ghany Aziz;	Co-operatives)

This is not an exhaustive list. Many of the indigenous business groups which later became prominent under Guided Democracy and the New Order had their origins in the Benteng period, but were then only of minor significance. Nevertheless, an examination of the development of the most significant of these groups gives some insight into the process of the formation of the indigenous capitalist class in this period.

Tamin, Dasaad and Aziz all came from Sumatran trading families whose business interests were based upon trade in small-holders' rubber, tea, coffee and pepper. Dasaad was born into a South Sumatran trading family with connections through marriage to Filipino trading families. Aziz came from a Palembang aristocratic family which had been engaged in trade for several generations, whilst the Tamin family was, until 1914, involved in trade on a scale which amounted to little more than peddling.[27]

These local trading groups soon expanded into inter-island and international trade. In the mid-1930s, Dasaad combined with other Sumatran traders, Djohan, Djohor and Aziz, to break the Chinese monopoly on the import of textiles from Japan and to begin importing raw cotton for the Indonesian textile industry. At the same time Dasaad began exporting small-holder rubber as distinct from merely being involved in its local collection.

Expansion of the Tamin group began in 1914 when Haji Tamin opened a small office in Bukitinggi to deal with the trade in small-holders' produce between Bukittingi and Padang. This was followed by an office in Padang itself in 1928, and by 1929 the business was being run by Agoes and Rahman Tamin who had established trading links with Chinese firms in Singapore. Involvement in the Singapore/Padang/Jakarta trade made it necessary for the firm to move its headquarters to Jakarta in 1932. As the Tamins moved beyond the local Minangkabau sphere they became increasingly involved in networks dominated by Chinese merchants, even establishing their head office in Pintu Kecil, the centre of Chinese commercial activity in Jakarta. With Chinese domination of trading, credit and distribution within Indonesia and of the Indonesia/Singapore trade, access to these Chinese networks and to Chinese credit was of crucial importance to the Sumatran traders.

The Benteng programme offered the Sumatran traders the opportunity to expand into sectors formerly controlled by the Dutch, notably the import of capital goods and manufactured consumer commodities from Europe. Aziz and Dasaad were so successful in securing import licences in foreign-exchange credit and government contracts for the supply of machinery that they were both able to enter sole agency agreements with foreign manufacturers. Aziz established N.V. Masayu, which became involved in the import, assembly and distribution of railway rolling stock, agricultural machinery and road-building equipment. The most important of these sole agencies for Masayu was that of International Harvester. By 1965, Dasaad had established a range of sole agencies which included Fiat, Lockheed, Westinghouse and Kaiser Aluminium. Throughout the 1950s, he operated one of the largest textile mills in Indonesia, P.T. Kancil Mas, a former German-owned mill secured in 1942. The Tamin group used Benteng licences to expand their position in the Jakarta/Singapore trade and in importing for the textile industry. Although the Tamins purchased a hotel in Bukittingi and a Dutch printing press in Surabaya in 1952 and 1953, the major transformation of the group was not to come until 1957 with the establishment of the Ratatex textile mill in Surabaya.

Other Sumatran traders were able to use Benteng licences and state credit to extend their business activities. Haji Sjamsoeddin was already established in trade, rubber re-milling and textiles by the end of the colonial period and his major expansion in the 1950s was into shipping. Sidi Tando, an established trader, opened a paint factory with credit from BNI and was to move into shipping in the early 1960s. Wahab Affan expanded from trade into banking and shipping.[28]

The success of these Sumatran trading groups must largely be attributed to the fact that they had an established capital base and trading structure of national significance and were therefore well placed to take advantage of the general policies of preference for indigenous capitalists. Nevertheless, personal and political association with influential officials and party leaders was important. Dasaad, for example, was a financier of the nationalist movement from the early 1930s and was a personal friend of Sukarno.[29] Wahab Affan was related to Sukarno's first wife, Fatmawati; Sukarno himself was a shareholder in one of Affan's early companies; and one of Affan's shipping companies in the early 1960s was a joint venture with the provincial government of West Irian.[30]

An important feature of the 1950s was the movement of officials and former officials into business. Among the first of these was R. M. Kusmuljono, a close associate of PNI party leaders and a leading PNI member of the National Advisory Committee, KNIP, in the late 1940s. He was born in 1905 into a central Javanese *priyayi* family. Both his father and grandfather had been officials with the Dutch colonial administration and the Kusmuljono children were educated at tertiary level in Holland. After returning to Indonesia as a lawyer, Kusmuljono spent the 1930s practising law in Kalimantan and advising indigenous rubber re-millers and exporters. From 1942 to 1943 he was director of a coconut oil plant in Tegal. With this business experience he returned to Jogjakarta in 1945 to establish a bank for the newly proclaimed republic, Bank Perniagaan, whose directors were to include Dasaad and Hashim Ning.

In 1951, Kusmuljono established P.T. Indoplano, together with Kussarjono, an associate of PNI Prime Minister Wilopo. Indoplano was a small-scale manufacturer of pencils, water pumps, and sugar cane processing machinery. It also operated a cast iron foundry, which never expanded beyond small-scale production. The thrust of the Indoplano group soon focused upon securing sole agencies for the import of manufactures, including those of Krupp, Hawker and Cummins Diesel. These involved the import of railway rolling stock, mining machinery, prime movers, tools and instruments, diesel engines and aeroplanes. The move into the field of sole agencies involved not only the capacity to obtain the licence from the government for sole agency importing status, but also the ability to secure contracts from the government for the supply of equipment.[31]

A second major party client was Hashim Ning, a West Sumatran born in 1916 into a family of small traders of rubber, tea and pepper. Before the war he worked in the family business and for several Dutch firms including the automobile importers, N.V. Velodome. However Ning, unlike Dasaad, Aziz and Tamin, did not become a figure of national business significance until the 1950s and is more clearly a product of political patronage. In the period 1946–47 he was personal assistant to Moh. Hatta, a fellow Minangkabau, and throughout the 1950s developed close associations with both the PNI and PSI.

After independence, Ning took over Velodome Motors from the Dutch, continuing to import automobiles but also successfully securing contracts for the servicing of military vehicles.[32] In 1952 he was appointed President Director of the Indonesian Service Company, which imported and assembled Dodge trucks and Willeys jeeps and which was owned by BNI and its subsidiary, C.V. Putera. During the period of PSI dominance within BNI, the Indonesian Service Company was able, along with several private PSI companies, to secure important government import contracts.[33] Together with Agoes Dasaad, Ning also established P.T. Daha Motors which secured the sole agency for the import of Fiat cars. Among his other business partners were Kusmuljono; Soetan Sjahsam (the brother of leading PSI figure Sutan Sjahrir), who also owned the successful import company, N.V. Soetan Sjahsam Corporation and, in later periods, the government of Jakarta; Pertamina director, Ibnu Sutowo; and the Arab/Indonesian businessman, Bakrie.[34]

Soedarpo Sastrosatomo entered business in 1952, after three years in the Foreign Service from 1948 to 1951. He began by establishing the import and export company, N.V. Soedarpo, which was able to secure Benteng licences.[35] Soedarpo was associated with the PSI, being a brother of the chairman of the PSI group in parliament, Subadio Sastrosatomo, and a personal friend of Sultan Hamengku Buwono. It was alleged in parliament that N.V. Soedarpo, along with other PSI companies, had received contracts to import vehicles and arms for the military which should have been channelled through the BNI subsidiary, C.V. Putera. At the time, the PSI controlled the Ministries of Trade and Finance, the BNI, and the state trading companies CTC and Putera.[36]

Unlike most of his contemporaries, Soedarpo quickly lessened his dependence upon the import sector and laid the foundations for the shipping companies he was to develop over the following decades. In 1953 and 1954 he established the Indonesian agency for two major international shipping lines and followed this with investments in stevedoring. After the mid-1960s he ventured into ship-owning and operation.[37]

The final business group to be examined is GKBI, a national association amalgamating the five major regional batik co-operatives. As mentioned in the previous chapter, indigenous batik merchants resisted Chinese incursions in the 1920s and 1930s by forming co-operatives to secure control over distribution of cambrics and, to a lesser extent, dyes and other raw materials. From 1949 to 1952, GKBI, through its subsidiary N.V. Batik, held the monopoly on cambric imports. In 1953, GKBI took over the functions of N.V. Batik, and although the total monopoly was terminated when Masyumi influence declined in the cabinets, regional batik co-operatives continued to depend upon affiliation with GKBI for supplies of cambrics.[38]

Because enterprise was largely based upon access to import licences and state-bank credit allocated by specific officials and political factions, the position of the Benteng trader was precarious. As parties and factions rose and fell and offices of authority within state banks and government departments changed hands, there was a tendency for licences, contracts and concessions to be re-directed to new sets of clients associated with the new party in power. The fragility of this situation encouraged short-term speculative and high profit adventures.

For those who were able to use Benteng as a basis for long-term survival, the keys to success involved the development of a combination of durable economic and political alliances and successful exploitation of political patronage for purposes of capital accumulation. Importing in a period of currency overvaluation and inflation provided excellent opportunities to make large profits which might provide the basis for capital accumulation. Overpricing of imports allowed reserves of capital to be built up overseas in foreign currency, and it was this source, according to several businessmen, which provided much of the finance used for domestic investment after 1967.[39] Some businessmen were able to combine import facilities with manufacture or assembly and this combination was particularly valuable for textile manufacturers such as Tamin, Dasaad and Pardede. Finally, some Benteng importers were able to build relatively stable relationships with foreign companies which provided sources of finance and corporate organisation and a degree of insulation from domestic political upheaval.[40]

Increasingly there developed a polarisation within the indigenous bourgeoisie, between those able to gain access to state facilities and political patronage and able to secure access to the finance and distribution networks of foreign and Chinese capital, and those who remained within the confines of a declining petty trade and commodity production sector. This latter group has, over the three decades since independence, constituted a persistent element of political resistance to the development of the politico-economic alliance between indigenous politico-bureaucratic power and foreign and Chinese capital.

THE DECLINE OF INDIGENOUS PETTY CAPITAL AND POLITICAL RESISTANCE

In the commodity production industries of *kretek*, batik and textiles, the transient success of a series of politically connected licence holders was thrown into contrast with continuing and serious decline among indigenous producers. The increasing application of capital and technology in these fields was shifting the bulk of manufacture into the hands of the Chinese.

In the *kretek* industry, import activity flourished on the basis of a clove import monopoly given to P.T. Pusat Pembelian, the shareholders of which were members of the Congress of Indonesian Cigarette Manufacturers Associations, Garpri. Castles commented that:

> The leading figures in this arrangement were politically connected with the parties supporting the Wilopo Cabinet and in October, 1953, after the fall of that cabinet, PPTI (Pusat Pembelian Tjenke Indonesia – Indonesian Clove Purchasing Centre) lost its monopoly.[41]

Subsequently, until the imposition of a government monopoly in October 1954, importers of cloves were 'selected' national importers, supporters of the Ali Sastroamidjojo Cabinet. However, while those able to secure import licences flourished either through the profits of the import trade or simply by selling licences, the indigenous *kretek* producers entered a period of serious decline. Castles found that in 1950, 65% of the production of *rokok putih* (Western style cigarettes) was in the hands of foreign and Chinese producers while the bulk of *kretek* production was now carried out by Chinese in Semarang, Surabaya and Malang, displacing indigenous producers in the traditional *kretek* production areas of Kudus and Brantas.[42]

In the textile industry, imports of cloth and cotton were reserved for Benteng importers, but individual indigenous producers, with a few notable exceptions, lacked the capital to purchase licences and make prepayments themselves. Consequently, large numbers of indigenous producers with access to licences actually abandoned manufacture and lived off the sale of import licences and raw material allocations. The decline of indigenous producers was also hastened by their inability to compete with fully manufactured textiles imported by Benteng importers or to compete for government orders with the more highly mechanised Chinese and European mills.[43]

Indigenous producers/exporters in Sumatra and the outer islands in general were also hard hit by a combination of high inflation rates with an artificially high rate of exchange for the rupiah. Importing in such a situation gave opportunities for massive profits in rupiahs after the landed goods were sold. In effect, the state was providing the importer with finance, a monopoly position and the conditions for super profits. Such a situation, as Schmitt noted, contrasted with that of the producer/exporters.

> Combined with fixed exchange rates, domestic inflation threatened the incomes of indigenous exporters in the Outer Regions, where the bulk of the exports originate. Dwindling real incomes there caused increased resentment towards populous Java, where most of the nation's imports were being absorbed.[44]

The question of inflation is an important one because it clearly distinguished the interests of the bulk of the indigenous producers engaged in export and manufacture, from those of importers. It was not only the outer island traders who were hard hit by inflation. Schmitt reports that traders in the Javanese textile industry:

> . . . found that they had to pay inflationary prices for supplies from abroad at the same time that they were harassed by sporadic price controls. Furthermore, even at high prices supplies became uncertain as the over valued exchange rate caused exchange reserves to dwindle.[45]

Grievances of the indigenous merchant bourgeoisie extended beyond the issues of inflation and foreign exchange rates. Increasingly their political associations demanded more thorough-going government action in creating a national economy in which the private indigenous businessman was to be the principal actor. Because the capital resources of the indigenous merchant bourgeoisie were so meagre, the state was expected to provide significant amounts of subsidy and protection. More important, economic nationalism, for

the indigenous business associations, was a notion which did
not include Chinese, whether *peranakan* or *totok*, citizen or
alien. Consequently indigenous business leaders and associations increasingly demanded economic exclusion of the Chinese by state decree.

The first post-colonial business association was the Association of Economic Workers (PTE), formed in 1946 to act as a
business arm of the revolution, transferring and smuggling
rice, arms and medical supplies. After Independence, the
PTE was replaced by the Indonesian Economic Board (DEI)
under the chairmanship of R. Rudjito, president director of
the indigenous-owned insurance company, Bumiputera.
While business associations like DEI, Ikini and Gapindo
were established to secure and distribute credit and licences
for members, they were also concerned with resisting continued foreign and Chinese dominance of the economy.[46]

By late 1955 the continuing frustrations of the declining
elements of the indigenous capitalist class found increasing
political expression. Anti-Chinese feeling was the main current for political unity but, as Schmitt noted, the basis for a
political coalition of indigenous capital also related to resentment of import-oriented state policy and those who benefited
from it.

The overvalued exchange rate benefited importers – bureaucrats
who controlled the exchange allocations and their friends – but did
not reduce costs for trading interests outside the import sector, to
whom imports were resold at high and rising prices. Price controls
added further irritation. Trading groups outside Java therefore won
political allies among their less powerful counterparts within Java.
In combination, the trading interests provided the core of indigenous support needed to put force behind the demand for retrenchment at the top.[47]

In 1956, the All-Indonesian National Economic Congress
(Kensi) was formed as a kind of political and ideological wing
of the indigenous business community. Under the leadership
of Asaat, formerly chairman of KNIP in the federal period,

Kensi passed resolutions calling for protection against Chinese economic dominance and expressing the view that the Chinese should be treated as an integral component of the colonial economy.[48] Despite the widespread enthusiasm for the resolution among the indigenous business community, particularly outside Java, Kensi failed to receive support from any of the major political parties. The PSI and Masyumi took the view that indigenous capital could only develop with the aid of Chinese and foreign capital, while the PNI refused to legislate legal rights and obligations on a racial basis. The PKI distinguished, not between indigenous and Chinese bourgeoisie, but between national and imperialist bourgeoisie.

The parties rejected the Asaat position partly on ideological grounds, but more importantly because it implied a massive extension of state financial and political intervention on behalf of a class which had demonstrated its weaknesses. In political terms the indigenous bourgeoisie and petty bourgeoisie had failed to secure a significant degree of direct political power, and even those parties and factions who hoped they would play a significant role in the development of Indonesian capitalism began to lose influence over policy-making from the mid-1950s.

In 1956, a year after Benteng was opened to Chinese importers, the state began to impose a tighter degree of regulation and control of indigenous business associations. DEI was replaced in 1956 with the Board of Trade and Business, DPP, a government-sponsored and regulated body with a structure parallel to that of the state bureaucracy. Such a move was the forerunner of increasing state co-ordination and incorporation of the political organs of the business community which continued under Guided Democracy with Bamunas (National Council of Businessmen) and under the New Order with Kadin (Office of Trade and Industry). At the same time the state discontinued a whole variety of programmes of state investment and subsidy such as the Economic Urgency Programme, and dissolved a variety of government-sponsored organisations, such as the Yayasan Kopra, which had been intended to channel finance and political protection to the indigenous bourgeoisie.

THE MOVE TOWARDS STATE-DOMINATED NATIONAL CAPITALISM

By the mid-1950s the new Indonesian republic was left with two options:

(a) To retreat from nationalism and indigenism and look once again to foreign and Chinese capital as the main generating force of capitalist development.

(b) To extend the process of economic nationalisation and socialisation by expropriating the remaining Dutch enterprises and using the state as the engine of national capital accumulation and industrialisation.

The first of these positions was urged by a loose coalition of parties including the PSI, Masyumi and the moderate wing of the PNI. In addition to their inability to halt the growing influence of Sukarno and his allies in the rarified atmosphere of Jakarta politics, they were unable to mobilise any social or economic coalition of sufficient political force to support their gradualist policies. The indigenous bourgeoisie, including the party clients, supported the gathering momentum of moves towards nationalisation. The expropriation of the extensive Dutch interests held out hopes (illusory as it turned out) of a bonanza for domestic capital. The PNI clients saw no reason to expect that nationalisation would do anything other than increase the largesse in the hands of their patrons.

Given the vacuum of social power in which parties operated, only the peasant and labour fronts of the PKI represented any cohesive socio-political force, and the political power of the military became decisive. Throughout the 1950s important elements of the military had made clear their dissatisfaction with the instability of party government, the corruption of political leaders and the ineffectiveness of formulation and implementation of policy. Further, they developed claims to a legitimate role in political and economic decision-making.[49] By the late 1950s, General Nasution had imposed an increasingly cohesive and centralised structure of authority upon the Army, a process which was assisted by the effectiveness with which the Central Command was able to retain the loyalty of the bulk of Army units and suppress the PRRI/Permesta regional revolts in 1958/59. Sukarno's moves to dismantle cabinet government and establish presidential authority, which began with his appointment of a working cabinet in 1958, were fully supported by the military. Indeed, it would be more accurate to say that the military was a prime mover in the establishment of Guided Democracy, ensuring in the process of negotiations that it secured a legitimate and strategic position in the new power structures.[50]

Similarly, the military supported policies of state capitalism and economic nationalism proposed by Sukarno and the radical nationalists because, as will be explained at greater length in the following chapter, the circumstances surrounding the expropriation of Dutch enterprises resulted in military control of the bulk of the new state corporations and independent sources of revenue and economic power.

The weakness of the moderate parties was such that they were able to offer no resistance to the 1957-58 nationalisation of Dutch enterprises, nor were they able to resist the replacement of parliamentary cabinet government with what was effectively presidential rule in the period 1958–60.

CONCLUSION

The party governments in the period 1949–57 had attempted to alter the structure of the colonial economy from reliance on export of estate and small-holder crops to a more self-sufficient industrial economy. They had also attempted to achieve varying measures of transfer of ownership of capital from foreign to national and from Chinese to indigenous. In essence, they sought to achieve these objectives by allowing the basic structures of production and ownership to remain intact while, at the same time, using the state to appropriate specific and crucial sectors of the economy such as banking and public utilities and to provide the engine of national capital formation. Central to the thrust of these policies was the intention to establish a strong indigenous capitalist class by providing state finance for indigenous investors and by introducing regulations giving indigenous investors preferential access to licences which, in some cases, excluded non-indigenous capitalists.

In general we may say that these policies failed. Structurally, the economy remained much as it did in the late colonial period, with industrial investment making little headway. Industry declined from 12% to 11% of national income between 1953 and 1958, and even export crops declined from 12.4% to 6.8%. The big gain was made by the government sector which moved up from 7.9% to 13.7%. Peasant agriculture increased from 36.2% to 40.4%.[51] Although precise figures are not available, the data we do have suggests that Chinese and foreign capital ownership was not substantially reduced and that the expansion of indigenous capital was largely that of state capital.

Nevertheless, we do see the beginnings of a small indigenous bourgeoisie. It was reliant on the protection and subsidy of general state policy such as that embodied in Benteng and on access to state capital and authority appropriated by centres of politico-bureaucratic power. The appropriated authority of state itself provided the main source for capital accumulation by indigenous rentiers, brokers and capitalists. Apart from access to the political and economic resources of the state, indigenous capital relied heavily on integration with established foreign and Chinese capital and networks of distribution. The beginnings of an alliance between indigenous politico-bureaucratic power and foreign and Chinese capital are apparent.

However, there was no inevitability about the plunge into national state capitalism which was to occur from late 1957.

The immediate problems of capital shortage, stagnating production and declining foreign earnings could have been
equally tackled by opening the door wide to international
and Chinese capital and abandoning ambitions to the establishment of a national economy. Indeed this is precisely what
occurred from late 1965 onwards. The choice of a nationalist
path in the late 1950s was one which grew out of the political
conditions of the period.

1. The complex manoeuvrings and structure of party politics in this
period are best explained in H. Feith, *The Decline of Constitutional Democracy in Indonesia* (Ithaca, 1962).

2. Sutter 1959, pp. 317, 117–19.

3. Sutter 1959, pp. 1184–91 and 1124 provides material drawn from
Sjafruddin's paper; 'Is Foreign Capital Dangerous for our Nation and
State?' from the Java Bank Report, 1951–52 and from resolutions of the
Sixth Congress of Masyumi, August 1952.

Sjafruddin's concept of religious socialism is treated in Sjafruddin, *Politik
dan Revolusi Kita* (Jogjakarta, 1948). Summaries of this are to be found in
K. Thomas and J. Panglaykim, *Indonesia — the Effects of Past Policies and
President Suharto's Plans for the Future* (Melbourne, 1973), pp. 44–6, and in
B. Glassburner, 'Economic Policy-Making in Indonesia, 1950–1957', in B.
Glassburner (ed.), *The Economy of Indonesia* (Ithaca, 1971), p. 81.

4. Sutter 1959, pp. 1179–83 and 1193–1201. Statement of PNI party
principles from Jakarta, Ministry of Information, *Kepartian dan Parlemen-
taria*, 1954, in H. Feith and L. Castles (eds), *Indonesian Political Thinking:
1945–65* (Ithaca, 1970), pp. 161–4.

PNI policy towards foreign investment, state investment and central
planning represented a triumph of the views of Wilopo over those of
Hadikoesoemo, Sidik and Mangunsarkoro who proposed a much more
hostile atttitude towards private enterprise in general and foreign capital in
particular. The tension between these two positions was a constant factor in
PNI politics in the 1950s.

5. The views of Wilopo are outlined in Sutter 1959, pp. 1179–83.

6. Dr. Sumitro Djojohadikoesoemo was the most prominent of these.
He was PSI Minister of Trade in the Natsir Cabinet (Sept.–March 1951),
Minister of Finance in the Wilopo Cabinet (April 1952–July 1953) and in the
Harahap Cabinet (August 1955–March 1956). For summaries of his econ-
omic policies originally developed in Sumitro, *Ekonomi Pembangunan*
(Jakarta, 1957) see: K. Thomas and J. Panglaykim 1973, pp. 44–6 and
Glassburner 1971*a*, pp. 81–2.

7. Glassburner 1971*a*, p. 80.

8. For details of the development of state corporations in the 1950s prior
to the nationalisations of 1957, see M. Sadli, 'Structural and Operational
Aspects of Public (especially industrial) Enterprises in Indonesia', *Ekonomi
dan Keuangan* 13, 5/6 (1960).

9. Sutter 1959, pp. 775–7; R. Anspach, 'Indonesia', in F. Golay, et al. (eds), *Underdevelopment and Economic Nationalism in Southeast Asia* (Ithaca, 1969), p. 163.

10. Anspach 1969, p. 141; Sutter 1959, p. 1037.

11. Sutter, p. 999. Mulyomiseno was a prominent NU politician who became Minister for Trade in 1958 and 1959 and issued the infamous regulation No. 10 (PP10) which prohibited Chinese from engaging in retail activity outside *kabupatan* capitals.

12. Sutter 1959, pp. 805–8, 908–22, 956.

13. Anspach 1969, pp. 142–3.

14. Sutter 1959, p. 702.

15. Anspach 1969, p. 182.

16. Sutter 1959, pp. 805–8; Anspach 1969, p. 184.

17. Sutter 1959, pp. 1101–4.

18. Anspach 1969, p. 183.

19. Information on the development of the Benteng policy is drawn from Anspach 1969, pp. 171–9; Sutter 1959, pp. 1017–35; Thomas and Panglaykim 1973, pp. 47–8. For comments on the type of importer produced by Benteng, see Castles 1967, p. 11; J. Panglaykim, 'Marketing Organization in Transition' *BIES* 9 (1968), p. 47.

20. See, among others, Panglaykim 1968, p. 48 and Feith 1962, p. 123.

21. J. Rocamora, Nationalism in Search of an Ideology: the Indonesian Nationalist Party 1946–65 (Ph.D. thesis, Cornell University, 1974), pp. 181–5; Sutter 1959, pp. 997–1000.

22. For details of business interests of Members of the Provisional Parliament of the Unitary Republic who served before 1955, see Sutter 1959, p. 1311 (Appendix W).

23. Ibid., pp. 791–8.

24. Rocamora 1974, p. 188.

25. Sutter 1959, p. 1072; Panglaykim 1968, pp. 48–50.

26. Panglaykim 1968, p. 48.

27. Information on these three groups was obtained from:
    (a) Interviews with Eddy Dasaad, son of Agoes Dasaad (Jakarta, 23.10.74); Darwis and Sofyan Tamin (Jakarta, 13.3.74); Ali Noorluddin, President Director of the Masayu Group (8.3.74 and 14.9.74).
    (b) H. A. Ghany Aziz, *Wasiat Pada Hari Ulang Tahun ke - 78, 79, 80* (Bandung, 1973).
    (c) A precis of the history of the Tamin Group prepared by Sofyan and Darwis Tamin for the author.
    d) Sutter 1959, pp. 289; Panglaykim 1969, pp. 48–50.

28. H. Dick, The Indonesian Inter-island Shipping Industry (Ph.D. thesis, Australian National University, 1977), pp. 170–5.

29. M. Nishihara, *The Japanese and Sukarno's Indonesia* (Honolulu, 1967), p. 153.

30. Dick 1977, p. 170.

31. Interview with Kusmuljono, 19.2.74. See also Sutter 1959, p. 792.

32. Sources for the Ning group in this period are G. Roeder, *Who's Who in Indonesia* (Jakarta, 1971); *Kompas*, 7.7.73; *Suara Karya*, 22.6.74.

33. Sutter 1959, pp. 981–3.

34. For ownership data on the Ning group see: R. Robison, Capitalism and the Bureaucratic State in Indonesia 1965–75 (Ph.D. thesis, Sydney University, 1977), Appendix B. p.v.

35. Interview with Soedarpo, 6.11.74.

36. Sutter 1959, pp. 1052–4.

37. Dick 1977, pp. 154–5.

38. Interview with Jusuf Moeid, Trade Manager of GKBI, 28.10.74. See also: Economic Research Bureau of the University of Gadjah Mada, 'The Batik Industry in Central Java', Ekonomi dan Keuangan, XI, 7 (1958).

39. Interviews with businessmen who operated in the 1950s: Eddy Dasaad — 23.10.74; Darwis and Sofyan Tamin — 13.3.74; Ali Noorluddin — 8.3.74 and 14.9.74; R. M. Kusimuljono — 19.2.74; B. R. Motik — 28.9.74; Harlan Bekti — 5.3.74; Mrs Sita — 12.10.74; Omar Tusin — 28.10.74; Soedarpo — 6.11.74; Idham — 6.11.74.

40. Apart from distributorships already mentioned, involving Kusmuljono, Aziz and Dasaad, joint ventures and agencies included: Soedarpo — agent for Hamburg America Line and Tokyo Senpaku Kaisha; Fritz Eman (N. V. Udatin) — joint venture with the German company Borgward to assemble automobiles.

41. Castles 1967, pp. 71–2.

42. Ibid., pp. 20, 38.

43. Interviews with Sukar Sjamsoeddin, Chairman of Perteksi (Indonesian Textile Producers Association) Bandung, 1.11.74; and J. C. Tambunan, Chairman of Perteksi Indonesia and a prominent textile producer of that period. See also Sutter 1959, p. 804.

44. Schmitt 1962, p. 288.

45. H. Schmitt, 'Post-colonial Politics: A Suggested Interpretation of the Indonesian Experience, 1950–1958', The Australian Journal of Politics and History 9, 2 (1963).

46. See resolutions of the 1945 Bandung Business Conference listed in Sutter 1959, pp. 260–4. Interviews with Omar Tusin (28.10.74), B. R. Motik (28.9.74) and Sutomo (25.10.74), three of the most politically active of indigenous business leaders in this period, confirmed that indigenous capitalists in this period viewed their situation as one of progressive deterioration primarily at the hands of Chinese and foreign capital.

47. Schmitt 1962, p. 289.

48. Anspach 1969, pp. 186–7; Feith 1962, pp. 481–7. See also Asaat's speech to the All-Indonesian National Importers Conference of March, 1956, reproduced in part in Feith and Castles 1970, pp. 343–6.

49. See D. Lev, The Transition to Guided Democracy: Indonesian Politics, 1957–1959 (Ithaca, 1966), pp. 182–201; H. Crouch, The Army and Politics in Indonesia (Ithaca, 1978), Chapter 1; R. McVey, 'The Post-Revolutionary Transformation of the Indonesian Army', Indonesia 11 (1971) and 13 (1972).

50. From 1958, the political power of the military was embodied in:
   (a) The emergency powers contained in the provisions of the martial law introduced in 1957, terminated in 1963 but reintroduced in modified form in 1964.
   (b) Representation in cabinet and parliament from 1958. In July

68 THE RISE OF CAPITAL

1959, one-third of cabinet ministers appointed were drawn from the military.
(c) The importance of military-dominated bodies which co-ordinated martial law and the West Irian Campaign.

51. D. Paauw, 'From Colonial to Guided Economy', in R. McVey (ed.) *Indonesia* (New Haven, 963), p. 176.

3
State Capital and Guided Economy: 1958–1965

THE STRUCTURE OF POWER UNDER GUIDED DEMOCRACY

IN the years from 1957 to 1960 the political structures of liberal democracy were dismantled and replaced with an authoritarian regime, loosely built around two centres of authority: the President and the Army. The authority of an elected parliament was replaced with the authority of the President who ruled through a variety of appointed bodies, the most important of which were the Cabinet, the Supreme Advisory Council, the Supreme War Authority (Peperti), which supervised martial law, and the Supreme Operations Command (KOTI), which dealt specifically with the West Irian campaign. The role of the parties was diminished not only by the emergence of these appointed bodies, responsible to and, in the last analysis, advisory to the President, but by the fact that the membership of these bodies was determined, not by the party hierarchies, but by the President and the military High Command. Party power was further eroded with the emergence of the concept that democracy was best served not by party representation but by the representation of functional social groups. In the 1960 parliament, 129 members were appointed to represent the parties, compared to 154 appointed to represent functional groups including the Army, peasants, trade unions, women and youth.[1] While power became authoritarian, its ideological expression became a kind of populist corporatism in which the social and political conflict embodied in the party system was to be replaced by a consensual system of mutual co-operation presided over by the President.[2]

In 1952 and 1956 elements of the armed forces had attempted to overthrow the existing system of party/cabinet rule. Although the High Command had suppressed these attempted coups, the military as a whole continued to be critical of the parties and developed claims to a central and legitimate political role for itself.[3] When Sukarno began his moves to replace cabinet government with presidential rule in the mid-1950s, the military was to become not only an enthusiastic partner but the main driving force in the enterprise. Military officers were attracted by the prospect of both strong government after a period of indecisive and vacillating party rule, and direct access to offices of authority. In March 1957 the military secured a critical source of authority with the establishment of martial law, under the provisions of which it was able to promulgate regulations, including those expropriating Dutch property and banning strikes. As the new structures of authority took shape, the military were able to secure strategic positions in Cabinet, the Supreme Advisory Council, the Parliament and in regional and local administration. Most important, the military secured authority over most of the expropriated Dutch estates and trading enterprises, and the state oil companies.[4]

The regional rebellions of 1958–59 were also important to the consolidation of power. Their failure demonstrated in a devastating fashion that neither regional military commands nor political parties sympathising with the regional separatists or producer/exporters were able to challenge the ultimate authority of Jakarta. The defeat of rebellious generals gave

General Nasution the opportunity to establish a stronger and more centralised military authority within the framework of Peperti. The failure of the rebellions also signalled the end of both the PSI and Masyumi, the parties which most strongly resisted Sukarno's moves to Guided Democracy and Guided Economy. Several of their leaders, including Natsir, Sjafruddin and Sumitro, had defected to the rebel cause, and such association enabled Sukarno to ban both parties. This meant the eclipse of those political forces constituting, in however haphazard a fashion, the interests of the Muslim merchant bourgeoisie in the outer islands together with those political forces advocating economic growth within the framework of international capital accumulation. The central state apparatus, both civil and military, was considerably strengthened, and in the outer islands the military were able to establish tight control over regional administration.

GUIDED ECONOMY AND STATE CAPITAL

There has been no single and authoritative definition of the term Guided Economy, but its elements may be gleaned from various economic policy statements and programmes, the most important of which are the Eight Year Plan of August 1960, and the Economic Declaration (Deklarasi Ekonomi — Dekon) of March 1963.[5] In broad terms, the principles of Guided Economy may be summarised as follows:

(a) The co-ordination and regulation by the state of all sectors of the Indonesian economy, state, private and co-operative, to ensure the integration of investment and production into the wider social and political goals and needs of Indonesia. State leadership would be provided both in the form of central planning and control over distribution, credit and production and by direct state investment.

(b) The destruction of imperialism and the subordination of foreign capital to national social and economic goals. Subordination of foreign capital was to be achieved by a combination of expropriation, preference for government-to-government loans and, where direct investment could not be avoided, joint ventures and production-sharing agreements.

(c) Replacement of the colonial import/export economy with a more self-sufficient and industrialised economy.

The state had always occupied a crucial position in the economy of post-colonial Indonesia, but it was thrust more directly into ownership of capital with the expropriation of Dutch enterprises in 1957/58. This process began as a spontaneous and unilateral takeover of some Dutch firms by workers and unions in December 1957, but this syndicalist movement was quickly halted by the military, and in December, General Nasution ordered all Dutch property to be placed under military supervision. A year later, the expropriation was formally endorsed by Parliament.[6]

The expropriations were a major blow to foreign capital in Indonesia and fundamentally transformed the structure of the economy. They involved the transfer of ownership of 90% of plantation output, 60% of foreign trade, some 246 factories and mining enterprises, plus banks, shipping and a variety of service industries.[7] These firms were not handed over to domestic private enterprise but were transformed into state corporations. There were several reasons for this. Indigenous capitalists had in general proven themselves too weak to assume ownership of such a massive slab of the colonial economy, consuming state credit and concessions throughout the 1950s without providing any serious evidence that they were able to establish the basis for a national industrial economy. At the same time it was clearly out of the question, in political terms at least, to hand the confiscated assets to Indonesian Chinese capitalists. In addition to these considerations, Sukarno and the leading PNI policy-makers believed indigenous private capital had proven itself unworthy of continuing government protection and subsidy. Thomas and Panglaykim[8] note that:

In the months between 'take-over' and nationalisation, private businessmen made a bid to persuade the Government to transfer certain of the ex-Dutch companies to the private sector. This was a rather forlorn hope because leaders of several political groupings had launched a strong attack on the performances of private enterprise at a National Economic Conference in November–December, 1957. Ex Vice-President Hatta had discussed the roles of Government and the private individual in furthering economic development and had sympathised with those who wanted the private entrepreneur to play the leading part. But he argued that the opportunity for the Indonesian capitalist had come too late. 'Freed from the shackles of colonialism, newcomers came forward in droves . . . but bitter experiences over the last eight years had entirely shattered those sentiments favourable to the private entrepreneur.' Hatta had been an ardent opponent of the Benteng system and it was the 'bitter experiences' of that programme to which he was referring.

For the military, state ownership was attractive because it offered the prospect of direct military control over economic resources. Neither the indigenous nor the Chinese national bourgeoisie or petty bourgeoisie were able to politically challenge these prevailing sentiments.

In April 1958, the confiscated Dutch trading houses were incorporated into six new state trading corporations (STCs) which, together with the two existing STCs, CTC and Usindo, constituted the state-owned 'big eight' and were given a monopoly on the import of thirteen basic commodities (including rice and textiles). They now effectively controlled 70% of imports.[9] Not only were STCs intended as a means of state control over pricing and supply of basic necessities, but were also to provide revenue for development, channelling 55% of profits, after depreciation and other deductions, into state revenue and special development funds.[10]

At the same time, the Dutch estates and a wide range of Dutch enterprises in the manufacturing and service sector were taken over by the state. The policies of all state companies, including pricing, investment and production, were controlled by supervisory boards — Bappit (industry), BUD (trade) and PPN Baru (agriculture). These were replaced in 1960 by BPUs (General Management Boards), which co-ordinated state enterprises in specific sectors, e.g. trade, estates, industry.[11]

In 1960 the Eight Year Plan laid down the basic strategy for economic development, designating two categories of economic activity. Category B included oil, rubber and other export sectors, which would earn income to repay foreign loans and provide the capital for investment in the Category A projects, which would promote the welfare of the people: education, public works, transport, health and production of basic necessities.[12]

Some state corporations did operate effectively and Moh. Sadli, later to become one of the main economic advisers of the Suharto Government, pointed out that those dealing with coalmines, ports, electricity, pawnshops and other public utilities and transport systems contributed Rp446 million in profits to the treasury in 1958 despite a loss by the railways.[13] Panglaykim notes that some STCs, particularly CTC and Gresik Cement, were efficient and profitable. But on the whole, state enterprises were a failure and were to preside over an alarming decline in Indonesia's existing capital stock. The United States Economic Survey Team to Indonesia stated in 1963 that: 'Indonesia has been living on its capital by failing to maintain inventories, to keep capital equipment in repair, and to replace over-age rubber trees, oil and coconut palms'.[14]

The decline in production of export crops was most serious because it significantly reduced Indonesia's export-earning capacity and destroyed the whole basis of the Eight Year Plan. Foreign earnings from estate crops declined from US$442.5 million in 1958 to US$330 million in 1966.[15] Prior

to independence, export earnings had been approximately
33% oil and minerals, 33% estate crops and 33% small-
holder crops. However, estate production of export crops
declined dramatically after independence. By 1963 they constituted less that 25% of total export earnings.[16] Mackie
reported that production of rubber, the main export crop,
was in serious difficulty by the early 1960s due to lack of
investment in planting and processing, lack of adequate
management and wide-spread smuggling.[17]

Industry also fared poorly and Mackie reported that:

. . . smaller investments in the light consumer goods industries,
which have been left implicitly to private businessmen, only attained a modest volume even during the favourable years of the
mid-1950s; since 1961 they seem to have dried up almost entirely
because of the intense uncertainty of prices, supplies and government regulations.[18]

Where industry was taken over directly or financed indirectly
by the state through BIN or co-operatives, the results were
also disappointing and most factories operated in the early
1960s well below capacity. This was due to a variety of
factors, including problems of capital formation, lack of
capital investment and maintenance of capital stock, and lack
of foreign exchange for machinery and raw material
imports.[19]

These problems were recognised by the state, and in May
1963 regulations were introduced which removed from the
STCs the monopoly on imports of essential goods and required
them to operate on a more autonomous basis. State
banks were ordered to direct at least 50% of credit to the
production sectors, thereby reducing the flow of credit to
importers.[20] In 1964, Sukarno introduced the Berdikari programme, which placed emphasis on the development of
import-substitution industrial production, focusing around a
new steel mill and other state investment projects which
included ship-building and fertiliser production. In 1965 the

government placed pressure on the private sector to get out of trade and into production. Introducing legislation associated with the Berdikari programme in April of that year, President Sukarno stated that:

> Private businessmen will be forbidden to import except in the Government's name. They will only be allowed to endeavour to become 'producer exporters' who must export under the government's leadership. This is the revolutionary task conferred on private business as an essential element in the Indonesian socialist economic structure.[21]

However, the government proved unable to replace a declining estate export sector with some kind of national industrial capitalism. A primary reason was its failure to generate the capital formation required for investment in industrial production and the provision of the necessary infrastructure. Declining export production earnings combined with burgeoning foreign borrowings and imports to produce severe balance of payment crises. Indonesia's export earnings had declined from $750 million in 1961 to $450 million in 1965, while import requirements for 1966 were estimated at $560 million to cover rice imports and raw materials and spare parts for industry. At the same time Indonesia's foreign debt had reached over $2 000 million and debt servicing for 1966 was estimated to be $530 million.[22] Obviously an impasse had been reached. Combined with increased government expenditures largely involved in the attempt to finance state enterprises, and a limited capacity to collect taxes, the state was forced to resort increasingly to inflationary policies to finance development projects and the requirements of the military.[23] Attempts to redress the balance of payments problem by withholding state credit from state and private importers and forcing a slowdown of sales by STCs created acute shortages of raw materials and spare parts for manufacturers.

Apart from difficulties with capital formation and the

chaos of monetary policy, the state corporations faced severe management problems. These were of two types. First, a lack of trained managers, and second, a tendency for managerial appointments to be made on the basis of political requirements to secure the economic position of the military and the political parties. Castles commented that: '. . . managers of state corporations were able to treat the property entrusted to them as in some respect private property and to extract private profits from the abuse of their authority'.[24]

Finally, state enterprises encountered structural problems which hindered the ability of individual firms to set prices, obtain credit and expand the scope of their operations to secure the advantages of vertical integration of marketing, production and finance. Perhaps the most detailed case study of state corporations was that made by Panglaykim[25], and some of his findings are worth recounting for the light they throw on the difficulties faced by the state enterprises as a whole.

Panglaykim argued that the decision to break up the vertical structure of the old Dutch trading houses and separate the import/export sections from production and distribution was a grave error. It meant that the STCs were structurally isolated from international distribution networks and regional and local production units. Inflexible credit arrangements with banks meant that they were unable to extend the same type of credit to producers as to private traders. With the deepening balance of payments crisis the government took action in 1963, forcing the banks to cut credit to the STCs, which were also required to slow sales of imports. STCs were unable to compete with private capital in the export sector in particular, and in both rubber and copra export, private capital remained dominant.[26] Even the dominant position of the STCs in import was ended in 1963 with the removal of the monopoly on essential goods imports.

Management was also a problem. Inefficiency was one major factor, but political appropriation of office was also damaging.

. . . the appointment of top executives was usually not in the hands of the top executives of the state trading corporations or of the General Management Board but lay with other decision centres. Often informal channels were used and informal pressures exerted by some group or other in order to obtain the appointment of its own candidates.[27]

In general, this meant that many of the crucial operating decisions within the STCs were not made on a commercial basis but were intended to provide finance for political power centres and individual officials. Service was often dependent on personal notes from influential persons, and many private firms received poor treatment from the STCs, both as a result of the general organisational inadequacies of STCs and their own inability to secure political patronage. Contributions of STCs to state revenue did not match the levels expected, partly because the difference between the official price and the market price of goods was not passed on to general revenue but expropriated by officials.[28]

By 1965, Indonesia had reached a point where the operation of state capital had to be recast. There were two possibilities:

(a) The constitution of political power and state capital under the PKI which would provide at least the organisational and ideological framework for capital formation and production under the ownership of the state. If necessary, foreign loans and joint ventures could be integrated within such a centrally planned system.

(b) The reconstitution of the relationships between state power, state capital and the various elements of the capitalist class in Indonesia – foreign and domestic – which would relocate the primary responsibility for capital accumulation and production with the private sector.

GUIDED ECONOMY AND FOREIGN CAPITAL

Expropriation of foreign capital in the period 1957–65 destroyed the dominance it had enjoyed within the structure of the colonial economy. In 1957 and 1958 the Dutch trading and estate enterprises, the core of Dutch colonial capital, were expropriated together with Dutch shipping, banking and industrial enterprises. These were followed by expropriations of British, American and other Western capital in 1963–65.

However, the expulsion of foreign capital was neither as complete nor as permanent as might have seemed. While it is true that nationalisations were politically inspired retaliation for Dutch policies in West Irian and British involvement in the formation of Malaysia, the Indonesian government did not seek to eliminate foreign capital but to change its form. In part, this meant dismantling investments which were considered exploitative and replacing them with more benign forms of investment such as production sharing or government-to-government loans.[29]

In the vital petroleum sector, state-owned oil corporations did not assume the production functions of foreign capital as did the PPN Baru in the estate sector. Instead, foreign oil companies worked as contractors to the state oil companies, retaining management control and providing the capital investment but entering into profit and production sharing agreements with the Indonesian state.[30] Foreign capital remained dominant in the petroleum sector because, unlike the estate sector, it was clearly recognised to be beyond the capacity of the Indonesian state to maintain production in such a highly capital and technology intensive sector. Naturally, the government was reluctant to put at risk such a vital source of foreign exchange. Earnings from petroleum exports were expected to provide 70% of the capital for the Category A projects in the Eight Year Plan, compared to 12% for earnings from rubber exports.[31]

The principle of production sharing was extended to investments in tin, timber, mining, fishing, edible oils and estate crops. Overseas investment or credit was to be repaid from the net increases in production which resulted from the investments. By the end of the Guided Economy period, capital commitments of US$72 million had been made, of

which Japan had contributed US$30.35 million.[32] Despite
the fact that investment in petroleum by the major oil companies, Caltex, Stanvac and Shell, is not included in this
figure, $72 million represents an extremely modest invest-
ment, indicating the reluctance of foreign capital to enter
production sharing agreements when more lucrative pickings
lay elsewhere.

Direct government-to-government loans were also problem-
atic when declining export earnings put Indonesia's growing
debt increasingly beyond its capacity to service.[33] With
politically hostile creditors, especially amongst the Western
creditor nations, rescheduling was not possible.

The experience of Guided Economy demonstrated that it
was politically possible to expropriate unacceptable forms
of foreign capital investment and to restructure the terms
under which foreign capital entered the economy. Indeed,
many of the structural devices introduced to deal with foreign investment were retained by the Indonesian government
after 1966. But the Indonesian state proved unable to establish a national economic structure strong enough to absorb
foreign capital selectively into a coherent programme of
investment and production:

DOMESTIC PRIVATE CAPITAL

The intention of Guided Economy was to construct a national industrial economy around state-owned capital. The
seizure of the Dutch-owned trading houses and the establishment of a state monopoly on the import of essential commodities was a clear indication that the private sector,
indigenous or Chinese, was to be excluded from the most
lucrative of trading monopolies. Correspondingly, state
credit was directed primarily to state-owned corporations,
ending the BIN experiment in state financing of a domestic
capitalist class.

Domestic capitalists were subjected to a variety of political
and economic controls by state agencies largely based upon

the power of the state to allocate raw materials and other imports. Most important here were the government-appointed co-ordinating bodies, GPS (Federation of Homogeneous Enterprises) and OPS (Organisation of Homogeneous Enterprises). Whole industries came under the control of GPS (e.g. textiles), while sub-categories of industries (e.g. weaving or spinning) were controlled by OPS. Although intended to provide regulation and rationalisation of production, OPS and GPS tended to become instrumentalities through which officials and political factions could make exactions from business in return for allocations of raw materials and other imports necessary to the production process.[34] The government also established the National Council of Businessmen, Bamunas, and appointed R. M. Notohamiprodjo, a PNI-associated businessman and former Minister of Trade, as chairman. Bamunas was intended as the offical channel of communication between business and the state and the agency through which government policy on private business could be implemented, especially the attempts under the Berdikari policy to push national investors out of importing and into production. However it operated more as a body which raised funds for the government from the business community. Castles reported that Bamunas raised Rp125 million from business for the Development Fund in 1964.[35]

Private business also suffered from the general process of economic dislocation, collapse of infrastructure, inflation, shortages of spare parts and other imports essential to production. These affected the national manufacturers and exporters most severely. Inflation and the over-valuation of the rupiah in particular made it costly to purchase imported raw materials and machinery. The very same factors that made importing and speculation in commodities economically attractive, also made manufacture less attractive. This was particularly so for the smaller commodity producers with limited capital resources, who were in the main indigenous commodity producers. Palmer and Castles described the difficulties confronted by the smaller indigenous textile producers:

> Most of the smaller producers did not have enough funds to purchase their quotas (of raw cotton) which had to be indented for in advance and they found bank credit hard to obtain. Consequently, they either processed the yarn on a commission basis for a middle man who financed the purchase of the raw material, or paid part of the quota to a money lender as interest, or sold the entire quota to the middleman who financed its purchase. In this way the greater part of the yarn allocations of small and many medium producers was channelled to the larger and more efficient factories.[36]

It was a common practice among smaller textile producers to exaggerate their production capacity in order to gain larger allocations, the majority of which they could sell in order to finance the purchase of enough cotton to keep production going. Many smaller producers gave production away completely and became sellers of allocations rather than manufactures. By purchasing the excess allocations from the smaller producers, larger manufacturers, predominantly Chinese, established an increasingly dominant position in the industry in this period. However, despite their advantage in the black market, even the larger-scale operators were forced to operate below capacity because of overall shortages of foreign exchange for imports of yarn and other raw materials. Investment in new machinery was minimal and most power looms in operation had been installed in the colonial period.[37]

Those indigenous capitalists who did manage to establish large textile manufacturing plants were drawn less from the traditional textile producers of Pekalongan and Majalaya and increasingly from the ranks of those businessmen who had built import firms around Benteng licences and who maintained association with political leaders, thereby guaranteeing privileged access to both import allocations and state-bank credit. The largest textile mills of the period were

not those of the traditional textile Hajis but those of Rahman
Tamin, Pardede, Dasaad, Ir. Aminuddin, Bram Tambunan
and General Almunir, who was director of the mill, P.T.
Ratna, established by the Department of Veterans Affairs
under General Sambas Atmatinata.

A further difficulty confronted by private investors was the
rapid rate of inflation and the arbitrary government policies
towards the exchange rate and monetary reform. Feith notes
that Indonesian private business was dealt another severe
blow by the monetary purge of August 1959, when all bank
deposits of over Rp25 500 lost 90% of their value.[38]

Accumulation of finance capital within Indonesia also
proved difficult in the extreme. Omar Tusin, leading a group
of Sumatran investors, established a private industrial credit
bank (Bank Pembangunan Swasta) in 1959 with a capital of
US$1 million. Largely due to inflation and government
monetary readjustments, the value of real assets had shrunk
to 5% of the original investment by 1966.[39] The lesson was
clear: accumulation and long term industrial investment was
not an attractive proposition. Many businessmen survived by
keeping funds tied up in diverse commodities such as nails,
screws and spare parts, selected as much as possible in
anticipation of shortages. If possible, capital accumulated
was to be located outside Indonesia. This was generally done
by overpricing imports, splitting the difference between the
real cost and the foreign exchange allocation with the overseas supplier, and depositing the profits in overseas banks.[40]
According to several businessmen it was this capital, brought
back into Indonesia after 1965, largely by Chinese, which
provided much of the finance for investment in the early New
Order period.

The tendency for national capital to concentrate in the
import sector was summarised by Castles in the following
terms:

Rapid price rises, transport bottlenecks, seasonal fluctuations
and imperfect information services, aggravated by sweeping revi-

sions from time to time of price controls and subsidies, made it possible for a man with money, information and connections to make large profits by buying, selling and hoarding.[41]

The government had attempted to minimise the role of private capital in the import sector by reducing the number of importers to 400 and reserving for the state corporations the right to import essential commodities. However, the STCs proved unable to cope with the import sector, for reasons discussed earlier, and the government had deprived itself of an important source of revenue previously gleaned from the private importer. Restrictions on private importers were therefore eased. In June 1960 permission was given for private importers to import formerly restricted commodities on indent to STCs, and in August, Rp1 billion of foreign exchange at favourable rates was made available for private import of goods on the free list. In May 1963 private importers were given permission to import commodities previously reserved for STCs.[42]

At the same time the government, faced with dwindling foreign exchange reserves and stagnating domestic investment in production, attempted to force private capital out of the import sector. In mid-1963 it was announced that 50% of bank credits to private business were to be reserved for the productive sector and 20% for export. In April 1965, President Sukarno ordered private firms out of the import sector except when importing in the government's name.

It is agreed by most commentators that by 1965, taking into account the generalised economic dislocation, the domestic bourgeoisie had not advanced since the 1950s although its dominant element, the Chinese, were probably in a stronger relative position.[43] Private capital continued to concentrate in trade, and the STCs had proven unable to establish their control over this sector. In the export sector especially, the STCs could not match the capital resources or organisational structures of the private firms.[44] But domestic capitalists also survived because, outside the perimeters of

state policy there developed strong politico-economic alliances between political leaders, state officials and private
business groups. Within the framework of these arrangements, which will be discussed in detail later in the chapter,
import licences, foreign exchange allocations, contracts and
other facilities were made available by politico-bureaucrats
to private businessmen.

THE STRUCTURE OF THE DOMESTIC BOURGEOISIE

Four major segments of the domestic bourgeoisie may be
identified:

(a) The traditional indigenous capitalists and petty capitalists located principally in petty trade and commodity production but with some penetration into
medium-scale enterprises.

(b) Chinese traders, retailers, commodity producers and
those engaged in service industries on a small scale.

(c) Indigenous capitalists operating on a medium to
large-scale, with access to state credit facilities and
licences, and with political connections and, often,
business partnerships with Chinese capital.

(d) Chinese capitalists operating in the medium and
large-scale sectors, with access to state resources and,
in many cases, finance from overseas.

Indigenous commodity producers in textiles, *kretek* and
other areas of petty commodity production were in this
period confronted by problems of inflation and shortages as
well as increasing competition from Chinese manufacturers
possessing superior capital resources. Outer island producer/
exporters found themselves in a similar situation. Since the
failure of the PRRI/Permesta rebellions and the banning of
Masyumi, they also found themselves bereft of whatever

meagre political protection and patronage they enjoyed in the 1950s.

In 1956, Kensi had demanded wide-ranging programmes of indigenisation, directed primarily at Chinese economic dominance. Masyumi's Sjafruddin had advocated a restricted programme in which small shops would be indigenised within two years, arguing that indigenisation should begin at the lower levels where the need for finance and experience were at a minimum. Entrenchment of a strong indigenous capitalist class at this modest level, it was argued, would create a base for capital accumulation and the establishment of trade networks. Despite the lack of interest and sympathy for such a proposal by the military and the major parties, PNI and PKI, a regulation embodying this philosophy was introduced unilaterally by the NU minister for trade, Rachmat Mulyomiseno, in 1959. This regulation, which became known as PP10 (Peraturan Pemerintah, No. 10, 1959), revoked licenses for alien Chinese in the retail trade at village level. At that time an estimated 83 783 out of 86 690 retail shops in villages were owned by Chinese and an estimated 25 000 were directly affected.[45] The effects of PP10 are interesting and reveal the dynamics of the balance of economic power between Chinese and Indonesian bourgeoisie and petty bourgeoisie.

The immediate consequence of PP10 was to create an exodus of the poorest Chinese traders from the countryside into the cities. An estimated 120 000 departed Indonesia altogether.[46] However, the larger Chinese capitalists had already left the countryside to fill the void progressively left by the Dutch in the cities and towns between 1945 and 1958. In the countryside, many Chinese aliens simply established joint ventures with indigenous former employees, often on an Ali Baba basis similar to that which characterised many Benteng importing companies, or with Chinese *warga negara* (Indonesian citizens).[47] The essential problem was the inability of indigenous capitalists to take up the role formerly filled by the Chinese. The Secretary of the Department of

Co-operatives estimated a need for Rp17 billion in credit if the co-operative movement was to replace the Chinese retailers.[48] Not surprisingly, such an amount was not forthcoming. In the long term the government proved unwilling to enforce PP10 rigorously and the Chinese dominance of this sector was gradually re-established.

As was the case with attempts in the 1950s to transfer rice milling, stevedoring, warehousing and bus transport to the indigenous bourgeoisie, PP10 failed because this group lacked the capital and the organisation to take advantage of preferential legislation. However, the strength of the Chinese position was also reinforced by the fact that none of the major centres of political power, including the military, the PNI, the PKI or Sukarno himself, were anxious to purge the Indonesian economy of Chinese capital because it was clear that such a move, if pursued comprehensively and vigorously, would create irreparable economic damage to the economy as a whole and to the many economic relationships between larger Chinese business groups and centres of party and military power.

Finally, the historical development of the Chinese bourgeoisie in Indonesia had provided a capital and structural basis which contained an inbuilt resilience in the face of political assault. Family and kinship organisations provided mutual access to distribution and credit networks. Among the bigger Chinese capitalists there existed links with Chinese traders and industrialists in Singapore and Hong Kong who provided access to finance, international trade networks and foreign havens for capital in difficult times. The very strength of the capital and organisational base of Chinese capitalists made them a more acceptable credit risk to banks and other financial institutions both within and without the country. An assault upon their position required deliberate and sustained political intervention.

Despite severe problems, there did occur a slow and steady development of a small but significant group of indigenous capitalists throughout this period. It is not possible to estimate the strength of this group as a component of the domestic bourgeoisie as a whole through any quantitative assessment of capital assets or profits, but several of these indigenous capitalists operated on a substantial scale. The particular importance of indigenous businessmen as opposed to Chinese is essentially political. Whereas a dominant Chinese capitalist class may impose the general interests of capital upon the state, an indigenous capitalist class possesses the potential for direct and public political action. Chinese capital may impose constraints and imperatives upon the policies of the state, but a powerful indigenous capitalist class has the potential to transform the very structure of power.

The most important indigenous capitalists of this period had established their position in the Benteng period with preferential access to licences, contracts, and state-bank credit, with the protection of political patrons. Their business groups continued to be built upon trade, particularly sole distributorships for foreign machinery and automobiles, because their access to political patrons meant government contracts and purchases for the foreign manufacturers. Some indigenous capitalists were able to move into areas vacated by the departing Dutch, particularly in shipping and steve-doring, and in several cases expanded their investments in manufacture, especially textiles. The general difficulties of manufacturing outlined earlier were to some extent offset by access to government credit and by restrictions on the import of manufactures competing with local products. Where manufacturers also imported their own raw materials, they were able to take advantage of the favourable exchange rates and build industrial enterprises upon a basis of cheap raw materials and capital equipment. Where no integration of importing and manufacture occurred, such advantages eva-porated in profit-taking by the importer.

The structure and dynamics of the indigenous capitalists are best looked at in specific case studies. The most promi-nent indigenous business groups of this period are those of:

Agoes Dasaad	Panggabean	Wahab Affan
R. M. Notohamiprodjo	Titiheru	Pardede
H. A. Ghany Aziz	Markam	Bram Tambunan
Rahman Tamin	Ir. Aminuddin	Suwarma
Omar Tusin	Hashim Ning	Aslam
Soedarpo Sastrosatomo	Moh. Tabrani	Mardanus

Probably the biggest and certainly the most interesting of these was Agoes Dasaad, whose business fortunes reached their high point in the period 1958–65. Although he entered the Guided Economy period with an established trading empire and a textile mill, his activities became increasingly associated with the operation of sole agencies for import and distribution of foreign technology, notably those of Westinghouse and Lockheed. In David Boulton's[49] analysis of the global operations of Lockheed, Dasaad is portrayed essentially as a fixer, organising pay-offs for AURI (Indonesian Air Force) generals and others involved in deciding aircraft purchases. For his trouble, Dasaad received generous commissions and 'special payments', including one of $152 000 in 1964. Despite the fact that Dasaad also represented the rival aircraft group, Sud-Aviation, and played one company off against the other, Lockheed officials were unable to do anything about the situation. Boulton quotes a Lockheed memorandum explaining their dilemma:

> To be realistic we both agreed nothing should be done about it since Dasaad does occupy a unique position in dealing with the Indonesian Government and Sukarno himself. As long as Dasaad can be equally effective in the sale of Lockheed products whenever we can sell to Indonesia, we seem to have no alternative but to continue to work with him.[50]

A significant new component of the Dasaad business group was his 15% shareholding in the property and construction firm P.T. Pembangunan Jaya, which was partly owned by the government of Jakarta, a major source of construction contracts. Other shareholders were the state-owned Chrysler automobile assembler, ISC; the state trading bank, Bank Dagang Indonesia; and the Bank of Indonesia. Another private indigenous shareholder was Sucipto Amidharmo of Bumiputera Insurance, who held 15% of shares and was also a leading official in Bamunas and Minister for Insurance. Hashim Ning of ISC was the President Director (*BNPT* 289/64). This was the most formally structured example of corporate partnership between the state and indigenous domestic capital.

The basis of large and medium-scale indigenous enterprise clearly continued to be trade, particularly import. The Benteng entrepreneurs, Aziz, Ning, Dasaad and Kusmuljono, continued to hold the important agencies secured in the 1950s, and several other indigenous capitalists rose to prominence on the basis of import and export. Aslam, of Arab Sumatran background, built up an extensive business group based upon import licences and foreign-exchange credits. Bram Tambunan similarly acquired a dominant position in the import sector, and was particularly involved in tyre imports. Other sole agency-holders included Panggabean, who owned P.T. Piola, the sole Volkswagen agency secured in the Benteng period; and Suwarma, who held the sole Mercedes agency, P.T. Permorin.

R. Mardanus, a former naval officer from a Javanese *priyayi* background, was involved in a complex interrelationship of state and private interests. He had established a shipbuilding firm in the Benteng period with BIN credit.[51] It is not clear whether this was a joint venture with BIN or was wholly owned by Mardanus. Under Guided Economy he was appointed to take charge of a major state project to establish a shipyard capable of building ocean-going vessels up to 50 000 tons, and became Minister for Naval construction in the Dwikora Cabinet. Again, it is not clear whether the proposed state shipyard was connected with that with which Mardanus had been associated in the Benteng period.

However, it is clear that much of the import of machinery and equipment for the new state shipyard was channelled through an import company privately owned by Mardanus.[52]

A further figure of some significance and interest is Markham, a former army lieutenant who established a multi-million dollar operation, P.T. Karkam, on the basis of exclusive rights to export rubber from South Sumatra to Singapore and Malaysia during the confrontation period. He also held several import licences, notably those for Nissan jeeps and Asano Cement.[53]

There are several problems for the long-term viability of enterprises based upon access to political patronage and monopoly positions in the import sector. The fall of the patron carries the risk that the licences will evaporate. Indeed, this is exactly what happened after 1965 with the fall of Sukarno, Yusuf Muda Dalam, Chaerul Saleh and other patrons of such businessmen as Dasaad, Markam, Aslam and Mardanus. In September 1965, Yusuf Muda Dalam, the Governor of the Bank of Indonesia, was convicted on four charges which included:

(a) Issuing import licences for US$270 million on special 'deferred payment' terms to certain firms and corporations and granting 'special credits' of Rp338 000.

(b) Manipulating Rp97 000 million from the 'funds of the revolution' which he loaned to certain firms, retaining Rp4 000 million for himself.[54]

Yusuf Muda Dalam was imprisoned and most of the major non-military patrons of the Sukarno regime were removed from positions of authority. With the fall of these patrons, many of the most prominent indigenous business groups also collapsed. The enterprises of Aslam and Markam were confiscated and handed over to the military to constitute the basis of the new trading group, P.T.P.P. Berdikari (*BNPT*, 145/66). Aslam and Markam were imprisoned, as was Mardanus. Charges against the first two included making illegal payments to officials in return for import licences and credit, and those against Mardanus included the use of a private trading company to import materials for the state shipyard. Bram Tambunan was also charged with making illegal payments for credit and licences.

After 1965, a large number of sole agencies were transferred from businessmen who had secured them in the Benteng and Guided Economy periods, including Suwarma, Panggabean, Dasaad and Aziz, to new business groups, mostly associated with the military. Although I wish to leave detailed consideration of these transfers to a later chapter, they raise the question of how indigenous capitalists may accumulate capital on a basis of political concessions and survive the collapse of political patrons. One answer is to establish a spectrum of patronage sufficiently broad to avoid dislocation in power shifts. The traumatic nature of movement from party government to Guided Democracy and finally to military rule, accompanied by the obliteration of the PKI and the suppression of Masyumi and the PNI, has tended to obscure the fact that there is a significant degree of continuity. Military patronage has been crucial and stable since 1957, and the old PSI group, among which we must include Sultan Hamengku Buwono and a large number of senior officials and economic planners, has been remarkably resilient.

However, the most important factor of survival is to minimise reliance on sectors particularly dependent on patronage, such as import, and to move into sectors where an independent capital base may be developed. This may involve joint ventures with other indigenous capitalists, or, more importantly, with foreign or Chinese capitalists. Of course it is impossible in the Indonesian situation to escape entirely from the importance of political patronage. Even large industrial projects require licences, construction ventures require contracts, state banks supply a significant proportion of credit, and these are all subject to varying degrees of manipulation by politico-bureaucratic factions.

Several indigenous capitalists were able to move successfully into manufacture, especially textiles, or to expand investments there. These included Bram Tambunan (P.T. Manboprint), Rahman Tamin (P.T. Ratatex), Dasaad (P.T. Kancil Mas), Pardede (N.V. Pardede), and Ir. Aminuddin (P.T. Tekstil). As we will see in later chapters, these enterprises confronted problems related more to competition with Japanese and Chinese capital than to loss of patronage.

Perhaps the most successful indigenous capitalist of this period was Soedarpo. As mentioned in the previous chapter, Soedarpo established an import company which was able to secure some lucrative import contracts and provide a capital base for other ventures. In 1953 he purchased the Dutch shipping agency ISTA, which secured the agencies for the Hamburg America and Tokyo Senpaku Kaisha lines which subsequently became two of the most important shipping lines to operate out of Indonesia. In 1957–58 he took advantage of the departure of the Dutch to secure interests in stevedoring and warehousing (Desta – *BNPT* 298/59). In 1964 Soedarpo purchased several tugs and barges (P.T. Bhaita – *BNPT* 238/64) and in the same year was given permission under Regulation 5/1964 to set up a deep-sea shipping line which was established in 1971 as P.T. Samudra Indonesia.[55]

Soedarpo's major enterprises were joint ventures with other national shipowners, including Sjamsoeddin Baso and Abdul Moeis, and with the Jakarta shipbuilding company, Indomarin. Indomarin was closely associated with the Bank of Indonesia and PSI figures within the bureaucracy. Such diversity of shareholding may also have been protection against arbitrary action to withdraw licences or refuse credit.

However, the majority of indigenous businessmen in this period remained within the lucrative import sector and therefore heavily dependent upon patronage. For those attempting to develop a capital base, the general economic situation, characterised by massive inflation, balance of payments problems and infrastructure collapse, was not favourable to long-term investment and accumulation.

POLITICO-BUREAUCRATIC POWER AND CAPITAL

Political power may be used to assist the process of capital accumulation and the development of a bourgeoisie in a variety of ways. The state may provide infrastructure in the form of roads, ports, energy, telecommunications, education and health systems. It may directly invest capital in sectors unprofitable to private capitalists but necessary to their general interests. It may provide a legal and political basis for private property and capital accumulation. The state may act as the financier of the bourgeoisie and it may intervene on behalf of certain elements. This form of state intervention is a regularised and, in Weberian terms, a 'legal' form of interaction between state and capital. As explained in the previous chapter, the Indonesian state possessed certain patrimonial characteristics whereby political factions appropriated strategic sectors of the state apparatus. Whereas in the Benteng period parties fought for control of departments such as Trade or Economic Affairs, under Guided Economy the independence of parties was virtually eliminated; the political and bureaucratic dimensions became inseparable. It became difficult to identify either the PNI or the military as distinctly political or administrative entities. In fact, to a significant degree they were both. Feith makes the following comment:

> Before 1956, if one may oversimplify for purposes of argument, politics was a struggle between a Masyumi led group of forces linked with independent business and a PNI led group with ties to the bureaucracy and bureaucratically dependent business. By 1958 the group linked with independent business had sustained a major political defeat and so politics became principally a matter of conflict between different segments and 'empires' of the civilian and military bureaucracies and their offshoots.[56]

Such a situation led to major contradiction in the development of Indonesian capitalism. The political and personal interests of the politico-bureaucrats often came into direct conflict with the objectives of general state policy. This proved to be a contributory factory in the poor performance of state corporations, most of which were controlled by the military and regarded in part as a modern day appanage benefice: a source of income for the military and for individual officers. As pointed out by Panglaykim, the profits of the STCs were severely reduced by means of selling goods at market prices, declaring profits based on sale at the official price and appropriating the difference. Another technique was to hoard commodities and sell at the original official price without adjustment for inflation in return for a 'commission' from the purchaser.[57] On a more general level, the mere fact that state corporations were regarded as vehicles for appropriating public wealth and securing a share of the surplus of private profits gave a lower priority to the process of reinvestment, maintenance of capital and regular book-keeping.

Military, and to a lesser extent party, satraps controlling state corporations became popularly known as 'bureaucratic capitalists' and were an increasing object of debate and concern not only because of their blatant role in appropriating the legal property of the state but because they constituted a significant element of the new and conspicuously rich, the OKB (Orang Kaya Baru).[58]

The impact of bureaucrat capitalism upon the reconstitution of a bourgeoisie in Indonesia was considerable. Allocation of credit, import and export licences, contracts and foreign-exchange allocations was often made according to the needs of the politico-bureaucratic faction in control of allocations. This led to unpredictability and compounded the reluctance to invest capital in long-term ventures. Capitalists were forced to pay dearly for the licences and other concessions. In one sense this may have merely compensated for the regime's inability to collect normal taxes, but the payment of 'taxes' by specific companies to specific politico-bureaucrat factions rather than by 'capital' to the 'state' gave a different character to the relationship. Revenue raised by the state might be reasonably expected to be used for the provision of economic and administrative infrastructure, but revenue raised by the politico-bureaucrat factions was primarily destined for financing their own political survival. Quite often, access to licences was not simply a matter of bidding on a one-off basis but of belonging to a longer-term politico-economic alliance. Specific alliances often persisted over extended periods and those domestic capitalists who were part of such alliances were able to secure considerable rewards from the patronage provided. This was especially true for some indigenous businessmen including Dasaad, Ning, Affan and others who could not hope to compete with Chinese or foreign business in a general auction of licences and concessions. However, it did mean that access to political patronage became another factor in successful business operations and that the normal processes of competition became distorted by politically allocated monopolies such as Markam's control of the export of rubber from South Sumatra or the various illegal export monopolies of the military.

The most important development in the relationships between power and capital from 1957–65 was the emergence of the military as the most powerful politico-bureaucratic force in Indonesia. By the time the Nationalisation Bill had been introduced at the end of 1958, the Army was already controlling former Dutch banks and agricultural estates, distribution of rice and allocation of foreign exchange, as well as assuming control of oilfields in North Sumatra. On 25 June 1958, a new Ministry of Economic Stabilisation was established under the chairmanship of Colonel Suprajogi, a close associate of General Nasution. Together with Lt.-Col. Suhardiman, the chairman of the STC, P.T. Jaya Bhakti, and the head of the Army-sponsored trade union, Soksi, Suprajogi was also in charge of the authority supervising the process of nationalisation, Banas.[59] Control of many of the regionally based Dutch enterprises which had been nationalised was given to a Board of Control of Regional Enterprises, Bappeda, headed by General Baramuli of the Department of the Interior and operated under the authority of regional governors, usually military officers. Distribution of imported commodities to private companies at the regional level, officially in the hands of the OPS and GPS, was often controlled by local offices of the Financial and Economic Sections of the Military Commands, Finek.

Finally, the military directly established business enterprises of its own, sometimes in partnership with Chinese capitalists. In some cases, former Dutch estates were taken over, not by the state but by individual commands (Kodam and Kodim). The operation of transport or construction companies using military equipment was a common form of enterprise.[60]

Most extensive of all military enterprises, however, was smuggling, especially during the period of confrontation when it was illegal to export to Malaysia or Singapore. The best known and probably the largest operation was carried out by Opsus (Operasi Khusus – Special Operations), an intelligence group associated with Kostrad under the command of Colonel Ali Moertopo.[61]

THE OVERTHROW OF SUKARNO AND THE ENDING OF GUIDED DEMOCRACY

The events of September and October 1965 which led to the destruction of the PKI and the ending of the Sukarno regime were political in nature, involving at one level the military's defeat of its opponents and, at another level, the victory of the propertied classes over the challenge posed under the PKI umbrella. But to a certain degree they were predicated on economic collapse and chaos on a scale which divested the former regime and its policies of the bulk of its early support. Most important was the desertion of the urban middle classes, hard pressed by inflation and the general decay of infrastructure. It was their support in 1966 which made the final discrediting of Sukarno easier.

It is possible to view the New Order as a counter-revolution against 'socialist' forces, and to the extent that the PKI was seen as a threat to the propertied classes, it was. But upon close inspection there is little that was genuinely socialist about Guided Economy; rather, it was a ramshackle, underpowered form of state capitalism operated by, and largely for, the benefit of the politico-bureaucrats who dominated the state apparatus, notably the military themselves. The problem was that it was a stagnating form of capitalism no longer able to serve the interests of those who were most powerful within it. The revenue crisis of the state was compounded by the fact that capital accumulation was almost impossible.

The years 1949–65 had seen the failure of Indonesia to build its own national capitalist economy through either a domestic capitalist class or state-owned capital. The most fundamental step taken by the New Order after 1965 was a simple one: it provided the conditions for the re-entry of international capital. The result may be seen as revolutionary rather than counter-revolutionary in that it broke out of the decaying colonial stage and lifted the capitalist revolution to a new state of development, providing the conditions for the entry of finance and industrial capital on a scale far beyond anything hitherto. For the victors of 1965 — politico-bureaucrat, middle class, capitalist and petty capitalist — the problem was to be one of accommodation and survival in the new capitalist era.

1. A comprehensive table of parliamentary representation in 1951, 1956 and 1960 is provided in H. Feith, 'The Dynamics of Guided Democracy', in McVey (ed.) 1963, p. 345.

2. For a selection of primary sources which criticise parliamentary/party government and explain the objectives of Guided Democracy, see Feith and Castles 1970, parts II and III, especially Sukarno's, 'Let Us Bury the Parties' (p. 81) and 'Returning to the Rails of Revolution' (p. 98).

3. Lev 1966, pp. 182–201.

4. Nasution was deputy to Sukarno in both Peperti and KOTI. In the 1960 parliament the military (including police) had 34 representatives. Five Army officers were appointed as provincial governors in 1960.

5. For summaries of these, see T. K. Tan, 'Sukarnian Economics' in T. K. Tan (ed.), *Sukarno's Guided Indonesia* (Brisbane, 1967).

6. J. van der Kroef, 'Indonesia's Economic Future', *Pacific Affairs* 32, 1 (1959), pp. 53, 54. Conflict between the military and the workers in the period 1957–58 and the establishment of military control of nationalised Dutch enterprises is dealt with in Sanusi Achmad, The Dynamics of the Nationalization of Dutch Owned Enterprises in Indonesia (Ph.D. thesis, Indiana University, 1963).

7. Anspach 1969, p. 193.

8. Thomas and Panglaykim 1973, pp. 56–9. Also, van der Kroef 1959, pp. 60–2, 83.

9. Thomas and Panglaykim 1973, Chapter III. Details of the so-called 'big ten' or 'big eight' Dutch trading houses and their Indonesian successors, the STCs, are given on pp. 63 and 64.

10. J. Panglaykim, *An Indonesian Experience, Its State Trading Corporations* (Jakarta, 1967), p. 11.

11. Thomas and Panglaykim 1973, pp. 62–6.

12. Category A prospects were estimated to require investment of Rp240 000 million over the eight year period, of which half was to be in foreign currency, 70% of which would be derived from petroleum exports and 12% from rubber exports (Tan 1967, p. 35).

13. Sadli 1960, pp. 230–2.

14. United States Economic Survey Team to Indonesia, *Indonesia: Perspective and Proposals for United States Economic Aid* (New Haven, 1963), p. 12.

15.   Exports by Principal Commodities (not including petroleum) 1958, 1960 and 1966 (in $millions).

Year	Total	Estate Rubber	Small-holder Rubber	Copra	Coffee	Tea	Tobacco	Palm Oil	Tin
1958	477.9	108.8	153.2	18.2	18.5	24.8	30.2	23.7	35.4
1960	620.0	134.0	243.2	29.1	13.7	27.7	33.3	20.0	50.6
1966	360.0	53.5	112.2	20.0	17.0	13.5	29.7	27.0	30.0

Source: Tan (ed.) 1967, Table 12, p. 154.

16. United States Economic Survey Team to Indonesia 1963, p. 35.

17. J. A. C. Mackie, 'The Indonesian Economy, 1950–1963', in Glassburner 1971, pp. 28–34.

18. Ibid., p. 42.

19. Thomas and Panglaykim 1973, pp. 93–9; A. R. Soehoed, 'Manufacturing in Indonesia', *BIES* 8 (1967).

20. Panglaykim 1967, p. 237–8.

21. Quoted in L. Castles 'The Fate of the Private Entrepreneur', in Tan (ed.) 1967, p. 85 (henceforth 1967a).

22. H. Arndt 'Economic Disorder and the Task Ahead', in Tan (ed.) 1967, pp. 130–1.

23. Sadli 1960, p. 252; Mackie 1971, pp. 62–6; Anspach 1969, p. 198.

24. Castles 1967a, p. 77. See also Thomas and Panglaykim 1973, pp. 65–7.

25. Panglaykim 1967.

26. Ibid., pp. 12 and 164, 165.

27. Ibid., pp. 247, 248.

28. Ibid., p. 295.

29. See J. Gibson 'Foreign Enterprise and Production-Sharing', in Tan (ed.) 1967.

30. A. Hunter, 'The Indonesian Oil Industry', in Glassburner (ed), 1971.

31. Tan 1967, p. 35.

32. Ibid., pp. 156–7.

33. Tan 1967, p. 163.

34. Castles 1967, 1967a, and Panglaykim 1973, p. 66.

35. Castles 1967a, p. 83.

36. I. Palmer and L. Castles, 'The Textile Industry', *BIES* 2 (1965), p. 43.

37. Palmer and Castles reported that the West Java mills, for example, were receiving only enough yarn to use 11% of capacity and that $134 million worth of raw cotton and yarn were required to bring production up to capacity (Palmer and Castles 1965, pp. 36–41).

38. Feith 1963, p. 374.

39. Interview with Omar Tusin, 28.10.74.

40. Interviews with Indonesian businessmen active in the Guided Economy period, including: Omar Tusin, 28.10.74; Ali Noorluddin, 14.9.74; Darwis Tamin, 13.3.74; Eddy Dasaad, 23.10.74; Sucipto Amidharmo, 20.9.74; Harlan Bekti, 5.3.74; Machdi, 15.3.74 and 29.10.74; Soedarpo, 6.11.74.

Nishihara (1967, p. 102) reports that reparations deals with Indonesia, involving capital equipment and commodities, were of interest to Japanese businessmen because they could easily persuade Indonesian businessmen or government officials to agree to overpricing and a division of the profits thereby derived.

41. Castles 1967a, p. 85.

42. Thomas and Panglaykim 1973, p. 57–60.

43. Of course the major beneficiary of the confiscated Dutch assets was the state, but the domestic capitalists, particularly the Chinese, also benefited by either purchasing or politically obtaining access to some of these assets or by stepping into gaps left by the Dutch which the state could not adequately fill. See Thomas and Panglaykim 1973, p. 60; Castles 1967; and Palmer and Castles 1965. The movement of national capital into sectors of the shipping, warehousing and stevedoring industry vacated by the Dutch is treated in detail in, Dick 1977.

44. Panglaykim 1967, pp. 238, 282–3.

45. Anspach 1969, p. 194. Mackie suggests that Rachmat's decision may have been a unilateral one, out of harmony with the feelings of many colleagues within the NU and certainly a move not intended, either in that form or at that time, by Sukarno ('Anti-Chinese Outbreaks in Indonesia', in Mackie [ed.] 1976, pp. 84–5).

46. This followed upon an earlier move against the Chinese when Chinese firms whose owners were suspected of being aligned with the KMT were confiscated. This was in retaliation for Taiwanese assistance to the

PRRI/Permesta rebels. Among the Chinese firms to be expropriated was the Oei Tjong Ham, probably the largest and longest lived Chinese business group.

47. Thomas and Panglaykim 1973, p. 71.

48. Ibid., p. 71.

49. D. Boulton, *The Lockheed Papers* (London, 1978), pp. 111–34.

50. Ibid., p. 116.

51. Sutter 1959, p. 800.

52. Politico-economic relationships between such political figures as Chaerul Saleh, Sukarno, Subandrio, Yusuf Muda Dalam, and businessmen including Mardanus, Markam and Aslam were treated exhaustively in the Jakarta press during 1966 and 1967, especially during the trial of Yusuf Muda Dalam. *Warta Berita*, 7.1.67, *Kompas*, 6.2.67 and *Sinar Harapan*, 16.2.67 give details of the contributions by businessmen to a special revolutionary fund for monopoly positions in the import sector.

53. Markam was alleged to have worked with local military officers to enforce what were, in effect, compulsory purchases from rubber smallholders at low prices. Markam's career is treated in Nishihara 1967, p. 154, and Castles 1967a, p. 85. Castles quotes an interesting defence of Markam by Sukarno.

54. *FEER*. 7.4.66.

55. Dick 1977, pp. 155–6.

56. H. Feith, 'The Politics of Economic Decline', in Tan (ed.) 1967, p. 54.

57. Castles cites the case of one STC which hoarded Rp200 million worth of motor parts from 1960 to 1964 and then sold to a private firm at 1960 prices although a 600%–700% price increase had occured in the meantime (Castles 1967a, p. 80).

58. Within the military itself there were important elements opposed to the large-scale appropriation of state funds and authority. General Nasution implemented a programme to recover illegally expropriated funds of state corporations. Known as 'Operation Budhi', it had, by 1964, recovered Rp11 million (*Tempo*, 19.6.76).

The PKI was active in identifying and condemning 'bureaucratic capitalism' because it eroded and discredited state ownership of capital as well as constituting a source of finance for the party's political oppononets. D. N. Aidit, 'Mismanagement, Corruption and the Bureaucratic Capitalists', quoted in Feith and Castles (eds) 1970, pp. 400–4; D. N. Aidit, 'Dekon Dalam Udjian' (Jakarta, 1963), quoted in part in Castles 1967a, pp. 77, 79.

59. van der Kroef 1959, p. 53.

60. I will be dealing with the origins of the military business groups and the details of their development in this period in a later chapter. For some general references to military business in the Guided Economy period, see McVey 1971, especially pp. 152–3; Crouch 1978, pp. 38–42.

61. Crouch 1978, pp. 74–5.

PART II
Capital and State Policy Under the New Order

4

State and Capital under the New Order: Theoretical Considerations

THE state has played a crucial role in shaping the development of capitalism in post-colonial Indonesia. Its influence has been decisive, not only in providing the political conditions for capitalist development but in providing the fiscal framework and even much of the investment capital. It is not enough, however, to simply catalogue the way in which the state has intervened in the process of capitalist development. It is necessary at this point to offer some explanation for the actions and policies of the state through an analysis of the relationships between state, economy and society in its Indonesian context. In an important sense, this chapter is an intermezzo which steps back from the subject matter and both reviews and looks forward in a fairly general way. Many of the aspects dealt with in broad sweeps in this chapter are treated in detail either in earlier or later chapters.

The outstanding features of the New Order regime as it has developed in the past eighteen years, have been: the entrenchment and centralisation of authoritarian rule by the military, the appropriation of the state by its officials, and the exclusion of political parties from effective participation in the decision-making process. Due to the absence of strong political parties, there exists no apparent mechanism of political dominance or influence over the state by any class or class coalition. Therefore difficulties have arisen in explaining the relationship between politics, society and economy. The tendency has been for analysts to examine the motivations and interests of the politico-bureaucrats themselves — ideological, political, cultural and economic — in order to understand the logic behind the general policy direction taken by the New Order.

Before going on to demonstrate the inadequacy of these approaches and to establish an alternative theoretical framework for the analysis of state policy it is necessary to outline the political structure of the New Order. There is already a large body of writing which deals with this subject and it is not my intention to make yet another lengthy foray into the field.[1] Rather, I intend to draw out the major features in order to establish a political context for analysis of the relationship between state, economy and society. These major features are:

(a) Retention of the 1945 constitution, effectively locating power in the office of president and reducing the parliament to little more than an advisory body.

(b) The control of parliamentary elections by the state through its veto over candidates, and its power to ban, amalgamate and determine the structure of political parties. In 1973, the political parties were forced to consolidate themselves into two uneasy and unlikely groupings of Muslim and non-Muslim parties which effectively diminished their specific character and electoral appeal. At the same time, a state party, Golkar (Golongan Karya), was formed, representing state policy and contesting the elections backed by the resources of the state to coerce, intimidate and offer patronage.[2]

(c) The consolidation and centralisation of military power within the Department of Defence and Security (Hankam), and the consolidation of effective political power in military-dominated, extra-constitutional bodies appointed by the president. These included the body of personal presidential assistants (SPRI, later Aspri) which was formally abandoned in 1974 but continued to operate in effect as an inner cabinet to the president. Also officially abandoned in 1974 was General Ali Moertopo's special operation group, Opsus, the political and economic intelligence body which planned and oversaw the Act of Free Choice in West Irian, the 1971 election and the formation of Golkar, and which operates a think tank on political and economic strategy dominated by right-wing catholic Chinese including Harry Tjan, Liem Bian Kie, Liem Bian Koen and Panglaykim. The other crucial body is the Command for the Restoration of Security and Order, Kopkamtib, which exercises authority over internal security.

(d) The widespread movement of military personnel into positions of authority within the state bureaucracy. This process is popularly known as *penghijauan* (making green).[3]

(e) Continuation of the Guided Democracy practice of establishing state-sponsored corporatist political organisations, within which the activities of social and economic interest groups are contained. Such corporate, or functional, groups operate as institutions of control, mobilisation and patronage in the fields of labour, business, the civil service, youth and a variety of other areas.

(f) The appropriation of the state apparatus by its officials in contravention of the constitutional and legal restrictions on the exercise of authority. In legal terms, the military politico-bureaucrats have not allowed the general rule of law to limit their authority, while allocation of licences, concessions, contracts and credit has been commonly appropriated for the personal and political objectives of individuals and factions of the politico-bureaucrats.[4]

(g) The establishment of an ideological basis for legitima-
     tion which presents the state as the executor of a
     scientifically conceived strategy for the development
     of Indonesian society and economy. Authoritarian
     rule in this context is presented as a necessary compo-
     nent of development, thereby lifting the state above
     the realm of politics and denying legitimacy to politi-
     cal activity, political opposition and critics of the
     regime.[5]

THE NEW ORDER AS A TECHNOCRATIC STATE

The dominant conservative interpretation of social and economic policies under the New Order has been that they have
been formed on the basis of 'rational' and universal economic criteria transcending political and social interests.
Such a position has been reinforced by the fact that considerable power over economic decision-making lies in the hands
of a group of economists, many of whom were trained in the
US, originally located within the National Development
Planning Board, Bappenas, but who have subsequently held
power in a variety of key economic ministries and boards.[6]
The criteria for their appointment, it is argued, were not
political but based upon their economic expertise.

The New Order itself has seized upon this notion of a state
operating above politics as a crucial ideological justification
of its legitimacy and a powerful weapon to use against its
critics. At the same time, apologists operating from the
theoretical position of Western liberal economics have also,
explicitly and implicitly, argued that New Order economic
policy can largely be explained as the product of purely
'economic' criteria.[7] New Order ideologues use this notion to
argue that *any* state economic policy is formed in the national
interest and is based on objective and universal 'economic'
criteria, therefore casting critics as subversive in their actions
and sectional in their interests. In contrast, Western liberal
economists implicitly assign the labels 'objective' and 'econ-

omic' only to specific policies: those which are guided by
free-market, private-enterprise, open-door economic principles as argued by the IBRD and the IMF. Consequently,
when there occurred a resurgence of economic nationalism
and state interference in the economy in the mid-1970s,
Western liberal economists became increasingly reluctant to
bestow the legitimacy of 'economics' upon the New Order.[8]

In effect, Western neo-classical economists have attempted to lift one particular set of economic strategies and
policies from their political and social context, and see conflict over economic policy as one between 'economics' as an
objective and universal set of criteria, and 'politics', representing ideological, sectional, short-term interests of specific
groups and classes. There are two critiques which must be
made of this artificial division of politics and economics.
First, the set of economic policies and philosophies regarded
as objective 'economics' by the conventional Western economists was introduced into Indonesia in 1965–67 only after
the political victory of the military over the PKI and the
Sukarno regime, which in turn secured a victory at the social
level for the propertied classes over the threat posed by the
landless and the urban workers. Therefore the policies of the
late 1960s had a specific political and social context and were
constrained by the social and economic interests of the new
rulers.

This leads to the second point: economic policies formed
on the basis of free-market economic philosophies did more
than address immediate fiscal and monetary dilemmas in
Indonesia in the mid-1960s. They were the necessary basis
for the rehabilitation, entrenchment and expansion of the
existing capitalist social order and the survival of those
classes whose dominance was embedded in the existing set of
social and political relationships. In other words, these policies were not selected because they were the best, in any
objective and universal sense, but because they promised
growth within the sort of social and economic order acceptable to the new political rulers of Indonesia. It had become

apparent by the latter years of the Sukarno era that the
survival of the existing social order and the continuing dominance of the propertied classes and non-communist politico-
bureaucrats required the political intervention of the military
and the reintegration of the Indonesian economy with the
international capitalist system. At the same time, the infusion of massive amounts of foreign capital investment,
finance, aid and technology offered the basis for growth
without redistribution of wealth or power. International
capital had become essential to the survival of capitalist
society in Indonesia.

If we extend this line of reasoning to a consideration of the
conflicts over economic policy which have punctuated the
last decade and a half, it is clear that they can in no sense be
regarded as conflicts between 'economic' rationalism and
irrational 'politics', with the IBRD/IMF free-market philosophies constituting the former, while contending economic
strategies are dismissed as the latter. Instead, as will be
demonstrated in following chapters, they represent disputes
within Indonesian capitalism in which the various elements
of capital — international and national, Japanese and US,
Chinese and indigenous, large and small — struggle to give
shape to Indonesian capitalism.

Finally, some mention should be made of the position of
the technocrats. Although we can, in the early 1980s, no
longer talk of the technocrats as a unified group, either in
terms of their economic philosophies or political attach-
ments[9], until the mid-1970s the technocrats adhered to
the type of free-market, open-door economics advocated by
Western liberal economic orthodoxy in general and the IMF,
the World Bank (IBRD) and the Inter-Governmental Group
on Indonesia (IGGI) in particular. Their power derived not
from their monopoly of knowledge but from their role as
managers of the sorts of economic policies acceptable to the
New Order, specifically as managers of the process of debt
renegotiation, and as authors of policies designed to allow
international capital access to Indonesia.

In general, we can say that their power, at a most fundamental level, has risen and fallen with the Indonesian need
for international capital investment, loans and aid. As rising
oil income in the years 1973–81 lessened this dependence and
provided opportunities for economic nationalist policies, the
technocrats were forced to give way. As economic nationalism has confronted crises (for example with the massive
debts of Pertamina in 1975–76) or where structural factors
have weakened its position (as oil revenues declined and the
international recession began to deplete government revenues and Indonesia's foreign exchange position in the early
1980s), the relative strength of IGGI, IMF, IBRD and
international capital in general has increased, along with that
of the mainline Bappenas technocrats and the influence of
liberal capitalist economic policies.[10]

THE NEW ORDER AS A BUREAUCRATIC POLITY

Just as conventional Western neo-classical economists have
attempted to divest economics of its social and political
dimension, so conventional Western political science has
attempted to divest politics of its economic and social dimension. Much of the confusion stems from the appropriation of
the state by its officials and its apparent autonomy from social
forces. There are several streams within this approach, but
perhaps the most pervasive and institutionalised is that which
stems from North American political science and constitutes
an amalgam of cultural and comparative political science,
structural functional social theory and the political order
theories of Samuel Huntington. This approach has been
applied to the New Order in its most systematic form by Karl
D. Jackson, who relies heavily upon the work of Fred
Riggs.[11] Its central feature is the division of society into an
'elite', defined by its position within the state bureaucracy,
and an amorphous and undifferentiated mass, defined by
exclusion from the bureaucratic apparatus. Political activity
within this model is determined by the 'traditional' nature of

the psychological and cultural attachments of the political actors. These produce political behaviour which, in terms of the Parsonian variables of behaviour distinguishing 'traditional' from 'modern' societies, are diffuse, ascriptive and particularist rather than specific, achieved and universalist. In Weberian terms, the political system remains patrimonial rather than progressing to the stage of 'rational' and 'legal' authority.

In turn, this means that political conflict is not characterised by disputes over questions of *general* policy or conflict between political parties seeking to secure the *general* interests of social classes but by a scramble by political factions for personal advantage. Consequently, politics is characterised by two phenomena: first, the appropriation of public office and the powers attaching to such office by political incumbents, and the fusing of political power and bureaucratic authority; second, the organisation of political activity within patron-client structures, which are mechanisms not for securing the adoption and implementation of particular policies but for gaining access to the distribution of benefices. The cement of such groups is not the common economic or social interests of those in the network but the personal relationships between patrons and clients, which in turn are built upon the effectiveness of the network as a mechanism for securing and distributing benefices.

The implications of such an approach are significant. To begin with, it focuses political analysis upon conflict between political leaders and factions and upon the capacity of the bureaucratic state to maintain itself: that is, the maintenance of political order. In reality, however, such conflicts are of limited significance, for the rise and fall of individuals and factions have no necessary general social or economic implications, only implications for the individuals in emerging or declining patronage networks. So there is, in the body of this approach, no conscious recognition, let alone systematic analysis, of the role of the state in securing the political conditions for the existence of a specific economic or social order or for the dominance of specific classes or social groups. The 'polity' in this sense is transcendental to society, seeking only to reproduce itself and to secure the privileges of those who occupy the apparatus of power.

Escape from such a patrimonial paradigm is seen to lie in the transformation of the consciousness and the behaviour of individual actors, deriving not from changes in the material conditions of their existence but by means of autonomous generation of new forms of behaviour within the ideological sphere itself, implicitly through a process of diffusion of values from 'modern' societies.[12] This approach avoids the options of either radical structural change to society or the political overthrow of the New Order.

The vision of a state appropriated by bureaucrats who rule in their own interest confronts many theoretical and practical difficulties. How can this approach explain, for example, the time, the resources and the energy state officials in Indonesia put into the planning and implementation of policies such as rehabilitation of the irrigation system, the development of complex tariff schedules or even the running of railway systems, which would appear to have little to offer patron-client networks chasing lucrative sources of spoils. We therefore confront the fact that a state has certain minimum obligations to provide material, legal and ideological infra-structures necessary for the reproduction of a specific social order which cannot simply be explained in terms of the immediate interests or predelictions of its officials. To dis-cover the link between state and society we cannot confine ourselves to analysis of social origins or ideological attach-ments of officials, nor should the existence of an economic and social component to political action be dismissed simply because no effective political parties exist. Limits upon the autonomy of the state are imposed by the very social and economic context in which it is located. These structural relationships between politics, society and economy are the missing element in the bureaucratic-polity approach.

THE NEW ORDER AS A COMPRADOR STATE

A third major approach to the relationship between state, society and economy has been based upon dependency theory. In general, the dependency argument has been that reintegration of Indonesian capitalism into a global system has meant a subordination of the structure of the Indonesian economy to the needs of international capital and a subordination of the Indonesian domestic bourgeoisie, either by their incorporation as compradors or their elimination (for example, in the textile industry). As for the government and its officials, these too are drawn into the relationship with international capital as compradors — facilitating the entry of international capital to obtain pay-offs (Franke's 'cargo cult' concept) or because of ideological attachment to the 'economics' of international capitalism (Ransome's 'Berkeley Mafia' interpretation of the Bappenas technocrats). Mortimer combines both these approaches in a more complex interpretation.[13]

There is evidence to support individual observations of the dependency theorists, especially when most dependency writing was produced before the upsurge of economic nationalism in Indonesian policy-making in the mid-1970s. Its weakness lies in its explanatory value as a theory. In concrete terms, the dependency approach is unable to explain the development of Indonesia's economy or of the New Order's economic policies. As I will demonstrate in later chapters, Indonesia's economic policy did change to one which placed severe constraints on foreign capital, and protected, subsidised and financed the national bourgeoisie and the development of state capital, although how much longer this can be sustained in the economic and political conditions of the 1980s has yet to be seen. It is also clear that the 1970s saw a substantial development of national capital and a national bourgeoisie despite the continuing dominance of international corporate capital and finance, especially in the resources and energy sector.

In theoretical terms, the weakness of the dependency approach lies in its emphasis upon the circulation of capital on a global basis as the crux of the development/underdevelopment process.[14] Consequently, the actors in the process of economic exploitation become countries: metropoles and satellites in which the latter are bound into an immutable process of underdevelopment and economic deformity imposed by their relative position in the international economy. This has led to a denial of the very real developments which have occurred in Indonesian capitalism and in the development of a domestic capitalist class.

The struggle over economic policy in Indonesia has not been a simple reflection of global relations of dependency in which technocrats become ideological slaves of the US, IBRD or IMF; compradors scramble for the crumbs offered by multinational corporations; while national bourgeois, in the process of obliteration at the hands of foreign capital, conduct a losing political struggle against the multinational corporations and the compradors. Instead, the development of capitalism in Indonesia has involved a process of accelerated domestic capital accumulation, both private and state. The very development of national capitalist forces has produced a resurgence of economic nationalism. The relationship between national and foreign capital has therefore been a complex one in which various elements of national capital seek selectively to integrate with foreign capital in cases where international capital and corporate resources are required (oil, gas, minerals and more complex industrial processes), or to exclude foreign capital where these resources are no longer so essential (increasingly in light industry). The balance of power in this relationship is contingent not only upon the development of the national bourgeoisie and the strengthening of the political forces of national capital, but also upon certain fluctuating factors in the international economic relationships. For example, the leap in the price of oil greatly strengthened the hand of national capital in the mid-1970s, just as the dramatic levelling of the rate of increase in oil income and the international recession in the early 1980s has weakened it.

THE NEW ORDER AS 'STATE QUA STATE'

Politico-bureaucrats in Indonesia are a cohesive and coherent socio-political force in their own right, with interests and power deriving from their position within the state apparatus. Three important factors which motivate their actions are the maintenance of the state itself, the maintenance of military dominance and the maintenance of their individual and factional positions within the state apparatus. The struggle between the PKI and the military can be seen as a struggle between contending politico-bureaucratic 'elites'. Similarly, the suppression of political parties by the military is a defence of military hegemony over the state apparatus and the dominance of its politico-bureaucrats.

Most important, however, has been the drive to secure a revenue base for the state itself, for the military and for the politico-bureaucrat factions. With an ailing economy and a national balance of payments and debt crisis, a fiscal crisis of the state existed in 1965. The need to reconstitute a revenue base for the state was a prime consideration for the generals, and reintegration with the international capitalist economy offered a solution. The renegotiation of foreign debts, the development of substantial aid programmes and the generation by foreign companies of taxes derived from oil, gas and timber production for export did indeed produce a firm revenue base for the state by the mid-1970s. So, in one important sense, state policy towards international capital must be seen as a consequence of the need to establish a revenue base for itself. International capital has also acted as the financier of the military politico-bureaucrats who dominate and appropriate the state through such mechanisms as joint venture partnerships, company directorships, and the extortion of illegal payments for contracts and concessions.

But can we extend this argument to suggest that the New Order can be fully explained in terms of the abiding impulses of the state imposing upon its officials sets of interests which transcend the social and economic context in which it operates? Can we fully explain the actions of the politico-bureaucrats in terms of an abiding logic generated by the state, transcending history? This is clearly the implication of Anderson's *state qua state* thesis.[15] His conclusion is worth quoting at some length:

> I hope to have shown that Suharto's policies are incomprehensible from the point of view of any articulation of popular-representative national interest, but are perfectly rational from the point of view of a state with an ancestry much older than Indonesia's. I am tempted to go still further. Despite the attractions of a straightforward class analysis of the policies of successive regimes in Indonesia, there is something peculiarly classless about ex-sergeant President Suharto and his entourage. Such men are creatures of the state and articulate its abiding impulses, through the Dutch, Japanese, revolutionary, liberal-parliamentary, Guided Democracy and New Order regimes. I would not like to swear that, had the PKI somehow peacefully come to power, Suharto would not now be found functioning capably within the state through which it ruled. (pp. 54–5)

Although the preservation of their institutional base (the state, the military, the faction) is an important factor in decision-making by the politico-bureaucrats of the New Order, to proffer this as a general explanation of the New Order state is quite inadequate. Rather than engaging in a direct critique of the Anderson model, I would like to proceed instead to an explanation of why the New Order state cannot be understood as some ahistorical, universal Javanese[16] state transcending its specific historical and social environment. Contrary to this, I will argue, the New Order can only be understood and explained within its specific historical and social context in which class is a crucial factor.

STATE AND CLASS

Quite clearly we cannot explain the class nature of the New
Order state in any simple instrumentalist way. Politico-
bureaucrats rule autonomous of any formal or *de facto*
ascendancy by class-based political parties. Nor can we argue
that most of the politico-bureaucrats are in reality also capitalists and thereby act in defence of their own personal class
interests. This may be an increasing trend now but it was not
so in the mid-1960s and even the early 1970s when the state
was acting so forcibly in the re-establishment of capitalism in
Indonesia.

Can we then understand the emergence of the New Order
as a capitalist revolution from above secured by state officials
ideologically committed to capitalist modernisation in a society where no consolidated ruling class existed?[17] In the first
place, the New Order did not bring about a capitalist revolution; it reconstituted an existing capitalist social order and
consolidated existing class structures as well as the political
authority of its own officials. Second, the precise form of
capitalist reconstitution was not the creation of the imagin-
ation of the new political rulers but was forged out of a
complete process of political and social conflict and coalition
involving not only domestic class and political forces but the
forces of international capital: the IMF, the World Bank,
IGGI and international corporations. The New Order state
did not emerge in a vacuum, a society in such a condition of
entropy that it presented neither constraints nor imperatives
upon state action.

While we must stress that state power in capitalist society
is not immediately reducible to class power and that the state
is a system of political domination relatively autonomous of
class forces, the fact that the state exists in the context of a
particular system of class relationships does limit and shape
the form and exercise of state power. In specific terms, my
first point is that the state is limited in its capacity to tamper
with the existing social, economic and class structures unless

these are already in an advanced stage of decay and/or a new set of vigorous social and political forces has emerged as the basis for the political revolution. The events of 1957–65, considered in the previous chapter, provide a concrete illustration of this problem. Under Sukarno, attempts were made to break the power of foreign capital and replace it with national state-led capitalism. A less structured attempt was made to replace Chinese merchant capital in the countryside with indigenous merchant petty capital. At the same time the state provided the legal conditions for the PKI farmers' front organisation (BTI) to attempt to redistribute land and break the social and economic dominance of the rural landlords.

These attempts to transform the social and economic structure of Indonesia had disastrous consequences, both economic and political, contributing significantly to the eventual collapse of the Sukarno state. National state capital proved unable to replace foreign capital, partly because it was a task beyond its resources and partly because of the ineptitude and corruption of the military managers of the state corporations. Similarly, the indigenous petty bourgeoisie were to prove unable to replace the entrenched Chinese distribution and rural credit networks in Java. In the countryside, the entrenched social and economic power of the landlords proved formidable obstacles to the BTI reformers. By the early 1960s the Sukarno state found itself presiding over a struggling economy and growing hostility from the urban middle class, the national bourgeoisie and the rural landowning class. It was not simply a case of foundering upon the resistance of entrenched class structures and established economic systems but also one of the failure of revolutionary and nationalist reformist forces to mobilise and organise political and economic power. Sukarno and those who imagined that he provided some form of protection had attempted major social and economic alterations to a weak but nevertheless resilient capitalist social order without the necessary political and social resources. They had confronted the limits of state autonomy.

Of course the nature of the Sukarno-state itself contributed to this result. Not only did the military, the major pillar of power, prove largely incapable of undertaking the complex administrative tasks of managing the development of a state capitalist system, but it was politically unwilling to contribute to any exercise which threatened to strengthen the hand of the PKI, its only rival as a national political and administrative organisation.

The point remains, however, that despite the weakness of classes and their failure to constitute themselves as a political force at the national level, Indonesian society was not in 1965, nor is it today, in a state of entropy. Whereas the Sukarno regime confronted the structure of class power, the New Order has consolidated it. While it may politically exclude the dominant social forces from direct access to political power, it rules nevertheless, with their general acquiescence and in their general interests. It provides the conditions for economic growth and the stability of the existing social order. When the urban middle classes, the national bourgeoisie, the landowning classes and rural traders, and indeed the extensive lower ranks of the state bureaucracy itself, see no economic rewards to balance against the burdens of arbitrary and authoritarian military rule, one may expect the social base of support for the New Order to erode, leaving it increasingly dependent upon the capacity of its security apparatus. Indeed, as will be argued in the following chapters, the New Order is extremely sensitive to discontent amongst those classes which constitute its base of social support. The broad interests of those very classes, which supported the military counter-revolution of 1965, in effect constitute a limit to the autonomy of the New Order state.

Just as the state is negatively constrained from confronting the long-term interests of an entrenched, existing social order, so it is forced to intervene in conflicts and respond to crises within the system and to provide the political, legal and, often, the economic infrastructure necessary for its survival and development. In doing so, the state may act contrary to the immediate interests of the propertied classes, but it is just this separation of political and social power that constitutes the basis of the capitalist state's effectiveness in ensuring the long-term interests of capitalist society.[18] This is not to argue that the state is a powerless cipher whose responses are predetermined by some structural mechanism. Policies are a matter of both judgement and response to specific pressures, but they are in the last analysis conditioned by the social order in which the state is located.

While the New Order state may face fundamental constraints upon its options for policies dealing with the interests of capital at their most general level, including the protection of private property, the subordination of labour and the provision of certain minimum levels of fiscal, monetary and economic infrastructure, there remains a vast potential for manoeuvre in formulating policies dealing with the more specific interests of capital. This is partly because capital does not constitute a monolithic structure or set of interests. The state has become a central element in the mediation of these conflicting interests and, at times, has thrown its weight behind one element of capital against others. At other times, where there is no fundamental threat to the social order as a whole, the state may indeed override the immediate interests of all elements of the capitalist class. Politics may operate here autonomous of social forces. It is the process of conflict within capital itself and the role of the state in this process which gives shape to the specific form which capitalism has taken in Indonesia. There is no general and necessary direction for state intervention at this 'non-antagonistic' level. Each situation presents its own set of options and constraints for the state and the precise form of policy is determined by political action. It may be useful to outline in general terms some of the more important contradictions in Indonesian capitalism which confront the New Order State and present it with real policy options which are thrashed out at a political level.

(a) The contradiction that exists between domestic and international capital involving the state in measures to constrain selectively the entry of foreign capital and to establish the conditions for its integration with national capital. On the one hand, international capital constitutes a crucial and necessary source of finance and direct capital investment and seeks to direct its resources with minimal restraint into those sectors of the Indonesian economy which are appropriate to the logic governing the global distribution of its capital investments formed at the corporate level. This means a concentration of investment in the resources and energy sector or in relatively labour-intensive, protected import-substitution manufacture. From the national standpoint, state planners place priority on the development of basic industries and integrated industrial development outside the logic which governs the international division of labour from the position of international corporate capital. To what extent can national constraints be imposed upon foreign capital without damaging necessary inflows of finance and direct investment? This depends in part on other factors, most importantly, the level of foreign exchange earnings, particularly oil. At the same time, national capital, within which the politico-bureaucratic leadership is increasingly integrated, demands selective protection and preferential access to credit, contracts, licences and concessions. To ignore these demands would be to invite hostility from domestic class forces and to erode the state's claims to constituting the national interest — an important component of its legitimacy.

(b) The contradictions that exist within international capital, particularly that between the US and Japan which, to some extent, reflects itself in the confrontation between the Bappenas technocrats and the CSIS technocrats, between policies of economic liberalism and state-led economic nationalism. While Japan clearly wishes to establish itself in the hitherto US dominated resources and energy sector, the CSIS economic nationalists have attempted to use Japanese finance, outside the normal channels of IGGI finance, to build a national industrial sector in basic industries and resources processing.

(c) The grievances of medium and small-scale indigenous bourgeois and petty bourgeois. These have two main components: the confrontation between small and large capital; and the confrontation between indigenous and Chinese capital, a political and cultural confrontation with origins in the early nineteenth century. On the one hand, economic policy is based upon the maximisation of growth through development of the forces of production, and therefore, of productivity as well as production levels. Giving credit, protection and subsidy to a potently inefficient sector of the economy contradicted this intention. Similarly, it made sense to build upon the most productive and effective element of national capital, the Chinese. However, these policies confronted significant political problems involving the hostility of the extensive indigenous petty bourgeoisie and the erosion of the state's claims to being nationalist, or even Indonesian. To complicate matters, leading elements of the military and the politico-bureaucrat factions had established business links with large-scale capital, predominantly Chinese.

(d) The contradictions between the practice of appropriation of state power and resources by the officials of the state and the demands of capital for rational, codified and predictable laws governing the economic activities of the state. This has been a persistent and bitter contradiction throughout the post-colonial period, particularly in veiw of the fact that the political rulers of Indonesia have themselves embodied the interests of the politico-bureaucrats, the state and capital, and the associated conflicting needs for finance for personal and political purposes, state revenues and legal administration.

(e) Contradictions between the political rulers and the 'middle classes' over the issues of authoritarianism, democracy and rule of law. Essential to the regime, the middle classes embody a tension between resentment of authoritarian rule, an attachment to the continuing economic growth provided by the New Order and fear of the political alternative — radical populism.

A final, but crucial, factor which gives the state a substantial degree of freedom in its choice of policies is its freedom from reliance upon domestic sources of revenue. Whereas in post-feudal Europe the need to come to terms with a domestic class which provided the bulk of its revenues severely constrained the autonomy of the absolutist state, no such reliance has occurred in Indonesia. Taxation has not become a major issue of conflict and debate in domestic politics. The revenues of the Indonesian state, as Anderson has pointed out,[19] come primarily from foreign sources. Tax derived from oil and gas production together with aid receipts constituted 73.3% of total state revenues in 1981/82.[20] Domestic class forces therefore possess no leverage against the state deriving from state's need for revenue.

From time to time, however, contradictions reach a crisis point which poses a fundamental threat to the system as a whole and demands resolution by the state. For example, the contradiction between declining and petty indigenous capital and larger, state-backed corporate capital in the early 1970s constituted such a potential for social unrest that the government judged it necessary to extend protection and support to the former in order to diffuse disorder, even at the cost of channelling scarce resources into less economically productive sectors.

In 1975/76 the state was forced to intervene in the operations of the state oil company, Pertamina, which had accumulated $10 billion in debts. Because of the threat this posed to the fiscal viability of the Indonesian economy as a whole, the state moved to regularise Pertamina's operations and dismiss Sutowo even though this contravened the interests of the military and influential politico-bureaucrats who relied on Pertamina as a major source of non-budgetary income.[21]

The most recent and perhaps most far-reaching crisis has been sparked by the decline in oil revenues, which in turn has threatened the revenue base of the state and Indonesia's balance of payments position.[22] As an immediate reaction, the state cut energy and food subsidies at the risk of social unrest.[23] There is pressure to reduce the protection of favoured business groups in the import-substitution manufacturing sector even though these groups are closely associated with politico-bureaucrats. There is also pressure to develop a domestic revenue base through taxation and to regularise bureaucratic procedures. In this instance the interests of the politico-bureaucrats and their business associates are in collision with the state's need for revenue and the economy's need for fiscal survival in the international economy.

The function of the state must also be considered in relation to changes in the nature of demands placed upon it as a consequence of changes in the structure of the economy. Robin Luckham has argued that the state project changes as the economy progresses from petty capitalist commodity production to enclave commodity production, import-substituting industrialisation (ISI) and hence to export-oriented industrialisation (EOI).[24] The final EOI stage requires a higher level of state activity in disciplining labour, providing complex fiscal legal and physical infrastructure and managing fiscal and monetary crises.

Pressures upon Third World states to move from ISI to EOI have been increased by the development of a new international division of labour in which capital is able to locate itself more freely and divide different production functions on an international scale. This has resulted in a widespread movement of relatively labour-intensive manufacture, especially textiles, electronics assembly and more recently, iron, steel and other heavy sectors, to the Third World.[25] In the case of Indonesia, pressures to move to EOI, and the types of demands made by international capital as a basis for Indonesia's inclusion in the New International Division of Labour as a 'Newly Industrialising Country' were clearly stated in the 1980 World Bank Report, and among its demands were the liberalisation of the economy and the regularisation of the state apparatus.[26]

The whole question of the relationship between the industrialisation of the Third World and the development of highly organised and institutionalised repressive and authoritarian regimes is beginning to be the subject of increasingly systematic attention.[27]

CONCLUSION

The operation of the state in Indonesia is conditioned by a complex variety of factors:

(a) The interests of the politico-bureaucrats as officials of the state committed to securing its continued fiscal viability, as members of the military committed to securing its continued political dominance, as members of factions committed to maintaining and extending positions of relative influence and power.

(b) The interests of politico-bureaucrats in relation to class interests as owners of capital and land, as partners and associates of capitalists, as dependants upon finance provided by corporate groups, and as individuals influenced by particular capitalist ideological and cultural forms.

(c) The restraints, obligations and imperatives imposed upon the state by the very configuration of class power and conflict inherent in the specific social and economic order over which it presides. These include: the need to mediate conflict, resolve crises, provide the legal, political and fiscal conditions essential to the process of economic growth and capital accumulation.

1. Crouch 1978; B. Anderson, 'Last Days of Indonesia's Suharto?', *Southeast Asia Chronicle* 63 (1978); K. D. Jackson, 'Bureaucratic Polity: A Theoretical Framework for the Analysis of Power & Communications in Indonesia', in K. D. Jackson & L. W. Pye (eds), *Political Power & Communication in Indonesia* (Berkeley, 1978).

2. K. Ward, *The 1971 Election in Indonesia: An East Java Case Study* (Melbourne, 1974); Oey Hong Lee (ed.), *Indonesia After the 1971 Elections* (London, 1974). The latter contains several articles on the role of Golkar and the political control of elections by the state. An excellent, and more recent, collection of articles on Golkar, the parties and elections is to be found in *Prisma* 25 (June 1982).

3. J. MacDougall, 'Patterns of Military Control in the Indonesian Higher Central Bureaucracy', *Indonesia* 33 (1982).

4. This aspect will be dealt with at length in the following chapters. On the question of rule of law, see also, T. M. Lubis and F. Abdullah, *Langit Masih Mendung: Laporan Keadaan Hak-Hak Asasi Manusia de Indonesia, 1980* (Jakarta, 1981). On the appropriation of the economic powers and resources of the state see R. Robison, 'Towards a Class Analysis of the Indonesian Military Bureaucratic State', *Indonesia* 25 (1978); H. Crouch, 'Generals and Business in Indonesia', *Pacific Affairs* 48 (1975).

5. A. Moertopo, *The Acceleration and Modernization of 25 Years' Development* (Jakarta, 1973) — a statement of the government position on the development role of the state and its implications for politics; K. Ward, 'Indonesia's Modernisation: Ideology & Practice', in Mortimer (ed.) 1973.

6. The leading members of the Bappenas technocrats were: Widjojo Nitisastro, who was head of Bappenas from 1967 to 1983 and Minister of State Co-ordinating Economics, Finance, Industry and Development from 1973 to 1983; Moh. Sadli, who has been Minister for Transmigration and for Mining; Emil Salim, deputy director of Bappenas, 1971–78, Minister for Development Control, 1978–83, Minister for the Environment since 1983; Ali Wardhana, Co-ordinating Minister for Economics, Finance and Development Control since 1983; Johannes Sumarlin, Minister for Rehabilitation of the State Apparatus in the 2nd and 3rd Development Cabinets and Minister for National Development Planning and Head of Bappenas since 1983.

7. 'But if government attitudes and the climate of public opinion in Djakarta meant anything, a new era had certainly begun. There was a willingness to eschew slogans and ideology, to face economic facts, to be pragmatic, which had not been in fashion in Indonesia for many years.' (Arndt 1967, p. 130).

Glassburner talks of the long political conflict between 'pragmatic', 'development-minded' politicians and 'radical' politicians viewing Guided Democracy as the triumph of the latter and the New Order as a return of the former: B. Glassburner, 'Economic Policy-Making in Indonesia, 1950–57'

128   THE RISE OF CAPITAL

(hereafter, 1971*a*) and 'Indonesian Economic Policy-making after Sukarno' (hereafter, 1971*b*), in Glassburner (ed.) 1971. See also, G. J. Pauker, 'Indonesia; the Age of Reason?', *Asian Survey* 13, 2 (1969). J. M. Allison, 'Indonesia: Year of the Pragmatists', *Asian Survey* 9, 2 (1969).

8. Perhaps the most persistent criticism of the economic policies of the New Order has been that which focuses upon the development of a highly protected and fairly inefficient import-substitution industrialisation (ISI) sector rather than pursuing an export-oriented industrialisation (EOI) strategy which would, it is argued, in the long term produce a more efficient industrial sector, less reliant on protection and subsidy and less vulnerable to the limitations of the domestic market. The choice of ISI strategy is seen as both a case of incorrect 'economic' analysis and the result of the political influence of those vested interests enjoying protection. See, P. McCawley, *Industrialization in Indonesia* (Canberra, 1979). These are also the views of the IBRD. See, G. Sacerdoti, 'Overdraft of Inefficiency', *FEER*, 29.5.81, pp. 44–9.

9. As will be demonstrated in Chapters 5 and 6, the influence of CSIS, both as a political base and source of competing ideas about development has been significant.

10. See Chapters 5 and 6.

11. For a more detailed critique, see Robison 1981.

12. It is interesting that Indonesian student protestors in 1970–71, 1973–74 and again in 1977–78, heavily influenced by North American social science, couched their critiques largely in behaviouralist terms. They have only begun to make structural analyses recently, i.e. to realise that the problems they sought to address were not the consequence of the moral turpitude of the political leaders but a product of factors integral to the structure of the system itself. This is discussed by Max Lane in his 'Voices of Dissent in Indonesia', *Arena* 61 (1982).

13. R. Mortimer, 'Indonesia; Growth or Development', in Mortimer (ed.) 1973; D. Ransome, 'The Berkeley Mafia and the Indonesian Massacre', *Ramparts* 9 (1970); R. Franke, 'Limited Good and Cargo Cult in Indonesian Economic Development', *JCA* 2, 4 (1972).

14. There is an enormous body of literature critical of dependency theory. See, for example: C. Leys, 'Underdevelopment and Dependency: Critical Notes', *JCA* 7, 1 (1977); Brenner 1977.

15. B. R. Anderson, Nationalism and the State in Modern Indonesia (Tokyo, 1982).

16. B. R. Anderson, 'The Idea of Power in Javanese Culture', in C. Holt (ed), *Culture and Politics in Indonesia* (Ithaca, 1972). Anderson argues that traditional Javanese notions of 'Power', in its mystical and spiritual sense, were actually fundamental in shaping political behaviour, and indeed, the political structures and the nature of political conflict, in contemporary Indonesia.

Such apparently discrete aspects of Javanese political thought and behaviour in the contemporary period as the rejection of parliamentary democracy, the characteristic traits of Djakarta's inter-ethnic and international politics, the patterns of administrative organization and internal bureaucratic relationships, the styles of post-independence leadership, the forms of corruption, and the ambiguous political position of the urban intelligentsia can and indeed should be seen as inextricably related to one another and that link is precisely the continuing cultural hold of traditional conceptions, including conceptions about Power. (p. 63)

17. This concept has been developed in K. Trimberger, 'A Theory of Elite Revolutions', *Studies in Comparative International Development* 7, 3 (1972), and applied in particular to explaining the emergence and policies of the Meiji state.

18. This is the consequence of the contradiction between the short-term interests of individual capitalists and the long-term survival of capitalism. Unfettered operation of the market system would devastate both the labour force and the physical environment. As mediator of intra-capital conflict and conflict between capital and labour, and as provider of infrastructure for accumulation, the state is forced to introduce policies which impinge on the property rights of capitalists: taxation, regulation of labour and welfare measures. See, F. Block, 'Beyond Relative Autonomy', *Socialist Register* (1980), pp. 231–2. There is a long-standing debate on the nature of the state and its relationship to society, beginning with the Milliband-Poulantzas exchange. One of the more recent and interesting pieces is Block's, but for a general overview, see, B. Jessop, 'Recent Theories of the Capitalist State', *Cambridge Journal of Economics* 1 (1977).

19. B. Anderson, 'Old State, New Society: Indonesia's New Order in Comparative Historical Perspective', *Journal of Asian Studies* 42, 3 (1983).

20. Budget figures in various issues of *BIES*, especially C. S. Gray, 'Survey of Recent Developments', *BIES* 18, 3 (1982), pp. 8, 9, 13.

21. The Pertamina debts had reached $10.4 billion by 1975, significantly larger than the debt inherited from the Sukarno period or the debt incurred by the state through its regular borrowing programmes: P. McCawley, 'Some Consequences of the Pertamina Crisis in Indonesia', *Journal of Southeast Asian Studies* 9, 1 (1978); D. Davies, 'Sutowo: Down but not Out', *FEER*, 30.5.75, pp. 52–8.

22. Due mainly to the decline in the value of oil exports, from $19.0 billion in 1981/82 to a projected $17.2 billion in 1982/83, the current account deficit in 1982/83 is projected at $7.0 billion, compared with a deficit of $2.4 billion in 1981/82 and a surplus of $2.1 billion in 1980/81 (Gray 1982). This aspect will be treated in detail in the final chapter.

23. The oil subsidy was reduced from Rp1 510 billion in 1981/82 to Rp924 billion in 1982/83, bringing about a 60% increase in the price of petrol. Food subsidies were reduced from Rp310 billion to Rp188 billion. The consequent 7% reduction in the routine budget allowed for a 35% increase in the development budget in that year. See, H. Dick, 'Survey of Recent Developments', *BIES* 18, 1 (1982).

24. R. Luckham, 'Militarism: Class, Force and International Conflict', *Institute of Development Studies Bulletin* 9,1 (1977). See especially pp. 28, 29.

25. See F. Frobel, 'The Current Development of the World Economy', *Review* 5, 4 (1982); F. Frobel et al, 'The New International Division of Labour', *Social Science Information* 17, 1 (1978).

26. IBRD, *World Bank Report, 1980*, Annex 5, *Indonesia: Selected Issues of Industrial Developments & Trade Strategy; Direct Foreign Investment in Indonesia*, 1981 (hereafter IBRD 1981). The report is treated in detail in Chapter 11.

27. See, H. Feith, 'Repressive Developmentalist Regimes in Asia', *Prisma* 19 (1980). This article draws on the work of O'Donnell, Schmitter & Cardoso who have developed this approach in their analysis of authoritarian regimes in Latin America.

5
The State, International Capital and Economic Nationalism: 1965–1975.

BROADLY speaking, economic strategy and the policy of the state towards the various elements of capital were to pass through three stages:

(a) A period influenced by *laissez-faire*, open-door econ-omic philosophies, aimed at producing maximum economic growth and relying heavily upon investment by international corporate capital. This period lasted from 1965–74/75, although significant cracks began to appear as early as 1970. It is this period and the decline of these policies which is the subject of this chapter.

(b) A period of resurgent economic nationalism, in which the state played a more aggressive and active role in financing, protecting and subsidising domestic capital and in direct investment. In addition, state policy focused heavily upon the creation of a national indus-trial sector based upon major resource projects in steel, natural gas, oil refining and aluminium and upon an import-substitution industrial sector. This increasingly contradicted the logic which underlay the newly emerging international division of labour and the policies of the IBRD and the IMF, which stressed comparative advantage, free trade and export-oriented industrialisation. This period spanned roughly the years 1974/75 to 1981/82, and will be treated in Chapter 6.

(c) A period of faltering in state-led economic national-ism and national industrialisation, caused by declining foreign investments, and a decline in the capacity of Indonesia to finance, or to attract finance for, its programme of national industrialisation. This period has just commenced in the early 1980s and will be treated in the final chapter.

The dynamics of conflict over the direction of policy towards international and domestic capital is complex, affected by such external factors as Indonesia's changing balance of payments and the changes in the available amount of capital for invest-ment. But it was also affected by political struggles both within the capitalist class and within the state apparatus. In this process neither the capital nor the state proved to be mono-lithic entities. Capital comprised various elements — interna-tional and domestic, large and small scale, Chinese and indigenous, while the state was divided into contending policy groups, the most prominent of which were the Bappenas and CSIS groups, and contending political factions, each of which had specific relationships to certain elements of capital and lines of economic strategy. A broad picture of the major forces at work and their positions are indicated in the following table.

THE BAPPENAS TECHNOCRATS AND ECONOMIC POLICY TO 1973/74.

The period 1965 to 1974 marks a definite stage in the devel-opment of economic policy in Indonesia, because it begins with the coming to power of the New Order and ends with a combination of events and circumstances (the 1974 riots, the influx of revenue into the state as a consequence of oil price

rises) which led to a significant change in the direction of
economic policy. Yet even within this time-span it is difficult
to find a single label to describe the thrust of policy. Not only
are there conflicting directions in policy but there are conflicting interpretations of the overall effect of Bappenas policy. Dependency theorists such as Mortimer and Ransome
see it as one of subservience to the IMF and the IBRD
involving the facilitation of foreign capital entry and the
restructuring of the Indonesian economy to suit the needs of
international capital. Glassburner[1] sees a much greater legacy from the Guided Economy period and from the 1950s,
arguing that economic nationalism, state intervention and
protectionism continued to be major elements of policy.
Others, notably McCawley[2] and Rudner[3], argue (from different perspectives) that Bappenas policy provided a protective
framework for the emergence of domestic capital
dominated by state corporations and by companies owned by
the military and their domestic Chinese corporate clients.

   In the years 1965 to 1968 there is little doubt that the
Bappenas technocrats were convinced by the IMF/IBRD
ideology of 'free-market' economics, which limited the state
to providing the fiscal and monetary conditions for capital
accumulation, and trusted in the mechanisms of the market
to generate maximum growth and efficiency. The major
writings of the Bappenas technocrats in this period were
concerned primarily with concrete problems of growth, currency stabilisation and rehabilitation of the infrastructure.[4]
Faith in the spontaneous radiation of social and economic
change relieved the government of the responsibility for
protecting and financing any particular fraction of capital.
Sadli illustrates this approach:

   There should be a fair and equitable treatment of private business
   and a guarantee of freedom of management. The tax regime should
   enable business to grow through ample cash flows. The foreign
   exchange regime should not be too tight and should prevent over
   valuation of currency. Labour laws should observe the proper

TABLE 5.1

DIMENSIONS OF IDEOLOGICAL, POLITICAL AND ECONOMIC CONFLICT OVER ECONOMIC POLICY

	Liberal capitalist orthodoxy	State-led economic nationalism	Liberal reformism	Petty bourgeois nationalism
IDEOLOGICAL	Laissez-faire. Free trade. Comparative advantage. Early emphasis on ISI shifts to EOI as the New International Division of Labour takes shape.	Development based upon industrialisation. Foreign capital subordination to national economic plan co-ordinated by state. Influenced by Meiji and Singapore models and selective legacy of Guided Economy.	A mixture of dependency theory, basic needs strategy, concepts of New International Economic Order and growth with equity.	Preservation of indigenous petty capital and commodity production.
POLITICAL	IMF, IBRD, IGGI, US State Department. Power derives from the key position of these institutions as financiers of Indonesian capitalism.	Opsus/CSIS. Ibnu Sutowo to 1975. State-led national capitalism integrated at a political level with authoritarian corporatism.	Intermittent student movements. Various groupings of urban middle-class intelligentsia including former Masyumi, PSI intellectuals, former military and their secretariats.	Generally unorganised elements of the indigenous petty bourgeoisie — largely Muslim. Spasmodic outbursts of anti-Chinese sentiment. Scattered support in DPR and the press.
		Bappenas, Hankam and Suharto. Fluctuation between the two approaches with Indonesia's capacity to finance economic nationalism		

ECONOMIC

International capital interested in free access to Indonesian economy	Japanese capital seeking control of access to Indonesian resources and energy via state-sponsored projects	Opposition to state economic policy a component of a broader opposition to the political-economic coalition of generals, national and international bourgeoisie.

Indigenous petty bourgeoisie

Large-scale Domestic Capital (state and private)

Integrating with foreign capital in free joint ventures and distribution agreements.	Integrating with state and foreign capital in state-sponsored major resource and industrial projects.

balance between the requirements of capital and the protection of
the rights of labour. Indigenous firms will flourish in such a climate.
The existence of foreign firms will have a catalytic effect upon
further growth of the national economy. The charge frequently
heard in ex-colonial economies that foreign business stifles the
growth of indigenous business will be avoided.[5]

Crucial to this 'trickle down' approach was the assertion
that the intrusion of foreign capital would spontaneously
generate a process of growth and that the climate of vigorous
competition would ensure that only healthy domestic businesses survive, in contrast to the inefficient and corrupt
enterprises that flourished under state protection and subsidy
in the 1950s and under Sukarno. Perhaps the central statement of adherence to the notion of spontaneous 'trickle
down' is to be found in Sadli's rejection of Boeke's dual
economy thesis in which Boeke argued that foreign capital
invariably formed enclaves which had little influence upon
the host economy in general. Sadli argued that economic
accumulation, integration and replication could occur as a
result of foreign capital investment in post-colonial societies
because of the existence of an indigenous 'elite' which would
act as a 'social reference group'.[6]
   The Bappenas technocrats themselves argued that they
rejected both the economically paralysing effect of etatism
and the social irresponsibility of liberal free-fight capitalism,
preferring instead what they called 'economic democracy' or
'pancasila economy'. This appeared to be some form of
capitalism in which the energy of market forces was un-
leashed to produce maximum growth but at the same time
restrained in the interests of social justice.[7] At this point it
becomes apparent that explaining Indonesian economic policy in terms of the expressed ideological attachments of the
Bappenas technocrats is limited in its effectiveness. This is
not simply because we are dealing with a whole array of
contradictory and vague statements, but because the development of policy and the flourishing of particular economic

ideologies relates to specific and concrete stages in the development of the political economy of Indonesia and the changing political and economic dominance of specific forces. Different aspects of technocrat economic ideology became dominant at different times.

Free-market, open-door ideologies were able to flourish in the early years of the New Order because, given the political options open to a counter-revolutionary regime presiding over a debt-ridden economy in a state of chaos and collapse and desperately seeking to renegotiate debts and attract foreign investment, there was little choice but to accept the IMF/IBRD/IGGI policy prescriptions.[8] Before IGGI and the IMF were willing to renegotiate loans and foreign capital was willing to re-enter Indonesia, the new policy-makers had to convince foreign creditors and potential foreign investors that they would give a high priority to debt rescheduling, infrastructure rehabilitation and currency stabilisation as well as removing controls on private investment, curtailing the activities of state corporations and regulatory bodies (such as OPS and GPS) and providing guarantees to foreign investors. During 1966, several official statements were made indicating acceptance of these priorities. The most precise statement was made in December 1966, by the Indonesian Government delegation to the Paris conference of IGGI. The main points were:

(a) That market forces were to play a central role in rehabilitation.

(b) State enterprises were to be placed on a competitive footing with private enterprise, ending preferential access to state credit and foreign-exchange allocations. State monopolies in the import sector were to be ended. On the other hand, state corporations were freed from the requirement to sell at artificially low prices. They could now charge market prices, operate economically and thereby no longer require subsidies.

(c) The private sector was to be stimulated by the removal

of import licence restrictions on raw materials and equipment.

(d) Foreign private investment would be encouraged by the introduction of a new investment law which would provide taxation and other incentives and guarantees.[9]

With this statement and the beginnings of moves towards a return of most of the foreign assets seized in the period 1963–65, the foreign creditor nations appeared satisfied that Indonesian economic policy was moving in an acceptable direction.

The immediate consequence of the negotiations with the IGGI was the rescheduling of existing debts and the reopening of access to international networks of finance from private and governmental sources and from international finance and monetary institutions such as the World Bank and the IMF. In the short term, foreign loans, particularly in the form of import credits, were to enable the government to finance the extensive commodity imports in the late 1960s which were so crucial in bringing inflation under control.[10] In the long term, foreign loans were to enable the government to embark on a programme of investment projects, primarily in rehabilitation of infrastructure, through the development budgets. They account for around 60% of the projected development budget expenditure for the first Five Year Plan (hereafter Repelita I — Rencana Pembangunan Lima Tahun), 1969–74.[11]

The most important pieces of legislation shaping the structure of capital ownership under the New Order have been the Foreign Capital Investment Law No. 1 of January 1967 (PMA) and the Domestic Capital Investment Law of July 1968 (PMDN). The major features of the PMA Law were:

(a) A guarantee that there is no intention to nationalise foreign assets and a guarantee of compensation payment if nationalisation does occur (Articles 21 and 22).

(b) That the duration of the operation of each foreign enterprise is thirty years with extensions beyond this period dependent upon renegotiation.

(c) Exemption of foreign investors from dividend and corporation tax for up to three years and provision for carry-on of losses into the post tax-holiday period (Article 15).

(d) Exemption from import duties on machinery and equipment and from duties on the import of raw materials for two years (Article 15).

(e) Full authority to select management and to recruit foreign technicians for jobs which Indonesian labour is not yet capable of undertaking (Article 11).

(f) Free transfer of profits, depreciation funds and proceeds from the sale of shares to Indonesian nationals (Articles 19 and 24).

It was not until August 1968, sixteen months after the introduction of the PMA Law, that the PMDN Law was introduced giving similar taxation and import duty concessions to domestic investors. In the intervening period foreign investors operated at a considerable advantage to domestic investors, but even after the introduction of the PMDN Law, domestic investors still operated from a position of structural disadvantage. BKPM required that companies investing under the PMA or PMDN programmes deposit 25% of their intended investment as collateral in state banks. For non-priority sectors, generally those outside forestry, agriculture or import substitution, the required collateral deposits were 50%.[12] Few domestic firms possessed such liquid assets after the high inflation and economic difficulties of the decade from 1957 to 1967. In any case, faced with high interest rates and competition from cheap foreign imports financed by commodity aid, potential domestic investors in manufacture tended to join the scramble for lucrative import credits or simply placed their money in the banks where savings interest rates were extremely attractive. Banks overflowed with funds and some were even forced to restrict deposits.[13]

Despite the increasingly desperate position of small capital in this period, particularly among indigenous petty manufacturers in the textile sector, there did occur a strong growth of domestic investment in the medium and large-scale sector. The survival and development of these elements was built around centres of politico-bureaucratic and state power. In particular, such state- and bureaucrat-sponsored capital was able to gain a privileged position within import-substitution manufacturing which, from 1968, became an increasing concern of Bappenas policy. One of the major contradictions in the political structure of the New Order is between the Bappenas technocrats and the major, military-dominated, politico-bureaucratic factions over the control of economic policy itself and, more specifically, control over the resources of the state. By the late 1960s, state managers, notably Ibnu Sutowo of Pertamina, together with various generals and officials involved in business, were using the state's considerable economic powers to allocate licences (for trade and manufacture), credit and contracts to build large corporate conglomerates, usually with Indonesian Chinese partners. This rising, state-sponsored domestic capitalist force found the IBRD/IMF policies a restraint upon their development. They relied upon maximum but selective use of the power of the state to intervene in the economy to underpin their corporate interests, not only to provide contracts, credits and licences, but also to secure strategic or lucrative joint venture partnerships with foreign companies. At the same time, these emerging groups required general fiscal policies which supported economic growth.

Pressure for growth-oriented policies also came from those who were in decline, both politically and economically — the national petty bourgeoisie and important elements of the urban intelligentsia.[14] Consequently, pressure from all sides made it politically untenable for the Bappenas technocrats to continue monetarist policies of financial retrenchment or to ignore demands for protection of national capital. The first major policy change was the introduction of Repelita I in 1969.

Although ostensibly following the IMF/IBRD strategy of broad-based agricultural rehabilitation, Repelita I set a high priority on the development of import-substitution manufacture, listing as priorities industries which would provide inputs into agricultural rehabilitation (fertilisers, chemicals, cement) and industries which would provide the basic consumer necessities (textiles).[15] However, Repelita did not involve specific and direct investments but rather set broad objectives to be achieved through the development budget and fiscal policies.

Expenditure under Repelita I projections comprised state investment channelled through the development budgets together with expected foreign and domestic capital investments. These investments were concentrated in three main areas:

(a) Agriculture — including rehabilitation of irrigation systems and finance for fertilisers and pesticides under the Bimas projects (Rp305 billion).
(b) Industry and mining (Rp380 billion).
(c) Communications (Rp265 billion).

Social Welfare (Rp172 billion) and Electric Power (Rp100 billion) constituted the other major areas of expenditure out of a total of Rp1 420 billion.[16]

Martin Rudner argues that Repelita I became predominantly a programme for the rehabilitation of industrial infrastructure in West Java. This must be seen in the context of state encouragement of industrialisation through preferential fiscal and monetary policies, including preferential effective foreign-exchange rates, direct concessionary bank credits, tax holidays, customs exemptions, protective tariffs, subsidised infrastructure, administrative services and assistance and a variety of protective tariff measures.[17] Before the 1973 tariff reforms, McCawley cites an overall protection rate of 66% in the import competing sectors.[18]

The crucial question to be asked from the perspective of this study is the effect of these policies, and especially those embodied in Repelita I, upon the structure of capital owner- ship in Indonesia. Essentially, there are two categories of capital investment — those in oil and gas, which do not come under the auspices of PMA and PMDN, and the remainder, which do. Total realised investment under PMDN and PMA was approximately US$2 billion by December 1973. Capital investment in oil and gas was estimated at twice this figure,[19] and was dominated by foreign corporations because of the high demands for both capital and technology. Of the re- maining third of capital investment under the PMA/PMDN programmes, slightly less than half was domestic.

Although domestic investment also constituted approxi- mately 6%–9% of PMA,[20] much of this was financed and

TABLE 5.2
APPROVED CAPITAL INVESTMENT UNDER PMA/PDMN TO DECEMBER 1973

Sector	Total investment approvals (in US$ million)[a]		% of Total investment approvals	
	PMA	PMDN	PMA	PMDN
Forestry	495.5	356.8	58	42
Agriculture)				
Fisheries)	113.0	232.5	33	67
Mining	860.5	46.2	95	5
Manufacture	1 045.1	1 740.9	38	62
(textiles)	(436.9)	(749)	37	63
Tourism, Hotels,)				
Real Estate)	195.9	200	50	50
Other (inc. infrastructure/ construction)	118.3	207	37	63
Total Approved	2 828.3	2 978.5	49	51
Total Realised[b]	1 131.2	876	56	44

Source: Palmer 1978, Tables 5.3 and 5.4. pp. 110–11, citing BKPM sources.
a based on the 1971/72/73 exchange rate of Rp415 = US$1.
b based on the realisation rate of 40% for PMA and 34% for PMDN applying over the period 1967–80. See I. Suhartoyo, Penanaman Modal dan Industrialisasi (Jakarta, 1981).

controlled by the foreign partner. In any case it does not significantly affect the general picture which emerges from the statistics. The most important factor to emerge from the pattern of PMA/PMDN investment is the significance of investment in manufacture and the apparent dominance of domestic investors in this sector. Can these figures be interpreted as a reflection of the growth of a powerful domestic industrial bourgeoisie, in turn the consequence of protective policies towards import-substitution manufacture?

In the first place, the apparent domination of domestic capital investment in manufacture is modified by the fact that the realisation rate of domestic investment in manufacture is only 29.8% compared with 41.9% for PMA, meaning that PMA constituted 46% of realised investment and PMDN 54%.[21] Foreign investment is also concentrated in expanding and capital-intensive areas, while the bulk of domestic, private capital investment was in declining labour-intensive areas producing lower value-added.

TABLE 5.3

OUTPUT, VALUE-ADDED AND EMPLOYMENT BY OWNERSHIP

	Total	Foreign	Government	Private Domestic
Number of Firms	6.758	282	547	5 929
Output				
Rp billions (%)	1.341 (100)	283 (21.2)	261 (19.5)	795 (59.3)
Value Added				
Rp billions (%)	555 (100)	127 (23)	126 (22.8)	301 (54.8)
Employment				
Total (%)	683 (100)	71 (10.4)	135 (19.8)	477 (69.8)

Source: IBRD 1981, citing the 1974 Industrial Census and BKPM approval lists.

Foreign capital, predominantly Japanese, concentrated in the heavily protected import-substitution sector, manufacturing goods for domestic consumption, mainly textiles, and investing in large integrated mills. By 1980 realised foreign investment in textiles totalled US$513 million compared with approximately US$89 million domestic investment.[22] Other favoured sectors of investment were automobile assembly and pharmaceuticals. In effect, these were industries which processed imported components and used imported technology. The object of the foreign investors at this stage was to dominate the local market from behind trade barriers.

From the data in Table 5.2 we can see that foreign firms were, on average, larger, more capital intensive and more productive than domestic firms. They accounted for one-fifth of manufacturing output, 23% of value-added but only 10% of employment. They were, on average, twice as large as state firms, and seven times as large as domestic private firms in terms of output per firm. Value-added per worker in foreign firms was twice that of public sector firms and almost three times that of private domestic firms.

State corporations constituted about one-fifth of output, value-added and employment. They were particularly dominant in the basic industries sector, where they continued their role as the spearhead for large-scale investment, considered necessary for building a national industrial economy but beyond the scope of private domestic investors. Data from the 1974/75 industrial census shows state firms producing 75.2% of cement, 51.9% of paper and paper products, 40.4% of food manufacturing and 52.0% of machinery.[23]

Private domestic investment constituted the largest sector, with 59.3% of output, 54.2% of value-added and 69.8% of employment. These firms were, on average, smaller and less productive.[24] It is important, however, to point out a significant division within domestic investment in industry. Several major domestic business groups with political patronage had emerged in this period and were operating on a large scale, in such sectors as textiles, electronics and pharmaceuticals, often in joint ventures with foreign partners. The bulk of private domestic enterprise and employment was, however, in smaller ventures such as textiles, rubber milling, sugar milling, sawmilling, rice milling, weaving, brick making, *kretek* and furniture manufacture.

The largest component of private domestic investment, in numbers of both firms and workers, was in the small and cottage sector, which was relatively small in terms of production and value-added. McCawley estimates that approximately 3.9 million of Indonesia's 4.9 million industrial workers were located in the cottage sector, although only Rp75 billion of Rp596 billion of value-added is produced in this sector.[25]

Given that the domestic market proved to be a finite one and that import substitution rapidly became saturated, the rapid gains by foreign investors were losses for the smaller indigenous firms. State protection of the ISI sector and provision of infrastructure had to a considerable degree benefited foreign capital and had not, in itself, created a large domestic industrial bourgeoisie. Bappenas technocrats were, however, reluctant to take specific steps to alter this situation.

The Bappenas position was was most clearly put by Sadli[26] in 1970, when he argued that foreign investors should be given more favourable treatment because domestic investors were in Indonesia in any case while foreign investors had to be lured. On the other hand, unequal treatment was recognised to be politically dangerous, particularly because of the increasingly strident reaction of the declining indigenous petty bourgeoisie. The reluctance of the Bappenas technocrats to provide protection and subsidy for domestic investors resulted from their deep suspicion that the inefficient and corrupt enterprises, both state and private, which had previously emerged in the 1950s and under Sukarno, would again emerge and weaken the recovery effort. It was felt that the more domestic firms were forced to operate in an open and competitive economy without monopoly privileges, the stronger they would become.

In conclusion, although the growth of an indigenous business class is a policy commitment of the present government, execution will be a difficult and slow exercise and the private indigenous entrepre-

neur will have to continue his struggle for survival and growth
against competition from foreign and alien enterprises and from the
public sector. But this will probably guarantee a more healthy
growth for them.[27]

Nevertheless, the increasing political unrest over the issue
of economic nationalism forced the government to introduce
legislation specifically protecting domestic investors. In 1970
the government refined its protection of import-substitution
manufacturing under Repelita I, by legislating to exclude
new foreign investment from thirty areas of light industry.
Further restrictions in other fields including trade and forestry, together with special credit schemes for domestic
investors, were to follow.

These reluctant steps towards economic nationalism satisfied no one and the Bappenas technocrats were to come
under increasing attack for their alleged *laissez-faire*, open-
door approach. On the one hand they were attacked for
providing a policy framework which had the effect of increasing inequality and concentrating economic and political
power in the hands of a coalition of foreign capitalists,
Indonesian generals and their Chinese business associates
(*cukong*). This criticism might be described as reformist/
nationalist, and the unlikely coalition of forces which expressed it comprised radical and reformist elements of the
civilian intelligentsia along with the leadership of the declining indigenous bourgeoisie and petty bourgeoisie. On the
other hand, the technocrats were attacked precisely for not
allowing the state fully to realise its capacity to develop a
powerful national bourgeoisie and a strong national industrial economy. Such a position might best be characterised as
bureaucrat nationalist. It envisaged a state-led, corporatist
society in which the economy was driven by large-scale state
investment in industry with economic power vested in the
hands of a domestic corporate bourgeoisie. Meiji Japan and
Singapore were the models here.

Technocrat policy had faltered in political terms because it

permitted a catastrophic economic decline among large segments of the indigenous bourgeoisie while at the same time
not providing emerging major domestic business conglomerates with the full potential support of the state.

THE RE-EMERGENCE OF ECONOMIC NATIONALISM

The resurgence of economic nationalism was a complex
movement influenced less by a declining petty bourgeoisie
demanding state protection against the superior forces of
foreign capital than by emerging political and economic
forces demanding the removal of political and economic
constraints upon their potential for development. The type
of economic nationalism which emerged in the early 1970s
aimed not merely to secure a share of capital ownership for
domestic capitalists within an economic structure determined
by the logic of international capital accumulation or driven
by crises of accumulation in metropolitan investor countries.[28] Instead, it envisaged a programme of state-led capitalist development to form an integrated national industrial
economy which included capital, intermediate and consumer
goods industries.

Such a strategy contradicted the logic embodied in the
emerging international division of labour within which Indonesia was most suitably placed to provide low-wage labour
for labour-intensive production of exports in such sectors as
textiles and electronics assembly, while importing goods
manufactured in the more technologically complex and
capital-intensive processes. It sought to subordinate foreign
capital to a set of national economic and political priorities
and to the interests of domestic capital. For the bureaucrat
nationalists who led the resurgence of economic nationalism,
it was clear that Indonesia possessed the capacity to generate
a national industrial economy using its energy resources
either to produce investment capital directly or as a form of
collateral to secure loans. Their objectives were to involve

the state in direct economic intervention for the purposes of
co-ordinating and financing national capital investment with
the long-term intention of building a broad industrial base
for the Indonesian economy.

Opsus/CSIS and Economic Policy

The bureaucrat nationalists operated from two major bases
within the political and bureaucratic apparatus of the New
Order state: the state oil company, Pertamina, and Opsus,
the political and intelligence centre operating under the
leadership of General Ali Moertopo. The broad ideological
position of the bureaucrat nationalists has been most clearly
and comprehensively presented by intellectuals associated
with the CSIS which constituted the only co-ordinated policy
opposition to the technocrats in Bappenas. Of these intellectuals, Jusuf Panglaykim, a Chinese academic and businessman, was the most important economic theorist. The
following summary of Panglaykim's economic thought in this
period encapsulates the general thrust of the bureaucrat
nationalist position.[29]

Panglaykim's initial point is that foreign capital operates
through multinational corporations which often also work in
a co-ordinated relationship with the governments of their
home country. Without a co-ordinated economic strategy of
its own, tying together state and business, the penetration of
foreign capital will be an exploitive and destructive exercise
for Indonesia rather than one in which foreign capital is
harnessed to long-term national economic goals. In 1974,
Panglaykim was arguing that Bappenas' policy repeated the
errors of earlier periods, attempting to confront the multina-
tionals in a fragmented fashion. Where the state had intervened in the economy, it all too often had done so not to
assist the general process of capital accumulation but to
squabble over economic spoils, often reducing the business
sector to a plaything of competing political groups.

What then were Panglaykim's prescriptions for the development of the Indonesian economy? He was heavily influenced by two models for development established in Meiji Japan and in Singapore in which the state played a central role in determining investment priorities, providing infrastructure, mobilising finance and investment capital and co-ordinating domestic investment. A second crucial feature of these models was that both countries developed a national economy based upon industrialisation in contradiction to the prevailing comparative advantages in international trade.

It followed from this focus upon a total national economic strategy that reliance upon spontaneous 'trickle down' of benefits from foreign investments channelled through the joint venture was inadequate because it simply achieved a share of capital investment in an economy whose form was determined by foreign capital. In any case, Panglaykim argued, the local equity in joint ventures was often financed by either foreign banks or foreign partners which meant that the local partner never actually received control of the limited equity he nominally held.

At the heart of Panglaykim's economic prescriptions was the notion of the nationally integrated economic unit (NIEU), a state-coordinated economic structure within which finance and production could be co-ordinated to achieve national planning goals. Such a structure owes much to the concepts which underlay the establishment of the OPS, GPS and the state corporate structure in the Guided Economy period. Indeed, Panglaykim saw in the state corporate sector a good deal of potential creative power. The NIEU was conceived as a vertically integrated structure in a specific industry, integrating processing of raw materials, production of capital goods and the manufacture of consumer goods, thereby constituting a set of reinforcing backward and forward linkages. The state would play a central role, providing finance, purchasing raw material imports, allocating production quotas and generally co-ordinating production. Through its leadership, the state would establish the basis of a domestic bourgeoisie by financing the participation of private business and providing the cohesion and protection necessary to avoid total domination by foreign capital. As the private domestic bourgeoisie began to accumulate capital, it would be expected to repay loans and purchase state-held equity, a process which would sort out the opportunists from the accumulators.

A crucial component in the success of such units in manufacture was to be the development of a state-led, nationally integrated financial sector incorporating state and private banks, merchant banks and financial institutions, and a money market. It was through such a complex financial sector that the private domestic components of the NIEUs could be financed in the initial stage. Without this national finance sector, Panglaykim argued, the NIEUs would simply be financed and controlled by foreign banks.

Apart from being an instrument for achieving an integrated, industrialised economy, the NIEUs were to be a means of rationalising the distribution of the ownership of capital between the contending factions, domestic and foreign, Chinese and indigenous, large and small units of capital. Tensions between the Chinese and indigenous investors could be relaxed if both enjoyed a guaranteed and defined place within the NIEUs. At the same time, the participation of foreign capital could be restricted to sectors where foreign capital and technology were necessary within the framework of a set of priorities determined by Indonesian economic planners.

The Panglaykim critique and strategy has been taken up by several other writers in various CSIS publications. Among these, Kwik Kian Gie adds some interesting detail to the Panglaykim critique in an article which appeared in 1975.[30] According to Kwik, Bappenas strategy had proved inadequate for generating the formation of domestic capital and for subordinating foreign capital investment to a national set of economic priorities. Foreign investors continued to capitalise their investments with domestic credit, and to dominate 'closed' sectors of investment through control of production of the capital goods and commodities used in these sectors. Finally, Kwik argued that transfer of equity from foreign to domestic ownership achieves little in itself because the foreign investor has usually recovered original capital investment several times over and simply hands over equity when the tax holiday has expired. Local investors therefore sink their finance into near obsolete companies whose taxation and other concessions no longer operate and are therefore placed at a competitive disadvantage in relation to new foreign investment.

Like Panglaykim, Kwik saw the answer in the establishment of nationally integrated units, combining state power and resources with private business interests and building 'national giants' in an attempt to counterbalance the power of the 'foreign giants'.

In political terms, the push towards state-led national capitalism came from a loose coalition comprising Ibnu Sutowo, the President Director of the state oil company, Pertamina, together with Generals Ali Moertopo and Soedjono Hoemardani, the dominant figures in the Opsus group. All three were convinced of the need for state economic intervention for the purpose of creating a national industrial economy. In the political sphere, as we have seen, Opsus had already initiated the beginnings of corporatist state structures designed to monopolise legitimate political activity and impose a state ideology based upon the concept of the state as developer, stabiliser and dynamiser. Such a corporatist, authoritarian structure was the natural political framework for the corporatist economic structures envisaged in the Panglaykim model. Hoemardani and Moertopo were explicit in their support for economic intervention by the state as the linchpin in the formation of NIEUs and a nationally integrated financial consortium.[31] However, the NIEUs as envisaged by Panglaykim required such a co-ordinated, complex and cohesive set of policy initiatives and implied such a degree of political discipline and administrative organisation that they were beyond the scope of Opsus, or indeed of the state itself.

Instead, the focus of state-led economic nationalism was much less ambitious, and settled on attempts to establish major resource and industrial projects seen as necessary for the formation of a national industrial economy. For this purpose, Pertamina became the focus of activity by the bureaucrat nationalists because it represented the only source of finance, or means of raising loans, which was both significant and outside the control of the Bappenas technocrats.

Sutowo, Pertamina and National Capitalism

In formal terms, the function of Pertamina was that of managing Indonesian oil resources through the allocation of drilling concessions, the administration of work-contract and production-sharing contracts and the co-ordination of the oil industry as a whole. Actual investment in production was a minor part of Pertamina's activities. However, Pertamina developed into the most powerful centre of economic power in Indonesia because, as production and oil prices rose, it came to control the single most important source of wealth. Between 1969/70 and 1974/75, government revenue from oil jumped from Rp66.5 to Rp957.2 billion and, as a percentage of total revenues, from 19.7% to 48.4%.

Pertamina was used as the spearhead for the creation of industrial capitalist accumulation in two ways. First, Sutowo extended the activities of Pertamina to include investment in a wide range of activities through subsidiary corporations. Most prominent among these was P. T. Krakatau Steel, which operated in 1974 with a capital of US$10 million of which US$6 million was provided by Pertamina. Other Pertamina subsidiaries were involved in petrochemicals, metal fabrication, engineering, telecommunications, real estate, air services and shipping. The second thrust of Sutowo's nationalist policies was to use potential access to Indonesia's oil and natural gas as a means of raising finance for the development of major projects in petrochemicals and natural gas.

Significantly, Sutowo turned to Japan, rather than to the IGGI, IMF or IBRD channels, to raise finance and attract investors. The liquid natural gas project was the most important of these. Japan was a natural source for loans because IMF/IBRD policy was not sympathetic to Sutowo's nationalistic programme of large-scale resource and industrial project development. For its part, Japan was willing to finance resource projects outside the IGGI/IMF which would provide privileged access to cheap energy sources.

By 1976, Robinson had noted that:

. . . the grand total of official energy related loan finance transfers comes to $2,303,683,000. This is nearly one and a half times total realised foreign investment in Indonesia for the whole post–1966 period and more than twice Japan's direct investment.[32]

It was clear that Sutowo's policies received support from the President himself, who has been a most enthusiastic supporter of large and generally Japanese-financed resource projects. His enthusiasm, particularly for the Asahan aluminium refinery and the Dumai hydrocracker, continued into the late 1970s and early 1980s, well after Sutowo's demise. In 1974, at the height of Sutowo's activities, presidential approval was given to Sutowo to raise special loans (for example, $500 million for Krakatau Steel) and presidential authorisation was given to Pertamina to withhold $800 million in oil taxes from the Bank of Indonesia to sustain the momentum of special projects.[33]

However, the momentum of state-led economic nationalism and industrialisation under the direction of Sutowo came to an abrupt halt in 1975/76. In March 1975, Pertamina found itself unable to meet payments on one of its short-term debts, forcing the President to appoint an investigation team under the Bappenas technocrat, Sumarlin. The investigations revealed a complex and compounding debt, initially estimated at US$10.5 billion. The serious implications of the massive Pertamina debt strengthened the hand of the Bappenas technocrats in their struggle to make Pertamina accountable and responsible to the formal state institutions with legal authority over its operations, including the Ministry of Mines, the Bank of Indonesia, the Ministry of Finance and the National Auditing Board. After investigations, it became clear that, although injudicious borrowing for resource projects had been the main cause of the financial crisis, there were spectacular examples of waste, incompetence and corruption.[34] This further strengthened the hand of the Bappenas technocrats, and in 1976 Sutowo was dismissed as President Director of Pertamina and a major shake-up of higher staff took place in which several of the officials closest to Sutowo lost their places.

There are several dimensions to the struggle between Sutowo and the technocrats. At one level it may be seen in terms of Weberian categorisation of bureaucratic types, as a conflict between patrimonial and legal bureaucratic authority, with Pertamina as a vestige of the appanage benefice. At another level, it suggests a free-wheeling robber baron capitalist, chafing under the dead weight of an incompetent and ponderous bureaucracy. Both of these interpretations are in some senses valid, but certainly not sufficient in themselves. The conflict was also part of the broader ideological confrontation with Western economic orthodoxy, manifested in the IMF and IBRD, which stressed free-market, free-trade approaches. Within this scenario, the role of the state was to be limited as much as possible to providing appropriate fiscal and monetary policies. The bureaucrat nationalists saw this as a sinister policy, inhibiting industrialisation and holding back the true development potential of Indonesia. Instead, they looked to state-led capitalist investment in major resource, energy and industrial projects designed to give Indonesia a broad industrial base and a degree of economic autonomy. However, the move towards nationalist industrialisation was by no means the simple consequence of an ideological vision of powerful bureaucrats. There were important material reasons for the move to such a strategy.

Most important were the limits on capital accumulation
imposed by a policy which focused on rehabilitation of the
agrarian sector and import-substitution manufacture for agricultural inputs or the consumer market. The opportunities
for expansion by both private and state-owned domestic
capital lay in the vertical extension of manufacture into
heavy industry and intermediate goods. Large-scale industrial and resource projects offered the prospect of substantial
expansion for contractors and suppliers and, indeed, Pertamina's moves in this direction in the early 1970s had already
spawned business groups which fed on this. There was,
however, no public and co-ordinated political move on the
part of those major domestic capitalists likely to benefit from
nationalist industrial policies in support of such strategies. B.
M. Diah, the newspaper publisher, developed and published
complex critiques of US and other foreign economic dominance and manipulation of the Indonesian economy, as well
as a recommendation for nationalist industrialisation.

Two trends are now clear. One leads via the Bappenas technocrats
to a 'free-fight' and laissez-faire pattern of development in the
Western and American fashion. Another trend takes the form of
co-operation with Japan on the basis of one's own strength without
loans from IGGI, the IMF and the World Bank with Pertamina as
guarantee.[35]

Although Diah had important interests in trade, manufacture and hotels,[36] his nationalist views extended back into
the 1950s and he cannot be regarded as speaking on behalf
of domestic capitalists in any formal sense. However, the
absence of a public position by domestic capitalists did not
mean indifference. For the most part they derived their
economic position from personal relationships with political
patrons rather than organised public moves to influence
policy in defence of general class interests. Nevertheless, the
major domestic capitalists clearly recognised that their interests lay in the development of industrial deepening.

However, it must be remembered that Panglaykim was himself a businessman of some substance and, given the cohesive
relationships between the business and political elements
associated with Opsus, his position can be assumed to represent a wider consensus, especially among the Chinese business groups. The young indigenous clients who surrounded
Sutowo and who were connected with the Young Businessmens Association of Indonesia (Hipmi) were not only supportive of the industrial deepening strategy but enthusiastic
about the worth of Pertamina as a model for state business
relationships.[37]

The conflict over policy also had political dimensions, in
Japan's thrust to replace the US as the major foreign investor
in Indonesia and the internal conflicts of the 1970–74 period.
Bappenas technocrats, educated in the orthodoxy of Western
liberal economics, worked closely, in the period to 1974/75,
with the IGGI, IMF and IBRD. A Harvard Advisory Group
worked within Bappenas itself. This coalition was crucial to
Indonesia's development plans. Indeed, it is no exaggeration
to regard IGGI, IMF and IBRD as the major financiers of
Indonesia's economic rehabilitation after 1966. To break out
of this restriction and secure the finance for major projects, it
was necessary for the Pertamina/Opsus group to look to new
international partners, notably Japan. Ali Moertopo had
been active in encouraging the development of an 'Asia-
Pacific Triangular Axis' linking Japan, Indonesia and
Australia.[38] Soedjono Hoemardani had, by 1974, become
the focal brokerage point for Japanese capital investment in
Indonesia. Japan, anxious to supplant the United States as
the dominant investor in the resources and energy sector,
was a willing accomplice.

IMF policy was firmly against the large resource project
loans sought by Pertamina in the early and mid-1970s. It was
at the IMF's insistence in 1972 that Indonesian state corporations were restricted in their capacity for independent foreign
borrowings for between one and fifteen years.[39] Such a
regulation hit directly and particularly at Pertamina, forcing

Sutowo into short-term roll-over loans which were to prove his undoing. Indeed, both Sutowo and *Merdeka* were to allege that the loans crisis had been engineered because Sutowo had to make a commitment of funds on the basis of a US$1 200 million, twenty-year loan which had mysteriously evaporated at the last moment.[40]

The bureaucrat nationalists also saw the student unrest of 1973 as part of the political thrust of the Bappenas/IMF/ United States axis. This view was expressed in B. M. Diah's journal, *Ekspres*, on 18 and 26 January 1974, claiming that student criticisms and demonstrations of 1973 and January 1974 were the work of PSI and Masyumi remnants operating in league with Bappenas technocrats against Opsus and Japanese business in Indonesia. It was suggested that the CIA was also involved to secure the interests of United States capital against the nationalist threat to its continued domination of the Indonesian economy. This interpretation was also proposed in the Opsus-sponsored weekly, *Topik*:

> There were speculations amongst political observers that the orga-niser of the first student action against Pronk was a high govern-ment official who objected to the technocrats guaranteeing the inflow of foreign capital and aid, including IGGI aid, in the last couple of years. The technocrats retaliated as soon as Pronk had left the country. By mobilising the Bandung students, they backed the demonstrations against Japanese capital, demanded the abolition of the ABRI institution and warned against the conspiracy between 'Japanese economic animals' and the sellers of the country.[41]

It was quite true that the criticisms and anger of the students and many of the middle-class intelligentsia were directed primarily at Sutowo (in 1970/71) and at Moertopo and his Chinese advisors, Liem Bian Koen, Liem Bian Kie and Harry Tjan, in 1973 and 1974. It is also true that demonstra-tions against foreign capital were directed primarily at the Japanese. But there is little evidence to suggest that their actions were part of a co-ordinated push by any Bappenas/

United States/IMF alliance against bureaucrat nationalist economic policies as such, although the US would, at that time, have welcomed the political decline of those who urged economic nationalist policies and the political entrenchment of Bappenas policy even, perhaps, if it meant bringing General Sumitro to power. The Japanese naturally attracted more Indonesian resentment, not only because of their closed style of operation and the close connections between Japanese companies and leading generals, including Hoemardani, Sutowo and Mrs Suharto, but because they were especially active in manufacture where confrontation with declining national producers was concentrated. On the other hand, United States investment was concentrated in oil and mining, where domestic capital did not operate. Similarly, resentment of Opsus by the middle-class intelligentsia had less to do with economic policy than with the fact that Moertopo and his Opsus associates and advisors, including Liem Bian Kie, Harry Tjan, Daoed Joesoef and General Benny Murdani, were the key figures in the move towards more authoritarian forms of state control.

While the Pertamina crisis dealt a body-blow to economic nationalism in the sense that it constituted a swing in the balance of influence over economic policy from the bureaucrat nationalists to the Bappenas technocrats, it did not spell the end of economic nationalism under the New Order. On the contrary, economic policy between 1975 and 1982 was to be dominated by the very sorts of policies urged by the bureaucrat nationalists in the period before Pertamina's collapse.

In the short term, however, the first major reassessment of economic policy, which occurred in the mid-1970s, was brought about not by pressure from the bureaucrat nationalists but by a variety of economic nationalism which called for a more equal sharing of economic resources and a focus upon basic needs rather than the corporatist industrialisation and concentration of power and wealth implied by the bureaucrat nationalists.

NATIONALIST REFORMISM AND ECONOMIC POLICY

By the early 1970s the economic strategy of the New Order had become the subject of active political protest from forces which may be grouped into two major categories. First, those who regarded themselves as direct victims of existing economic strategy: the declining indigenous capitalists and petty capitalists. Second, those who saw themselves as an alternative governing class and whose questioning of economic policy was part of a larger protest against the political rule of the New Order. This latter category comprised various elements of the civilian urban intelligentsia, many of whom had been figures of some influence in the party governments of the 1950s, as well as students and groups associated with former military officers shouldered aside in the power struggles between factions within the New Order itself.

The critique of economic policy by these groups must be set in a wider political context. While the New Order had attempted to incorporate the non-military, urban middle class within the various corporatist organisations and the state administrative apparatus itself, it was adamant in its exclusion of independent political parties from effective participation in the political process. For the bulk of the middle-class intelligentsia, particularly those associated with the former political parties, or those adhering to liberal or democratic socialist ideologies, opposition to the regime focused upon the monopolisation of political power and bureaucratic authority by the military and the increasingly arbitrary and authoritarian exercise of political power. Their critique of the economic policies of the New Order was a crucial component of this general political opposition because it thrust directly at the legitimacy of the regime, disputing its nationalist, populist and developmentalist claims, arguing instead that the regime presided over a process of increasing inequality and concentration of wealth in collusion with foreign economic interests. The New Order, they proposed, was elitist, comprador and possessed a view of development which did not extend beyond the interests of those who controlled it.

The first political protests occurred in 1970–71. They were essentially a reaction against the New Order by students and intellectuals who, just four or five years earlier, had played a major role in its legitimation, as trenchant critics of the Sukarno regime and enthusiastic supporters of military intervention. However, despite increasing frustration at their continued exclusion from political participation, the critique mounted by the students and intellectuals in 1970–71 had not yet become one which questioned the whole basis of the regime, and concentrated instead on what were considered excesses and aberrations.[42]

Of these moral aberrations, corruption was the most politically sensitive and spectacular manifestation. Not only was it conspicuous in material terms, and damaging to those outside the state apparatus who were its victims, but it symbolised a separation of the state from the people: the appropriation and abuse of power. Corruption was also portrayed as an impediment to the administration of development and as the mechanism of collusion between Indonesian political leadership and Chinese business.

The first major target of the protest was Ibnu Sutowo. *Indonesia Raya*, a newspaper owned by Mochtar Lubis, a liberal nationalist and former Sukarno critic in 1969 and 1970, ran a series of detailed exposés of Sutowo's methods of operation: alleging that Sutowo treated Pertamina as his personal fief, dispensing contracts and revenues to various clients and political allies on the basis of their political or financial importance to the regime or to Sutowo himself.[43] The point here was that the legal framework had been overturned and, in this case, the resources of the country used for the purposes of consolidating the wealth and power of the individuals who controlled the state apparatus. A second major issue of this period concerned Mrs Tien Suharto's plans to build a costly, Disney-like entertainment centre, the miniature Indonesia project. This was portrayed as a symbol of waste and as a frivolous, even obscene, disregard for the existence of widespread poverty.

Under the leadership of former "generation of '66" students, notably Arief Budiman, protests were mounted by the student Committee Against Corruption which held regular demonstrations and protests in 1971. When the protests against the activities of Mrs Suharto began to escalate in December 1971 and January 1972, the President moved decisively, arresting student leaders and newspaper editors and threatening a major use of force to crush the critics.[44] This had the desired effect, dissolving organised protest for the next eighteen months. Arief Budiman left for overseas shortly afterwards.

By early 1973, the protests and criticisms had emerged once more but with fundamental differences. The generation of '66 students who had led the 1970–71 protests were replaced by a new generation who had not experienced the period of alliance with the military. Protest and criticism now involved a wide variety of groups ranging from the various student factions to former party leaders and intellectuals, leaders of the weaker elements of the indigenous business community and intellectuals associated with dissatisfied elements of the military.[45] These protests were no longer simply moral rebukes directed at the excesses of a basically sound regime. The critics were now arguing that the Bappenas economic strategy was inherently damaging to Indonesian society, providing a structural framework for concentration of wealth and entrenchment of mass poverty. The regime was no longer criticised simply for its excesses but for being an integral participant, in collusion with foreign capital and the larger Chinese business groups, in the exploitation of Indonesia. Corruption, extravagance and incompetence were transformed from a morally regrettable aberration to a necessary and integral component of this larger system of exploitation.

The critiques revealed a mix of Indonesian socialist and

nationalist sentiment of the 1950s together with Latin American dependency theory, basic needs strategy and the more narrowly based interests of the declining indigenous bourgeoisie. Such direct challenges to the Bappenas concepts of development through spontaneous diffusion of capital, technology and growth were most clearly spelt out by intellectuals including Sarbini Soemawinata, the economist Dorodjatun Kuntjorojakti and, to a lesser degree, Subjatmoko. Their analyses, widely publicised in the press and highly influential with students, focused upon the creation of enclaves of privilege, capital-intensive foreign investment directed at the resource needs of the West or the production of luxury consumer goods, and reliance on oil income. As solutions they prescribed the subordination of foreign capital to a national economic strategy which stressed development with equality, employment, appropriate technology, agricultural development and industrialisation for Indonesian requirements.[46]

These critics, representing the more wealthy and secular elements of the urban middle-class intelligentsia were joined by others representing different sources of social power and influence, but also pursuing a liberal/social democrat critique. Moh. Hatta, the elder statesman of Muslim politics and long-time champion of the co-operative system, entered the debate, refuting the arguments of Ibnu Sutowo and other government spokesmen that distribution of wealth could not proceed until the size of the cake had reached a certain level.[47] Sjafruddin Prawiranegara, former Masyumi cabinet minister and Governor of the Bank of Indonesia, had since the late 1960s turned his attention from a concern for the military's refusal to permit a return of the Islamic parties, to matters of economic policy focusing upon the decline of the indigenous bourgeoisie, the growing gap between rich and poor, government corruption and foreign manipulation of the Indonesian economy through such bodies as the IMF.[48]

A most interesting development was the entry into the debate of social democrat intellectuals associated with the officer corps. General Simatupang, a former chief of staff in the early 1950s, participated in the debates of the Cibulan Discussion Group at the University of Indonesia in November 1973, arguing that foreign industrial powers determined the process of development in Indonesia, that the Bappenas strategy ignored the poor, the weak and the disorganised and, in any case, the strategy could not be implemented because of massive corruption of the administrative apparatus.[49]

Slamet Bratanata, former Minister of Mines and a member of the military-associated group, BPS Siliwangi, argued that Indonesia was caught in a neo-colonial process in which growth benefited a trio of foreign investors, *cukong* and officials, excluding indigenous capital and the bulk of the population. It was a mixture of the dual economy thesis with dependency theory. By implication, the New Order became the executors of the new colonial order. But neo-colonial Indonesian society, according to Bratanata, contained seven time-bombs:

(a) National demoralisation as a consequence of the formation of the adventurer-*cukong*-official trio.
(b) The bureaucrat/business complex.
(c) Government bank credit policy.
(d) Destruction of forests and other natural resources.
(e) Eviction of people from their lands by the 'feudalism of money'.
(f) Economic colonialism.
(g) Growing unemployment.[50]

Despite the fact that the critics included liberal intellectuals, Muslim leaders and sections of the military, they were all, in the final analysis, drawn from the middle-class, urban intelligentsia and without a real base of political power or political alliances with popular forces. Even their alliance with the declining indigenous petty capitalists was more symbolic than real. Yet the protests and criticisms of the

1973/74 period were to have a significant effect upon government economic policy. The reasons for this are complex, but
one factor was clearly the extent of press ownership by the
liberal/social democrat intelligentsia which enabled them to
dominate and define the public debate. A second factor was
the success of students and artists such as Rendra in creating
popular images, through demonstrations and performances,
to convey their interpretation of the regime as bloated,
corrupt and extravagant and of foreign capital as exploitive
'economic animals'. Third, the protests came increasingly to
embrace a vigorous, anti-Chinese, nationalist sub-movement
of declining indigenous bourgeois which not only linked the
protest to the populist resentments of the Muslim petty
bourgeoisie but illustrated in a very concrete way the nationalist and anti-foreign elements of the broader protest. Not
only did leaders of the declining indigenous capitalist class
such as J. C. Tambunan, Sutomo and Rachmat Mulyomiseno
become more vocal, but such issues as foreign take-over of
the textile industry became *causes célèbres* for the critics of
the regime's policies. Finally, in a very complex way, the
protest became enmeshed in a power struggle internal to the
New Order itself, enabling the critics to gain, for a few
months, patrons and forums which would not have been
available had the regime been unified.

THE MALARI

The struggle was to be crystallised in the demonstrations
against the visit of Japanese Prime Minister Tanaka of 15 and
16 January 1974 (the Malari). The significance of the violent
riots which followed have been the subject of considerable
debate.[51] Many commentators have seen them as primarily a
political power struggle between the Commander of Kopkamtib, General Sumitro, and the existing hierarchy, dominated by Suharto and Moertopo, in which the students were
manipulated by competing political forces. Certainly there is
evidence of involvement by troops and associated political

groups in the burning of the Astra building (owned by William Soerjadjaja, a Chinese business associate of both Mrs Suharto and Ibnu Sutowo) and the Senen shopping centre, indicating an interest by some elements of the regime in provoking violent conflict. The Opsus, as mentioned, had publicly argued that General Sumitro's civilian supporters represented pro-US forces intending to stop moves to build a national industrial economy. However, despite the political manipulation of the events of January 1974, it is clear that deep social frustrations burst to the surface on the streets of Jakarta, manifesting themselves in anti-Chinese and anti-government actions which clearly shook the government.

The government reaction was swift and effective. Critics and student leaders were arrested or placed under house arrest and the most prominent tried and jailed. Five of the most critical newspapers were closed down: *Indonesia Raya, Abadi, Nusantara, Harian Kami, Mahasiswa, Indonesia* and *Pedoman*. The middle-class intelligentsia had proven unable to develop a basis of power which constituted any real political threat to the military. They proved unable and perhaps unwilling to establish political alliances with workers and peasants or even to mobilise effective commitment from the urban middle classes, most of whom benefited from the policies of the New Order in material terms and would be unlikely to be enthusiastic about a radical redistribution of wealth. Instead they chose to flirt with the Sumitro faction of the military, whose commitment to their objectives was unlikely to be any different to that of Suharto. Such a flirtation was purely political and mutually cynical. Indeed, for the liberal intellectuals, 1974 was to be the beginning of the end. Since that time the New Order has successfully devoted its energies to controlling the bases of liberal influence: the universities, the press and the civil service. By the 1980s the apparatus of control and co-option has reached a level of efficiency and effectiveness far beyond that of the early 1970s.[52]

While the weight of the New Order was brought against

the liberal intellectuals, the regime moved to accommodate the indigenous petty capitalists. Large sections of the indigenous petty bourgeoisie, particularly in the textile sector, were in a decline, popularly attributed to the actions of larger foreign and Chinese capital. The consequent resentment against both the Chinese capitalists and the government had been foreshadowed in the participation of indigenous petty capitalists in the anti-Chinese Bandung riots of August 1974. Most worrying for the government was the prospect that a populist opposition would form, fuelling its resentment with both the economic grievances of a declining petty bourgeoisie and the religious grievances of fundamentalist Islam. The indigenous petty bourgeoisie could no longer be ignored.

Government modification of its economic policy was made necessary for two reasons. First was the need to ameliorate social and economic tensions which had obviously deepened in the years of New Order rule. In particular, provision of credit and protection for the indigenous petty bourgeoisie was to become a central plank in the government's economic policy after the Malari. In effect, the New Order was forced to widen the socio-economic basis upon which its political power rested. Along with international capital and the larger elements of the domestic capitalist class, the smaller, generally Muslim-oriented capitalists and petty capitalists were now to be drawn, however marginally, into the dominant class alliance in Indonesia. A second reason for the modification of economic policy was the need to repair the damage wreaked upon the legitimacy of the government and the ideology upon which it based its claims to authority. As a result of the student and press campaigns over the previous two or three years, it was now generally accepted, in the cities at least, that the New Order was no less corrupt than the old and that specific economic alliances linked the Indonesian leaders of the New Order, including the presidential family, with foreign and Chinese business groups. Consequently, policy measures to restrict the activities of foreign and Chinese capital became necessary if the New

Order was to retain some claims to the populist and nationalist symbolism which underpinned much of its ideology. There were, of course, contradictions emerging. Because international and Chinese capital were so crucial to continuing economic growth in Indonesia and to the generation of state revenue and economic resources for the political factions and individual families which dominated the New Order, there were limits to the extent to which their activities could be circumscribed.

Nevertheless, one week after the Malari, major changes to investment and credit policy were made by a hastily assembled meeting of the National Economic Stabilisation Board.[53] These changes were:

(a) Capital equity in new joint ventures to be progressively transferred to Indonesian partners so that they achieve 51% ownership within ten years.

(b) All foreign investment projects to be in the form of joint ventures with indigenous Indonesian partners.

(c) Where local partners are not indigenous Indonesians, the 51% national equity shall be achieved in a shorter period through the stock market, and 50% of national shares disbursed to indigenous Indonesians.

(d) The number of investment areas closed to foreign capital to be increased, taking into account the degree of saturation of the sector and the potential of domestic investors to take over investment and production.

(e) Investment credits by state banks to be allocated only to indigenous investors.

(f) Domestic investment projects are required to contain 75% indigenous equity or, where management is largely in indigenous hands, 50% of equity.

These regulations signalled an important change to the existing free-market, open-door approach and a fundamental shift in the balance between domestic and international capital.

International capital now faced increasingly stringent demands to ensure domestic equity participation and, more importantly, to submit to increased Indonesian government control over the areas in which it could invest. Foreign capital was now much more closely harnessed to the process of domestic capital accumulation. Ironically, however, it was not the indigenous petty capitalists who benefited most but the larger domestic capitalists and state-owned capital, which moved into the second half of the 1970s in a much stronger position *vis-à-vis* international capital.

TOWARDS A CORPORATE CAPITALIST ECONOMY

The mid-1970s were an important watershed in the political and economic history of the New Order. Although the reformist critics of the urban intelligentsia were to be effectively and progressively obliterated as a political force over the following years, the New Order was brought to a sudden realisation that social tension was an integral component of an economic strategy which focused solely on maximum growth. In the period after 1974/75 we see much greater attention paid to investment at local and village levels, at least in official policy, although the reformist critics did not consider that these moves in any way altered what they considered to be accelerating economic and political inequalities. State policy did not move in the direction desired by liberal and student critics but towards authoritarian corporatism both in the political and economic spheres. Rather than a 'basic needs' type of economic nationalism, we see the emergence of state-led industrial development policies and greater state intervention in the planning process, the most important aspects of which were:

(a) Priority for the development of industry focused upon major projects involved in the processing of resources (natural gas, metals, petrochemicals, oil refining) and basic industries (steel, paper, cement).

(b) Protection of domestic capital through extension of

closed and priority sectors for foreign capital and
stringent joint venture regulations.

(c) A more structured central role for the state in financ-
     ing infrastructure, providing credit and indirect in-
     vestment.

The question is, why did economic policy take this turn?
There are several factors to be considered. First, the need to
mediate tensions within the capitalist class, which called in
turn for greater protection of domestic capital from international capital and greater protection and subsidy of small-
scale capital. Second, the rapidly growing, large-scale
domestic business groups found their interests increasingly
served by state investment in resource and industrial projects
and state management of their integration with international
capital. The influence of such business groups stemmed not
only from the increasing size of their capital and corporate
bases but from their structural integration with centres of
politico-bureaucrat power. It was not only private capitalists,
but managers of the extensive state and military-owned
corporations, who developed interests in state-led national
industrialisation.

A third factor was the increasing political prominence of
CSIS/Opsus identities and their movement into authority in
the state apparatus as Ministers and Directors. Moertopo
became Minister for Information and Deputy Director of
Bakin, Daoed Joesoef became Minister for Education and
vigorously set about dismantling student opposition. Ir.
Soehoed has been especially influential in economic policy-
making, first as Director of BKPM and then, from 1978, as
Minister of Indusry. Bureaucrat nationalists were able more
directly to translate their strategies into actual policy.

At the same time, Bappenas technocrats themselves had
modified their earlier beliefs in the spontaneous effects of
'trickle down' and the benign nature of foreign investment.
Moh. Sadli admitted the excessive generosity of the original
PMA Law:

When we started out attracting foreign investments in 1967, everything and everybody was welcome. We did not dare refuse; we did not dare to ask for credentials. We needed a list of names and dollar figures of intended investments to give credence to our drive.[54]

The technocrats also confronted contradiction between international capital and national interests over such questions as the most appropriate location and form of capital investment. Naturally, national concerns for employment generation and investment in resource processing contradicted the profit-based criteria for investment used by international capital. By 1974, Sadli was claiming that foreign capital could not be expected to play a major role in the process of development because of its unwillingness to enter socially necessary but economically unprofitable sectors of investment.[55] Speaking in 1975, at an Indonesian-US Chamber of Commerce Seminar, Ir. Soehoed criticised the hit-and-run activities of some foreign investors, especially in the forestry and textile sectors:

Certain countries send people out to do a quick job, and after a couple of years get out again. Some of the persons notorious in this field are the so-called timber contractors . . . there is no retribution except for a couple of empty forests on this concession.

You know for what reason textiles have been a target. There are a lot of operators coming . . . for a quick operation, and then after a couple of years, without training any people, they just go out again.[56]

Despite these criticisms, the Bappenas technocrats remained committed to foreign capital investment as an indispensible catalyst of development. The difference was to be the introduction of more stringent regulations governing its entry and its subordination to more clearly defined national economic objectives. Once again we confront inconsistencies in the public statements of economic philosophy by the technocrats, and there is evidence to suggest that they felt pushed by political forces to restrict foreign capital to a greater degree than desirable. Referring to the closure of some sectors to foreign investment, Ir. Soehoed told participants at the 1975 Indonesian-US Chamber of Commerce Seminar in New York that: 'The Government has entered into this exercise essentially to avoid possible friction between foreign and domestic business circles and for no other reason'.[57]

Perhaps the most important development has been the increase in state revenues which occurred in the late 1970s. The introduction of policies of economic nationalism in the post-1975 period became a realistic proposition partly because domestic capital, both state and private, had developed to the stage where it could effectively exploit protective policies and state subsidies and credit. At the same time, massive increases in state revenue generated by oil export earnings provided a basis for a degree of independence from foreign capital investment, for state investment in infrastructure and production, and for government finance of development on a scale required by the new policies of industrialisation. This is illustrated in Table 5.4.

TABLE 5.4

SOURCES OF GOVERNMENT REVENUE

(in Rp billions; figures in brackets indicate % of total revenue)

	Non-Oil Domestic		Oil		Aid		Total
1969/70	178.1	(53.2)	65.8	(19.7)	91.1	(27.2)	334.8
1970/71	245.4	(52.8)	99.2	(21.3)	120.5	(25.9)	465.1
1971/72	287.3	(51.0)	140.7	(25.0)	135.5	(24.0)	563.5
1972/73	360.1	(48.1)	230.5	(30.8)	157.8	(21.1)	748.4
1973/74	585.5	(50.0)	382.2	(32.6)	204.0	(17.4)	1 171.7
1974/75	789.1	(39.9)	957.2	(48.4)	232.0	(11.7)	1 978.3
1975/76	993.9	(36.4)	1 248.0	(45.7)	491.6	(18.0)	2 733.5
1976/77	1 287.0	(34.9)	1 619.0	(43.9)	784.0	(22.1)	3 690.0
1977/78	1 286.0	(32.3)	1 949.0	(48.7)	764.0	(19.1)	3 999.0
1978/79	2 057.4	(37.0)	2 308.7	(43.5)	1 035.5	(19.5)	5 301.6
1979/80	2 436.0	(30.1)	4 260.0	(52.7)	1 381.0	(17.1)	8 077.0
1980/81	2 625.2	(24.8)	6 430.1	(60.9)	1 501.6	(14.2)	10,556.9
1981/82	3 699.0	(26.6)	8 575.0	(61.7)	1 626.0	(11.7)	13 900.0
1982/83 (projected)	4 635.0	(29.7)	9 122.0	(58.4)	1 850.0	(11.9)	15 607.0

Sources: McCawley 1978; Indonesian Government Budget Statements provided in BIES: various issues.

From 1967 to 1972, oil exports constituted around 40%–50% of total export earnings, but this figure rose sharply after the 1973/74 oil price rises and presently rests at around 70% of export earnings. Similarly, the percentage of state revenues derived from corporate oil taxes has risen from 19.7% in 1969/70 to over 60% in 1980/81 and 1981/82. In the same period, non-oil domestic revenues have declined from over 50% of total revenues to around 25%, while the aid component of revenue has dropped from 27% to around 12%. Clearly, the outstanding factor has been the emergence of oil taxes as the dominant element of state revenue. It has reduced dependence upon aid (although it must be remembered that it is foreign capital which produces the oil), and has significantly increased the funds available for development expenditure.

For policy-makers in the period 1974/75–1981/82 the enormous sums made available to the state through oil company tax meant that the state could finance and directly invest in economic development, on a scale previously impossible, either through the creation of infrastructure, the provision of credit to national corporations and direct state investment in major resource, or through industrial projects. It is not an exaggeration to say that the state was awash with funds.

1. B. Glassburner, 'Political Economy and the Suharto Regime', *BIES* 14, 3 (1978).

2. P. McCawley, 'The Growth of the Industrial Sector', in A. Booth and P. McCawley (eds), *The Indonesian Economy During the Suharto Era* (Kuala Lumpur, 1981).

3. M. Rudner, 'The Indonesian Military and Economic Policy', *Modern Asian Studies* 10, 2 (1976).

4. Probably the most complete statement of the economic philosophy which was to form the basis of Bappenas policy is to be found in W. Nitisastro (ed.), *Masalah-masalah Ekonomi dan Faktor-faktor Ipolsos* (Jakarta, 1965). This collection contains key articles by Widjojo ('Persoalan-persoalan Ekonomis-Teknis dan Ekonomis-Politis Dalam Menanggulangi Masalah-masalah Ekonomi') and by Salim ('Masalah Ekonomi yang Timbul [Atau Ada] Sekitar Coup G-30-S'). Problems discussed include the economic problem of the Sukarno period — monetary approach vs. production approach and the problem of inflation, fiscal and monetary policy and the limit of government intervention.

5. M. Sadli, 'Indonesian Economic Development', *Conference Board Record* 6 (1969).

6. M. Sadli, 'Boeke's Theory of Dualistic Economies', in Glassburner (ed.) 1971.

7. E. Salim, *Tulisan-tulisan* (Jakarta, 1971) and 'Kearah Demokrasi Ekonomi', *Indonesia* (Jakarta) 5 (1970).

8. For analysis of the period of negotiation between the Indonesian government and the IGGI, see Thomas and Panglaykim 1973, Chapters V & VI; *FEER*, 29 December 1966, pp. 679–81; I. Palmer, *The Indonesian Economy Since 1965* (London, 1978), Chapter 3; K. Thomas and J. Panglaykim, 'The New Order and the Economy', *Indonesia* (Cornell) 3 (1967).

9. Thomas & Panglaykim 1973, pp. 135–9.

10. Palmer 1978, pp. 45–52; Glassburner 1971*b*.

11. J. Panglaykim and K. Thomas, 'The Five Year Plan', *BIES* 5, 2 (1969).

12. 'Kredit PMDN — Antara Koneksi dan Investasi', *Tempo*, 9 December 1972, pp. 44–8.

13. Palmer 1978, pp. 52–8.

14. The first public debate over economic policy occurred in 1967/68, when contractionary monetary policies were criticised by those urging structural change in the economy, including development of infrastructure and industrialisation. For an overview of this debate, see Thomas and Panglaykim 1973, pp. 139–44.

The major critic was Sarbini Soemawinata, a former PSI intellectual. See his 'Non Economic Aspects of Development' in Fakultas Ekonomi Universitas Indonesia, *Five Papers on Indonesian Economic Development* (Jakarta, 1970).

15. Industrial priorities were listed as follows:

Industries supporting the agricultural sector.

Industries earning and saving foreign exchange by producing substitutes for imported goods.

Industries processing more domestic materials than imported materials.

Industries which use relatively more manpower than capital.

Industries which incite more regional development activities because of their character of being cumulative in effect.

16. For data on allocation of expenditures through the development budgets in the first Five Year Plan, 1969/70–1973/74, see Thomas and Panglaykim 1973, p. 169.

17. Rudner 1976, p. 271.

18. McCawley 1981, p. 80. Even after the 1973 reforms, McCawley points out that protection rates, especially in textiles, automobile assembly and pharmaceuticals remained high.

19. This figure was quoted by Ir. Soehoed, the Deputy Chairman of BKPM, in *FEER*, 17.12.76, p. 48. This situation has continued into the 1980s. In 1981 it was reported that investment in oil and gas constituted 60% of direct foreign investment in Indonesia (Richard Cowper, 'US leads Japan as Indonesia's top Investor', *The Financial Times,* 13 October 1981).

20. Ir. Soehoed in *Kompas*, 23.2.74, and P. R. Silalahi, 'Perimbangan Modal Swasta Nasional di Indonesia', *Analisa Masalah-masalah Internasional* 3, 5 (1974).

174   THE RISE OF CAPITAL

21. Suhartoyo 1981, Tables 3 & 4.

21. Suhartoyo 1981, Tables 3 & 4.

22. Compiled from Tables 1, 2, 3 & 4 in Suhartoyo 1981. Total **PMDN** investment in industry from 1968–March 1980 was Rp1 062 488 billion, of which 17.5% was in textiles, of which 23.9% was realised. On a rough exchange figure of 500 we arrive at the figure of $89 millions.

23. IBRD 1980, p. 23, Table 1.

24. Ibid.; McCawley 1979, pp. 26, 27.

25. McCawley 1979, p. 15, Table 8.

26. Moh. Sadli, 'Development Policies for the Private Sector', in *Five Papers on Indonesian Economic Development* (Jakarta, 1970), p. 41.

27. Sadli 1970, p. 46.

28. Wayne Robinson argues that the Indonesian policy-makers failed in this objective; that industrialisation in Indonesia was conditioned by the needs of industrial economies to locate certain components of their manufacturing processes in the Third World to take advantage of cheap energy. He suggests that industrialisation in Indonesia was determined by the needs of international rather than national capital: 'Imperialism, Dependency and Peripheral Industrialization: the Case of Japan in Indonesia', in R. Robison and R. Higgott (eds), *Southeast Asia: Essays in the Political Economy of Structural Change* (London, 1985).

29. The works by Panglaykim referred to in the summary are: 'Organisasi Bisnis dalam Rangka Pembangunan Ekonomi di Asia Tenggara', in J. Panglaykim, *Persoalan Masa Kini: Perusahaan Multinasional* (Jakarta, 1974); 'Struktur Domestik dalam Interdependensi Ekonomi Dunia', *Analisa Masalah-masalah Internasional* 2, 12 (1973); *Indonesia's Economic and Business Relations with ASEAN and Japan* (Jakarta, 1977), especially Part I, Chapter 3, 'Foreign Enterprise in the Indonesian Economy', and Part II, Chapter 2, 'Investment, Japanese Business Practices and Economic Dependence'; personal interviews, 12 March 1974 and 21 October 1974.

30. Kwik Kian Gie, 'Foreign Capital & Economic Domination' *Indonesian Quarterly*, April 1975.

31. Hoemardani, 'Indonesia-Japan Relations in the Future', *Suara Karya*, 23, 24 and 26 January 1974.

32. Robinson 1985.

33. Ibid.

34. Perhaps the most important examples were the purchase and hire of tankers at well above market prices (*FEER*, 22.10.76; *Tempo*, 25.9.76) and excessive prices for contracting at Krakatau steel (Arndt, 'P. T. Krakatau Steel', *BIES* 11, 2 [1975]). The Tahir case has given an extraordinary insight into appropriation of Pertamina funds (*AWSJ*, 30.7.80, 17.7.80, 5.2.80).

35. *Ekspres*, 18.1.74 (*USPRT*). For other relevant articles, see *Merdeka*, 1.10.70, 20.11.70, 5.12.70, 14.9.71 and 15.9.71.

36. Among the Diah family holdings are the Hotel Aryaduta and joint ventures in the manufactures of cardboard, paper and adhesives. See *BNPT* 169–1969, 264–1969, 159–1970 and 395–1973.

37. Interviews with Hipmi members. See also *Topik*, 25.4.74 and *Sinar Harapan*, 18.6.74. Hipmi will be dealt with at greater length in Chapter 10.

38. These ideas are reported in the article 'Japan-Indonesia Corruption; Part II: The Building of an Underdeveloped Economy', *Ampo* 8, 2 (1976),

p. 43. *Ampo* quoted its sources as an article written by Moertopo entitled, 'Indonesia's position in relation to Japan', *Kokusai Keizai* (December, 1974).

39. McCawley 1978, p. 10.

40. *Merdeka*, 13.1.76. Ibnu Sutowo, quoted in the article, 'Saya tidak pernah berfikir ingin jadi Dirut seumur hidup', *Tempo*, 17.1.76.

41. 'Demonstration, Fire and Interrogation', *Topik* 3, 4 (1974) (*USPRT*).

42. Lane 1982, pp. 111–12.

43. See especially *Indonesia Raya*, 15.12.69.

44. *Tempo*, 29.1.72; *Pedoman*, 25.1.72; *Indonesia Raya*, 28.1.72.

45. It is not my intention to deal in detail with the Byzantine nature of the politics of this period. See G. Harper, The Politics of Opposition under the New Order, 1970–74 (BA Hons thesis, Murdoch University, Perth, 1983), and C. van Dijk, 'The Hariman Siregar Trial', *Review of Malay & Indonesian Affairs* 9, 1 (1975).

46. Sudjatmoko, International Relations in a New Era — Japan and the Economic Development of Asia (Tokyo, 1973); Sarbini 1970, and 'Some Notes on the Perspectives of Long Range Development Planning in Indonesia', *Indonesia* (Jakarta) 22 (1973).

The economic critiques of the New Order were widely discussed in the press in this period. See: *Indonesia Raya*, 28.9.73 and 29.8.73, for a comparison of Sudjatmoko and Barli Halim of BKPM; *Pedoman*, 9.11.73, for Dorodjatun; *Tempo*, 1.12.73.

47. *Tempo*, 21.2.76.

48. *Angkatan Bersenjata*, 28.6.68; *Operasi*, 25.9.68; *Kompas*, 27.5.69; *Pedoman*, 25.6.69; and *Harian Kami*, 3.8.70.

49. *Jakarta Times*, 24.11.73, 3.12.73; *Tempo*, 21.2.76.

50. Slamet Bratanata, *Menundjang Perekonomian Pribumi* (mimeo) (Jakarta, 1972) and Praktek Demokrasi Dalam Peralihan (paper given to a meeting of BPC Siliwangi, Cipayung, 10–12 April 1970). The time-bomb thesis is outlined in *Sinar Harapan*, 18.5.76.

51. *FEER*, 28.1.74; C. van Dijk 1975. For the Opsus view, see Arifin, *Fakta Analisa Lengkap dan Latar Belakang: Peristiwa 15 Januari* (Jakarta, 1974).

52. An example of successful control has been Daoed Joesoef's taming of the university campuses between 1978 and 1982 (*Asia Week*, 1.2.80).

53. Resolution of the National Economic Stabilisation Board (Dewan Stabilisasi Ekonomi Nasional) on 22.1.74 and directives issued by the President on 21 September 1974. See *Business News* 1, (Jan/Feb. 1974), pp. 16–18 and Kartini Mulyadi, Some Notes on the Joint Venture Agreement (Jakarta, March 1982).

54. *Insight* (Hong Kong), March 1971, p. 48. See also Ir. Soehoed's statement in *Tempo*, 16.2.74.

55. *Kompas*, 13.4.74.

56. Embassy of the Republic of Indonesia in the United States of America and the American Indonesian Chamber of Commerce, Inc., *Seminar on New Opportunities* (New York, 1975), p. 121.

57. Ibid., p. 19.

6
Economic Policy, Domestic and Foreign Capital: 1974/75–1981/82

WHEREAS the first decade of the New Order was a period of rather *ad hoc* moves towards the establishment of political order and economic growth, in the second decade the New Order has been able much more systematically to integrate its political, ideological and economic goals. Politically its character became more stridently one of authoritarian corporatism in which the apparatus of the state either incorporated or crushed its critics and potential opponents. Not only had the state effectively silenced the middle-class intelligentsia; it was able to defuse much broader grievances by the infusion of funds made available by the oil boom into the small business and landowning classes. In the sphere of economics, the New Order was able to move closer to state-led industrialisation. Apart from the consolidation of state power, the period from 1974/75 has been one of rapid growth of large-scale domestic corporate capital under the umbrella of the state and within the framework of import-substitution industrialisation. By the end of the 1970s the picture of domestic capital as weak, dependent and subservient could no longer be sustained. Nurtured by the state, and spearheaded by several major business conglomerates, domestic capital had gained a sizeable hold on investment in a variety of sectors, constituting a new and significant focus of socio-economic power.

THE RESURGENCE OF ECONOMIC NATIONALISM AND INDUSTRIAL POLICY

Economic policies after 1974/75 may partly be interpreted as a direct response to foreign economic dominance, involving transfer of capital ownership from foreign to domestic bourgeois in those sectors in which domestic capital was most highly developed: in import-substitution manufacture of consumer goods and intermediate goods, in trade and distribution, and in the timber industry. New regulations governing the formation of joint ventures and assigning levels of exclusion and priority for foreign investment were the mechanisms for such a transfer.

However, changes in policy extended beyond ownership to the question of the structure of the Indonesian economy. As it stood, the economy was characterised by export of oil and gas, minerals and timber, import of capital and intermediate goods, and the domestic manufacture of relatively low value-added consumer goods in a protected and subsidised import-substitution sector. R. B. Suhartono observed that:

... much of the newly established manufacturing industries, including those in the category of heavy industries, are engaged only in simple, final stage processing. These industries are not fully grafted on to the Indonesian economy; in fact some subsidiaries of foreign enterprises are totally dependent on imported inputs from their parent companies abroad. Since the backward linkages of these industries are weak or simply non-existent, their growth did not have much effect on the growth of other related industries.[1]

The difficulties of ISI could not be solved by exporting what was already produced, because of the inefficiency of Indonesian manufacturers and the over-valued rupiah. For Indonesian capitalism to progress, the stage of import-substitution manufacture in the consumer goods sector had to be transcended. While the IBRD and international corporate interests were to urge Indonesia to seek the solution by opening the door to international capital and integrating into the new international division of labour, Indonesian economic planners, with seemingly infinite resources made available by oil earnings, decided instead to extend ISI by building a fully integrated industrial economy in which the dynamic of growth was to be internally generated by forward and backward linkages between capital, intermediate and consumer goods sectors. Their perceptions of the problems posed by the existing ISI stage are well illustrated by the following analysis of the economic relationship between Indonesia and Japan made by the Minister for Industry, Ir. Soehoed, and his remarks bear quoting in some length[2]:

Japan's trade with Indonesia has been basically stimulated by the drive to secure the supplies of natural resources along traditional lines on its imports side, and to provide market outlets for manufactured products on its export side.

About 92 percent of Indonesia's exports to Japan are in the form of fuel (75 percent) and crude materials including timber (17 percent); Japan's imports of manufactures represented only a little over 2 percent of its total imports from Indonesia.

Corollary to the pattern of trade, Japan's investment is partly dominated by projects to secure the supplies of natural resources, which generally are at the very earliest stage of processing.

Another category of investments, constituting the majority in terms of the number of projects, but much smaller in amount, stems directly from Japan's drive to secure the market for its manufactured products in Indonesia, which has led Japanese firms to set up assembling or manufacturing plants catering for Indonesia's domestic market but with all materials supplied from Japan. Hence these investments are generally in import substitution type of industries, from processed food to electronics, textiles, motorcycles, cars, etc. In a number of cases the plants so established engage only in the final stage of processing operation. The industries so established are in effect a mere trade arm of the Japanese parent companies to penetrate the local market, and in general have so far not shown any inclination for export.

Accordingly, strategy was designed to attack the problem on several fronts. Exploiting comparative advantage in resource based, energy-intensive industries, capital investment was channelled into large projects which processed raw materials to a higher stage of value-added for export and for domestic use. At the same time the structure of industry was to be deepened rather than simply broadened. Capital and intermediate goods sectors were to be developed to link with established consumer goods manufacture. By the end of Repelita II in 1979, production in these sectors had risen from 20% to about 35% of total manufacturing production.[3]

The embodiment of the concept of progressively deepening the structure of manufacture is to be found in the policy objectives of the various Repelita.[4]

Repelita I: 1969–74

Concentration on manufacture supporting agriculture (fertilisers, pesticides and agricultural implements) and provision of basic needs (textiles, footwear).

Repelita II: 1974–79

Concentration on the processing of raw materials to a higher stage of value-added (rubber, timber, oil and minerals).

Repelita III: 1979–84

Resource processing plus the establishment of capital goods (engineering) industries.

Repelita IV: 1984–89

Resource processing, capital goods and the manufacture of technology.

Underlying the changing emphasis was a set of priorities based on such factors as foreign exchange savings, employment generation and creation of higher value-added as well as the 'deepening' of the industrial structure. These priorities were explained by Soehoed, in the following terms:

Top priority projects mostly consist of basic production complexes producing primary industrial raw materials — such as petrochemicals, base metal — and those which have a strong effect on the balance of payments. These are usually highly capital-intensive requiring high technology. Furthermore, since their location will

usually be near the source of raw materials, the large capital outlays
involved will be further augmented by the requirements for support
of infrastructure. Special facilities will be negotiated and may be
granted, and the projects usually involve direct Government participation and/or public corporations.

The second level priority projects usually involve those producing
capital goods, intermediate products, parts and components which
have a critical role to play for further industrial development.
Government participation will not be improbable, although private
initiative will be given first option. The extension of incentives may
include the granting of tax credit.

The third level priority projects include a vast array of projects
for which the Government is still prepared to grant certain facilities
and incentives. Basically, the area is to be kept open entirely for
private enterprises, with speedy procedures for handling applications and clarity in regard to the extent of facilities and incentives
to be granted.[5]

This strategy thrust the state further into the core of the
development process in Indonesia, both as a financier and a
direct investor, and its importance is illustrated in figures for
anticipated investments required for Repelita III.

(a) Public investment — Rp993 billion
(b) Private Foreign Investment — Rp265 billion
(c) National Capital Participation — Rp30 billion
(d) Domestic Private Investment (including state enter-
     prises) — Rp800 billion[6]

The massive increases in oil taxes and the strong balance of
payments position created by oil export earnings enabled the
government to undertake these investments, mainly through
the development budget which had grown by an average
rate of 32% per year from Rp164.8 billion in 1970/71 to
Rp8 605 billion (approx. US$13.8 billion) in 1982/83. Total
development budget expenditure over this period reached
Rp46 875.7 billion (US$75 billion approx.).[7]

The spin-off for domestic capital has been significant, particularly in the construction industry. Around half of the development budget is spent on building and civil construction,[8] including both major construction projects and village-level public works funded through the Inpres and Banpres schemes.[9]

At the heart of the government's new industrial strategy were large resource-based and industrial projects involving oil refining, LNG production, petrochemicals, fertilisers, hydro-electric and steam power, minerals processing, steel and paper mills and engineering works. By 1982 several were already coming on stream, including Krakatau steel and Asahan aluminium. But there were also thirty-seven major industrial projects in the process of development, including twenty-seven projects in basic chemicals with a total investment of $9 198 million and ten projects in basic metals with investment of $2 226 million. The largest of these were the Olefin Centre in Aceh ($2 800 million) and the Aromatics Centre in Plaju, South Sumatra ($1 785 million).[10]

To these we must add other major projects, including the Palapa satellite communications system (US$1 400 million), Asahan aluminium smelter (US$2 000 million), the oil refineries at Cilacap, Balikpapan and Dumai (a total of US$3 000 million), the LNG expansions at Banteng and Arun (US2 000 million). Other projects to be funded through the development budget and with IGGI aid in 1982 include the Bintan alumina plant, the Bukit Asam coal mine, the Pomala ferro-nickel plant in South Sulawesi, the Siruar and Sadang hydro power plants and the Gresik steam power plant. These totalled US$19 394.8 million.[11]

Finance from these projects comes from three major sources: 1) the Indonesian government through the development budget, state corporations or investments outside the state budgets; 2) IGGI loans and aid; 3) foreign, 'government to government' or private loans, and foreign private investments. By the early 1980s the scale of investment involved in these projects had become too large for individual private domestic companies or even many private foreign companies, whose participation was increasingly as contractors, suppliers, managers or consortium members. The debt: equity ratio in most of these projects is around 80:20 to 70:30, with the Japanese and US Export-Import Banks and other government agencies prominent in providing loan finance for the resource ventures. Given their interest in securing access to resources such as LNG, oil refining and aluminium, foreign companies have been willing to arrange extensive loans as export credits.[12]

In effect, the oil boom has made it possible for the state to begin establishing the sort of economy envisaged by nationalist economic planners since the 1950s — an economy built upon a large industrial base with a capacity to produce both capital goods and basic industrial inputs. The change in the overall structure of GDP[13] is not yet apparent because the full impact of most of the projects will not be felt until the mid-1980s. Consequently, the industrial base remains comparatively small and the growth rate in industry is not spectacular. In 1980, manufacturing constituted 13.4% of GDP, and industry as a whole (including mining and construction) constituted 28.8%. The growth rates for the period 1972–80 were 12.6% and 10.6% respectively. As Soehoed pointed out:

> Despite the progress, industrial development in Indonesia is still at a very early stage. Manufacturing value added in the Philippines is some 15% higher, although Indonesia's population is over thrice larger. Per capita manufacturing value added in Thailand, the lowest in ASEAN outside Indonesia, is still about three times that of Indonesia, while that of Singapore is nearly twenty times. Within ASEAN, Indonesia is the least industrialised.[14]

Nevertheless, the implications and the new economic policies for the structure of capital ownership and economic power in Indonesia are significant. There has been a major shift of international capital from direct equity investment in the ISI sector to larger-scale finance capital investment in major resource and industrial projects with participation increasingly taking the form of construction and management contracts. At the same time, state capital has established a massive predominance both as financier and capital investor while domestic private capital has enjoyed relative boom conditions within which it has expanded investment and production.

DOMESTIC AND FOREIGN CAPITAL: 1975–82

The significant development of domestic capital, both state and private, in this period was, in part, achieved by forcing foreign corporations to provide local investors with a degree of equity in their investments under the new joint venture regulations. But it was probably more significant that foreign investors were forced out of protected import-substitution industries into sectors which required a level of capital or technology not available domestically.

This process began as early as 1976. In an interview with the *Far Eastern Economic Review*, Soehoed noted that foreign investment in manufacture tended to be concentrated in import-substitution manufacture of consumer goods that increased imports rather than reducing them, and that ' . . . the Government feels Indonesians have now acquired enough capital and experience and can probably do more of this themselves, and that lowers the amount of foreign investment coming in'.[15] Foreign investment was to be concentrated in areas which contribute to upstream operations: the manufacture of intermediate industrial products. In an interview with *Asian Business* in 1982, the Chairman of BKPM, Suhartoyo, expanded on this position:

It's the same in any developing country. The first motivation for foreign investment is in the consumer sector, but very soon the consumer sector becomes saturated. So they have to go over that into [downstream] high technology, huge investment projects.

Asian Business summed up the new situation:

> To put it another way, the consumer sector — the soft option for investment — is now the domain of the domestic investor. Those [foreign] companies still stranded in it and wishing to stay will have to play the game by different rules from now on. That may mean incorporating cooperatives — the putative 'backbone of the Indonesian economy' — into the manufacturing process. It may mean floating shares on Jakarta's nascent stock exchange — the now customary trade-off for permission to expand. Or it might mean both these options. What it will certainly mean is operating with a minority shareholding, and not a specious one either.[16]

Since the introduction of the PMA Law No. 1 of 1967, the government has sought to influence the overall structure of investment by closing certain sectors to new investment, by placing specific conditions upon investment and by offering taxation and other incentives for investments in specific sectors. From 1976, these policy controls have been co-ordinated and formalised through investment priority scales (DSP-Daftar Skala Prioritas) issued by BKPM.[17] The DSP have been a policy instrument for achieving a pattern of investment which accords with long-term economic objectives; for example, moving capital from the ISI consumer goods sector into industries which process raw materials or manufacture capital or intermediate goods. But the DSP also constitute a response to political demands made by the various elements of the domestic bourgeoisie. They have been used to protect domestic capital, including *pribumi* and small-scale capital investors, by either reserving entirely some sectors for them or making foreign investment conditional upon some form of participation for local business. Investments in some specific sectors are conditional upon investment outside Java, or production for export only.[18]

As mentioned earlier, the PMA Law of 1967 closed certain sectors to foreign investment, mainly in the fields of transport, communications and public utilities, on strategic rather than economic policy grounds. However, the changing structure of the Indonesian economy produced a new basis for foreign investment regulations. Some sectors in the import-substitution field were closed simply because production had exceeded the demand of the domestic market. The primary example here is the textile industry, which grew rapidly from 1967 with heavy protection from imports and constant crack-downs on smuggling but had become saturated by the mid-1970s and, as well, offered few backward linkages. Levels of imported inputs for the industry in 1974 were 99% for cotton, 100% for synthetic fibres, 50% for yarns, 95% for textile dyes, 99% for machinery and 95% for spare parts.[19] In that year a ban was placed on new investments in low quality textile manufacturing in Java, while investments in the outer islands were restricted to *pribumi* investors. Investments in fully integrated mills were given priority.

Other sectors were closed or restricted in order to protect established national enterprises with the potential to expand. The banking industry is in part such a case, although more ideological and nationalist motives are also involved. Foreign banks were restricted to two branches in Jakarta, although regulations introduced to facilitate the establishment of financial institutions permitted joint ventures between domestic and foreign banks.[20] In trade, foreign companies were excluded from the import sector since 1970 and from the end of 1977 were totally excluded from acting as domestic distributors. Foreign factories located in Indonesia and producing for the domestic market were required to appoint national companies as local distributors.

In the construction industry, which has boomed with the growth of the development budget and the heavy investments in large resource-processing projects, Presidential Decree No. 14A of 1980 (Keppres 14A) has imposed precise controls on access to contracts, closing all contracts with a value of less than Rp200 million to foreign contractors and giving the economically weak (indigenous) group preference in allocation of contracts under Rp100 million.[21]

A final form of operation of DSP involves the use of

taxation and import duty concessions and penalties to attract investment into desired fields of investment. In Law No.11 of 1970, which amended the PMA Law of 1967, tax holidays and exemptions for two years were to be awarded to firms in the following categories: 1) investments which enabled foreign exchange savings; 2) investments located outside Java; 3) large-scale capital investments; 4) investments considered special priorities, including introduction of high technology production. As the objectives of the technocrats became more clearly defined, further periods of exemption were awarded for fulfilment of specific priorities. Tax concessions were also given if foreign investors offered shares for public purchase through the Jakarta stock exchange.[22]

By use of the DSP, the government has been able to encourage investment to enter those sectors which have been given priority in the five year plans. In the case of Repelita III, these were projects with potential to stimulate further industrial growth, such as primary processing of natural resources, or industries which add value to domestic raw materials by secondary processing.

An important example of how DSP were used to transform an industry, both by excluding investments in certain sectors and applying specific incentives and disincentives to particular forms of production, is the forestry industry. This was one of the boom areas of investment in the period 1967–75, and to this stage was concerned almost exclusively with the export of logs, an export earner second only to oil. Companies were initially formed by the granting of concessions by the Ministry of Forestry and various local governments. Large numbers of these concessions fell into the hands of the military and their Chinese clients, who in a large number of cases entered joint ventures with foreign companies which financed the ventures but often subcontracted the actual operations out to Philippine or Malaysian loggers. This, however, was one area where domestic investment grew, and by 1975 it exceeded foreign investment. Nevertheless, the intention of the technocrats was to have all log production

processed in Indonesia because the export of raw logs
created little value-added and provided no forward linkages.

However, whereas domestic capital could cope with logging, it was less able to move into higher value-added timber
production. A paper plant producing 170 tons of paper and
150 tons of pulp per day, for example, was estimated to cost
between $125 and $250 million, beyond the scope of most
local investors.[23]

In May 1975, new foreign capital investment in logging was
prohibited and tax incentives were offered as an inducement
to draw foreign capital into pulp, paper and plywood manufacture. But their efforts to force local log exporters to
consolidate into joint ventures in plywood manufacture,
milling, pulp and paper production met with severe resistance. Controls over logging and log exports were initially
limited and relatively ineffective because log exporting was
lucrative and involved little investment or management for a
large number of extremely powerful concession-holders. Japanese importers also preferred to process the logs in Japan,
and had imposed a 20% tax on imports of processed logs.[24]

By 1980 a decline in the timber market had weakened the
position of log exporters and many concessions ceased operations altogether. At the same time, some of the larger
domestic companies were developing a capacity to enter into
the field of processing, and the government was determined
to assist this process. In December 1980, log exports were
limited to 32% of total output, and in May 1981 no log
exports were allowed for companies with no investments in
processing. Companies with mills were permitted to export
one log to every four processed locally and companies establishing mills were permitted to export two logs for every one
processed locally.[25] With the gradual implementation of the
regulations, there is occurring a merger of PMDN companies
and the development of joint ventures in the processing
sector. The Japanese appear to have accepted the inevitable
and begun a concerted move into joint ventures in plywood
milling.[26] The larger US and European logging firms have

not been willing to make the increased investments in the required plywood and other processing mills and have dropped out of the industry (the most recent of these was the US giant, Weyerhauser), to be replaced by investors from Taiwan, Japan, South Korea and Hong Kong.

A further interesting example of shifts in ownership in the ISI sector is the milk industry.[27] Of the eleven companies operating in milk processing, the four PMA companies established by large multinational dairy conglomerates (Friesche Vlag, Foremost, Nestle and the Australian Dairy Corporation) account for 90% of production and a sales turnover of Rp150 billion.[28] What is more, the PMA companies have traditionally imported the bulk of their raw materials, and 95% of the milk sold in Indonesia is either reconstituted or repackaged milk powder.[29] Consequently, in the DSP of 1981, expansion of existing foreign-controlled milk processing plants has been prohibited and new foreign investment in the industry has been closed unless the foreign investor is prepared to: 1) locate the plant outside Java; 2) establish a dairy farm to supply the raw materials from within Indonesia; 3) involve the 'economically weak' category and/or co-operatives; 4) refrain from the production of powdered milk.[30]

The moves are intended to give opportunities for domestic producers to expand while PMA investors remain limited, and to give opportunities for the development of co-operative dairy farming. In fact, the new regulations appear to be at the heart of the decision by the largest foreign producer, ADC (Australian Dairy Corporation), to leave Indonesia. As reasons for the pull-out, ADC management cited apprehension at increasing controls on PMA companies, transfer of management control and a sales slump prompted by higher costs as domestic milk replaces imported powder.[31]

The second major instrument of control used to influence the relative share of capital ownership by domestic and foreign capitalists was the joint venture. When the PMA Law of 1967 was introduced, no hard requirements concerning joint venture arrangements were included, although it was generally considered desirable that foreign investors take local partners. The lack of attention to the joint venture as an institutional means of ensuring that domestic capital would benefit from the infusion of foreign capital and technology reflected Indonesia's weak bargaining position at this time, as well as confidence in the spontaneous workings of 'trickle-down' on the part of the Bappenas technocrats.

By the early 1970s it was clear that the technocrats had adopted a much more cautious attitude towards the spontaneity of the diffusion process and were more amenable to direct intervention to promote it. But the immediate catalyst for review of the joint venture requirements was the intensity of political agitation against foreign capital domination in the early 1970s and, in particular, the anti-foreign dimension of the violence of 15 January 1974. On 22 January, just one week after the riots, a series of regulations aimed at ensuring domestic equity in foreign investments was issued by the National Economic Stabilisation Board (Dewan Stabilisasi Ekonomi Nasional) and confirmed in subsequent official instructions and directives in the course of the year. As mentioned in the previous chapter, these regulations required domestic partners in all new foreign investments, beginning at a minimum of 20% domestic equity and rising to 51% within ten years. Where projects had a long construction period, the ten years would commence from the date of commercial operation. Local partners were required to be indigenous Indonesians. Where existing local partners were Chinese, 50% of their equity had to be sold to indigenous Indonesians. This latter resolution was in accordance with requirements that 75% equity in all national companies be transferred to indigenous owners within ten years (or 50% where indigenous Indonesians control management), preferably by selling shares through the stock exchange. These regulations emanated, not from the technocrats themselves, but from the President.

The immediate reaction of both Bappenas technocrats and those charged with implementing the resolutions was one of scepticism. It was the opinion among observers in Jakarta, in January and February 1974, that the regulations were instant political reactions made without a sufficiently serious consideration of their economic feasibility. Although the technocrats felt the new regulations were both economically impractical and against the spirit of their economic strategy, they were nevertheless required to find ways of implementing them.[32]

The most troublesome problems were those of financing the transfer of equity. According to Soehoed, the chairman of BKPM at the time, achieving the targets set would require investment of Rp100 billion per year for ten years. Such a sum appeared to be beyond the immediate capacity of national investors, and for the government to finance the transfer would require a major redirection of funds away from new investment.[33]

However, the problem for foreign investors was not as formidable as it first appeared. Requirements could be relaxed in special circumstances, including a) high technology investment, b) substantial investments, c) investments creating substantial employment opportunities.[34] New foreign investment was being increasingly directed into large projects excluded from the strict requirements of the joint venture legislation which applied in the ISI sector.

A second method of securing equity transfer was by offering substantial tax incentives for companies willing to place a portion of the equity on the capital market.[35] *The Far Eastern Economic Review* reported in 1980 that:

> The huge issue (US$26.4 million) in 1979 by P.T. BAT Indonesia, the cigarette manufacturer, will help it garner the approvals necessary for a major plant expansion project in its Java factories. By coming to the market with 30% of its equity, BAT was also able to reduce its tax liabilities from 45% to 35% on profits over Rp10 million (US$16 000) during the first five years it was listed.[36]

Nor has there been any shortage of subscribers to these public share issuings, partly because of the interest shown by life assurance companies and financial institutions as well as the state-owned underwriter P.T. Danareksa, created for the purpose of purchasing up to 50% of public shares.[37]

Most important in both the capital market and in direct national purchase of equity were the eight investment banks formed in the mid-1970s as joint ventures between foreign banks and local capital. Although foreign equity in the banks was as high as 80% in some cases, they were regarded as national enterprises permitted to take up equity as domestic partners. Speaking at the Indonesian-US Chamber of Commerce Seminar, Bank of Indonesia official T. M. Sjakur Machmud explained to the American business community that:

> The financial institutions are also given an opportunity to participate in equity in any foreign investment company and the financial institution is considered as an Indonesian partner even though you may have 80% owned by foreigners. So I don't think it would be a great problem for you to find local partners.[38]

A final and crucial factor lies in the willingness of foreign companies to finance the equity of their local partners. This leads us to the question of the nature of joint ventures and their role in the development of a domestic capitalist class. Did joint ventures give rise to a class of domestic compradors or provide the basis for the development of a genuine domestic capitalist class?

The dominant pattern in the 1970s was a shortage of potential indigenous partners with capital, skills, or even interest in management. Consequently there was a preference for Chinese partners and, as this became more difficult, the use of indigenous front men. Where indigenous partners were sought, they generally contributed political resources — access to government contracts, forestry concessions and monopoly positions, protection from harrassment by government departments. In other cases, foreign manufacturers established joint ventures with former domestic distributors. The role of the local partner is well illustrated in two studies, one on Japanese investment by Yoshi Tsurumi and the other on Australian investment by Kate Short.[39] Tsurumi found that:

A typical Indonesian partner of a Japanese venture is a single individual, an Indonesian of Chinese ancestry, who used to be an importer of Japanese goods, and who paid for a 10-20% ownership in a joint venture either in cash or in kind (plant sites, building or the cash value of goodwill), or with funds borrowed from a Japanese partner. Out of 87 Indonesian partners, 61 (70%) paid for their equity share either in cash or in kind. The remainder, whose equity shares had been financed by Japanese partners, were involved in larger ventures, whose average equity was approximately 2.3 times as great as that of subsidiaries whose Indonesian partners paid in cash or in kind. This may well indicate a future trend; as the Japanese subsidiaries expand further, financially hard-pressed Indonesian partners may need either to have Japanese (and other foreign) partners lend them ever increasing amounts or resign themselves to seeing their relative equity position in Japanese (foreign) subsidiaries decline.[40]

From his research, Tsurumi provides the following table (p. 306).

Background of Indonesian Partners of Japanese Subsidiaries

Chinese Indonesian (former importer-agents)...................... 35
Chinese Indonesian Manufacturers.................................... 22
Indonesian Manufacturers 2
Indonesian with Government Contacts[a]............................ 28[b]

[a]Government-owned businesses and government-related groups (for instance, organised by retired naval officers) are included as well as those who had concessions for natural resources.
[b]These subsidiaries engaged in mining, logging and fishing.

Tsurumi notes that, with some notable exceptions, Indonesian partners are generally not involved in the management of foreign subsidiaries.[41] Various reasons are given by Tsurumi for this silent role, including the unwillingness of Indonesian partners to put up cash for long-range projects where interest rates are 1.5% to 2.0% per month, preferring to concentrate both their capital and their energies into distributing the products.

Kate Short's examination of Australian joint venture companies emphasises that local partners rarely pay for equity in cash. What functions then do local partners perform? At the most general level, Short argues, the local partner performs an ideological function by giving the impression that Indonesians share in foreign investment. At a more concrete level, they are a possible defence against nationalist reaction to foreign capital, particularly if the local partner is a *pribumi*. Political functions of local partners are important, providing influence and contracts. Knowledge of local conditions and procedures and ability to deal with officials are also valuable where bureaucratic entanglement and obstruction can potentially absorb vast amounts of time, money and energy. Finally, local partners are useful where they have a knowledge of the local market and access to domestic distribution networks.

Short's findings on the financing of local equity reinforce those of Tsurumi: payment in kind, usually factories or land, and promises of payment out of future profits were the most common forms of local equity contribution. Consequently there were serious doubts as to whether the joint venture has proven to be the conveyor belt for capital accumulation by domestic investors hoped for by economic planners. As mentioned, local capital resources have been generally inadequate for purchasing local equity shares or keeping up with increased demands for investment made as the company expands its operations. Foreign loans become an increasingly important part of the joint venture operation, not only in respect of the domestic equity component but as a means whereby foreign investors can reduce the total equity component and therefore the impact of the 1974 regulations requiring transfer of equity. The comment of a Japanese researcher on the increasing use of high debt equity ratios is illuminating:

There are certain to be a large number of Japanese and other foreign investors who use the high debt-equity ratio device to retain firm control over their joint ventures. However, the prevalence of this phenomenon can also be perceived as an unwitting, rather than deliberate, development brought about by the general economic conditions prevailing in present-day Indonesia, namely, scarcity of local capital and entrepreneurs, and the government's firm guidance regarding increased local ownership of equity capital. Under these circumstances, a foreign investor may have no realistic alternatives but to limit the size of total capital, lend his partner the money to be paid in a local equity capital, and to make long-term loans to the joint venture in order to supplement its funds.[42]

The average loan component in PMA investments has risen from 37% in 1967–69 and 56% in 1970–74, to 63% in 1975–79, giving an average loan component of 60% in the period 1967–79.[43]

Such dependence on foreign loans, either in the form of cash, raw materials or machinery, has placed the local partner in a vulnerable position. It has been usual for the foreign partner to retain control of management and make decisions concerning technology and production, prices and distribution which accord with the logic of operation of the multinational corporation in a global context. Financially and organisationally dependent, the local partners are forced to fit in with the multinational corporation, meaning that the local company is viewed as a trade arm of the international manufacturer or, increasingly, as a manufacturer of specific and usually more labour-intensive elements of the product.[44] As the organisation becomes larger and more complex, smaller local partners who prove unable to cope with the needs of the company have found themselves dropped in favour of a larger domestic company more able to provide the necessary distribution networks, corporate resources or political influence. The most recent case has been the replacement by Nissan of its local partner, Wahab Affan, with a military-associated company. The automobile industry as a whole has been subject to a progressive replacement of smaller local partners with larger and more politically in-fluential domestic business groups.[45]

In Panglaykim's view, the answer to the problem lies in a consolidation and rationalisation of domestic corporate structures and in the creation of a cohesive financial system able to provide a countervailing force to the MNC:

> The small family firm which has become the typical mode of Indonesian business operation is no longer appropriate in the new environment of multi-country interaction. Domestic entrepreneurs must set aside their typical aversion to the loss of direct control inherent in mergers and associated business amalgamations and instead join in united bodies enlisting the support of the government and domestic financial institutions in an endeavour to form a viable countervailing force capable of meeting the incoming MNC and negotiating with them as equal or preferably dominant parties in seeking to determine the conditions under which to implement joint business activities.[46]

The government has recognised this problem and has made several initiatives to provide a mechanism facilitating the access of domestic business to joint venture partnerships. Of these, the state-funded investment underwriter, P.T. Dana-reksa; the state investment trust, P.T. Bahana; and the proposed Domestic Investment Company, in which state and private banks and financial institutions would participate, are the most important. But the operations of these institutions and of the capital market have not yet developed to the stage where they have been able to make a significant impact upon the financing of domestic equity.

However, to assume that the joint venture is a structure which inherently preserves the economic subservience of domestic capital to international capital is incorrect. The joint venture can, alternatively, operate as a mechanism for capital accumulation by a domestic capitalist class and the eventual movement of the leading elements of this class into the sphere of international capital. The relative position of domestic capital within the joint venture stems from a variety of factors, notably the strength of their capital and corporate base at the time of their entry into the joint venture. So the relative weakness of domestic joint venture partners in Indonesia in the years 1967–75 is the product of a specific historical situation and not the inevitable consequence of global economic relationships. Since 1974/75, domestic capitalists have developed their corporate and capital bases largely as a consequence of state intervention on their behalf. From this much stronger base, the position of several of the leading business groups within the joint venture has changed significantly. Not only have these groups been able to secure a larger share of equity control, but they have been able to exert a greater degree of influence over decisions affecting investment and production. The joint venture has been an important element in the further expansion of their capital base and in their move out of the sphere of trade and distribution into manufacturing and finance. It is best to examine this process in the context of case studies of specific business groups, which will be made in later chapters. In the meantime a few general observations will be made.

(a) The movement of domestic business groups from import and distribution into manufacture has generally been achieved within joint ventures with foreign companies. For example, the movement from import of motor vehicles to assembly and, finally, to actual manufacture of components and engines has been carried out in conjunction with foreign motor companies: Toyota, Suzuki, Daihatsu, Mitsubishi, Mercedes and Nissan. The same is true in pharmaceuticals, chemicals, the milk industry, metal fabrication and engineering. Recently, domestic foreign-exchange banks have entered arrangements with foreign banks in order to boost their operations.

(b) Although relying on foreign partners to provide finance and equity capital in the early years, it has become increasingly common for major domestic capitalists to be able to raise finance equity on their own behalf. Such giants as Astra, Berkat and Liem Sioe Liong have no trouble in raising 51% equity for large joint venture projects. It is also of significance that some domestic groups are now able to raise their own finance independently through loans or on issues on the international market. Liem Sioe Liong recently raised $120 million whilst the Astra group has issued a $25 million floating dollar loan in Singapore as a basis for further corporate expansion, much of which is concentrated within joint venture arrangements.

(c) In several instances, domestic capitalists have bought out their foreign partners in a variety of industries, including forestry, cement manufacture, log carrying and property. This indicates both an increased capacity for capital investment by domestic capitalists and a declining interest in equity capital as a form of investment and control by foreign capital.

The point I am arguing, which will be demonstrated in subsequent case studies, is that the joint venture does not lead inevitably to the subordination and decline of the domestic partner. Integration with foreign capital through the joint venture may equally be the mechanism where domestic capital moves to a higher stage of capital accumulation, corporate organisation and technological complexity. The outcome depends not only upon the framework of state policy but upon the degree of corporate development and the extent of the capital base of the domestic partner. Domestic partners, as will be demonstrated in later chapters, range from generals and their relatives who regard their equity as a form of tribute to genuine businessmen and women who utilise the partnership as a basis for expanded accumulation.

THE STRUCTURE OF CAPITAL OWNERSHIP AT THE BEGINNING OF THE 1980s

The conflict over economic policy-making in the 1970s was concerned at one level with the structure of the Indonesian economy: whether it would adhere to the principles of 'comparative advantage' and 'free markets' or conform to the bureaucrat nationalists' vision of an integrated industrial economy. But at another level the struggle was internal to capital in Indonesia and related to the determination of the relative position of each of the elements: foreign capital and domestic capital, Chinese and indigenous capital, state and private capital, large-scale and small-scale and petty capital.

What was the relative position of foreign and domestic capital ownership in Indonesia in the early 1980s and in what sectors were foreign and domestic investments concentrated?

Several broad categories of capital investment may be identified:

(a) Investment in the oil and gas sector.
(b) Foreign capital investment under the Foreign Capital Investment Law (PMA). This covers investment in agriculture, forestry, mining, manufacturing and the tertiary sector.
(c) Domestic capital investment under the Domestic Capital Investment Law (PMDN) which covers domestic investment in the same sectors mentioned above under PMA.
(d) Domestic capital investment under the Company Regulation Ordinance of 1934 (BRO). We may assume that investments in this sector are mainly small scale, including petty trade and cottage industry. Normally it is desirable for domestic investors to invest under the PMDN programme to obtain taxation and import duty concessions as well as bank credit. Those who invest under BRO either are not in a position to derive much advantage from the concessions or facilities, or are unable to meet BKPM requirements concerning capital structure or even to afford the mandatory feasibility studies.

For the purposes of this study we are concerned with large and medium-scale capital, i.e. the first three categories above.

If we define capital investment in the oil and gas sector as capital funds spent on exploration, development and facilities, then it totalled US$5.8 billion between 1971 and 1980, out of a total expenditure by oil companies of US$9.5 billion.[47] In the period from 1967 to 1970 inclusive, oil and gas investment may be reasonably estimated at a further US$880 million.[48] Realised PMA investment in 1967–80 was US$3.7 billion, while realised PMDN investment in the same period was approximately US$3.8 billion.[49] The breakup of capital investment in 1967–80 therefore appears as follows:

Oil & Gas	*PMA*	*PMDN*
US$6.7 billion	US$3.7 billion	US$3.8 billion
47.5%	26%	26.5%

The oil and gas sector is dominated by foreign capital because of the huge amounts of investment and the nature of the technology required. Domestic involvement has been confined to the state oil company, Pertamina, through the medium of production-sharing contracts, although Pertamina has very recently switched to 50% joint ventures.[50]

It is in those sectors of investment covered by PMA and PMDN that real interaction, integration and conflict between domestic and foreign capital has occurred, and it is in these sectors that a domestic bourgeoisie is emerging. The following table enables a comparison of the main features of PMDN and PMA investments. The PMDN figures are approximate because they have been converted into US$ to enable comparisons to be made.[51]

Two provisos must be taken into account when assessing these figures. First, the domestic component of PMA investment is 11%. This, however, must be balanced by the consideration that a proportion of capital invested under PMDN is not domestic in origin, especially where domestic Chinese enter partnerships with Hong Kong and Taiwanese investors. It has already been noted that foreign financing of domestic equity is also common.

TABLE 6.1

REALISED CUMULATIVE CAPITAL INVESTMENT. 1967–80

(in US$ millions)

Sector	Total Investment		% of Total Investment		% distribution of investments		Realisation %	
	PMA	PMDN	PMA	PMDN	PMA	PMDN	PMA	PMDN
PRIMARY Agric./ Forestry/	1 173	1 070	52	48	31.9	28.3	47.9	47.9
Fishing	337	625	35	65	9.2	16.5	33.8	31.6
Mining	836	445	65	35	22.7	11.8	57	173
SECONDARY Industry Constr.	2 235	2 240	50	50	60.8	59.1	36.7	29.8
TERTIARY Trade Comm. Tourism R. Estate Service	266	475	35	65	7.2	12.5	40.1	41.3
Total	3 674	3 785	49	51	100	100	39.9	34.7

Leaving these considerations aside, total realised investment under PMA and PMDN is almost equal, the obvious
differences being the predominance of PMA in mining (65%)
and the predominance of PMDN in the agricultural and
tertiary sectors. However, these raw figures tend to distort
the relative position of international and domestic capital.

Foreign investment has generally been concentrated in
higher technology projects with higher value-added, while
domestic investment has tended to be located in the more
labour-intensive and smaller-scale enterprises. This division,
which was quite clear in the industrial census of 1974, has
continued into the 1980s in certain key areas of import-
substitution manufacture. For example, in textiles PMA
realised investment to 1980 totalled US$837 millions com-
pared to US$297 millions under PMDN, giving a clear su-
premacy to foreign capital in large-scale integrated spinning
and weaving mills.[52] In the automobile industry to 1980,
Japanese equity and loan investment totalled US$129 million

compared to Indonesian equity investment of only US$17 million. This was before the new investments in engine manufacture.[53]

We can therefore say that domestic capital investment, in the medium and large-scale sectors, is not only smaller than foreign capital investment but has a lower rate of realisation, tends to be concentrated in less capital and technology intensive sectors, and is reliant upon international technology and finance. However, it must be kept in mind that the development of the major resource and industrial projects will make a significant impact upon this picture, which will only become clear by the mid-1980s.

The crucial area of finance capital is not fully taken into consideration here because it lies largely outside the scope of PMA and PMDN. This form of capital derives from a variety of sources: the development budget, government investment outside the development budget, IGGI and other soft loans, and foreign commercial loans, as well as from informal overseas Chinese finance networks in Southeast Asia. It is difficult to disentangle these or to identify what proportion is directed into capital investment and what proportion is directed into investment in infrastructure. Commercial loans in 1979/80 and 1980/81 alone totalled US$2 159 millions[54] and, as pointed out in an earlier chapter, Japanese loans to the LNG projects were in excess of Japanese PMA investment to that date. On the other hand, the increased oil revenues have greatly enhanced Indonesia's capacity to provide finance capital. Of the US$10 billion investment requirement projected for the manufacturing sector in Repelita III, the government estimated that 65% of the funds would come from domestic sources and, of this, 40% would come from the private sector.[55]

The major point is not to develop a precise measurement of the balance between foreign and domestic capital or to assess it in terms of progress towards either some abstract level of control of ownership by domestic capital or towards the reproduction of an autonomous and integrated industrial economy within Indonesia. Both objectives are implicitly based upon notions of a universal measure of dependency and autonomy. The important question is the degree to which domestic capital is able to establish a basis of accumulation, capital ownership and control, and shape politically the terms of its own integration with foreign capital in pursuit of these objectives. There is no necessary contradiction between the development of domestic capital and a domestic industrial sector and continuing reliance upon international finance and technology.

What is important is that the policies generated by the structuralist and nationalist approach to economic strategy in the post-1974 period did provide a framework of protection, subsidy and investment policy which contributed significantly to development of domestic capital. Increases in the development budget enabled the government to finance private investors and its own corporations at an increasing rate. In particular, growth was substantial among state corporations and large private business groups with military patronage operating in the import-substitution manufacturing sector.

A second feature was the decline in foreign capital investment in the late 1970s. The rate of decline in foreign investment approvals after 1974/75 was significant: 34%, or 77% if we exclude the investment in Asahan.[56] Such a decline could be absorbed by Indonesia while oil revenues were growing at a rapid rate, but when the rate of increase flattened out, placing pressure on the balance of payments, the demands of foreign capital and the IBRD for a return to a more 'open-door' and 'free-market' economy gathered strength, placing the domestic ISI investors under considerable pressure. To an extent, however, this decline in direct capital investment was off-set by a movement in the role of foreign capital from direct equity investors to financiers and contractors for supply of technology, construction and management, largely within the framework of the major resources and industrial projects.

A dilemma for the government in its approach to the

question of international and domestic capital has been the problem of indigenous and Chinese ownership of domestic capital. Any planned retreat from foreign or state ownership was tempered by the knowledge that private domestic capital, particularly at the large-scale corporate level, was dominated by Chinese. As a consequence, the government was politically forced to apply resources and energy to the creation of a viable indigenous bourgeoisie, a strategy contrary to normal capitalist notions of rationality and efficiency.

Given that government policy in the period 1974/75 placed restraints upon international capital and provided more favourable conditions for the development of domestic capital, partly by changing the terms within which the integration of domestic and international capital was achieved, we must now turn to an analysis of the rise of domestic capital, both state and private.

1. R. B. Suhartono, 'Industrial Development in Indonesia', *Indonesian Quarterly* 8, 1 (1980), p. 7.

2. A. R. Soehoed, Japan and the Development of the Indonesian Manufacturing Sector (Seminar Tentang Industrialisasi Dalam Rangka Pembangunan Nasional, Jakarta, 1981), pp. 15 and 16.

3. Soehoed noted that, in the 1970s:

... there was evident change in the composition of manufacturing value added at market prices: the share of consumer goods in total manufacturing value added declined from over four-fifths to around two-thirds, while those for intermediate products and capital goods both increased from around one-seventh to over one-fifth and from insignificant to one-tenth respectively (ibid, pp. 3–4).

4. See A. R. Soehoed, 'Industrial Development during Repelita III', *Indonesian Quarterly* 10, 4 (1982), pp. 39–40.

5. Soehoed 1981, p. 13.

6. A. R. Soehoed, 'Commodities and Viable Economic Sectors — A Possible Basis for Development Planning', *Indonesian Quarterly* 5, 1 (1977), p. 63.

7. Compiled from budget statements, *BIES*, various issues.

8. Minister of Public Works, Sutami, quoted in *Eksekutif*, August 1981; Dick 1982, p. 12.

9. R. Daroesman, 'Survey of Recent Developments', *BIES* 17, 2 (1981), pp. 12–15.

10. Gray 1982, pp. 37–40 citing President Suharto's 16 August address.

11. *ICN* 182, 28.9.81.

12. Robinson 1985; D. Jenkins, 'Indonesia's Challenging New Frontier', *FEER*, 4.8.78, pp. 36–42; G. Sacerdoti, 'Joint Ventures: A mode in Indonesia Controversity', *FEER* 18.9.81, pp. 64–65; J. P. Manguno and A. Spaeth, 'Indonesia Says Exxon Chemical Will Join Pertamina in $1 billion Petrochemical Plant', *AWSJ*, 18.9.81.

13.   GDP Growth Rates by Broad Sectors
                            (1973 market prices)

Year	Agriculture	Industry		Services		GDP
		Total	(Mfg. only)	Total	(Excl. Trade & Transport)	
1972	1.6	20.1	(15.1)	12.6	(15.3)	9.4
1973	9.3	19.3	(15.2)	8.0	(5.9)	11.3
1974	3.7	11.2	(16.2)	9.6	(8.9)	7.6
1975	0.0	5.6	(12.3)	10.1	(17.0)	5.0
1976	4.7	11.1	(9.7)	5.9	(5.7)	6.9
1977	1.3	14.3	(13.8)	12.0	(14.5)	8.8
1978	5.2	6.3	(11.2)	8.9	(9.6)	6.9
1979	2.5	4.8	(8.8)	7.0	(5.9)	4.9
1980	5.0	6.1	(11.6)	9.5	(10.7)	7.1
1972–80	(3.7)	(10.6)	(12.6)	(9.3)	(10.8)	(7.5)
Percentage share of GDP						
1980	31.7	28.8	(13.4)	39.5	(17.3)	100.0

Source: Biro Pusat Statistik. From Daroesman 1981, p. 3.

14. Soehoed 1981, p. 3.

15. D. Jenkins, 'Foreign Investment: Indonesia's Aims', *FEER*, 17.12.76, pp. 48–49.

16. S. Astbury, 'Foreign Investors Reassess Indonesia: the Party's Over', *Asian Business* (February 1982), pp. 18–22.

17. The latest DSP come in 7 volumes and indicate sectors in which investment is permitted and the conditions which attach to such investments, including the type of production (e.g. assembly, component manufacture etc.), permitted locations, requirements for domestic participation, relevant tax and other incentives. See: BKPM, *Daftar Bidang Usaha Penanaman Modal Dalam Negeri* and *Priority List for Foreign Investment* (Jakarta, 1981).

18. See BKPM DSP lists of 1981 and the summary of the first DSP lists in R. C. Rice and H. Hill, 'Survey of Recent Developments', *BIES* 13, 2 (1977), pp. 14–16.

19. *ICN* 7, 12.6.74, p. 28.

20. 'The Development of the Banking Industry', *ICN* 203, 9.8.82, pp. 3–16.

21. For contracts or purchases less than Rp20 million, contracts are awarded without tender to firms in the economically weak category (at least 50% capital controlled by *pribumi*) and total company assets less than Rp25 million (trading firms) or less than Rp100 million (industrial or construction

firms). Contracts up to Rp50 million are tendered to local companies in the economically weak category. Contracts between Rp50 and Rp100 million are open to tender by all domestic firms but a 10% margin on the contract value is allowed for firms in the economically weak category. Contracts between Rp100 and Rp200 million are open for tendering on equal terms for all domestic firms while contracts above Rp200 million are open to tender from any firm, domestic or foreign, although the successful tenderer is required to provide opportunities for sub-contracting by companies regarded as economically weak (Daroesman 1981, pp. 15–16).

22. For details of these tax incentives, see BKPM, *Indonesia: A Guide for Investors* (Jakarta, 1982), pp. 65 and 74 and BKPM, *Indonesia Investment Guide* (Jakarta, 1980), pp. 95–110.

23. BKPM 1982, pp. 18–20.

24. R. Pura, 'Timber-Processing Plants Sprouting up in Southeast Asia as Japanese Firms Invest', *AWSJ*, 22.7.81, p. 8.

25. R. Pura, 'Jakarta's Timber Rules could Slash Shipments', *AWSJ*, 20.6.81.

26. R. Pura, *AWSJ*, 22.7.81.

27. The best short overview of the milk industry will appear in Chapter III of Thee Kian Wie's forthcoming monograph, *Regulating Foreign Investment in Indonesian Manufacturing*. Much of the material in this analysis is drawn from this work.

28. 'Susu Tambang Emas Dibagi PMA' (The Milk Gold Mine Carved up by Foreign Investors), *Bisnis* 6, 2 (1981), pp. 32–3.

29. *Asian Business*, February 1982, p. 21. The Australian Dairy Corporation explained its initial decision to establish in Indonesia as being concerned with the search for export markets for the Australian Dairy Industry. Indomilk, the ADC joint venture, was therefore a processing enterprise for Australian dairy exports. See J. P. Manguno, 'Australian Dairy Corp. to Sell its 50% Stake in Indomilk', *AWSJ*, 16.10.81.

30. *Business News*, 5.8.81, p. 17.

31. J. Manguno, *AWSJ*, 16.10.81. S. Astbury, 'Aussie Dairymen Call it a Day', *Asian Business* (February 1982), pp. 20–1. Domestic milk was selling at Rp276 per litre compared to Rp180 for imported.

32. See unpublished Bappenas document: *Perkiraan Kebutuhan Dana untuk Menunjang Program untuk Peningkatan Usaha Pribumi dalam PMA dan PMDN* [Estimate of Finances Needed to Establish a Programme to Increase Pribumi Participation in PMA and PMDN] (Jakarta, February 1974).

33. Soehoed in *Kompas*, 23.2.74.

34. Kartini Mulyadi, Some Notes on the Joint Venture Agreement (Jakarta, March 1982). This paper provides a good, general, overview of the development of joint venture regulations from 1967.

35. A company with 20% of shares offered to the capital market attracts a 20% tax on earnings up to Rp200 millions; 30%, Rp200–550 millions; and 45% above this. Companies with 30% of shares on the capital market attract a 35% tax on corporate earnings for 5 years. Companies with 51% of shares on the capital market attract 25% corporate tax earnings for 5 years. See BPKM 1982, p. 74.

36. G. Sacerdoti, 'A Boost for Jakarta's Market', *FEER*, 5.9.80, p. 81.

37. G. Sacerdoti, 'Three's Company in Jakarta', *FEER*, 23.11.79 and A. Rowley, 'The Indonesian Connection', *FEER*, 1.2.80.

38. ERI (USA) & AICC 1975, p. 82.

39. Y. Tsurumi, 'Japanese Investments in Indonesia: Ownership, Technology Transfer, and Political Conflict', in G. Papanek (ed.), *The Indonesian Economy* (N.Y., 1980); K. Short, *Australian Manufacturing Companies in Indonesia: A Case Study* (Sydney, 1977).

40. Tsurumi 1980, p. 304.

41. Ibid., p. 307.

42. See the comments by Takeshi Mori of the Institute of Developing Economies (Tokyo) in, *Japanese Direct Investment in Indonesia* (Tokyo 1978), pp. 153–4.

43. Foreign Investment Approvals: Total Investment, Foreign Equity, Indonesian Equity, Foreign Loans by Firms Classified by Initial Year of Application, 1967–79.
(in Millions of US$)

Year	Total investment[b]	Foreign equity	Indonesian equity	Foreign loans
1967–69	752	280 (37%)	31 (11%)	278 (37%)
1970–74	3 924	949 (23%)	505 (13%)	2 193 (56%)
1975–79	875[a]	200[a] (23%)	21[a] (14%)	5 551[a] (63%)
Total	(5 557)[a]	(1 429)[a]	(707)[a]	(3 022)[a]
% of total	100	23.5	11.0	60

Source: IBRD 1980, p. 31 citing data compiled from BKPM sources.
[a] Excludes Asahan hydro-electric aluminium complex. (Total investment = $1 878m in 1975.)
[b] Total investment does not add to Foreign equity, Indonesian equity and Foreign loans because some investment is financed from retained earnings and because of data omissions in some of the applications.

44. See the excellent discussion on joint ventures in Thee Kian Wie (forthcoming), Chapter III; Panglaykim 1977, pp. 51–75; F. B. Weinstein, 'The Multinational Corporations and the Third World: the Case of Japan and Indonesia', *International Organization* (Summer 1976).

45. The development of the automobile industry will be dealt with in Chapters 9 and 10.

46. J. Panglaykim 1977, p. 68.

47. R. Cowper, 'US leads Japan as Indonesia's top investor', *The Financial Times*, 13 October 1980. Cited in Thee Kian Wie (forthcoming), Chapter III.

48. This is an approximate figure and is based upon Soehoed's statement that two-thirds of foreign investment in the period 1967–76 was made in the oil and gas sector (Quoted in *FEER*, 17.12.76, p. 48) and the fact that realised foreign investment in PMA, 1967–71, was US$440 million

(*Indonesia Development News* 4, 12, August 1981). We can reasonably estimate oil and gas investment in this period as US$880 million.

49. Suhartoyo 1981, Tables 1 and 2.

50. In 1977 new arrangements began under which companies could apply for exploration rights in a 50% joint venture arrangement with Pertamina. Fifty percent of the production would be secured by Pertamina and, of the remainder, 85% would go to Pertamina and 15% to the contractors (*Asia Research Bulletin*, August 1977, p. 354).

51. Modified from Suhartoyo 1981, Tables 1 and 2. PMDN data is always given in Rp. The difficulty of converting Rp to US$ is largely related to the fluctuations in the exchange rates which have moved from 326 in 1968 and 1969, to 378 in 1970, 415 from 1971–78 and 625 from the end of 1978. While it is easy to break up *approved* investment on a yearly basis and so accommodate the fluctuations, this is not possible for *realised* investment. On the basis of PMDN approvals to 1978, I have calculated that approximately 17.5% of investment in the period 1967–80 has occurred between November 1978 and March 1980, which is the cut-off period of this data. To account for this I have used a general figure of 475 to make the conversion from Rp to US$. Quite obviously this will mean that the figures are not precise. However, the figures are adequate for the purposes of this table, i.e. to give a general comparison between domestic and foreign capital.

52. These figures are computed from the data in Tables 3 and 4 of Suhartoyo 1981 by Thee Kian Wie (forthcoming, Chapter III).

53. These figures have also been computed by Thee Kian Wie from, JETRO, *List of Japanese Investment Projects in Indonesia* (Jakarta, 1981).

54. *ICN* 181, 4.9.81, p. 18.

55. Suhartono 1980, p. 19.

56. IBRD 1980, pp. 29–45.

PART III

The Nature of Domestic Capital

7
The State Corporate Sector and State Managers of Capital

THE state-owned corporate sector is the largest and most crucial element of domestic capital in Indonesia. Despite the demands of the IGGI creditors and the proclamations of the economic planners within Indonesia in the period following the counter-revolution in 1965 that 'etatism' would be dismantled, state capital has been consolidated and, in some sectors, has experienced considerable growth. Officials and politico-bureaucrats who control and manage state corporate investment continue to exercise a strategic influence upon the nature of capital investment and production in Indonesia. We may identify four major reasons for this.

(a) Without the active development of state corporate capital, the political leaders and economic planners of the New Order were faced with the prospect that the ownership of the means of production would be handed, by default, to international capital and, to a lesser extent, to a select few Chinese corporate groups. State corporations constituted the only element of domestic, and *pribumi*, capital with the resources and structure to undertake large-scale investment activities.

(b) State corporations became the crucial element in the

strategies of national industrialisation which emerged in the early 1970s, constituting terminals for the collection of oil and gas taxes, and investment in the major industrial and resource projects financed by oil and gas earnings. Because investment decisions of the state corporations were amenable to determination by state policy far more directly than private capital, they became a central element in the state's efforts to impose specific directions upon economic development.

(c) State corporations became an indispensible element in the development of private capital in Indonesia, undertaking investment in sectors that were unprofitable, providing cheap infrastructure and inputs for private firms, as well as finance and contracts. Indeed, state capital was not merely complementary to private capital; it was a necessary precursor for its emergence. This is a reflection of the social and political context in which state capital developed in Indonesia from the 1950s, not as the product of a socialist revolution against an entrenched capitalist class, but as a component of a national capitalist revolution. Consequently, state capital has generally operated as an instrument for providing the conditions of accumulation for private capital and not as the instrument for its expropriation.[1]

(d) State corporations sit astride strategic sectors of the economy and have constituted important sources of revenue for political factions and military commands as well as providing a basis for the accumulation of personal wealth by individual political power-holders. Through the power of corporations to allocate contracts for construction, supply and distribution, and to allocate concessions for oil drilling and forestry exploitation, they also constitute a source of patronage for political leaders. So state corporations have been an integral component of the political dominance of the military, and the factions within it.

REASSESSMENT OF THE ROLE OF STATE-OWNED CAPITAL IN THE EARLY NEW ORDER PERIOD

As we have seen, state capitalist activity in Indonesia began as early as the mid-1950s under the guidance of Dr Sumitro. At that stage, state corporations were established primarily to serve the government's objectives of industrialisation in an economy where foreign capital (at that time mainly Dutch) and domestic capital (mainly Chinese) remained firmly embedded in trade and the production of primary products. With a few notable exceptions such as the P.T. Gresik Cement works, little progress was made until 1957, when the political context within which state capital developed changed dramatically.

To a large degree, the establishment of a state corporate structure in the years 1957 to 1959 was an *ad hoc* response to the nationalisation of Dutch enterprises. State corporations were formed to take over the confiscated enterprises because of the absence of a strong indigenous domestic capitalist class. Most of the new state corporations, particularly those involved in trade and plantation agriculture, were seized by the military, partly to forestall control by labour unions and partly to secure new terminals of economic power.

Nevertheless, state corporations were to become the crucial components within a strategy to industrialise the Indonesian economy. By the end of the Guided Economy period, state corporations occupied the 'commanding heights' of the Indonesian economy, controlling trade, agricultural estates, access to the oil sector and dominating investment in the capital goods sector. State industries in steel, shipbuilding, electronics and cement were commenced or extended. The state sector operated with extensive government subsidy and protection. Private capital, regulated by the OPS and GPS, played an ancillary role in trade, transport, light industry and the services sector. The extent to which state corporations fulfilled their role as engines of industrial growth or remained instruments for expropriation is contentious, but certainly there developed a tension between these two aspects of their existence which has continued into the present era.

After the counter-revolution of 1965, several new factors brought about a change in the role of state corporations. The most immediate of these was the increased influence of the IGGI and the IBRD, which placed strong pressures on the Indonesian government to open the economy to foreign investment and reduce state investment and intervention. Nor was there continued ideological commitment within Indonesia for maintaining the total fabric of Guided Economy and the principle of state economic leadership, after the political destruction of the PKI and the PNI left wing. The New Order government also took a more positive view of the role of private capital — an ideological position no doubt sustained by the extensive and growing economic relationships beween the military and private enterprise.

At the same time, however, there persisted ideas of economic nationalism and even of socialism of a populist variety. The state continued to be viewed as a mediator, preventing the excesses of 'free-fight capitalism'.[2] These conflicting considerations were manifest in the early policy statements of the New Order on the question of state and private investment. The MPRS Decision XXIII of 5 July 1966, on the Reform of Basic Economic, Financial and Development Policy, contained the following proposals.[3]

(a) 'Free-fight' liberalism of the period 1950–57 be excluded.

(b) Etatism be removed 'where the state and its economic apparatus fully dominate the economy and tend to push out and stifle the potential and creative powers of those economic units which operate outside the government sectors'.

(c) Exclusion of monopolies which are hamful to the people.

(d) Commitment to the principle that, ' . . . national private enterprise has the freedom to choose its own fields, provided that it does not dominate the basic needs of the ordinary people nor strategic fields, and it has the right to obtain reasonable service, protection and assistance from the government'.

(e) Confinement of government projects to fields which: i) require investment too large for national capital; ii) involve problems of management and skills too complex for private enterprise; iii) are unprofitable; iv) too risky; v) provide infrastructure — harbours, bridges, irrigation, public utilities, etc.

Part of the reason for the continued dominance of state corporate capital also lay in the difficulty of selling off the corporations. To sell them to foreign or Chinese interests was politically untenable, and private indigenous capital simply did not have the resources. Moh. Sadli, then Minister for Mines, stated in 1970 that:

At the moment the public sector is still very important because the Government is not disposed to sell its enterprises to the private sector.

The private sector is still weak in itself and there is no organised capital market as yet; hence it would be difficult to find buyers for these state enterprises.[4]

Nor did this position change quickly. Twelve years later the Minister for Industry, Soehoed, noted that:

Given the current inadequate capabilities of national private enterprise the necessity for the government to play a role in some sectors is clearly apparent, not merely because of the possibilities that exist for direct commercial profit for the government, but more particularly because of the politico-strategic considerations involving the need to preserve some shareholding in the interests of the national economy.[5]

The importance of state corporations was enhanced in the 1970s when they were used by the state as the core of the new industrialisation strategy. Only state corporations were sufficiently amenable to central planning or capable of operation at a loss if necessary in order to achieve state objectives of major investment in the capital goods sectors, steel, petrochemicals, metal processing, pulp and paper.

THE STRUCTURE OF STATE-OWNED CORPORATE CAPITAL UNDER THE NEW ORDER

There is no data to determine precisely the size and scope of state owned capital investment in relation to private domestic capital. Christianto Wibisono has calculated state-owned capital as constituting 9.24% of PMA investment and 58.75% of PMDN investment in 1980.[6] His figures are, however, based upon details of equity in the company registrations (*BNPT*), which tend to understate the size of foreign and Chinese investment and do not adequately reflect subsequent additions to investment.[7]

A better way of approaching the problem is to look at figures on gross domestic investment and to complement this with analysis of investment in specific sectors of the economy.

TABLE 7.1

GROSS DOMESTIC INVESTMENT PROJECTIONS, 1975–90

(1980/81 Constant Prices)

(% of GDP)	1975	1980	1985	1990
Public	7.4	10.0	14.8	14.3
Central Government	5.0	6.8	9.4	9.3
State Enterprises	2.4	3.2	5.4	5.0
Private[a]	10.5	11.6	12.4	13.3
Total	17.9	21.7	27.2	27.6

Average Annual Growth %	1975/76–1980/81	1980/81–1985/86	1985/86–1990/91
Gross Investment	11.7	12.5	7.8
Central Government	14.4	14.5	7.3
State Enterprises	13.9	19.2	5.9
Private	9.7	9.0	9.0

Source: From tables in Gray 1982, p. 5 and *FEER*, 24.9.82, p. 120, both citing as sources: World Bank, *Indonesia: Financial Resources & Human Development in the Eighties* (3 May 1982).

[a] A residual category including Pertamina and other state corporations for which no separate investment data is available.

Several interesting aspects are revealed in these tables. First, the World Bank itself, which drew up these projections, saw that the development of the necessary ratio of gross investment to GDP was a task primarily for state investment. Particularly striking are the projected high growth rates of investment by the central government and state enterprises in the period 1980/81 to 1985/86. Gross investment as a percentage of GDP also reveals a dominant role for the state. By 1985 it is expected that public investment will account for 14.8% of GDP, and private investment 12.4%. Although much of the public investment is in infrastructure and public works and not in corporate investment, this is counterbalanced by the fact that much of the domestic private investment lies in the small-scale and household sector, and the fact that the category 'private' is a residual category which includes public enterprises such as Pertamina which are substantial sources of investment.

The importance of state-owned corporate capital is not only to be seen in its relative size but in the strategic position state corporations occupy in specific sectors of the economy.

CATEGORIES OF STATE-OWNED CAPITAL

State Capital in the Resources Sector

State corporations in this sector include Pertamina (oil), Timah (tin mining), Aneka Tambang (general mining) and Inhutani (forestry). Essentially they are the terminals through which the state establishes production and work-sharing agreements with the foreign companies which make the bulk of investments and carry out production. Included in their responsibilities are the collection of royalties and taxes, the allocation of concessions and contracts, and the supervision of domestic supplies (in the cases of oil and gas). This sector is crucial because it embraces the major sources of foreign exchange earnings and state revenues.

State Capital in the Provision of Infrastructure

While the bulk of state investment in infrastructure goes through the development budget, there are also major state utilities such as PUTL (Public Works), P. T. Telkom (Tele-communications) and Perusahaan Listrik Negara (Electricity), which are important channels for the direct investment of state finance in infrastructure.

State Capital in the Banking Sector

As well as providing central banking facilities, state banks provide the bulk of commercial credits as shown in Table 7.2.

TABLE 7.2

BANK CREDITS BY GROUPS OF LENDING BANKS, 1977–81

	Rp Billions	%
Bank Indonesia	9 430	28.86
State Commercial Banks	18 618	56.98
Private Commercial Banks	2 310	7.07
Regional Development Banks	597	1.82
Foreign Banks	1 715	5.24

Source: 'The Development of the Banking Industry'. *ICN* 203 (9 August 1982). p. 8.

Wibisono, in a survey of bank records and company registrations provides more details (Table 7.3).

TABLE 7.3

ASSETS, DEPOSITS AND CREDIT OUTSTANDING OF CATEGORIES OF BANKS, 1981 (in %)

	Assets	Deposits	Credit Outstanding
State Banks	85.0	87.4	84.1
Foreign Banks	6.5	4.2	6.6
Private Domestic Foreign-Exchange Banks	5.4	4.7	5.3
Other Private Domestic Banks	3.1	3.7	4.0

Source: Summary of Wibisono's Banking Report in 'Bukan Non-Pri Tapi Negara'. *Tempo*. 28.11.81.

It must be remembered that neither of these tables take account of the large, informal credit networks which operate among the overseas Chinese business community at the local level and, on a much larger scale, at a regional, Southeast Asian level.

State Capital in Manufacturing

The New Order inherited a complex of state corporations in the manufacturing sector which had been established to implement industrialisation policies, producing intermediate goods inputs for the agricultural sector and the consumer goods and construction industries. The 1974 industrial census revealed that state-owned firms contributed around 20% of output, value-added and employment.[8] In comparison to private domestic investments, state enterprises were larger and more capital intensive, a situation that was to be further developed. They were consolidated and extended by the New Order. By the early 1980s all fertiliser production was state owned and P.T. Pusri held a monopoly on fertiliser trade down to the village level. In the cement industry, state-owned factories in joint venture with foreign investors constituted 5.55 million tons of the total 7.55 million tons' capacity of the industry in Indonesia.[9] As private firms began to move into industries such as cement, paper and engineering, the state moved into larger and more capital-intensive projects. The giant Krakatau steel complex, revised under Pertamina control in the early 1970s, was the first of these and was followed by such projects as the Asahan aluminium complex, major extensions to oil refining capacity and the building of new refineries, new petrochemical plants and new investments in heavy engineering. By 1982, after the completion of Asahan and the bulk of Krakatau, proposed and ongoing investments in basic chemicals totalled $9 198 million spread over twenty-seven projects, while investments in basic metals totalled $2 226 millions spread over eighteen projects.[10] Although these projects, particularly in oil refining and petrochemicals, were largely financed by foreign loans, the domestic equity was state owned. Out of an estimated $10 billion of capital funds required for manufacturing under Repelita III, $3.5 billion was to come from foreign sources, $2.6 billion from private sources and $3.9 billion from the state.[11]

State Capital in the Distribution of Basic Commodities

The state logistics board, Bulog, was established to control the price and distribution of basic staples, particularly rice, sugar and flour. As part of this duty it has a monopoly on the purchase and distribution of certain crops, although it is also able to appoint official distributors. The function of Bulog is primarily political: to mediate crises which might arise from shortages and price rises in basic staples, through purchasing and pricing policies, including subsidy.

State Capital in Other Sectors

State corporations continue to occupy a dominant position in agricultural estates, shipping and air transport, construction, and trade.

STATE CAPITAL AND THE FACILITATION OF CAPITAL ACCUMULATION IN THE PRIVATE SECTOR

State capital in the New Order Indonesia has not been an instrument for confrontation or expropriation of bourgeois capitalism but the central component of a state-led, corporatist form of capitalism, constituting a framework within which domestic private capital accumulation is nurtured. Indeed, the development of state-owned capital in New Order Indonesia must be viewed as a necessary precursor for private capital accumulation and the emergence of a strong domestic capitalist class.

Economic strategy from the early 1970s has been focused around the development of integrated industrialisation which included capital, intermediate and consumer goods industries grouped into units bound together by backwards and forwards linkages. Ideally, chains of processing and servicing industries were intended to feed off the central cores: the oil and gas industry, the alumina industry, the timber industry, the steel industry and agricultural estates. Cross linkages included those between iron mining and the steel industry, the steel industry and heavy engineering, the petrochemical industry and the textile industry. CSIS technocrats had long advocated formal, state-supervised co-ordination of 'nationally integrated economic units' or 'national trusts' or 'national holdings'. Part of the function of the state in these economic units or holdings was envisaged as financing investment, while providing for the gradual expansion of private participation by allocating roles for private companies within the 'holding' or issuing shares or 'participation certificates' for public purchase. There was a conscious intention that the 'units' or 'holdings' provide the nursery for the growth of a strong private domestic capitalist sector.[12] Soehoed commented that:

It must be emphasised at this point that the role and the participation of Government in the economy should preferably not extend over the whole field of economic activity, but should rather be restricted to a level at which it can exercise sufficient influences over the development of the national economy (controlling interests) in those sectors and areas where national private enterprise is not, or not yet, in a position of sufficient strength to safeguard its own interests.

and

It is to be hoped that the activities of the Government in this context be clearly directed towards the growth of national private enterprise, with the government in the role of primary supporter (prime mover), and not towards the establishment of government control just for its own sake (etatisme).[13]

Although such 'units' or 'holdings' have never been established in formal terms, many of the principles envisaged by
the CSIS technocrats do operate. The government is a financier of the private sector. There is a division of labour in the
industrialisation process in which the state makes the large,
capital-intensive investment while the private sector capitalises on the spin-offs in construction, supply and servicing,
or concentrates in the more lucrative consumer goods industries: textiles, automobiles or electronics. These state
functions are probably most clearly illustrated in the establishment of the major industrial and resource projects, in
banking and construction industries.

State-Owned Enterprises and the Development of Basic Industries

The key basic industry projects nominated by the government in 1980 were intended to be developed with state and
foreign capital. By 1982, industrial projects to the value of
US$2 billion had actually been commenced — all by public
corporations.[14] Soehoed explained that state enterprises
played such a central role because only they were large
enough to deal with MNCs, or ensure that the investment
'package' was opened to allow local manufacturing of plant
equipment and other engineering support. So direct investment by state corporations, in partnership with foreign or
domestic private capital rather than mere state provision of
infrastructure for joint ventures between foreign and domestic private companies was considered more desirable.[15]

. . . the path of development that promotes national enterprise
by calling upon the public corporation is probably the only path at
the moment to accelerate development and to strengthen the structure of national industrial production.

But Soehoed is quick to point out that:

In the implementation of this concept, the effort is always made for the public corporation, and the world of private business to develop side by side. It is at no time intended that the public corporations pressure the private. Basically the state owned corporation is based upon the following principles: to develop vital sectors in which the capacity of private investors is limited; participate in important commodity ventures to stabilise prices; to pioneer new sectors of enterprise in which the risks for private enterprise are still too great.[16]

Although the benefits for private capital generated by state corporate investment in basic industry lay primarily in spin-offs and subsidised inputs for downstream investment, there is clear evidence that real integration in some cases and division of labour in others is beginning to occur in the industrial sector between state-owned and private capital. A recent important example is the establishment of a steel rolling mill, P.T. Krakatau Cold Rolling Mill, with an investment of US$800 million in which 40% of shares were to be held by the state-owned Krakatau Steel, 40% by the Liem Sioe Liong group and 20% by the Ciputra group (P.T. Metropolitan). The finance was to be raised from export credits and commercial loans.[17] In another recent case, the government has decided to offer four government cement projects for sale to the private sector. The immediate reason for their sale is cutbacks on government expenditure forced by declines in oil revenue and by foreign-exchange difficulties.[18] But it is significant that these sales are in the cement sector where private enterprise, notably the Liem group, has already demonstrated a capacity to finance and operate.

State Capital, Private Capital and the Banking Sector

The top ten private banks remain minute in comparison to the state commercial banks although there has been rapid growth of a few of them, especially Bank Central Asia and

Panin Bank which are tied into major industrial groups. It is the state banking system which has provided much of the finance for the private sector. From 1973/74 to 1977/78, a total of Rp1 620 billion in bank credit was directed towards the private sector compared with Rp1 607 billion for public enterprises and entities.[19] State banks have been used in a deliberate fashion as instruments of government policy to build a strong domestic capitalist class, even where this has contradicted the 'normal' practices of banking and resulted in financial difficulties for the banks themselves. The most spectacular illustration of this has been the impact upon some of the state commercial banks of fulfilling the state's credit policies towards small and medium-scale indigenous business. Following the 1974 regulations, state banks were restricted to providing credit to firms in which indigenous shareholders had at least 50% equity, cutting out the big Chinese firms — in banking terms, the most creditworthy. State banks were also required to provide the credit for various government schemes to finance small business and Bimas credits to farmers. Small business credit — KIK and KMKP (Small Investment Credit and Working Capital Credit) — was limited to Rp10 million maximum loans to companies with a net worth of less than Rp100 million in industry and construction, and less than Rp40 million in other industries. From 1974 to 1980, KIK and KMKP loans totalled Rp526 billion. This represented only 6% of total bank credit in this period[20], but must be considered together with Bimas credits and government pressures upon banks to lend on a basis of viability rather than collateral. In 1980, Bank Rakyat Indonesia, for example, was extending 80% of its credits to small-scale indigenous farmers and businessmen, and 14% to big indigenous businesses. On top of this, the state commercial banks were placed under pressure to lend to companies with powerful political patrons. These so-called command loans were, in effect, gifts, not expected to be repaid.[21]

As a consequence of becoming heavily involved in providing loans to economically weak enterprises as well as to companies with political influence, the state commercial banks experienced a high rate of bad debts. In 1978, it was revealed that the Bank Bumi Daya estimated one-third of its outstanding loans, totalling US$948 million, to be either overdue or uncollectable. It had already written off US$177 millions as bad debts.[22] Some state commercial banks had been forced to become shareholders, and become involved in the management of many companies, a measure recommended by the central bank. Bank Bumi Daya, Bapindo and Bank Negara Indonesia 1946 had become entangled in this way with several declining companies in fields including electrical and telephone cable manufacture, textiles, aluminium extrusion and plastics. Some companies were alleged to involve banks in control and ownership deliberately, as a form of guarantee against bankruptcy.[23]

Bank Rakyat Indonesia's situation in June 1981 illustrates the way in which state banks' financing of private enterprise amounted to a virtual state subsidy to private capital. The President Director of the bank, Mr Permodi, explained the bank's continuing small profit margins as the consequence of government requirements that it provide low interest loans to priority categories of indigenous businesses. Ninety per cent (Rp884 billion) of its loans were provided for the indigenous group and 10% (Rp102 billion) to the non-indigenous group, to the end of 1980. In addition to the low level of profits deriving from adherence to government lending policies, credit backlogs at the end of 1980 totalled Rp133 billion, of which Rp65 billion was admitted to be unrecoverable.[24]

The problem aroused considerable concern and debate in the press and in business circles, even providing a suggestion from Hashim Ning, Chairman of Kadin, that the government banks should provide credit in the form of capital goods rather than cash, to ensure that it was not dissipated.[25]

The government was also anxious to develop a strong private banking sector, offering taxation incentives to encourage mergers in the hope that larger and more viable

banks would emerge.[26] The state also provided special financial assistance through the Bank of Indonesia to help the
private banks through periods of difficulty of the sort that
followed the 1978 devaluation. In a few cases, state banks
have entered joint ventures with private banks and businesses, but the use of state banks as corporate cores of
banking or financial conglomerates within which private
banks might grow is a strategy not yet fully exploited.[27]

The Construction Industry

The massive growth of oil income from the early 1970s was
accompanied by a boom in state investment. It is difficult to
measure the amount expended on construction but most estimates claim that it would amount to 45%–65% of the development budgets and 40%–50% of private investments.[28] The
large state resource and industrial projects of the 1970s and
early 1980s were essentially expenditures on construction
and equipment. The new projects ranged in size from US$20
million to US$2 billion, providing significant opportunities
for the construction industry, which grew at a rate of 12%
per annum in contrast to 6.5% for GDP as a whole.[29]

Although the bulk of these projects was financed either
directly by the state or by foreign lenders working in partnership with the state, contracts for both supply and construction became a major channel through which the state sought
to develop private capital. To 1967, all projects and contractors were government financed and owned. From this time,
private contracting firms developed, many gaining access to
consortiums with foreign and state firms as well as preferential allocation of contracts. Private firms such as P.T. Bangun
Cipta Sarana, which began under the Pertamina umbrella in
1968 with a capital of Rp2.5 million, are now able to make
capital investments of over Rp2 billion. Capital outlay of
Bangun Cipta Sarana rose from Rp33 billion in 1979 (Rp12
billion in real estate and Rp21 billion in construction) to Rp48

billion in 1980 (Rp9 billion in real estate and Rp39 billion in construction).[30]

The various regulations introduced in 1979, 1980 and 1981 (Keppres 14, 14A and 18) to ensure preference for economically weak firms in allocation of government contracts below Rp100 million created a glut of small, indigenous contracting companies: an estimated 3 000 contractors in Jakarta before Keppres, expanded to 10 000 after. Huge numbers of small contractors chased too few small contracts.[31] At the large-scale level above Rp200 million, the government was still forced to use foreign firms because of the shortage of domestic contractors able to undertake large projects. However, the government required foreign contractors at this level to co-operate with local contractors and suppliers, and we begin to see Indonesian participation in large construction projects, as sub-contractors in conglomerates of state-owned and private companies. State construction companies such as P.T. Pembangunan Perumahan, P.T. Waskita Karya and P.T. Hutama Karya were still the largest domestic constructors and a necessary and crucial component of these sub-contracting conglomerates.[32]

STATE CORPORATE CAPITAL AND THE FINANCING OF POLITICO-BUREAUCRATIC POWER

After 1965 it became clear that the military were not going to relinquish their control of selected state corporations established in the late 1950s. The most important centres of politico-bureaucratic power, particularly the Kostrad/Opsus/Palace alliance, quickly established their hegemony over the more strategic and lucrative corporations, especially Pertamina, Bulog and Timah. Expropriation took several forms: simple expropriation of state funds or the interest on state funds illegally deposited in banks; commissions received from private companies for access to contracts for construction; supply and distribution as well as kickbacks from the manipulation of contract prices.

It was also common for officials to favour private companies in which they had a personal financial interest with preferential access to contracts and monopolies. Indeed, it became an increasingly important function of selected state corporations to constitute the hub of corporate conglomerates, associated with prominent politico-bureaucrats and political factions.

These functions, of course, often contradicted the role allocated to state corporations in the implementation of long-term policy objectives. There developed a permanent tension between the demands of the economic planners on the one hand, and the military officials in charge of the corporations on the other, over the control of state funds and the exercise of the economic power of the corporations. In 1970 a Presidential Commission of Inquiry, the 'Commission of Four', was appointed to investigate corruption, and focused critical attention upon the expropriation of the state corporate appanages, Bulog, Pertamina, the Department of Forestry and P. N. Timah.[33] Investigations following the Pertamina debacle of 1975 disclosed massive corruption, wastage and inefficiency. Other crises in state banks and shipping companies have been brought to light by vigorous campaigns of criticism by the press and reformist elements of the urban intelligentsia. In 1978, for example, the entire board of directors of the state commercial bank, Bank Bumi Daya, resigned amid charges of corruption, revelations that US$984 million of credits were overdue, and allegations that former director R. A. B. Massey illegally provided US$37 million credit to a Chinese businessman, Endang Wijaya (Yap Eng Kui), in return for payments.[34] Instances of the expropriation of state corporations by their officials are provided in the Jakarta newspapers almost daily and there is little point chronicling them further. What is important is explaining how and why the process of appropriation and expropriation fits into the relationship between state, politico-bureaucrat, state corporation and private capital and into the conflicting demands of state economic policy and the fiscal needs of the politico-bureaucrats. This is perhaps best done in case studies of the two most strategic and lucrative state corporations: Bulog and Pertamina.

CASE STUDIES: BULOG AND PERTAMINA

Bulog

Through Bulog (Badan Urusan Logistik Nasional — National Logistics Board), the Indonesian state exercises monopoly control over the distribution and pricing of basic commodities, notably rice, sugar and flour.

The crucial function of Bulog is to provide the basis for political and social order by ensuring stability in the supply and pricing of basic commodities. But it has also been a major launching pad for domestic corporate capital, through its power to allocate distributorships and contracts, as well as a major source of funds for the private and political needs of the politico-bureaucrats who have controlled it. The head of Bulog, Bustanil Arifin, himself stated, 'After Pertamina, many people believe, it is here you can earn money'.[35]

Bulog was established in 1967 to purchase basic commodities for supply to the military, government agricultural estates and other state instrumentalities. In 1970 its function was broadened to include responsibility for the maintenance of price stability through policies of purchasing, importing, marketing and pricing.[36]

In its early years, Bulog was controlled by military officers close to the President, to Kostrad and to Opsus. It is not responsible to any ministry but reports directly to the President, who was himself 'Commander' of Kolognas, Bulog's predecessor, in late 1966 and early 1967. From 1967 to 1973, the head of Bulog was General Achmad Tirtosudiro, a former Kostrad officer personally and professionally close to Suharto and the Kostrad 'financial' general, Soerjo.

These years were fraught with difficulties. Until the mid-1970s, Bulog proved unable to control severe price fluctuations and encountered difficulties operating within its budget and repaying loans to the Bank of Indonesia. In 1968 and again in 1972, Bulog failed to make necessary overseas purchases to avoid severe domestic shortages. In other cases, rice was imported where domestic surpluses remained unpurchased.[37] These difficulties were related both to ineffective implementation and to the contradictions between Bulog's purchasing and marketing functions and its other functions as a source of finance and economic power for its officials.

In one early case, Bulog officials deposited credit obtained from the Bank of Indonesia at 3% interest into private banks at interest rates between 10% and 15%, the intention apparently being to withdraw the money in time to make last-minute purchases and appropriate the interest accumulated in the meantime from the illegal use of funds. Unfortunately for the manipulators, three of these private banks, including P. T. P. P. Berdikari's Bank Dharma Ekonomi, collapsed, leaving Bulog without the necessary purchases and exposing the manipulation.[38]

The Commission of Four on Corruption was extremely critical of Bulog's performance, recommending that its regional agencies be disbanded and that Bulog itself be made responsible to the Department of Agriculture. More trenchant criticism came from the Jakarta press in the early 1970s, accompanied by graphic examples of corruption, waste and incompetence.[39] Since this time, however, it has more successfully integrated its various functions. Despite continuing manipulation and embezzlement,[40] these have not been allowed to fundamentally undermine Bulog's primary function of providing stability of pricing, marketing and supply of basic commodities. In this case the need for social order has taken precedence over the interests of politico-bureaucrats.

A significant aspect of Bulog's operations has been its

capacity to facilitate access by private companies to a sector
of the economy which embraces the whole range of trade in
basic commodities: import, distribution and purchase, and
the manufacture and distribution of some basic foodstuffs,
notably flour. Bulog is well placed to provide the monopolies
which guarantee the growth of a domestic capitalist class
and, more specifically, to decide which companies gain
monopoly positions and which are excluded. Under the
patronage of Bulog, several private business groups have
flourished, mostly those of Chinese capitalists with long-
standing connections to Kostrad, a prime example of the
so-called *cukong* system under which Chinese businessmen
fulfil the role of financiers to the military in return for access
to licences, credit monopolies and political protection.

Bulog's authority to allocate distributorships was the primary means of channelling opportunities to private companies.
Indeed, for private companies, the only way to penetrate
trade in primary commodities was to gain access to the
monopolies controlled and allocated by Bulog. In the case of
sugar, distributorships could reportedly be obtained with
letters from influential Bulog officials and various generals.
The distributorships most in demand were those which gave
the right to businessmen to re-channel quotas through other
distributors rather than having to become directly involved in
trade themselves — a parallel with Benteng briefcase entrepreneurs which is striking. In the late 1960s and early 1970s,
client businessmen jostled for places in the syndicates established by Bulog to import and/or distribute sugar, flour,
wheat and rice. Among the early beneficiaries was the Mantrust group, headed by Sutantzo (Tan Kiong Liep) and
Sjarief Margetan. Mantrust had long been a major supplier
of foodstuffs to the Army and now that control of Bulog
rested in the hands of those who formerly dominated the
Army Logistics and Procurement Command, notably General Tirtosudiro, Mantrust's position in the distribution and
manufacture of foodstuffs was enhanced. It was even granted
extensive credits from Bulog to manufacture a rice

substitute.[41] The connection was further entrenched in a
joint venture with various Kostrad and Opsus officers in the
Volkswagen sole agency, P.T. Garuda Mataram.[42] The distribution industry, however, became increasingly Byzantine
and speculative[43], and by the early 1970s the Chinese businessman Go Swie Kie had emerged from the pack to secure
a lion's share of the importing and distributing monopolies.[44]

However, the economic power of Bulog and the nature of
relationships between the military, private capitalists and the
state corporation are probably best illustrated in the long
saga of P.T. Bogasari. The original decision to establish a
flour mill in Indonesia was taken in 1970 and a Singapore
company, P.T. Prima, was given the licence to begin milling. Then suddenly a company, P.T. Bogasari, was established by Liem Sioe Liong, the Suharto family business
associate, to enter the flour milling business also. It was
owned by the Liem group, in partnership with Sudwikatmono, the half-brother of President Suharto, who was also
President Director. The articles of association stipulated
that, in effect, 26% of profits be set aside for 'charitable'
foundations including Mrs Suharto's Yayasan Harapan Kita
and Kostrad's Yayasan Dharma Putra.[45] In essence, Bulog
and Bogasari both operated under the one political umbrella.
Five days after its establishment with a capital outlay of only
Rp 100 million, Bogasari received bank credit of Rp2 800
million and the licence from Bulog to mill flour for the whole
of Western Indonesia, including Java and Sumatra. At the
same time, Bulog revoked Prima's original licence and issued
it with a licence to mill for the less lucrative East Indonesia
market, including East and West Nusatenggara, Kalimantan,
Sulawesi, Maluku and Irian Jaya.[46]

Prima established a mill at Ujung Pandang with an investment of US$13 million and a licence to operate for thirty
years. However, from the beginning it faced difficulties in its
relationship with Bulog, whose policies appeared designed to
secure the whole of Indonesia's US$400 million annual flour
market for Bogasari. Between 1972 and the end of 1980,

Bulog allocated wheat to Prima sufficient only for operation at half capacity, whereas Bogasari's Jakarta and Surabaya mills were allocated sufficient wheat, allegedly of a higher quality, to maintain full capacity production. In 1980, BKPM informed Prima that its intention to divest itself of 25% of its shares to a private businessman, Mr Wirontono, could not proceed. Because flour was a strategic industry, Prima would have to sell to a state company, and it would have to sell 50%, not 25%. Coinciding with this demand, Bulog withdrew Prima's licence to market in Kalimantan. By now only Sulawesi remained of the original market area. Supplies of wheat were also cut back, to the extent that Prima was operating at 20% of capacity.[47]

It is alleged that Bulog chief, Bustanil Arifin, in negotiating Prima's final withdrawal from Indonesia, suggested in writing to the Singapore owners of Prima that the shares be divided 45% to Bogasari, 30% to the Bulog-controlled state trading company Berdikari, 20% to Sigit Suharto (the son of the President) and 5% to himself.[48] In the end, Prima sold 100% of its shares to Berdikari for US$31.5 million. As a result, the politico-military faction surrounding the President's family and its commercial associates now controlled access to the import, distribution and purchase of the bulk of primary commodities as well as directly operating the flour milling industry through the state corporations Bulog and Berdikari, and the private company Bogasari.

Pertamina

The saga of Pertamina provides the most extensive insight into the complexities of state corporate capital. The most important of its functions have been:

(a) The collection of oil revenues, co-ordination of work-sharing and production-sharing contracts with foreign oil companies and allocation of drilling concessions. This was its legal function in the narrowest sense, seen

as the desirable limit of its operations by the Bappenas technocrats and those who wished to submit Pertamina to the authority of the Ministry of Mines.

(b) The catalyst and financier of major development projects favoured by those advocating a nationalist, industrial and corporatist economy, including Sutowo and
economic planners associated with the Opsus group.

(c) Financier of the military.

(d) A source of wealth and power for Pertamina officials
and individual political and military leaders.

(e) A core around which private domestic capitalists
could expand through access to contracts for supply
and construction as well as the provision of services.
Conversely it gave those who controlled Pertamina,
notably Ibnu Sutowo, the power to determine which
private business groups gained access to the contracts,
concessions and monopolies.

In the years immediately following the establishment of
the New Order government, a struggle for control of Pertamina took place between those who wished to regularise its
operations and make Pertamina accountable to the Ministry
of Mines and those who wished to retain its autonomy. The
conflict came to a head in 1967 when Minister of Mines,
Bratanata, challenged Ibnu Sutowo's authority over allocation of drilling concessions, the process of tendering and the
investment of Pertamina funds. The President entered the
struggle in a decisive manner, making Sutowo directly responsible to Cabinet through the Cabinet Presidium. Pertamina's operations became closed to public scrutiny and im-
mune to public accountability. Annual balance sheets were
never published, nor was the DPR given the opportunity
to discuss the finances of the oil giant.[49] Suharto's and the
Army's interests in this were clear. Pertamina constituted the
channel through which the bulk of the state's revenue
flowed, as well as the largest and most concentrated source of
contracts for construction and supply. Pertamina therefore

was the strategic focus of economic power and the crucial source of revenue. The autonomy and hegemony of the military was closely dependent upon its ability to maintain its control over this terminal and to prevent its absorption by any regularised state apparatus.

By 1968, Pertamina had completed the incorporation of the other existing oil companies, Pertamin, Permina and Permigan, and was now solely responsible for domestic distribution and allocation of drilling concessions. This autonomy became a central target for reformist critics, including both students and the press, in the context of growing protest at military appropriation of the state apparatus, the resulting exclusion of civilians and political parties from political power, and the increasingly authoritarian and arbitrary nature of military rule.[50] Pertamina was correctly seen as a key element in these developments. The newspaper *Indonesia Raya* documented several instances where individual foreigners associated with Sutowo had been given oil leases as 'gifts' despite demonstrable inability to exploit the leases. In all cases the leases were quickly sold again to foreign oil companies. *Indonesia Raya* concluded that these 'gifts' were a device designed to achieve what Pertamina was legally prohibited from doing — selling leases. The device of the gift also avoided the normal signature bonds which, in these cases, would have amounted to a total of US$60 million.[51]

In 1970 the Commission of Four concentrated much of its attention upon Pertamina, and was particularly critical of Pertamina's continued immunity to the normal processes of accountability. The Commission showed clearly that Sutowo exercised considerable autonomy in the dispersal of Pertamina finances and that quite significant amounts of revenue were not accounted for. They listed several violations:[52]

(a) Pertamina did not pay taxes in 1958–63, and between 1967–69 at least Rp6.8 billion in taxes had not been paid.

(b) Pertamina had neglected to contribute to the Development Fund 55% of its profits as stipulated under Article 18 of Law 19, 1960.

(c) Liquid assets and foreign exchange earnings of Pertamina were not deposited as required in the Bank of Indonesia, but in foreign banks.

(d) Expenditure in excess of estimates had not been explained. (An example of Rp500 million unexplained excess for maintenance is cited.)

(e) Pertamina had not passed on to the government US$64 million in so-called 'data compensation' fees collected from foreign companies.

A series of attempts to bring Pertamina under the public control of the state was made in 1972 and 1973. In May 1972, Pertamina was placed under the supervision of a committee including the Minister of Finance, the Minister of Mining and the Chairman of Bappenas. From October 1972, all loans negotiated by Pertamina were required to be approved by the Bank of Indonesia and Bappenas, and Law No. 5, 1973, authorised the Financial Auditing Board to examine the budgets of state-owned companies.[53] These moves followed specific recommendations made by the Commission of Four in 1970, but in fact contradicted Law No. 8 of 1971 which gave the President Director of Pertamina full control over oil, LNG and foreign contractors, subject only to the authority of the President.[54] After the crisis of 1975, it became apparent that the attempted controls had not limited the personal direction and authority of Ibnu Sutowo. Loans had been sought and raised without the authority of the Board of Supervisors. One of the first moves of the Bappenas technocrats in 1975 was to abolish the right of state corporations to borrow independently.[55]

In the words of Heinz Arndt, long a defender of Sutowo and Pertamina:

The chief problem was that Pertamina, despite the establishment early in 1972 of a Ministerial Board of Commissioners, was amen-

able to no authority below the President. Unless and until the
President exercised this authority, Pertamina was, on many policy
issues, a law unto itself.[56]

Autonomy was used by Pertamina officials for various purposes, not the least of which was the expropriation of state
funds. Over-pricing has been a chief mechanism for such
transfers, and the most notable example concerns the purchase
of tankers for the Pertamina fleet. Prices paid by Pertamina
were far in excess of normal market prices at a time when the
tanker business was in a period of depression. Tankers were
bought from the ailing US builder, General Dynamics, at a
price of US$150 million when the same capacity tankers were
available from Norwegian yards for US$100 million.[57] After
the departure of Sutowo, the new authorities in Pertamina
charged that the charters signed by Sutowo for twenty-three
tankers totalling $2 750 million 'were far above the market
rate for comparable vessels and were on terms which defy
any conclusion that they were the result of arm's length
bargaining'. They cited the case of the charter of the tanker
Jalna. The original charter provided for a total cost of $56
million for a new tanker of 133 400 dead weight tons. Pertamina finally received a three-year-old vessel of 145 188 tons
for twice the earlier figure at a time when the tanker market
was at rock bottom. It was charged that Indonesian officials
were bribed to allow the deals to go through, by the Singapore
businessman Robin Loh, long an associate of Sutowo and a
tanker broker for Pertamina.[58]

A second example of conspicuously high costs concerns
the Krakatau steel project, where an investigating committee
reported that staff housing at Cilacap was costing $250 000
per unit and Siemen's charges for the construction of a power
station were three times the average.[59] The conservative US
magazine, *Time*, confirmed the opinion of informed observers in Jakarta by quoting estimates that most of Pertamina's contracts were padded by as much as 40%, and that
most oil shipping contracts contained a 30% 'kicker' clause,

providing a substantial private tribute for officials of the company.[60]

The appropriation of Pertamina's powers and resources by its own officials was not simply aimed at their personal enrichment. Politico-bureaucrat control of Pertamina facilitated introducing nationalist industrial strategies contrary to Bappenas policies, facilitated the development of select private business groups and provided an independent source of revenue for the military.

As I have argued in Chapter 5, Ibnu Sutowo became convinced that the appropriate path for economic development lay in the creation of a national economy built upon an industrial infrastructure which included the capacity to produce steel, petrochemicals, cement and fertilisers. Pertamina borrowed heavily on the international money market to finance investments in Krakatau steel, fertiliser and petrochemical plants, and the Pertamina tanker fleet. Funds earmarked to pay state taxes were diverted to servicing these debts, and future oil and steel production was used as a bargaining point for loans as export credits. In this way, Pertamina was able to by-pass both IGGI and the Bappenas technocrats and get projects off the ground that were regarded by them as economically undesirable.[61]

Some idea of the extent to which Sutowo used Pertamina to raise loans for investment can be gauged from the debts revealed after the crisis of 1975. Of the total US$10.5 billion debt, US$2.5 billion was owing for civil works contracts, US$3.3 billion for tankers, US$1.9 billion for LNG and oil refining projects, and US$2.1 billion for the Krakatau Steel project.[62] The massive size of these debts and investments becomes apparent if we compare them to the development budgets. For Repelita I, 1969/70–1973/74, the total development expenditure was Rp1 232.8 billion or just under US$3 billion, less than Pertamina's tanker debts. For Repelita II, 1964/65–1978/79, the total development expenditure, swollen by oil earnings, had grown to Rp9 126.5 billion or approximately US$22 billion, just over twice the size of Pertamina's US$10.5 billion 1975 debt.

Pertamina's monopoly position in the oil and LNG field and Sutowo's independence from ministerial control were secured in the mid- and late 1960s with the backing of the President and of Hankam. The reason for this support relates to the importance of Pertamina as a source of finance for the military.[63] Military expenditure in 1981 stood at the modest figure of US$2 122 millions, or 12.5% of the national budget, declining from 14% in 1977.[64] However, it is generally accepted that only 40%–50% of the military's real expenditures came from official budgetary allocations.[65] The shortfall is met through a variety of means including foreign military aid credits, a special military discretionary fund managed by Hankam but outside the formal budget, funds from military-controlled state corporations, and profits from military-owned private companies. Pertamina's role as channel for the major source of foreign earnings and state revenues made it particularly crucial.

Pertamina also acted as an unofficial banker for projects associated with major figures within the New Order, and was lavish in its dispersal of funds for the building of mosques and sporting complexes, government buildings and the development of a constellation of prestige projects, which include an airline, a real estate and land development company and a series of hotels.

State corporations have also provided a basis for the personal enrichment of officials and those who exercise political control over them. It was clear that Ibnu Sutowo, his family and other Pertamina officials built private business empires and partnerships which were difficult to disentangle from the operations of Pertamina itself, and this will be dealt with in Chapter 10. But it was not until 1977 that the enormity of the process of personal expropriation of Pertamina funds and the accumulation of personal wealth as a consequence of holding authority within Pertamina was revealed, in the course of a legal battle between Pertamina and the widow of Haji Thahir, the former personal assistant to the director of Pertamina.

After Thahir's death, his Chinese Indonesian widow, Kartika Ratna, withdrew US$45 million from personal accounts in her husband's name from the Chase Manhattan and Hong Kong and Shanghai Banks in Singapore. She was prevented from withdrawing a further US$35 million from the Sumitomo Bank by a writ from the Indonesian government claiming that the money was the property of Pertamina illegally expropriated by Thahir. Lawyers representing the Indonesian government claimed that Thahir had accepted bribes from two German firms, Siemens A.G. and Klochner Industries Anlagen, in connection with allocation of contracts valued at more than US$500 million for the Krakatau Steel Mill.[66]

Rejecting an Indonesian offer to let her keep the US$1.5 million interest on the Sumitomo deposit, Kartika fought the case in the courts of Singapore. She claimed that:

(a) It was a generally accepted practice for Pertamina officials to take gifts from successful contractors.

(b) Thahir's activities had been carried out with the full knowledge of Ibnu Sutowo, who also banked with Sumitomo. Her lawyers produced documents to show a US$3.8 million deposit in Sutowo's name. Thahir also kept a deposit of US$320 000 in Sutowo's private bank, P.T. Bank Pasifik.

(c) Thahir was part of a larger financial network including Sutowo, President Suharto and Mrs Suharto, and Liem Sioe Liong, the President's business associate. In evidence she cited the shareholdings of the construction company P.T. First Realty Corp., which had access to Pertamina contracts. Shareholders of the company were: Kwee Hian Long (Indonesian Chinese resident in Singapore), Sudono Salim (Liem Sioe Liong), Soedama Salim (son of Liem), Albert Salim

(son of Liem), Ibrahim Thahir (son of H. A. Thahir),
Bambang Tirtomuljono (associate of Suharto family).

Kartika also claimed that Liem and Thahir were partners
in the sale of 5 000 jeeps to the Indonesian Army by Liem's
Volvo agency and the Chrysler agency owned by the President's brother, Probosutejo, and Hashim Ning.

Putting aside the contentious claims and counter-claims, it
is clear and uncontested that Thahir had used his office in
Pertamina to accumulate a sum of US$80 million which was
deposited in personal bank accounts. It is unlikely that this
was all intended for Thahir's personal consumption. It is
more likely that Thahir was the 'banker' for a variety of
economic and political projects outside the state budget.
Nevertheless, if we put this case together with others involving Bulog, P.N. Timah and various government departments, the importance of state corporations as a source of
personal finance to individual officials becomes apparent.
There is undoubtedly a new category of politico-bureaucrats
who have built for themselves a lifestyle of staggering dimensions on the basis of their control of strategic terminals of the
state-owned sector of the economy. The major question is,
however, whether they used this money to reconstruct their
basis of power from control of political office to ownership of
capital. In other words, are the politico-bureaucrats using
wealth accrued during their period of office to reconstitute
themselves as a capitalist class? The potential certainly exists.

At a broader level, Pertamina has been a big factor in the
emergence of a domestic capitalist class under the New
Order because it is a major source of contracts for supply and
construction and generates a variety of manufacturing and
service industries. The rise of the major New Order business
groups, among them that of Ibnu Sutowo, has been connected with successful access to Pertamina contracts and
control over the allocation of Pertamina resources.

These connections and the detailed relationship between
Pertamina, its officials and the development of the major

business groups of the New Order will be examined in Chapters 9 and 10.

CONTRADICTIONS WITHIN STATE-OWNED CAPITAL

There have been remarkably few conflicts between private domestic capital and state-owned capital because the latter has generally operated in areas which are either unprofitable to private capital or beyond its resources. Indeed, state capital has proven to be an essential element in the development of private capital, providing infrastructure and opportunities to take part in large projects as contractors and suppliers. Nevertheless, state capital contains within itself contradictions which derive from the different functions it has performed. At one level, the state corporation is required to perform in an efficient manner in terms of normal business and financial criteria. Conversely, it may be required to operate in a broader strategy of national industrialisation in which the operations of the corporation become meaningful only in terms of the success of the strategy as a whole, deficit spending and borrowing by individual corporations justified in the context of broader strategy objectives. At another level, state corporations are required to act as financiers of the military and other centres of politico-bureaucratic power and as avenues for the accumulation of personal wealth and capital accumulation by private business groups.

Conflicts have been most bitter in those corporations which straddle strategic sectors of the economy, among them Bulog, Pertamina, Telkom, Inhutani and Timah. The Pertamina crisis of 1975/76 offers the best insight into the conflict over state capital and the nature of the groups competing for control of state capital. Pertamina was able to carry out the range of functions described above because of rising oil prices and revenue flows. But in 1975 a temporary recession in the oil market caught Pertamina overextended and unable to meet short-term debt-servicing obligations.[67]

Suharto was confronted with a situation which threatened to plunge Indonesia into a major debt crisis. Given Indonesia's reliance on international credit and her dependence on oil revenues to service these debts and finance the development budget, Suharto was forced to move quickly to clean up the Pertamina mess. In doing so, he was forced to give way to long-time critics of Pertamina's function as the financier of major industrial projects and the political and military centres of New Order power. These included critics within Bappenas and international financial and banking institutions.

A 'technical' team under Sumarlin, the Minister of State for Administrative Reform, was appointed to investigate and to reform Pertamina. By March 1976 the reorganisation was completed, Sutowo was discharged and replaced by a 'technocrat' general, Piet Harjono. Pertamina's role as an alternative engine of national industrial development was ended and its right to raise loans was removed and transferred to the Bank of Indonesia. Krakatau Steel and the Sumatra fertiliser project were removed from Pertamina control along with a host of Pertamina subsidiaries outside the oil/LNG sector, the most important of which was P.T. Patra Jasa which was entrusted with the building of the major Pertamina construction ventures. The Batam Island project, intended to challenge Singapore's dominance as an oil refining centre and free port, was suspended. At the same time, Presidential Decree No. 44 of 1976 established a new internal structure for Pertamina which greatly reduced the authority of the director, making it difficult for any future incumbent to act with the autonomy of Sutowo.[68] Many of the top Pertamina officials, including Sjarnubi Said and Haji Thahir, were dismissed.

Although Pertamina's problems were largely caused by massive commitments to industrial investment and a loan crisis brought about by a temporary recession,[69] the technocrats were able to present a picture of considerable incompetence and corruption. A wide variety of contracts were

accordingly renegotiated and reduced.[70] Production-sharing
contracts were also argued to be too generous to contractors,
and the technocrats renegotiated these.[71]

Minister for Mines Sadli also revealed that production
from Pertamina's own wells had declined because of declining investment and exploration. For the technocrats and the
reformist intelligentsia of Jakarta, the operation of Pertamina as a state within a state had not been justified. It had
been an inefficient, corrupt and gullible organisation.[72] Sutowo's fall was therefore seen as a victory for efficiency and
regularisation; *Kompas* commented, 'The removal of Sutowo shows that there is still accountability for officers assumed in Indonesia'.[73]

However, for supporters of economic nationalist policies,
the struggle had culminated in a victory by international
capital, anxious to keep Indonesia dependent. *Merdeka*
charged that Pertamina has been caught in a web of debt and
dragged down by an international capitalist conspiracy. As a
result, the postponement of the development of heavy industries would increase the dumping of foreign goods and perpe-
tuate the foreign-exchange drain.[74]

While the reformers and regularisers may have successfully taken advantage of the crisis to ensure that Pertamina
could no longer operate as it did under Sutowo, the events of
1975 and 1976 cannot be seen as a fundamental change in the
operation of state-owned capital or the nature of relationships between political power and state-owned corporate
capital. Nor can they be seen as a long-term victory for
reformers, regularisers and free marketeers over economic
nationalists or political appropriation of the state apparatus.
Rather, they were a short-term response to a situation which
temporarily posed a major threat to the Indonesian economy.

The regularisation of Pertamina has not been complete.
Large-scale thefts of oil involving Pertamina officials have
recently come to the surface.[75] More important, there are
persistent and insistent claims by well-informed sources in
Jakarta that illegal spot oil sales now constitute the primary

means of expropriating Pertamina for financing the major centres of politico-bureaucrat power. The replacement of Piet Harjono with Judo Sumbono in 1980 was also seen by many to be a retreat from a technocratic to an appanage style of authority. Nor has Pertamina, or indeed the state corporations as a whole, been required to operate on the basis of 'normal' capitalist market criteria and they have continued to constitute instruments of general policy whose effectiveness has not been evaluated in terms of profitability but in terms of facilitation of broad economic strategies.

This situation has been perpetuated by the continued political dominance of the military and the nationalists over the Bappenas technocrats and the continued flow of oil revenue which has made it possible for state corporations, particularly Pertamina, to fulfil a variety of roles at one time. However, with the decline in oil revenues and the accompanying balance of payments crisis which emerged in 1982, it would appear that a new crisis point has been reached. The fiscal crisis faced by the state now directly contradicted the interests of the officials, private corporations and political factions. Once again changes in Pertamina reflect these new contradictions. The replacement of Judo Sumbono in June 1984 was related to the need to make Pertamina more efficient and profitable. On 7 April 1983, President Suharto met with the Board of Commissioners of Pertamina and expressed concern over Pertamina's weak performance in selling oil overseas, wastage and the structure of control over Pertamina. Particularly worrying was the performance of the new refineries, which were operating at partial capacity, had failed to halt the import of distillates from Singapore, and had failed to establish the marketing of their oil products in foreign markets in the face of more efficient competition from refineries in Europe and the Middle East. The prospect of these expensive refineries becoming white elephants was horrifying to economic policy-makers.[76]

In short, the fiscal and economic crisis in Indonesia was making it increasingly essential that state-owned corporations operate efficiently, produce profits and/or achieve specific development targets. The threat of major dislocation to the economic order and to the interests of those political and social forces whose dominance was embedded within it was bringing pressures for regularisation not previously achieved by generations of critics and reformers.

1. The relationship of the form of state capitalist enterprise and state capitalism in general to the social and political context in which it operates has been more fully explored in: J. F. Petras, 'State Capitalism and the Third World', *JCA* 6, 4 (1976); R. Sobhan, 'The Nature of the State and Its Implications for the Development of Public Enterprises in Asia', *JCA* 9, 4 (1979); J. P. Perez Sainz, 'Towards a Conceptualization of State Capitalism in the Periphery', *Insurgent Sociologist* 10, 4 (1980).

2. Glassburner 1978. See also the statement of President Suharto of 17.4.70, published in the article, 'Indonesia Launches a Development Offensive', *Indonesia* (Jakarta) 4, (1970).

3. Thomas and Panglaykim 1973, pp. 100–106; B. Halim, 'Industrial Expansion in Indonesia During the Five Year Plan', *Indonesia* (Jakarta) 7 (1971).

4. Sadli 1970, p. 33.

5. Soehoed 1982, p. 50.

6. C. Wibisono, 'Saham "Pri" dan "Non-Pri"', *Tempo*, 14.3.81, pp. 70–2.

7. For a survey of some of the problems with Wibisono's methodology and assumptions, see: T. M. Lubis, 'Pleidoi Bagi Pengusaha Non-Pribumi', *Prisma* 4 (1981), pp. 90–4.

8. IBRD 1981, citing the 1974 industrial census.

9. S. Hambali, 'Semen: Profil Industri Yang Menguntungkan', *Eksekutif* (May 1981), p. 51.

10. Gray 1982.

11. Soehoed 1981, p. 12.

12. Soehoed 1977, p. 63.

13. Ibid., pp. 56, 59.

14. Soehoed 1982, p. 56.

15. Ibid., p. 55.

16. Ibid., p. 56.

17. 'Dulu Rockefeller Kini Taipan Liem', *Tempo*, 2.7.83, pp. 73, 74.

18. M. Habir, 'Stripping in Public', *FEER*, 23.6.83, pp. 84–6.

19. S. Grenville, 'Monetary Policy and the Formal Financial Sector', in Booth and McCawley (eds) 1981.

20. Daroesman 1981, pp. 17–20.

21. This issue has also been treated in D. Jenkins, 'Indonesia Adds Up After 10 Years of Bad Debts', *FEER*, 18.8.78, pp. 40–3.

22. Ibid.

23. 'Traps for the State Banks', *ICN* 166, 26.1.81.

24. 'Bank Rakyat Indonesia: Small Profit, Huge Credit Backlog', *ICN* 176, 22.6.81; and 'Bank Rakyat Indonesia's Outstanding Credits up 65.2%', *ICN* 202, 19.7.82.

25. 'Capital Goods Instead of Cash Credit', *ICN* 179, 18.8.81.

26. 'The Development of the Banking Industry', *ICN* 203, 9.8.82.

27. One of the early examples of a banking joint venture between state and private capital is P. T. Bank Dharma Ekonomi, which was a joint venture between the state-owned P. T. Berdikari and the Chinese Be Sulindro group. Another is the private foreign-exchange bank, Bank Niaga, in which shareholders include the Bank of Indonesia, Julius Tahija (businessman and former PD of P. T. Caltex Indonesia) and Soedarpo Sastrosatomo, a private indigenous businessman. A recent example is the financial institution, P. T. Private Development Finance Co. of Indonesia (PDFC), whose shareholders include the Bank of Indonesia as well as a wide range of major private business interests: Indonesia Research and Development Co., *Financial Directory of Indonesia* (Jakarta, 1980).

28. 'Masa Panen Kontraktor Besar', *Eksekutif* (August 1981).

29. 'The Development Prospect of the Construction Industry', *ICN* 182, 28.9.81, p. 4.

30. The rise of the Pertamina clients will be dealt with in Chapter 10.

31. *Eksekutif* (August 1981).

32. Details of the composition of some of these conglomerates are to be found in: *Eksekutif* (August 1981); *ICN* 182, 28.9.81.

33. Details of the Report of the Presidential Commission of Inquiry into Corruption, the 'Commission of Four', were published in *Sinar Harapan*, 18, 20, 21, 22, 23 and 24 July 1970.

34. D. Jenkins, 'Indonesia adds up after 10 Years of Bad Debts', *FEER*, 18.8.78, pp. 40–3.

35. G. Sacerdoti, 'Bulog Archipelago under Fire', *FEER*, 24.2.78, p. 36.

36. The most comprehensive analysis of the structure and operation of Bulog are to be found in the Report of the Commission of Four on Corruption in *Sinar Harapan*, 22.7.70, and in 'Ratu Pelita Sedang Gunduh', *Tempo*, 28.10.72.

37. Crouch 1975, pp. 613–14; *Indonesia Raya*, 16.10.69.

38. *Indonesia Raya*, 12.2.69; Crouch 1975, p. 614.

39. See the Report of the Commission of Four in *Sinar Harapan*, 22.7.70. Clearly the Commission saw corruption, as well as incompetence, playing a major part in Bulog's problems. It called for '. . . strict internal control and a sufficiently large number of skilled and honest employees'. See also: *Indonesia Raya*, 12.2.69 and 16.10.69; *Nusantara*, 19.10.72; *Abadi*, 20.10.72.

40. See Crouch 1975, pp. 612–14. One persistent claim made by informed sources in Jakarta is that Bulog's huge overseas purchases in 1978 were made at a price considerably below those officially notified and the difference syphoned off. This is a process similar to contract padding, which will be discussed in relation to Pertamina. The article 'Ratu Pelita Sedang Gunduh' in *Tempo*, 28.10.72 details numerous methods whereby Bulog funds are transferred to officials. One of the most common is the provision of down-payments for the sale of rice to contractors who never deliver and are never prosecuted.

One of the largest scandals involved the East Kalimantan regional chief, Budiaji, who expropriated 64 498 tons of rice worth Rp7.8 billion (US$18.8 million) in 1978 (see Sacerdoti, *FEER*, 24.2.78, p. 36).

41. Details of the operations of Mantrust in this period are to be found in Crouch 1975, p. 614, *Indonesia Raya*, 2.9.69 and 9.9.69; *Operasi*, 19.9.69; *Pedoman*, 25.9.69; *Kompas*, 25.9.69.

42. P.T. Garuda Mataram's shareholders were:

Kolonel Sofjar (Financial Officer, Kostrad)	25%
General Cokropranoto (Aspri)	25%
Herman Setyadi (Chinese businessman)	25%
Sjarief Margetan (Chinese businessman of the Maxim/Mantrust group)	25%
Sofjan Wanandi (Liem Bian Koen — financial organiser for Opsus)	Director

43. *Tempo*, 28.10.72.

44. Go Swie Kie's rise to prominence is discussed in *Tempo*, 28.10.72; *Nusantara*, 19.10.72; *Chas*, third week of October 1969. Details of his business group are given in Chapter 9.

45. *BNPT* 258–1970.

46. *Nusantara*, 11.2.71; *Indonesia Raya*, 3.11.72.

47. J. P. Manguno and S. K. Witcher, 'Suharto Relatives, Officials Gain Contol of Indonesian Flour Trade', *AWSJ*, 23.11.80, pp. 2, 3; *Tempo*, 20.3.82.

48. Ibid.

49. *Mahasiswa Indonesia*, third week of April 1967; *Indonesia Raya*, 22.11.69.

50. See *El Bahar*, 30.5.67; *Nusantara*, 30.8.69, 2.10.70; *Pedoman*, 23.6.69, 8.12.69; *Harian Kami*, 9.12.69; *Indonesia Raya*, 22.11.69, 25.11.69, 26.11.69, 27.11.69, 3.12.69, 15.12.69.

51. *Indonesia Raya*, 26.11.69.

52. See the 'Report' in *Sinar Harapan* (note 33, above), and the interview with Wilopo, the former chairman of the Commission, in *Tempo*, 22.5.76.

53. S. Grenville, 'Survey of Recent Developments', *BIES* 9, 1(1972).

54. *Kompas*, 1.5.74.

55. See Wilopo's comments in *Tempo*, 22.5.76; and the statements made to DPR Komisi I, VI and VII, and to the DPR Budget Committee by the Minister for Economic Planning, Wijoyo (*Kompas*, 26.6.75).

56. H. Arndt, 'Survey of Recent Developments', *BIES* 11, 2 (1975b).

57. *Tempo*, 25.9.76.

58. *FEER*, 22.10.76; *Tempo*, 25.9.76.

59. Arndt 1975b.

60. *Time*, 22.3.76.

61. Robinson 1985.

62. *Kompas*, 21.5.76, quoting Mining Minister Sadli's statement to the DPR.

63. Mackie states: 'It has long been common knowledge that a large part of Pertamina's oil revenues has not been paid into the state treasury but has remained under the control of Ibnu Sutowo who has made use of it in his own ways, either as unconventional finance for the armed forces and other parts of the government or for the diverse purposes of Pertamina or himself.' (J. A. C. Mackie, 'The Commission of Four Report on Corruption', *BIES* 6, 3 [1970]).

Crouch also notes: 'The secrecy surrounding the financial affairs of

Pertamina was intended to disguise its role as a major source of funds at the disposal of the military leadership . . . As long as Ibnu Sutowo continued to supply the funds required by the military leadership, they had not interest in restricting his autonomy in running Pertamina.' (Crouch 1975, pp. 610–11)

64. David Jenkins, 'The Military's Secret Cache', *FEER*, 8.2.80.

65. Ibid. See also A. Rieffel and A. Wirjasuputra, 'Military Enterprises', *BIES* 7, 2 (1972).

66. The summary of the Thahir case is taken from *Tempo*, 26.7.80; *Kompas*, 13.2.80; R. Pura, 'Fight for Mystery Fortune Embroils Pertamina', *AWSJ*, 5.2.80; R. Pura and S. K. Witcher, 'Two West German Firms are Named by Pertamina in Bribery Probe', *AWSJ*, 27.5.80; S. K. Witcher and J. P. Manguno, 'Suharto Received Kickbacks, Affidavit Charges', *AWSJ*, 17.7.80; J. P. Manguno, 'Suharto Denies Taking Payoffs on Arms Deals', *AWSJ*, 30.7.80; G. Sacerdoti, 'The Ghost in the Courtoom', *FEER*, 7.3.80, and 'The Revelations of a Widow', *FEER*, 1.8.80.

67. For a discussion of the financial difficulties which led to the crisis see: 'Pertamina, 1976: Penyesuaian Dengan Ikat Pinggang', *Tempo*, 17.1.76; H. Stockwin, 'Why the General Had to Go', *FEER*, 19.3.76.

68. 'Pertamina 1976: Penyesuaian Ikat Pinggang', *Tempo*, 17.1.76.

69. Interview with Sutowo, 'Saya tidak pernah berfikir ingin jadi Dirut seumur hidup', *Tempo*, 17.1.76.

70. 'Di Celah-Celah Hutang yang Itu', *Tempo*, 22.11.75; also *Tempo*, 31.5.75.

71. Renegotiation of production-sharing contracts was expected to bring in an extra $300 million in 1976/77 (*Tempo*, 7.8.67). For details of the new regulations, see D. Jenkins, 'Jakarta's Bitter Oil Men Weigh up their Future', *FEER*, 13.8.76.

72. The technocrats were careful in their criticism, no doubt because the President himself had been so deeply involved, but their concern was unmistakable. See: Sadli, in *Sinar Harapan* and *Kompas*, 26.3.75, *Sinar Harapan*, 3.9.75, 5.9.75, *Merdeka*, 8.9.75, *Tempo*, 13.9.75.

73. *Kompas*, 5.3.76 (*USPRT*).

74. *Merdeka*, 1.8.75, 23.12.75.

75. J. P. Manguno and S. K. Witcher, 'Pertamina Aides Probing Reports of Multimillion Dollar Fuel Theft', *AWJS*, 22.11.80; and J. P. Manguno, 'More Fuel Thefts Found in Pertamina Probe', *AWSJ*, 27.2.81.

76. F. Jufri, 'Pemimpin Baru — Untuk Sebuah Era Baru — di Pertamina', *Tempo*, 23.6.84. This article contains interviews with former Pertamina Director, Piet Harjono, and Minister for Mines and Energy, Dr Subroto.

8
The Military-Owned Business Groups

ORIGINS OF MILITARY-OWNED BUSINESS GROUPS

THE military have been involved in economic activities since the early 1950s, primarily to raise extra-budgetary revenue for the operations of individual commands and units as well as for the personal and political needs of individual officers and political factions. At its earliest and crudest level these economic activities took the form of illegal levies on businessmen, the imposition of various tolls on the transport of goods, and the enforcement of labour services from peasants.[1] At a more organised level the military have been involved in smuggling, providing protection and even trucks, guards and forged papers for the operations. Smuggling was a major means by which military commands raised revenue, especially in the Outer Islands during the period of Guided Economy when the artificially high exchange rate of the rupiah and other regulatory constraints made trade through normal export channels difficult and unprofitable. Units involved in the PRRI/Permesta rebellions as well as Kostrad raised funds in this way, and various regional commands continued to be involved in smuggling into the late 1960s and early 1970s.[2] The military were also involved in establishing systems of forced purchase of small-holder crops at below market prices, the most recent case of which has been the establishment of a military-backed company with a monopoly of purchase on East Timor coffee.[3]

The most significant movement of the military into economic activity took place in 1958/59 when they secured control of the bulk of the nationalised Dutch enterprises. After 1965 the military continued to develop its economic power, through control over such state-owned corporations as Pertamina, Bulog and Berdikari.

The element which concerns us here is the relationship between the military and private capital — in particular, the development of military-owned companies and joint ventures between the military and private capital, both domestic and international. These relationships did not begin in 1965, since it had long been necessary for private companies to come to some accommodation with local and regional military commanders, particularly in the Guided Economy era when the military wielded significant influence over the operations of the OPS and GPS. But more formal relationships were also developed between particular military commands and private business groups, invariably embracing close personal associations between individual military commanders and Chinese businessmen, which endured for long periods. Chinese businessmen who proved reliable and efficient became the economic operatives of military commands, acting as suppliers to the military as well as organising smuggling operations and more regular business activities on their behalf. These operations were coordinated by the Finek (Finance and Economic Section) officers within the commands (the 7th Assistants).

After 1965 the military commands began to formalise their private business activities by establishing military-owned companies. Previously scattered and uncoordinated business activities were centralised and incorporated. At the heart of this process were the 'financial generals' who emerged from the Finek sections of the old military commands, the Army Quarter Master Corps, and various military-controlled state corporations.[4] These financial generals now had almost unlimited access to the resources and facilities of the state and power to influence allocation of import/export licences, forestry concessions and state contracts. Among the most important were:

General Soedjono Hoemardani. Former Deputy Chief of Finek (Diponegoro Division) and Deputy Chief of Finek (Army Central Command). Director of P.T. Tri Usaha Bhakti (the largest military-owned business group), former Personal Presidential Advisor, the political linchpin of a complex network of Chinese and Japanese business groups, and an important member of General Ali Moertopo's political and intelligence centre, Opsus.

General Sofjar. Former Chief of Finek, Kostrad and head of the Kostrad business group, Yayasan Dharma Putra (YDP). Former Chairman of Kadin.

General Soerjo. Director of YDP and the state-owned Hotel Indonesia group. Former Chairman of the State Audit, and Personal Presidential Advisor (Finance and Economic). Director of the President's 'Team to Regularise State Finances' (Pekuneg), a body which also exercised authority over confiscated enterprises.

General Alamsjah. 7th Assistant, Finek (Army Central Command) 1963–65; Personal Presidential Assistant; State Secretary 1969–73.

General Tirtosudiro. Personal Presidential Assistant and Chief of Bulog to 1972. Previously head of Army Logistics.

General Suhardiman. Former head of the state trading company, P. T. Jaya Bhakti, and the military-sponsored, anti-PKI trade union, Soksi. Director of the state corporation Berdikari to 1972.

In the period immediately following the 1965 coup, military officers in strategic positions were able to manipulate export credits and state contracts to the advantage of Chinese-owned companies close to military commands. In one case, foreign exchange made available at a special low rate for the import of priority goods (BE exchange) was either used to import goods outside the priority list or simply resold in Jakarta. Estimates of the amount manipulated in this way vary from $35 to $100 million in 1968. Although several of the Chinese importers involved were deregistered, none of the unnamed government officials instrumental in the manipulations were brought to trial and only a minute proportion of the unused funds appear to have been recovered.

Another case involved Coopa, a company which had obtained a contract to supply fertiliser to the government's 'Bimas Gotong Royong' scheme intended to provide farmers with the inputs for the 'Green Revolution'. It was revealed by the Jakarta press that Coopa had failed to deliver fertiliser for which it had been paid approximately $711 000. Further investigations revealed that Coopa, registered in Liechtenstein, was owned by Arief Husni (Ong Seng Keng), the director of Bank Ramayana, in which Suharto's brother Probosutejo was a commissioner and shareholder and with which General Soerjo was associated.[5]

To these cases we must add numerous scandals involving smuggling and the overpricing of imports of equipment for the military.[6] The significance of these scandals is first and foremost the light they throw on political economic relationships between the military officers, to allocate credit and contracts to preferred business groups, and the power of these officials to bypass legal procedures. But these scandals also reveal a process of politically based accumulation at work. It may be argued that accumulation of this type was necessary in the situation confronting capital in Indonesia in the late 1960s. Indeed, the funds so raised probably formed the basis of capital investment by the Chinese business groups involved. However, there is little evidence that these or any other funds were used by the military to finance a corporate commercial infrastructure of its own. Rather, the formation of military companies appears to have been built upon three types of resource:

(a) Companies nationalised and taken over by the military in 1958, involved in warehousing, freight forwarding, salvage, towage, air cargo facilities, repair shops and shipyards. Although formerly state companies managed by the military, many of these were transformed by the mid-1960s into military-owned companies.

(b) Assets confiscated and handed over to the military which included cash funds, hotels, a shipyard and automobile sole agencies. The primary instrument of such confiscations and reallocations to the military was General Soerjo's Pekuneg which, in particular, supervised the redistribution of the assets formerly controlled by Yusuf Muda Dalam. A second important element was the breaking up of state-owned forestry concessions and their allocation as HPH (*hak pengusaha hutan* — forestry exploitation rights) to private companies. Around 600 HPH were issued and formed a key element in the constellations of most business groups. Military commands, groups of retired officers and individual generals were well represented among the recipients.

(c) Privileged access to military and government contracts for supply and construction, licences for import, and import credits.

THE MILITARY-OWNED BUSINESS GROUPS AND THE STRUCTURE OF SOCIAL AND ECONOMIC POWER IN INDONESIA

Military-owned businesses are significant in their own right as a component of corporate power and wealth. Although we have no precise figures on the relative size of the military corporate sector *vis-à-vis* the state-owned sector or the Chinese-owned sector, military companies operate in most areas of domestic investment and are partners in a range of joint ventures with foreign and Chinese partners. But the real significance of the military companies lies in the crucial role they play in relation to the state and to the structure of the emerging capitalist class.

Most analyses of military business interests have focused upon their role as terminals of revenue raising. Military spokesmen have admitted that the revenue needs of the military exceed formal budgetary allocations and that the military entry into business is designed to close this gap.[7] The ABRI newspaper, *Angkatan Bersenjata*, stated that the routine budget of the military only provided 50% of its needs, and therefore, 'To make up for shortages in its routine budget, the Army, for example, has been forced to establish limited liability companies outside the Army'.[8] Admiral Harjono explained how military economic activities could be divided into civic missions to upgrade infrastructure (*operasi bhakti*) and attempts to close the gap between official budget allocations and the financial needs of the military (*operasi karya*), which included local military economic activities in transport and contruction.[9]

Military business activities also became the subject of censure by critics. The right-wing Muslim newspaper, *Nusantara*, charged that:

> Military engage in trade and business to meet their budgetary needs which are not met by the state budget. It would be better to allocate ABRI sufficient funds since it will eliminate the excuse of ABRI elements that their dealings with Chinese bankers are done to earn extra income for the Government.[10]

and:

> General Panggabean has ordered eight Army directorates to set up P.T.'s to channel production activities into their own fields. Our experience is that state enterprises headed by military men collapse while their directors enrich themselves. ABRI should be provided with a budget which would make commercial activity unnecessary.[11]

However, the military-owned companies are not merely sources of revenue for the military; they act as mechanisms whereby individual officers can increase their own political and economic power, their resources for patronage and their personal wealth, as well as facilitate their personal entry into the capitalist class. The charges made by *Nusantara* above reflect a general belief that some military companies are run at a loss and operate merely as mechanisms for the depredation of the state purse by individual officers. Through their contacts with the capitalist class, many officers, both retired and serving, sit as directors on the boards of Chinese and foreign companies, while some establish companies on their own behalf.[12] As we shall see, it is often difficult to determine whether a company owned by retired officers is a private company, a company operating on behalf of a military command, or both. These companies are often enmeshed with military companies in a complex network of joint ventures.

Most important is the relationship between the state, the military companies and the capitalist class, both domestic and international. Despite the politically derived resources the military is able to call upon, the bulk of military companies remain small, under-capitalised and struggling. Generally they flourish only after entry into joint ventures with Chinese or international capitalists. It is the latter who provide the capital, the management and the broader corporate structures to turn these sets of political resources into real profits. Nowhere is this better illustrated than in the forestry industry.

As will be evident from case studies of military business groups later in the chapter, the military has been remarkably successful in obtaining logging concessions. Generally the concession-holding companies were established with a capital investment of only Rp2 or 3 millions, and only become involved in production after entering a joint venture arrangement with foreign or Chinese firms which boosted investment to levels around Rp100 million. There is substantial evidence to suggest that the contribution of the military to such joint ventures was the concession itself, a commodity to be traded in return for a share of the profits generated from its exploitation. The Commission of Four was particularly concerned with the mode of operation of indigenous concession-holders in the forestry industry:

> It has been indicated that there are national investors who have sold their exploration rights to foreign brokers for US$5 per cubic meter. These brokers have not conducted exploitation themselves but have engaged contractors . . .

In many joint ventures moreover. 'The rupiah share in the joint enterprise was nil, meaning that the Indonesian party gives only its name'.[13]

A study by Chris Manning in 1971 noted that over one million hectares of concession area had been given to five para-military organisations, representing 10% of the total forest area set aside for production and 20% of that in production at the time. Manning also notes the presence of 'non-business' elements in the forestry industry:

> At least two of the Indonesian companies nominally partners to a profit-sharing agreement, in practice received only a contract fee.
>
> It is the high level of present income that makes the contract fee system so attractive and undoubtedly explains the participation of non-business interests both in domestic corporations and in joint ventures.[14]

Throughout the 1970s virtually unrestrained exploitation and export of logs gave the concessionaires opportunities to make huge profits and military-backed companies opportunities to pirate logs from the concessions of companies with less powerful connections.[15] By the late 1970s, however, the 'wild west' situation was beginning to alter with the decline in the timber market and the successful moves by technocrats to restrict unprocessed log exports and force producers into sawmilling, plywood manufacture, pulp and paper. Large numbers of logging concessions now stand idle and others are being forced into amalgamations to raise the capital for investments required by the processing regulations. With greater demands on local partners to play a role in financing and managing forestry-based industry as foreign partners withdraw, the military find themselves in a role for which they are poorly equipped.

What then is the broader significance of the entry of the military into business? The military has become a corporate owner of capital and as such has developed a vested political interest in the perpetuation of conditions conducive to the accumulation of capital and the generation of profits. Consequently, the military's vigorous prosecution of anti-strike, anti-labour legislation is not only an ideological reflection of the social and political interests of the officer corps but also a product of the military's position as a major institutional owner of capital. But there is a much more concrete relationship between the military and the capitalist class. Through the mechanism of the company and the joint venture, Chinese and international capital effectively operate as the financiers of the military in that they provide the capital and organisational resources to turn the HPH, the licence, the contract or whatever concession into profits and, ultimately, income for the military. It is natural, therefore, that the military has become committed not merely to abstract ideologies of capitalism but to the social dominance of the capitalist class, even to the fortunes of particular companies. This is given another dimension of emphasis by the fact that increasing numbers of military men are moving into private business on their own behalf.

Military corporate ownership of capital also means that the military has a vested interest in a corporate environment in which the state plays a dominant role in determining access to the market, to resources, production and credit through a system of monopolies, concessions and direct state corporate control of strategic sectors of the economy. The entrepreneurial generals have been the foremost opponents of moves by the technocrats to regularise the economy.

THE DEVELOPMENT AND STRUCTURE OF MILITARY BUSINESS GROUPS

The dynamics of the relationships between military, state and capital are best illustrated by the way in which these factors have interacted in the rise of particular military business groups. There are literally hundreds of military-owned companies, although the bulk are very small-scale operations with limited capital investment and of doubtful profitability. Many continue to be owned by individual commands at the Kodim and Kodam level, although there has been an effort since 1965 to incorporate these into centralised business groups. Four military co-operatives were formed: Inkopad, Inkopal, Inkopau and Inkopak, constituting co-operatives of Army, Navy, Air Force and Police companies respectively. The Ministry of Defence, Hankam, established the Tri Usaha Bhakti business group as an umbrella to further consolidate the scattered military business holdings. Apart from these, business groups operated by the more important military commands continued to operate, the most notable being the Kostrad business group, Yayasan Dharma Putra (YDP); the Siliwangi group, Propelat; and the companies of the Diponegoro Division.

Diponegoro Division Associated Companies

Perhaps it is best to begin with the business interests of the Diponegoro Division, because more is known about the early history of this group, which occupies a central position in the constellation of military power. Suharto himself was commander of Diponegoro in the late 1950s and developed close associations with Chinese businessmen, including Liem Sioe Liong and 'Bob' Hasan. Suharto's removal from Diponegoro in 1959 was allegedly connected with moves by officers in Army Central Command, Generals Sunarjo and Pranoto, against 'excesses' in military-business relationships.

It would appear that the Diponegoro Division was involved in the ownership of agricultural estates before 1965, probably former Dutch-owned estates appropriated by the military. In 1967, ten of these plantations were consolidated into one company, P.T. Rumpun, large numbers of the shareholders being Diponegoro officers and family members.[16] Another Diponegoro venture was shipping and stevedoring. As early as 1958 Major Hoemardani on behalf of the Diponegoro Division entered a partnership with Bob Hasan and Sukatia, two Chinese businessmen, to form P.T. Pangeran Lines, which in 1960 became P.T. Wasesa Line. A similar partnership constituted the holding company P.T. Dwi Bakti, which in 1967 joined with other associated interests to form the deep-sea shipping line, P.T. Karana Line.[17] P.T. Karana, in turn, became a joint venture partner with Japanese investors in the log carrier, P.T. Garsa Line. The articles of incorporation of Karana include a dispersal of dividends to various foundations, including Mrs Suharto's Yayasan Kartika Jaya.[18]

None of these companies can be said to be substantial, and Wasesa was said to be in decline in the mid-1970s despite the considerable political facilities at its disposal.[19] The significance of the companies lies in their ownership structures. Management of the enterprises was carried out by the Chinese partners, who also held substantial business interests apart from these partnerships in Diponegoro. Several of the military shareholders are individuals with origins in the Diponegoro Division but who may well hold equity on their own behalf; for example, the late Diponegoro commander Gatot Subroto and his wife held shares in Karana and Wasesa separate from the Dwi Bakti shares (the official holding company). Certainly private shareholders from powerful military families are tied into the Diponegoro-Hasan interests. P.T. Pasopati, a shareholder in Karana, is a partnership between Hasan and Ibnu Hardoyo, a relative of Mrs Suharto.[20]

P.T. Tri Usaha Bhakti

P.T. Tri Usaha Bhakti is a holding company sponsored by Hankam, incorporated in 1969, and supervised by a board of managers consisting of military officers with a background in finance.[21]

The general pattern of military investments outlined earlier is well illustrated by the TUB operations.[22] Small trading, warehousing, trucking, manufacturing and coastal shipping companies use plant and facilities appropriated from the Dutch or which were formerly state or Army property. Low levels of capitalisation would suggest that most of these companies are running down. P.T. Wahana Bhakti Utama is a prime example of this aspect of TUB investment. Established in 1971 using a workshop formerly owned by the Army and former workshop employees, Wahana Bhakti Utama assembles motor vehicles and vehicle bodies. It has had trouble obtaining orders for the old Moskvitch sedans and Ford Mitrar it assembles and the vehicle bodies it makes. Ageing equipment and lack of investment have seen the company progressively pushed out of the market, and it produced only an average of 180 vehicle bodies per year in 1972–78.[23] This would suggest that TUB is interested only in exhausting inherited or appropriated capital stocks and not in accumulation, a pattern reminiscent of the military ventures into estate agriculture in the 1960s. An ambitious attempt to move into the cement industry in the early 1970s in partnership with Swiss Holderbank A.G. came to nothing when the licence for this venture was given to a company associated with the Suharto family, P.T. Gunung Ngadeg Jaya.[24]

The most extensive element of the TUB group is in forestry where, together with regional military units and groups of retired generals, it was successful in obtaining concessions. The capital and management required for exploitation appears to have come from Chinese partners (eg. P.T. Kayumas) or foreign partners, because it was only when these partnerships were concluded that substantial capital was injected.[25] While military companies have been prepared to act as sleeping partners in logging ventures, they have been unenthusiastic about buying out departing foreign partners when restrictions on logging were introduced and about entering the milling and plywood industry. It was the state bank, Bank Pembangunan Indonesia, not Weyerhauser's partner, P.T. TUB, which bought Weyerhauser's 65% share when the US company pulled out in 1981.[26]

More recently, with the exception of the agricultural estate company, P.T. Padi Bhakti, TUB has tended to concentrate its investments of significance in the construction and plant-hire industry, where it has entered six joint ventures with overseas partners.

TUB's corporate partnerships also exhibit some interesting political features. Apart from knitting together a network of fragmented military enterprises, P.T. TUB has cemented business alliances with several important domestic business groups, both Chinese and indigenous. P.T. Private Development Finance Corp. links several of the major domestic business groups, including those of Sutowo, Soedarpo (indigenous), Liem Sioe Liong, Mochtar Riady (Chinese), as well as the Bank of Indonesia, the government of Jakarta, and the Chinese/military auto sole agency, P.T. Gading Mas. P.T. Perkins Diesel, a company involved in the assembly and installation of diesel engines, is a joint venture between TUB, Perkins of UK and a private indigenous company, P.T. Masayu.[27] Through these corporate activities the military has become integrated with most elements of private and state capital in a vast and complex politico-economic network.

The Kostrad Business Group

The Kostrad group comprises the Yayasan Dharma Putra (YDP) and a smaller foundation, Trikora. Both were integrated into the command structure of Kostrad, and the responsibility for their operation given to the 7th Assistant[28], who until 1973 was General Sofjar, also the chairman of Kadin. After Sofjar's death, his position was taken by General Soerjo. Of all the military units in the post-1965 period, Kostrad was most closely associated with that group of officers which came to dominate the positions of real power and influence under the New Order. With the rise of Suharto, YDP, as well as the Chinese businessmen most closely associated with Suharto during his period as commander of the Diponegoro Division and Kostrad, notably Liem Sioe Liong and 'Bob' Hasan, were to experience a rapid rise.

The centrepiece of the YDP group was the Bank Windu Kencana, formerly owned by Liem Sioe Liong and, although transferred to YDP ownership, reputedly still managed by him.[29] Apart from this, YDP owns a forestry concession (P.T. Dharma Rimba Kencana), which became the basis of a joint venture in a logging operation (P.T. Asia Veteran); interests in airlines (P.T. Seleuwah and P.T. Mandala), together with assorted airforce officers; and a small trading and film producing company. Its largest company, however, is P.T. Garuda Mataram, the Volkswagen sole agent, in partnership with the Mantrust group, while a *komisaris* is Sofjan Wanandi (Liem Bian Koen), a Chinese financier/ businessman also associated with Opsus.[30]

The fortunes of the YDP group appeared to peak in the early 1970s. Thereafter, the airlines failed to expand, Bank Windu Kencana remained small and the Volkswagen agency declined with the arrival of the Japanese assemblers. In the early 1980s, Kostrad itself was disbanded and it is not clear exactly where its corporate property was distributed.

The P.T. Propelat Group (Siliwangi Division)

Propelat is a vastly different group to YDP. The latter is built upon a forestry concession, a sole agency and a bank, all obtained in the early years of the New Order and widely regarded as being in effect operated by Chinese managers, notably Liem Sioe Liong. In contrast, Propelat, although it benefited greatly from politically secured monopolies in contracting, appears to have been actively involved in management.

P.T. Propelat was established in 1967 when General Dharsono was Siliwangi commander. Although only 40% of its shares were directly held by the Yayasan Kartika Siliwangi (the Siliwangi Foundation), the remaining shareholders have always been serving or former officers and it is generally considered to be fully owned by the Siliwangi Division. The company was originally known as Propelad (Proyek Perhotelan Angkatan Darat) and its function was to build hotels, guest-houses and other accommodation for the military in Kodam Siliwangi.[31] Its activities soon extended to road construction, and it reportedly received all the contracts it could handle from the West Java Provincial Government. The degree of support from the provincial government in Bandung may be gauged by Governor Solichin's order to all mayors and *bupati* to give excavating permits for sand, rock and gravel solely to Propelat and its subsidiary, P.T. West Java Contracting and Engineering.[32]

In 1970, Propelat began to secure generous contracts from Pertamina as the oil company boomed. During the early 1970s, Propelat entered three construction joint ventures with Japanese; these were considerably larger than any of Propelat's previous ventures, involving investment of $5.5 million, although the Propelat equity investment for all three totalled only $750 000.[33] However, the crisis of 1975 left Propelat in considerable difficulty with many of its projects cancelled and others postponed.[34]

Since 1975, Propelat has been in decline, partly because of the losses it sustained with the collapse of Pertamina and partly because it has not been able to mobilise necessary political resources. Its most difficult problem has reportedly been an inability to obtain bank credit.[35]

In October 1978, General Dharsono, the former Siliwangi commander and Secretary General of ASEAN was ap-

pointed director of Propelat. This appointment can hardly
have filled Propelat with hope, because Dharsono had become one of Suharto's major critics and hardly likely to
receive sympathetic treatment. Despite Dharsono's optim-
ism, the outlook for Propelat grew bleaker as it became
increasingly bogged down in a road project in Bali, with
funds almost exhausted. Even military companies can lose
political influence and suffer the consequences.

Miscellaneous Military Companies

Outside the TUB, YDP and Propelat groups there are hundreds of military-owned companies. A large number of
these are military co-operatives, many of which have been
incorporated to some extent into centralised co-operative
organisations including Inkopad (Army), Inkopal (Navy),
Inkopau (Air Force) and Inkopak (Police). Other companies
are owned by the Yayasan of various Kodam and Kodim.
There is little point in attempting to track down each and
every military-owned company, but a few do offer interesting
insights into the nature and structure of military business
groups and these are worth looking at.[36]
   The formation of the Army central co-operative Inkopad
was greatly assisted by the operations of Pekuneg which
appropriated and confiscated assets of business groups associated with the 'old order' and in several cases transferred
them to newly emerging groups close to the new centres of
power.[37] Among these assets were those of P.T. Flat Blun-
tas, a company associated with Yusuf Muda Dalam, which
was involved in a hotel construction project in Jakarta. The
hotel was transferred to the Inkopad company P.T. Wisma
Kartika, which subsequently entered into a Rp1 200 million
(approximately US$3.6 million in 1968 figures) joint venture
with a foreign company to complete what is now the hotel,
Kartika Plaza.[38] In addition, Inkopad has a 20% share in the
small Bank Bukit Barisan with a Chinese partner, a second,
smaller hotel; and a 10% share with Japanese partners and

the local Sulawesi military command in a large-scale fishery and cold storage operation, P.T. Kartikamina.

Predictably, the Navy's business interests are primarily related to shipping, although it does have interests in two small banks (Bhumy Bhari and Dewarutji) and the usual forestry concessions (P.T. Sangkurilang). Most of the companies are very small and engaged in warehousing, freight forwarding, salvage and towage, but there have been moves into larger-scale shipping ventures. Following the military seizure of power in 1965, the Navy company P.T. Pelita Bahari took over the state-owned shipyard previously under the former Minister for Naval Construction and private businessman, Mardanus; while a Navy-owned inter-island shipping company, P.T. Pelayaran Nusantara Bahari, secured the transfer of five ships from the Navy to form the bulk of its commercial fleet.[39] These ships, relatively new when taken over by Bahari, were in poor condition by 1973 and rehabilitated only after the company secured World Bank credits. P.T. Bahari also entered a joint venture with Inkopal to form the deep-sea shipping line P.T. Ampera Lines (later P.T. Admiral Lines). P.T. Admiral was also fortunate enough to obtain five of its seven ships from the Navy. Not only were these two shipping lines initially capitalised by the transfer of ships from the Navy, but they were managed by a Chinese businessman, Moh. Hoesni, the major shareholder in P.T. Emdece, a fishing and shipping company. Chinese businessmen appear to have played a prominent role in operating the Navy's shipping lines. Like Inkopad, Inkopal is also involved in a joint venture in fishing and cold storage, holding a 6% share in a US$6.7 million operation of which its equity contribution has been $162 000.[40] Fishing can be likened to forestry in the sense that the licence to exploit a specific area can be used to constitute the basis for capital participation by a local partner.

The business activities of the Police and the Air Force reinforce these patterns, with small banks, logging concessions and, in the case of the Air Force, air services and freight handling companies forming the bulk of their interests.

CONCLUSION

The involvement of the military in business is significant from three perspectives:

(a) The military has become firmly locked into relationships with the business world, both on an informal basis and through direct corporate capital ownership. Military officers responsible for the raising of revenue operate as managers of publicly owned corporations and as shareholders in private companies and are therefore directly bound up in the process of capital accumulation. As a consequence, the military has developed an interest in establishing policies conducive to the general process of capital accumulation, including the control of labour. Similarly, the military's involvement with Chinese business groups in the import-substitution manufacturing sector, particularly after 1965, no doubt reinforced the enthusiasm of the government for the adoption of economic nationalist policies involving protection and subsidy for domestic firms.

(b) Military business activity has been primarily conducted in partnership with both Chinese and foreign capital, because these groups control the resources necessary to finance investment and manage corporate operations. Consequently, a politico-economic alliance between the military and major Chinese and international business groups affords Chinese and foreign capital in general a significant degree of political protection. As a consequence, the structure of business has tended to take the form of large conglomerates clustered around centres of politico-bureaucratic power, presenting smaller (particularly indigenous) business groups with significant structural disadvantages and entrenching the exclusion of that indigenous section of the capitalist class attempting to

accumulate through trade or small-scale manufacture.
(c) The entry of the military into business involved the
rise of a group of entrepreneurial generals who have
accumulated considerable economic and political
power through their ability to influence the allocation
of licences, monopolies and concessions and to appropriate state resources. Not only have these generals
operated as state managers of capital, or, in the terms
used by the PKI, as 'bureaucratic capitalists', but their
position as military entrepreneurs has also proved an
avenue to both personal enrichment[41] and entry into
the capitalist class on their own behalf.

It is significant, however, that military corporate activity
reached its height in the late 1960s and early 1970s. The
subsequent decline reflects an inability, and perhaps a lack of
interest, in extending, by a process of corporate management, capital accumulation and reinvestment, the corporate
resources and concessions obtained by the various commands in the aftermath of the change of power. The companies served primarily as terminals for the exploitation of
politically secured monopolies and concessions, and military
companies have been notorious for allowing a run-down of
capital stock. A second reason for the decline may be associated with the centralisation of military authority and the
decreasing ability of individual commanders to seize concessions and strike independent corporate arrangements with
private capitalists. This has been reflected in a centralisation
of the revenue-gathering apparatus and a move away from
corporate activity as a means of securing extra-budgetary
revenue.

1. For some illustrations of the types of practices still prevalent in the
late 1960s see: *El Bahar*, 26.9.67 and 8.12.76; *Ampera* and *Operasi*, 5.8.68;
Harian Kami, 11.5.68; *Mimbar Demokrasi*, 16.5.68; *Indonesia Raya*,
27.7.69 and 11.7.69; *Sinar Harapan*, 2.5.68.
2. Crouch 1978, pp. 291–5, *Indonesia: Angkatan Darat, Staf Umum,
PRRI*, Vol II (Jakarta, 1962) — this document outlined the smuggling

activities of units involved in the PRRI rebellion and included details of the Chinese businessmen who co-operated with the military in these operations.

    3. In East Timor P. T. Denok, an Army-controlled company managed by a Chinese businessman, Robby Sumampouw, and reportedly backed by General Murdani himself, has assumed a monopoly over the purchase of coffee. One report suggests that the Army (P. T. Denok) pays Rp400 per kg. for coffee it sells at Rp.1 700 in Singapore. *FEER*'s sources of information suggest that Denok buys at Rp250 kg. and sells at Rp1 000 kg., making an estimated profit of US$20–25 million between 1976 and 1980 (*FEER*, 23.5.80, and *Tempo*, 2.1.82).

    4. See 'Bintang Bintang di Gelanggang Dagang', *Tempo*, 3.2.73, pp. 44–5.

    5. On Coopa, see Crouch 1978, p. 290. For details of Bank Ramayana, see *BNPT* 604–1971.

    6. Crouch 1978, pp. 291–5.

    7. D. Jenkins, 'The Military's Secret Cache', *FEER*, 8.2.80. Crouch (1978, p. 274) also quotes General Hartono as claiming that only 40% of the Army's needs were met in the budget (*Pedoman*, 30.9.69) and the Chief of Naval Staff's statement that only 30%–40% of the Navy's needs were met by regular budgetary allocation (*Indonesia Raya*, 28.3.70). Referring to the transfer of the Caterpillar agency from an old indigenous company to P. T. Trakindo Utama, a company owned by former naval officers, Admiral Sudomo stated that he was willing to allow naval technical facilities to be used by Trakindo Utama as a basis for securing the sole agency in order to obtain badly needed finance for the Navy ('Bintang Apa Pula Itu', *Tempo*, 24.5.75, and 'Coba Dong Buktitan', *Tempo*, 7.6.75). The subject is also treated in detail in *Tempo*, 3.2.73, p. 45.

    8. *Angkatan Bersenjata*, 4.3.70.

    9. 'Kaum Militer Dalam Bisnis', *Ekspres*, 3.10.70.

    10. *Nusantara*, 27.5.69.

    11. *Nusantara*, 3.9.69.

    12. Former generals who have become businessmen in their own right include generals Ali Sadikin, Sumitro and Jassin. Several Chinese-owned companies boast lone former generals as directors or commissioners. General Sadikin (Ret.) sits as director of P. T. Bank Nasional (*BNPT* 562–1973), General Moh. Musa is director of the Chinese textile giant P. T. Daya Manunngal. *Kompas* noted that almost all national banks in Indonesia have senior ABRI officers as protectors, who act as directors or commissioners in return for a share in profits (*Kompas*, 3.9.69).

    13. *Sinar Harapan*, 21.7.70.

    14. C. Manning, 'The Timber Boom', *BIES* 7, 3 (1971), pp. 57–8, p. 49.

    15. G. Sacerdoti, 'Indonesia at the Crossroads', *FEER*, 30.11.79, pp. 64–5.

    16. See details in *BNPT* 1–1968. Many of the shareholders were the wives of Diponegoro officers, including Mrs Suharto and Mrs Gatot Subroto. The official advisors of the company were listed as General Munadi and General Surono, who were respectively Governor of Central Java and Diponegoro Commander at the time.

    17. *BNPT* 826–1959; *BNPT* 263–1963; *BNPT* 44–1968; *BNPT* 162–1970. See also Dick 1977, p. 168.

    18. *BNPT* 44–1968.

    19. Dick 1977, pp. 168–9.

    20. *BNPT* 662–1972.

21. *BNPT* 269–1969.

22. For details of TUB Companies, see Robison 1977, Appendix B.

23. *ICN* 113, 6.11.78.

24. Ibid.

25. P. T. Irda was formed with issued capital of Rp1million, but this increased to Rp200 million when the joint venture with Weyerhauser was formed. P. T. Sula, with shareholding of Rp2.5 million became involved in joint ventures with an investment of Rp800 million. P. T. Mulawarman Bhakti (Rp1million) entered joint ventures with investments of Rp560 million and Rp662 millions. For details, see Robison 1977, Appendix B.

26. *AWSJ*, 26.10.81.

27. Robison 1977, Appendix B.

28. Kostrad Dharmaputra, *Panitia Penyusun Sejarah KOSTRAD* (Jakarta, 1973), pp. 83–7.

29. The Liem Sioe Liong group and its connections with the military and the Suharto family will be treated in some detail in Chapter 9. The Bank Windu Kencana was reportedly established by Liem in the 1950s (*Insight*, May 1978, p. 13) but was reconstituted under military ownership in 1968 (see *BNPT* 74–1968). Liem's continuing management of the bank has been frequently referred to by the Jakarta press. See especially the interview with the then director of the Bank Umum Nasional, Njoo Han Siang, in the article 'Minoritas Tjina, Pintu Kecil dan Cukong Besar',*Ekspres*, 26.7.70, in which Njoo also acknowledged the general practice of indigenous political 'protectors' operating together with Chinese capitalists in the establishment of private banks.

30. Robison 1977, Appendix B.

31. *BNPT* 3–1971. See the article, 'Propelat dan Dharsono', *Tempo*, 13.1.79.

32. 'Bintang Bintang Dalam Gelanggang Ekonomi', *Tempo* 3.2.73.

33. P. T. Promits, P. T. Prominator, P. T. Prointal (see JETRO 1981, pp. 51–2).

34. 'Suara Kontraktor', *Tempo*, 22.11.79.

35. 'Propelat dan Dharsono', *Tempo*, 13.1.79.

36. Details of many of the military companies are to be found in Robison 1977, Appendix B.

37. Crouch 1975, pp. 639–40.

38. 'Bintang Bintang Dalam Gelanggang Ekonomi', *Tempo*, 3.2.73.

39. Dick 1977, p. 167–8.

40. JETRO 1981, p. 66.

41. For details on the personal lifestyles, collection of directorships and alleged corrupt activities of some of the major entrepreneurial generals in the late 1960s see: *Nusantara*, 20.8.69, 21.6.69; *Tempo*, 8.5.71; *Operasi*, 12.4.68; *Kompas*, 11.3.68; *Sinar Harapan*, 12.5.68; *Mimbar Demokrasi*, 16.5.68.

9
The Emergence of a Capitalist Class: Chinese-Owned Capital

THE domestic capitalist class in Indonesia may be divided into a number of overlapping economic and political categories. At one level we may discriminate between a widespread, petty-capitalist strata of traders and manufacturers, and a smaller corporate sector often inter-linked with international and state capital. At another level we may distinguish between different elements of capital: financial, manufacturing, merchant, agrarian. There is also economic and political competition between individual corporate groups to influence policy, secure patronage and integrate with international and state capital. But perhaps the factor which has proven most fundamental in the development of the Indonesian capitalist class has been the deep political and social divisions between Chinese and indigenous. It is this conflict which has invaded and often subsumed the others.

Before 1965, the major contradiction inherent in the domestic capitalist class was that its economically dominant element was at the same time politically weak and socially harassed. Chinese capitalists could not translate their dominance of domestic finance and production into class dominance. In the face of pressure from a declining indigenous merchant bourgeoisie, successive governments in the 1950s imposed restrictions on Chinese importers and rural retailers under the Benteng programme and the PP10 regulations. However, despite the attempts by various governments to encourage indigenous capital, both state and private, Chinese dominance of business and commerce persisted, due largely to a structure of tightly knit family firms integrated into well-developed credit and distribution networks both within Indonesia and, for the larger Chinese business groups, throughout the Southeast Asian Region.[1]

The counter-revolution of 1965 and the new political order which subsequently emerged offered Chinese capitalists a much more favourable environment. Economic growth and rehabilitation became a priority and the government turned to those best equipped to invest capital and expand corporate activity. The re-entry of foreign capital into Indonesia was especially favourable to Chinese capitalists, who were best able to take advantage of various joint venture arrangements to expand their capital and corporate bases. Finally, the emergence of the military as the dominant political force greatly strengthened the position of a substantial number of Chinese capitalists, the so-called *cukong*, who had long been their financiers and business operatives. Now that the military controlled state economic power, it was these *cukong* who were given opportunities rapidly to expand their operations and to become the major capitalists of the Suharto era. They secured trading monopolies and privileged access to state bank credit, Bulog distributorships, BE credits, and a wide variety of contracts for the purchase and supply of materials for state corporations and projects.

While alliances with politico-bureaucrat power have continued to be an integral and necessary part of the development of Chinese capital, other factors have been crucial. First, the access of the financial and corporate networks of overseas Chinese capital in Hong Kong, Taiwan, Thailand, Singapore and Malaysia has offered the Chinese a source of finance capital and corporate partnerships not generally available to indigenous capitalists. Second, the major Chinese business groups have been able to integrate at corporate level with international capital. Both generals and international investors were attracted to Chinese capitalists because they had the necessary corporate, capital and distribution apparatus in place, and the business 'culture' essential to the making of profits. Similarly, it was because of this existing infrastructure that the larger Chinese business groups were best placed to take advantage of government policy to boost import-substitution manufacture and control foreign investment through the DSP.

POLITICAL CHALLENGES TO THE CHINESE IN THE EARLY 1970s

In this relatively favourable environment, there emerged a number of large Chinese-owned business groups with investments in manufacture, forestry, trade, shipping and transport, banking, property and construction. By the early 1970s, in the context of the continuing decline of indigenous capital increasing opposition to Bappenas policies and to relationships between the military and capital, the Chinese capitalists came under severe pressure from a variety of sources. The state was confronted with a dilemma. The Chinese capitalists were essential to economic growth and to extra-budgetary revenues for the military and politico-bureaucrats. On the other hand, the legitimacy of the New Order was threatened if it allowed itself to be portrayed as the handmaiden of Chinese business interests.

The indigenous share of domestic investment (PMDN) was, by most calculations, a minor one. *Tempo* in 1972 quoted figures which placed the Chinese share of the value of PMDN investments at 47%, the indigenous share at 38%, with 15% mixed.[2] Credit, too, was a point of contention. The militant right-wing newspaper, *Nusantara*, charged that Rp200 billion of state credit had gone to Chinese, constituting 80% of total domestic credit allocations.[3] Neither of these claims was ever publicly established, but they were generally accepted as not far from the truth and, most important in political terms, were generally believed.

Government policy-makers pointed out that Chinese economic dominance was a historical legacy — they came into the New Order with a much larger capital base and an established distribution network. The bulk of indigenous enterprises were simply not credit-worthy in normal banking terms, unable to raise the required collateral and repay loans.

But the critics rejected these explanations, focusing instead on the importance of political protection in the success of individual *cukong*. In *Nusantara* and other papers, including *Abadi, Indonesia Raya* and various student publications, attention was drawn to relationships between such political figures as General Soerjo, Mrs Suharto, Ibnu Sutowo, and various *cukong*, including Robby Cahyadi, Liem Sioe Liong, Liem Bian Hwa, Liem Bian Koen, Go Swie Kie, Ong Seng Keng and Cokrosaputra. Not only did these men receive the bulk of credit, it was claimed, but in several well-publicised cases did not repay it. The *cukong* issue was taken up by indigenous business leaders, including J. C. Tambunan, Rachmat Mulyomiseno, Sutomo and Zachri Achmad.[4]

As outlined in earlier chapters, the *cukong* question became an effective and emotional rallying point for anti-government feeling in the complex struggle of 1973/74. Despite the political weakness of indigenous capitalist critics, the government was forced to place formal restrictions upon the economic activities of Chinese for reasons of legitimacy.

Before January 1974, government policy on indigenous and Chinese capital was vague. In 1972, President Suharto announced plans for the government to buy 50%–60% of the shares of non-indigenous enterprises and transfer these to indigenous businessmen.[5] Nothing substantial came of this, and subsequent comments by the President concentrated upon exhortations to Chinese business to include indigenous participation in their investments. In the Presidential Address of 16 August 1972, Suharto argued that:

. . . non-pribumi businessmen generally possess greater capital and skill resources, therefore they have greater opportunity to make use of facilities. Because of this, it will demonstrate that harmony has now become a reality if non-pribumi work together with pribumi when making investments.[6]

Officials and ministers were hostile to using compulsion to achieve *pribumi* equity because they generally believed that the weakness of the *pribumi* was due to lack of capital, skills and a business culture, which could only be addressed by direct assistance in the form of credit and education. Hence the policy emphasis was upon the formation of government bodies to provide credit and advice and to insure indigenous borrowers.[7]

When the extent of anti-Chinese feeling became apparent in the riots in Bandung and Jakarta in 1973 and 1974, the legislation described in Chapter 5 was hastily introduced. These measures, however, did not defuse the issue. Debate continued to rage about the inadequacy of special credit packages for indigenous investors, non-compliance with the regulations concerning indigenous equity, continued structural dominance by the Chinese, and the continued operation of the *cukong* system.[8] On the ground the major contradictions remained: political pressure to contain Chinese capital was balanced by the fact that Chinese capital was essential to the general process of capital accumulation and economic growth in Indonesia and remained politically secured by indigenous patrons within the ruling politico-bureaucratic strata. The inescapable fact was that Chinese capital was strong and indigenous capital weak and the implications of a systematic attack on Chinese capital were prohibitive. It was in this environment of conflict, tension and contradiction that Chinese capitalists were to expand significantly their corporate dominance of the Indonesian economy.

GROWTH OF CHINESE CORPORATE CAPITAL UNDER THE NEW ORDER

There is insufficient data to quantify in precise terms the relative shares of capital ownership held by the state and by indigenous and Chinese private capitalists. Most commentators have held to the belief that Chinese-owned private capital retained and developed its dominance of the non-state sector. PMDN Committee Chairman, Drs. Sri Pamungkas, claimed that 25% of PMDN investments in 1974 were indigenous.[9] The Chairman of BKPM, Ir. Soehoed, also estimated the indigenous share of PMDN investments to be 25%, as did Pande R.Silalahi who argued in the CSIS journal *Analisa* that Chinese dominance would increase.[10] Christianto Wibisono, in a research project he claimed destroyed the myth of Chinese economic dominance, produced figures which showed Chinese ownership of 65.5% of private capital investment under PMDN, compared with 27% for indigenous and 7.5% for 'other'. The major point of his research was his finding that 58.75% of all PMDN investment was carried out by the state. Private Chinese investment was therefore only 27% of all PMDN.[11]

While the state is clearly crucial, particularly in large project investment, Wibisono's figures are fraught with pitfalls and unanswered questions, some of which are acknowledged by Wibisono himself. For example, loan capital is much more important than equity capital in corporate investment in Indonesia, and the larger Chinese companies now tend to raise a large proportion of their loan capital overseas, in some cases through banks which they own in Hong Kong or Singapore. This loan capital does not appear in the data used by Wibisono.

To pursue the question of relative capital ownership by Chinese further is probably neither possible nor necessary. Suffice it to say that the Chinese own, at the very least, 70%–75% of private domestic capital and that Chinese business groups continue to dominate medium and large-scale

corporate capital. The domestic capitalist class remains predominantly Chinese.

The following lists are designed to give some sense of the
extent to which Chinese capitalists have established a significant corporate presence. It shows, where possible, the size of
corporate activities, the areas into which Chinese-owned
domestic capital has moved, and relationships with international capital as well as domestic centres of politico-
bureaucrat power. I have not attempted to list them in strict
order of importance. In the comments column I have included information on political and business links, relevant
history of corporate emergence, overseas links and joint
ventures, and size of investments.[12]

In the process of corporate concentration and consolidation that is clearly occurring, two groups stand apart,
progressively increasing the distance between them and the
rest of the pack, both Chinese and indigenous. These are
Tjia Kian Liong (William Soerjadjaja) of the Astra group
and Liem Sioe Liong (Sudono Salim) of the Liem group. An
analysis of the development of these two groups provides an
insight into of the mechanics of capital accumulation by
Chinese capitalists under the New Order.

THE ASTRA GROUP

The company which is now P. T. Astra was established in
1957 by William Soerjadjaja (Tjia Kian Liong) and his
brother Ben Soerjadjaja. Under Guided Economy it proved
successful in obtaining government contracts for the import
and supply of asphalt and other materials involved in road
building and construction, and was reportedly a major supplier of materials for the large Jatiluhur dam project in West
Java. By 1965 it was already an established company with
government contacts. In 1967 a contract held by Astra for the
import of General Motors generators was cancelled by the
government, but in their stead it was offered 800 Chevrolet
trucks which Astra was reportedly able to dispose of for a

278

TABLE 9.1
MAJOR CHINESE-OWNED BUSINESS GROUPS

Name	Major Companies	Sectors of Activity	Comments
Liem Sioe Liong (Sudono Salim)	P.T. Waringin	Trade	
	P.T. Unicor Prima	Auto sole agency & assembly	See case study.
	P.T. Indo Mobil Utama	"	
	P.T. Indohero	"	
	P.T. Bogasari	Flour Milling	
	P.T. Indocement	Cement	
	Bank Central Asia	Banking	
	P.T. Mega	Clove imports	
William Soerjadjaja (Tjia Kian Liong)	P.T. Astra	Auto sole agencies & assembly	See case study.
	P.T. Multivest	Auto components manufacture	
		Property & Construction	
		Agriculture	
Tan Siong Kie (Hanafi)	P.T. Roda Mas	Foodstuffs	The *Expo* lists report him to be the largest industrialist outside the automobile and cement industries. His largest ventures are his 50% shareholdings in glass manufacture with Asahi glass. Total planned investments are $56 million of which $8.5 million is equity investment by Roda Mas (JETRO 1980, p. 10).
		Detergents	
	P.T. Tumbak Mas	Metal works	
	P.T. Asahi Mas	Sheet glass	
		Airconditioners	
	P.T. Fadjar	Electrical equipment	
	P.T. Salonpas	Pharmaceuticals	
		Television screens	

Group	Companies	Activities	Description
The Kian Siang (Bob Hasan)	P.T. Karana Line P.T. Wasesa Line P.T. Garsa Line P.T. Alas P.T. Georgia Pacific P.T. Indo Logistic P.T. Indo Nikka P.T. Pasopati	Shipping " " Forestry " Offshore drilling Chemicals	Close personal and business relations with the Diponegoro Division and Suharto family. Hasan has been discussed to some degree in Chapter 8.
Yap Swie Kie (Sutopo Jananto)	C.V. Berkat P.T. Berkat Indah Agung P.T. Indah Kiat P.T. Berkat Cahaya P.T. Shorca Mer P.T. Bridgestone Tyre	Trade Rayon fibre Pulp and paper Timber-plywood Timber-sawmilling Tyres	Close links with the military in late 1960s. Lost the Mercedes sole agency to Sutowo and the clove monopoly to Liem Sioe Liong but built his group on extensive forestry concessions. Has recently entered joint ventures with Japanese partners.
Go Swie Kie (Dasuhi Angkosubroto)	P. T. Gunung Sewu P.T. Gpadak Indah Sari P.T. Gunung Sewu Kencana P.T. Duta Anggada P.T. Mainning P.T. Bank Bumi Arta P.T. Indo Sanggar Pacific	Processing and manufacture of foodstuffs – sugar, tapioca, corn oil, biscuits, tinned food. Importer of rice and soy beans. Contracting Property development - Hayam Wuruk Plaza - Wisma Gunung Sewu - Chase Plaza Leasing	Go Swie Kie's business group is based upon its activities as an importer; distributor, warehouser of rice, sugar and other primary products. According to the *Expo* lists he has business associations with the Chase Manhattan Bank and the Philippine corporation, Ayala, and it is further claimed that he now controls Bank Niaga, formerly controlled by Soedarpo. Politically, Go has maintained very close relations with Bulog and his business success has largely been due to his success

TABLE 9.1

MAJOR CHINESE-OWNED BUSINESS GROUPS

Name	Major Companies	Sectors of Activity	Comments
			in obtaining import and distribution licences, construction and management contracts from Bulog. Offices in Singapore, HK and USA.
Go Ka Him (Dharmala Gondokusumo)	P.T. Dharma Lampung P.T. Makasindo Dharma	Export of coffee and pepper Sole agent for heavy equipment including IHI.	Closely associated with Go Swie Kie. Reported by *Expo* to be financed by the Bangkok Bank.
	P.T. Kayu Eka Ria P.T. Bank Pasar Warga Nugraha P.T. Taman Harapan Indah P.T. Putra Surya Perkasa	Forestry Banking Property development Construction	
Ong Kang Ho	P.T. Ratu Sayang P.T. Unitex	Property development and construction - Ratu Plaza Textiles	One of the major office and shopping complex developers.
Kang King Tat (Yos Soetomo)	P.T. Meranti Sakti Indah P.T. Sumber Mas Timber P.T. Meranti Sakti Timber P.T. Sumber Mas Indah	Forestry and plywood " " "	One of the largest timber groups in Indonesia. Corporate interests of the company extend to Hong Kong, Singapore and Japan. Soetomo and other

	P.T. Kayan River Timber	"	figures in the Sumber Mas group recently arrested for tax fraud of Rp4.6 billion. ($4.5 million).
	P.T. Kayan River Indah	"	
Tan Tjoe Hing (Hendra Rahardja)	P.T. Bank Harapan Santosa	Finance & banking	The Harapan group has recently been investigated for alleged non-payment of Rp17.5 billion ($17.5 million) in taxes. The Yamaha agency is the core of the operation, with 26% of the motorcycle market and annual earnings of $150 million. P.T. Yamaha Indonesia Motor, for example, has planned investments of $10.1 million of which P.T. Karya Sakti Utama has invested $1.8 million in equity. Assets and earnings of the Bank Harapan Santosa are placed at Rp24.7 billion and Rp153 million. Harapan has just built the major office/shopping complex in Jakarta (Gajah Mada Plaza) and is reported to have purchased 44% of Town and City Properties Singapore for $46.6 million and to be planning investments of $900 million in Marina City, Singapore. He is reported by *FEER* to be the biggest Singapore hotelier but running into problems financing his projects in a declining market.
	P.T. Bank Tonsea Menado	"	
	P.T. Bank Pasar Gunung	"	
	P.T. Inti Harapan	"	
	P.T. Asuransi Harapan	"	
	P.T. Cahaya Harapan	"	
	P.T. Sumber Cipta Harapan Sakti		
	P.T. Arta Buana Sakti	Property development	
	P.T. Grand Paradise	- Wisma Harapan - Gajah Mada Plaza	
	P.T. Harapan Motor Sakti	Motor cycle sole agent, assembler, components manufacture	
	P.T. Karya Sakti Utama	"	
	P.T. Yamaha Indonesia Motor		
	P.T. Cipta Logam Sakti	"	
	P.T. Pembina Logam Sakti	"	
	P.T. Yamaha Harapan Sakti	"	
	P.T. Semen Sugih Harapan	Proposed 3 million tonne cement plant in Semarang.	

TABLE 9.1

MAJOR CHINESE-OWNED BUSINESS GROUPS

Name	Major Companies	Sectors of Activity	Comments
Ong Ka Huat (Ongko Kaharuddin)	Bank Umum Nasional Bank Surya Sakti P.T. Indo Kisar	Property development and construction	Bank Umum Nasional formerly owned by PNI, then Chinese business groups close to Opsus (Njoo Han Siang). Ong has business ties to T.D. Pardede, the indigenous Sumatran businessman.
Liau Bung Kay (Lembana Ali)	Bank Umum Nasional P.T. Tektona Lembana	Property development. Other interests include a shipping office, forestry and trade.	Also from Medan and close to Ong Ka Huat.
Pho Siong Liem & Tjia Hong Tiong	P.T. Southeast Asia Bank P.T. Tripoda	Property development and construction	
Lau Bi Su (Suleiman)	P.T. Sejahtera Bank Umum P.T. Harmoni Mas	Property and construction	Other interests reportedly include corn and coffee export and textiles.
Fu Kim Mu Lim Sui Lim Budi Hartono	P.T. Bentoel P.T. Sampoerna P.T. Jarum	Clove, clove cigarettes "	Some diversification into electronics, metal manufacturing and cooking oil.

Yance Lim (Yani Haryanto)	P.T. Gunung Madu Plant	Sugar plantations and sugar mill	Reputed to have established himself as a supplier of Hankam. Involved in a scandal relating to the import of landing craft for the military in the late 1960s.
Po Tjie Guan (Murdaya Widyawimarta)	P.T. Berca	Import and installation of telecommunications facilities	Major supplier of PLN — the state electricity authority. Has also contracted for construction and installation with Singapore partners. Sole agent for airconditioners, computers.
Mirawan HS	P.T. Iradat Puri	Forestry, furniture	Large concession-holder for Sulawesi 'black timber'.
Kang Ho (Sukanto, T.)	P.T. Raja Garuda mas P.T. Bina Karpel Bank Tani Nasional	Forestry & timber processing Construction and property development	Reported to have obtained very large Pertamina projects for construction of LNG facilities.
Lie Mouk Min (Mukmin Ali) Lie Mouk Kwang Kwek Ban An	P.T. Pan Indonesia Bank P.T. Panjatex P.T. Diamond P.T. Diamond Sarana Electric	Textiles Cold storage & ice cream Electronics	Panin Bank is the second largest private bank in Indonesia. Partner with Probosutejo in P.T. Subentra.
Ciputra			President Director of P.T. Pembangunan Jaya owned predominantly by the government of Jakarta. Ciputra himself

TABLE 9.1

MAJOR CHINESE-OWNED BUSINESS GROUPS

Name	Major Companies	Sectors of Activity	Comments
			owns 2% of Pembangunan Jaya, but it is unclear what proportion of its satellite companies he owns or how many privately owned companies developed out of Pembangunan Jaya subsidiaries. Ciputra has recently taken up a $29 million share in a cold rolling mill with Liem and P.T. Krakatau Steel. His metropolitan group is a major partner of Liem in the property sector.
Ng Ke Chun (Kiesi Masrim)	P.T. Lautanluas P.T. Findeco Jaya P.T. Indonesia Acid Industries Other companies in regional capitals	Chemicals for textiles, food and beverage industries	The major chemical manufacturer. Also has interests in Singapore and Hong Kong.
Yap Tek Ciang (Mulyono Hartono)	P.T. Ippilo	Importer	P.T. Ippilo is reportedly the biggest supplier for the domestic procurement office of Pertamina. Owns Peninsular Hotel in Singapore.
Indra Wijaya	C.V. Sinar Mas	Trade	The major producer of cooking oil. *Expo'*

	P.T. Bimoli P.T. Sawit Melindo	Manufacture of cooking oil	reports that Wijaya and Liem Sioe Liong now co-operate in a monopoly on cooking oil production through joint ownership of P.T. Bimoli and P.T. Sawit Melindo.
Lim Cu Kong (Agus Nursalim)	P.T. Kedaung Setia P.T. Kedaung Subur P.T. Kedaung Medan P.T. Kedaung Raya	Glass and adhesives " Cooking oil and butter "	Probosutejo (Suharto's brother) is a 35% shareholder in Kedaung Subur, *BNPT* 103–1974. Lim also owns the Mount Elizabeth Hospital in Singapore which caters for wealthy Southeast Asians.
Lim Eng Hway (Adil Nurimba)	P.T. Gesuri Lloyd	Shipping	*Expo* reports that Gesuri Lloyd has 14 ships, of which the oldest was built in 1975. The ships are from 12 000–15 000 tons, and are estimated to cost $18–$30 million each. The newest ship is 40 000 tons. See also Howard Dick's work on Lim.
Tjai Ko Tjiang (Th.D. Rachmat)	P.T. Gudang Garam	Clove cigarettes	Holds 30% of the clove cigarette market and generated $700 million in sales and $80 million in profits in 1982/3. *Expo* produces figures to show the size of the *kretek* industry: Gudang Garam's profits amounted to almost 50% of the Indonesian government's tax receipts, and its total sales earnings were equal to one-third of the value of Indonesia's LNG exports.

TABLE 9.1

MAJOR CHINESE-OWNED BUSINESS GROUPS

Name	Major Companies	Sectors of Activity	Comments
Djamzu Papan	P.T. Putera Toppan	Printing	Linked with the business group of Sultan Hamengku Buwono.
	P.T. Pupar	Timber and paper	
		Cardboard boxes	
	P.T. Pioneer Plastic	Plastics	
	P.T. Pioneer Kimica Agung	Chemicals	
	P.T. Pioneer trading	Agent for Yanmar Diesel tractors	
Sjamsul Nursalim	P.T. Daya Patoya		Nursalim was the main figure in a recent takeover of Sultan Hamengku Buwono's Bank Dagang Nasional Indonesia reportedly in association with Panin Bank.
	P.T. Daya Madya		
	P.T. Inoue	Crumb Rubber	
	P.T. Bank Dagang Nasional Indonesia		
Masagung	P.T. Gunung Agung	Printing and retail	Also holds the lucrative Dunhill agency.
	P.T. Jaya Bali Agung	Property	
Jarry Sumendap	P.T. Porodisa	Forestry and plywood	
	P.T. Kesume Karya Jaya	Forestry and plywood	
	P.T. Bouraq	Airline	
	P.T. Porodisa Raya Shipping		
	P.T. New Porodisa Utama Equipment	Agent for Clark heavy equipment	

Name	Companies	Business	Notes
	P.T. Nusa Lease	Leasing	
	P.T. Waringin Lloyd	Insurance	
Sik Sian Han (Suhendro)	P.T. Daya Manunggal	Textiles	
	P.T. Tiga Manunggal		
Tjokrosaputra	P.T. Batik Kris	Batik and textiles	
Lie A Kiat	P.T. Madona	Sewing machines	Formerly sole agent for Suzuki motor cycles.
	P.T. Bank Perkembangan Asia		
Jauw Tjong Kie	P.T. Yasonta	Manufacture of Sharp electronic products	
Gow Bun Liong (Bun Yung)	P.T. Gajah Tunggal	Tyre manufacture	
	P.T. Daya Indonesia Paint	Paint	
	P.T. Daya Indonesia Bank		
Gow Su Ho	P.T. Sinar Ancol	Soap and detergent	
A Liang	P.T. International Chemical	ABC dry battery manuf.	
	C.V. Central Food Industrial	Foodstuffs	
	P.T. ABC Central Food Industrial	"	
Tan Seng Eng	P.T. Suptan Film	Sole importer and distributor of Mandarin films	

288

TABLE 9.1
MAJOR CHINESE-OWNED BUSINESS GROUPS

Name	Major Companies	Sectors of Activity	Comments
Jusuf Panglaykim			Panglaykim is the main economic theoretician of the CSIS group, associated with Generals Moertopo (to 1983), Hoemardani, Moertono and Murdani. He is a director and shareholder of P.T. Sejahtera Bank Umum and is associated with the Pan Asia group of companies and the Parkati group which are involved in log-carrying, manufacture of batteries and adhesives.
Mochtar Riady	P.T. Bank Central Asia		Has 17.5% share in BCA which has assets of $1.5–2.0 millions.

substantial profit.[13] Shortly afterwards Astra obtained a 60% share in the state-owned G. M. assembly plant, P. T. Gaya. In the cut and thrust politics of contract and import-licence allocation that prevailed in the late 1960s, Soerjadjaja clearly had the skill and political patronage to compete.

By the early 1970s Soerjadjaja was increasingly seen by foreign manufacturers as a valuable local business associate. He obtained the sole agencies for Toyota, Fuji Xerox, Westinghouse, Kodak and Allis Chalmers. However, he was not to remain for long simply an importer and distributor, and moved quickly into property and construction, auto assembly and heavy engineering.

The group was built around two holding companies: Astra, wholly owned by the Soerjadjaja family; and Multivest, owned by the Soerjadjaja family and members of the Astra management.[14]

The most important component of the Astra group by the mid-1970s was vehicle import, distribution and assembly. It expanded into a vertically integrated conglomerate embracing component and engine manufacture. Auto assembly and component manufacture has been one of the fastest developing of the import-substitution manufacturing fields along with textiles, nurtured not only by tariffs on imports but by government restrictions on the import of fully assembled cars as well as the imposition of minimum local content levels in local assembly operations.[15]

In 1965, this lucrative field was dominated by the following: Bachtiar Lubis — National Motors (Leyland); Suwarma — Permorin (Mercedes); Panggabean — Piola (Volkswagen); Hashim Ning — Daha (Fiat); Fritz Eman — Udatin (Holden); Indonesian Govt — Gaya (General Motors).

However, the picture quickly changed, with Ibnu Sutowo, William Soerjadjaja and, most recently, Liem Sioe Liong moving in to dominate production through their sole agency and assembly activities with Japanese car makers. By 1981 the Astra group produced 41.7% of the total vehicle production of 173 297 units, including 34.7% of commercial vehicles,

TABLE 9.2

THE ASTRA GROUP

(William Soerjadjaja and Family)

HOLDING COMPANIES
P.T. ASTRA INTERNATIONAL
P.T. MULTIVEST
(a non-banking financial institution)

AUTO ASSEMBLY &
SOLE AGENCIES
P.T. TOYOTA ASTRA
(Toyota Sole Agent)
  P.T. Astra 36%
  P.T. Gaya 15%
  Japan 40%

P.T. INTER ASTRA MOTORS
(Daihatsu Sole Agent)
  Moh. Joesoef 8%
  Sjarnubi Said 8%
  Ibnu Sutowo 9%
  P.T. Astra 50%
  William Soerjadjaja 5%
  Ben Soerjadjaja 5%
  BNPT 281–1973

P.T. MULTI ASTRA
(Toyota Assembler)
  P.T. Astra
  P.T. Multivest

P.T. GAYA MOTOR
(Daihatsu Assembler)
  Indonesian Government 40%
  P.T. Astra 60%
  BNPT 560–1973

P.T. MULTIFRANCE MOTOR
(Peugeot, Renault Sole Agent)
  P.T. Multivest 75%
  Probosutejo 25%
  BNPT 591–1973

AUTO COMPONENT
MANUFACTURE
P.T. KABAYA
  P.T. Astra 50%
  P.T. Karya Sakti Utama 10%
  Japan 40%

P.T. TOYOTA MOBILINDO
  P.T. Astra 40%
  Japan 60%

P.T. GS BATTERY
  P.T. Multivest 51%
  Japan 49%

P.T. NIPPON DENSO
  P.T. Astra 22.5%
  P.T. Multivest 22.5%
  Japan 55%

P.T. DAIHATSU
  P.T. Astra 70%
  Japan 30%

P.T. INTI GANDA PERDANA

HEAVY EQUIPMENT
P.T. UNITED TRACTORS
(Komatsu Sole Agents)

P.T. TRAKTOR NUSANTARA
(Massey Ferguson Sole Agent)

MOTOR CYCLES
P.T. FEDERAL MOTOR
(Honda Sole Agent and Assembler)
  P.T. Astra 82.5%
  Ibnu Sutowo 17.5%
  BNPT 431–1973

P.T. HONDA FEDERAL
(Honda Components)
  P.T. Federal 40%
  Japan 60%

P.T. KGD INDONESIA
(Motorcycle Electronics)
  P.T. Federal 20%
  P.T. Prospect Motor 5%
  Japan 75%

MISC. MANUFACTURE
P.T. SURYA
(Trading and Engineering)
  P.T. Gading Mas 25%
  P.T. Astra 75%
  BNPT 923–1973

P.T. SILGA
(Metal Works)
  Sjarnubi Said 50%
  P.T. Astra 50%
  BNPT 426–1973

TABLE 9.2
THE ASTRA GROUP
(William Soerjadjaja and Family)

PROPERTY & CONSTRUCTION
P.T. INDONESIALAND
 P.T. Astra 33%
 P.T. Multivest 34%
  33%
 P.T. Indobuildco. 33%
  (Sjarnubi Said)
  (Ibnu Sutowo)
 BNPT 750–1973

P.T. MULTILAND

P.T. TOWN AND CITY
 P.T. Multivest 47.5%
 P.T. Indophing 47.5%
 BNPT 926–1973

P.T. WISMA HEGARMANAH

P.T. SUNGAI DELTA

ROAD BUILDING
P.T. NATIONAL ROADBUILDER

P.T. LEIGHTON INDONESIA

P.T. NUSA RAYA CIPTA

LEASING
P.T. WARDLEY SUMMA
 P.T. United Tractor
 Wardley Ltd HK
 Summa Int. HK

TRADE
P.T. RAMA SURYA INT.

P.T. LINDETEVES

P.T. JAYA PURISA

P.T. WINDUSURJA
(Sole Agent of Kodak)

P.T. ASTRA GRAPHIA
(Sole Agent of Fuji Xerox)

P.T. MIDAS OIL

BANKING
P.T. INDO COMMERCIAL BANK

P.T. BANK MALBOR

P.T. BANK UMUM BANTU

P.T. SUMMA INTERNATIONAL

FORESTRY
P.T. MULTI FOREST

P.T. UNI RIMBA

AGRICULTURE
P.T. MULTI AGRO
(Cassava)

P.T. HARAPAN TANI BHAKTI

P.T. HUMA INDAH MEKAR
(Cassava)

P.T. TUNGGAL PERKASA
(Oil Palm)

P.T. TAPOS

P.T. HORTINDO

JAMBI WARAS GROUP
(Crumb Rubber)

FISHING
P.T. INDEKS MINA

P.T. SINAR ABADI CEMERIANG

P.T. SAFCOL INDONESIA
(Tuna Canning)
J V Australia

Sources: BNPT where indicated; BKPM company investment approvals in. JETRO 1981; ICN 80 (27.6.77), 180 (31.8.81), 181 (14.9.81), 213 (10.1.83); AWSJ, 10.12.81; Expo 2, 18.1.84, p. 25; Tempo, Apa dan Siapa, 1984.

60.5% of passenger vehicles and 70.7% of multi-purpose vehicles.[16] To complement these vehicle assembly activities, Astra developed a strong grip on the components industry and on the assembly of motor cycles (Honda) and heavy equipment (Komatsu).

Astra's rise to prominence in the industry is due to a complex variety of factors. Sid Astbury in *Asian Business* emphasised Astra's attractiveness to foreign manufacturers as a reliable and efficient domestic partner. But corporate efficiency is only one aspect of the equation. Potential local partners must first possess the capacity to obtain the sole agency, a much sought after political benefice, and to distribute the products effectively, largely through contracts for supply to the government. Securing the government contract for the import of 800 Chevrolet trucks and then securing a 60% share of the Gaya assembly plant were clear indications that Soerjadjaja had the political backing and the plant to be a serious local partner. In the late 1960s he was approached by Toyota to become their local partner in import and assembly.

Political connections have been necessary where access to licences and contracts are so important. The very structure of Soerjadjaja's corporate holdings show that he has been able to work closely with powerful politico-bureaucrats. Among his business partners in the early 1970s was Ibnu Sutowo, while the Suharto group has been associated with him throughout the New Order period. Sutowo, Sjarnubi Said and Moh. Joesoef were partners in the Daihatsu sole agent, P. T. Inter Astra Motors, and the Honda motor cycle sole agent and assembler, P. T. Federal, as well as the engineering works, P. T. Silga and P. T. Surya. Apart from these joint ventures, Soerjadjaja joined with Sutowo in a major foray into property and construction through P. T. Indonesialand and P. T. Town & City. Soerjadjaja's shares in the Sutowo holding company, P. T. Indophing, also gave him equity in such firms as the Mercedes and Volkswagen assembler, P. T. Star Motors.

It is doubtful whether much of this business alliance has

survived Sutowo's gradual slide after 1975/76. Soerjadjaja himself indicated that he lost substantially on the property ventures, implying that these investments may no longer exist.[17] Nevertheless, such an economic/political alliance was crucial in the early and mid-1970s when Sutowo controlled the major source of government contracts for supply and construction.

The alliance between Soerjadjaja and the Palace, although widely discussed in Jakarta, is much less tangible. In corporate terms, it exists in the Peugeot and Renault sole agent, P. T. Multifrance Motors, which is a joint venture between P. T. Multivest and Probosutejo, the President's brother. Despite its low levels of production it was able to survive the cuts involved in the government's 1980 nationalisation of the industry.

Perhaps most interesting is Soerjadjaja's relationship with the Department of Industry, where policy relating to the auto industry and to the allocation of sole agencies is made. Ir. Suhartoyo, the Director General of this Department throughout the 1970s (and since 1983 head of BKPM) has also long been a *komisaris* of P. T. Astra.

A second factor in the rise of the Astra group has been access to investment finance. To a certain extent we must assume that early accumulation was assisted by access to government contracts for supply and licences for import. No doubt Astra was also able to gain access to other networks of credit which extended from Hong Kong to Singapore among the overseas Chinese. However, one thing is clear — once in joint venture with the big Japanese manufacturers, finance became no problem. Astra's move into large-scale automobile manufacture was made possible by the ability of the Japanese partner to raise the bulk of the investment through loans. A brief glance at the investment data of some of Astra's auto ventures will illustrate this. Out of a total investment of $138 223 000 in the companies listed below, Astra was required to provide only $9 063 000, or 6.6%.

TABLE 9.3
INVESTMENT DATA — SELECT ASTRA GROUP AUTO COMPANIES

Company	Indonesian Equity	Japanese Equity	Loan
P. T. Daihatsu Indonesia (components)	$1 050 000	$450 000	$4 000 000
P. T. Honda Federal (motor cycle components)	$1 200 000	$1 800 000	$2 005 000
P. T. Kayaba (components)	$1 200 000	$1 800 000	$7 500 000
P. T. KGD (electronics)	$1 050 000	$3 150 000	$5 886 000
P. T. Nippon Denso (auto electrics)	$675 000	$825 000	$3 000 000
P. T. Toyota Astra (sole agent)	$1 088 000	$1 044 000	$75 000 000
P. T. Toyota Mobilindo (components)	$2 800 000	$4 200 000	$18 500 000
	$9 063 000 6.6%	$13 269 000 9.6%	$115 891 000 83.8%

Source: BKPM investment approvals listed in: JETRO 1981.

However, as the Astra group was developed, it has accumulated a larger capital base and a capacity to both provide its own equity capital and raise its own loans. Even though the 6.6% figure mentioned in the above table is relatively small, it does represent an outlay of over $9 million, a figure well out of the range of any domestic companies a decade ago. In 1981 the Astra group made a profit of $54 million on sales of $986 million, indicating a healthy basis for capital formation but one which needed considerable additional loan capital. Astra's finance director, B. L. Tan, estimated Astra's outstanding borrowing at $326 million in 1980.[18] These needs were well beyond the scope of the domestic capital market, particularly in view of the credit ceiling on lending by domestic banks. Tan explained, however, that:

. . . even without the ceiling . . . the availability of Rp. is very thin. There's only about $13 billion of rupiah in circulation. If we wanted to borrow only $500 million in Rupiah that would be a big chunk of the total available.[19]

Astra has therefore gone overseas to raise its finance, establishing the finance bank, Summa International Finance, in Hong Kong. In 1982 Summa International, together with Wardley of Hong Kong, made a $25 million floating loan rate Asia dollar issue on the Singapore market to raise capital for the heavy equipment leading firm, P. T. Wardley-Summa. It would also appear that Astra now has little difficulty in raising finance on the international finance market, particularly through US banks.[20]

Once inside the auto assembly and components industry, Astra has benefited heavily from protective policies. Restrictions on import of components and of fully assembled vehicles, through tariffs, quotas and prohibitions, has given rise to the domestic components and assembly industries. Astra has also done well out of rationalisation programmes. In April 1980, the Directorate of Basic Industries cut into the 22 auto sole agents and 20 assemblers representing 57 makes and 140 models which constituted the auto industry at that time. Of the eight groups of sole agents/assemblers that survived, Astra controlled two: Toyota and Daihatsu. As a further development of vertical integration, the government now began to require Japanese manufacturers and local partners to move into engine manufacture. Astra are consequently involved in two of the five (possibly six) new engine plants which look like being the future basis of the Indonesian auto industry. Latest figures indicate that Astra will be involved in a Daihatsu plant with a planned investment of $80 million and a Toyota plant with a planned investment of $110 million.[21] It would appear from early figures that once again the foreign loan component will constitute the bulk of the investment.[22]

As far as future expansion is concerned, Astra is concentrating on deepening and consolidating the vertical integration of its auto interests with investments in the components and parts industry to the value of at least Rp46 billion ($57 million).[23] Apart from this, William Soerjadjaja has expressed the belief that the future lies in agro-business and has invested in estate cultivation of cassava and palm oil. One report predicts that up to 35% of Astra's investments will eventually be located in agriculture.[24]

While Soerjadjaja has been able to take full advantage of policies of protection and subsidy for import-substitution manufacture, he has also avoided many of the restrictions placed upon Chinese business. Policies to limit allocation of state-bank credit to indigenous capitalists appear to have been irrelevant to the processes of financing adopted by Astra. Nor is there any indication that Astra has been forced to divest any of its shares to indigenous partners as required by the 1974 legislation. In the years since the New Order came to power, Soerjadjaja has established a substantial corporate and capital base, close corporate partnerships with Japanese auto manufacturers and an organisation able to cope with the managerial and productive tasks of heavy engineering manufacture. It is these capital and corporate resources that now form the basis of his economic power, while the process of capital accumulation is the engine of the group's economic expansion.

THE LIEM GROUP

Not much is known of Liem's early career. Born in China in 1916, he arrived in the Central Javanese *kretek* (clove cigarette) manufacturing town of Kudus in 1936 to join his elder brother, Liem Sioe Hie, in a peanut oil trading business. He subsequently expanded into the clove trade as a supplier for the local *kretek* factories. By 1945 it would appear that his enterprises had expanded considerably because he was able to establish close connections with the Republican forces as a supplier of foodstuffs, clothing and medicines, and, according to one report, arms.

Liem's association with the Diponegoro Division in Cen-

tral Java grew out of these activities and continued into the
1950s when Suharto was Commander and Soedjono Hoemardani was Financial Assistant. In addition to his trading
activities in this period, Liem expanded into manufacture
(textiles, soap, nails, bicycle parts) and successfully established himself as a supplier of the Indonesian Army. In the
early 1950s he established the Bank Windu Kencana and
followed this in 1957 with purchase of the Bank Central Asia.
When Suharto came to power in 1965, Liem already presided
over an established and varied business group and had an
established history of association with the now dominant
Diponegoro Division and with Suharto himself.[25]

The Structure of the Liem Group Under the New Order

The Liem group has been able to take advantage of
policies designed to protect and nurture domestic capitalists,
particularly in import substitution, because of its capacity to
secure monopolies and access to the financial and organisational resources of international capital. But the Liem
group can no longer be regarded as a client or comprador
group hanging onto the coat-tails of Indonesian generals and
foreign bankers; it is a major regional and international
financial and industrial group with a substantial capital base.

The Liem group's onshore interests illustrate the significance of the politico-economic alliances discussed earlier.

(a) It is clear that joint ventures with foreign partners
     have been a crucial factor in the development of the
     group. In the larger industrial ventures, including the
     initial cement plant and the auto engine plant, foreign
     partners have been essential. In property, construc-
     tion and finance, Liem has also integrated with exist-
     ing international and regional groups. Apart from
     equity capital provided by foreign partners, the larger
     Liem projects have been dependent upon securing
     large amounts of finance from international banks.

TABLE 9.4
THE LIEM GROUP (INDONESIAN-BASED COMPANIES)

Trade	Automobile Distribution & Assembly	Manufacture	Property & Construction	Finance	Logging, Timber & Miscellaneous
P.T. WARINGIN KENCANA	P.T. NATIONAL MOTORS Partly owned by Liem Hino & Mazda Sole Agents	P.T. MULTIATEX (Textiles)	PROPERTIES: P.T. METROPOLITAN KENCANA Liem 50%	BANK WINDU KENCANA	P.T. KAYU LAPIS MURNI (Plywood)
P.T. WARINGIN KENCANA Liem 85% Sudwikatmono 5% Risjad 5% Bambang Tirtomuljono 5% BNPT 275–1970		P.T. INDAH KENCANA (Nails)		BANK CENTRAL ASIA Liem 24.0% Mochtar Riady 17.5% Sigit 16.0% Siti 16.0% Maryono 11.0% M. Thahir 8.5% Sumarjo 7.0%	P.T. DONO INDAH (Logging)
	P.T. UNICOR PRIMA Partly owned by Liem Hino & Mazda Assemblers	P.T. INDARA MAS (Bicycle Tyres)	P.T. WISMA METROPOLITAN Liem 25% HK & Sing. Partners 75%		P.T. OVERSEAS TIMBER PRODUCTS CORPORATION (Logging)
		Rubber refineries in Palembang and Jambi			
P.T. PERMANENT		P.T. TARUMATEX (Textiles)	P.T. METROPOLITAN DEVELOPMENT	P.T. MULTIFINANCE CORPORATION BCA 27.5% Foreign Investors 62.5%	INDACO LTD (Tin Mining) Liem Australia CSR
P.T. MEGA (Clove Imports)	P.T. INDO MOBIL UTAMA Suzuki Sole Agents & Assemblers	P.T. PANGAN SARI UTAMA (Food Processing)	P.T. JAKARTA LAND Hong Kong 25% Singapore 25% Liem 25% Jaya group 25%		
P.T. ARIMONO Liem 75% Sudwikatmono 25% BNPT 768–1973	P.T. CENTRAL SOLE AGENCY Volvo Sole Agents	P.T. BOGASARI (Flour Milling) Liem 67.6% Djuhar 24.4%		CENTRAL ANTAR JASA (Insurance Broking)	
P.T. HANURATA	P.T. SALIM JAYA		P.T. GREEN LAND	P.T. CENTRAL SARI	

(ISMAC)
Volvo Assemblers

P.T. HARAPAN MOBIL
NUSANTARA
Ford Distributors

P.T. INDOHERO
*Suzuki Motorcycle
Assemblers*

Risjad 4.0%
Sudwikatmono 4.0%
BNPT 258-1970

P.T. INDONESIA
CEMENT
Liem 45%
Djuhar 45%
Sudwikatmono 5%
Risjad 5%
BNPT 273-1974

P.T. DISTINCT
INDONESIA CEMENT
ENTERPRISE
Indocement 56%
HK Investors 44%

P.T. PERKASA
CEMENT

P.T. PERKASA AGUNG
UTAMA CEMENT

P.T. PERKASA INDAH
CEMENT PUTIH

P.T. PERKASA INTI
ABADI CEMENT

P.T. JAYA BALI
AGUNG

P.T. JAYA MANDARIN
AGUNG
(Mandarin Hotel)
Liem 40%
Hong Kong 60%

P.T. AGUNG UTAMA
PERMAI

P.T. PERWICK AGUNG
Liem 25%
Hong Kong 75%

P.T. ASIA
NUSANTARA

P.T. KABELE ASIA
NUSANTARA
Liem 25%
Hong Kong 75%

CONSTRUCTION:
P.T. CENTRAL SARI
INT. BUILDERS

P.T. NUGRAHA
KENCANA JAYA

METROPOLITAN
LEASING

P.T. ASSURANSI
CENTRAL ASIA
Liem
P.T. Gesurilloyd

P.T. ASSWANSI JAVA
CENTRAL ASIA RAYA
Liem
P.T. Gesurilloyd

TABLE 9.4

THE LIEM GROUP (INDONESIAN-BASED COMPANIES)

Trade	Automobile Distribution & Assembly	Manufacture	Property & Construction	Finance	Logging, Timber & Miscellaneous
		P.T. TRIDAYA MANUNGGAL PERKASA	P.T. CAHAYA TUGU KENCANA		
		Liem group			
		Sahid group			
		Jaya group	P.T. CENTRAL SALIM BUILDERS		
		P.T. KRAKATAU COLD ROLLING MILL	P.T. RIMBA KENCANA		
		Liem 40%	Liem 25%		
		Krakatau Steel 40%			
		Jaya group 20%	P.T. BUDHI AGUNG		
			Liem 50%		

Sources: BNPT – indicated in chart; Insight (HK), May 1978;
ICN 134–24.9.79, 162–17.11.80, 166–26.1.81, 179–18.8.81, 201–5.7.82, 202–19.7.82, 203–9.8.82; 'Dulu Rockefeller Kini Taipan Liem and Liem & Partner di Krakatau Steel, Tempo, 2.7.83 and 9.7.83; Rowley, 'Birth of a Multinational', FEER, 7.4.83; Habir and Rowley, 'The Extended (Corporate) Family of Liem Sioe Liong', FEER, 7.4.83.

The group also relies heavily on foreign management for the technical side of its operations. Nihon Cement and Taiwan Cement manage Indocement; US Steel manages the Krakatau Cold Rolling Steel Mill. It must also be kept in mind that the initial investments in the large cement and steel projects are largely for supply and installation of technical equipment and construction by foreign contractors.

(b) Liem has also developed a broad range of partnerships with domestic private and public business groups including the state-owned Krakatau Steel, the Ciputra/(Metropolitan) property construction manufacturing group, Sukamdani's Sahid group, and the declining auto assembler, National Motors, formerly owned by the Lubis family.

(c) The political and economic alliance between the Liem group, the Suharto family and Kostrad is also manifested in the concrete form of business partnerships. The President's step-brother, Sudwikatmono (Waringin, Indocement, Bogasari), and a son and daughter of the President, Sigit and Siti (Bank Central Asia), are among Liem's business partners.

The Liem Group's Early Trading Interests

The first step in the development of domestic business groups in Indonesia has traditionally been in the field of trade, where big killings could be made if monopolies could be secured. Similarly, the expansion of the Liem group after 1965 was initially focused upon the development of its existing trading interests through the acquisition of new and lucrative monopolies and preferential access to licences. The trading companies Waringin and Waringin Kencana, which were operated in partnership with Sudwikatmono and Bambang Tirtomuljono, an associate of the Suharto family, were the vehicles for such expansion. Waringin developed rapidly, particularly in the coffee and rubber export trade, with the aid of large government credits and export licences far in excess of its formal quota. It was mentioned by the Presidential Commission of Inquiry into Corruption (the Commission of Four) as one of the five cases requiring priority investigation, but the matter was never publicly pursued. However, the most lucrative monopoly secured by Liem was in the clove trade. In 1968 the government decided to restrict the import of cloves to two companies — P. T. Mercu Buana, owned by the President's brother Probosutejo, and P. T. Mega, owned by Liem.[26] Because of the large *kretek* industry in Indonesia, the clove trade is substantial, totalling US$60.9 million in 1980 and US$120.1 million in 1981. According to the terms of the monopolies, Liem and Probosutejo take a 5% handling fee and deposit the profits with the state as non-budgetary revenue for special projects. It was from the activities of Waringin and Mega that the capital base of the Liem group began to be formed.[27]

Automobiles

Perhaps the most lucrative trading activities were sole distributorships for imported technology and automobiles. After 1965, the old sole agency holders were quickly expropriated or marginalised, being absorbed or ousted by a new set of sole agents: Ibnu Sutowo and Sjarnubi Said from Pertamina (Mitsubishi and Mercedes), Kostrad's Yayasan Dharma Putra (Volkswagen), William Soerjadjaja (Toyota, Daihatsu), Probosutejo (Renault, Peugeot, Chevrolet), and Wahab Affan (Nissan). Propelled and protected by government policy and sustained by foreign partners, those licenceholders were transformed into assemblers and eventually manufacturers of components and engines.

Liem was a late entrant into an automobile sector increasingly concentrated in a few hands, but has nevertheless been able to secure a fair slice of the market as assembler and sole agent for Hino, Mazda, Suzuki and Volvo, absorbing the old National Motors, formerly a Lubis/Leyland joint venture, along the way. Most recently, in partnership with Hino Motors and Sumitomo, Liem has secured a licence to build Indonesia's sixth engine plant, with a planned investment of $33.32 million.[28]

Manufacture

It is in the field of manufacture that the Liem group has made its most spectacular advances. Nurtured by government policies which protect, subsidise and finance domestic manufacture, import-substitution industrialisation has proceeded apace in Indonesia, to the advantage of a relatively small group of domestic capitalists able to gain the licences, credit and contracts for supply to the massive government resource, construction and industrial projects.

Liem's general manufacturing activities, particularly in textiles, experienced healthy growth in the late 1960s and early 1970s, aided by government contracts for supply.[29] By 1979 P.T. Tarumatex had an authorised capital of Rp 4 billion (US$6 400 000 approx. at 1979 exchange rates), and loans of Rp 7.7 billion (US$12 320 000 approx. at 1979 exchange rates), of which Rp 9.6 billion were loans from government banks.[30] However, it is in flour milling and cement that the heart of the Liem manufacturing empire now lies.

In 1969 the government decided to establish a flour milling capacity in Indonesia and licensed two companies, P. T. Prima (Singapore owned) and P. T. Bogasari, to begin milling operations. By 1983, Bogasari had secured effective control of the US$400 million per year Indonesian flourmarket, by means set out in Chapter 7. This monopoly had been made possible in general terms by the use of state power to determine the allocation of licences, and in specific terms by Liem's alliance with the Suharto/Kostrad political faction.[31]

Liem has concentrated on cement manufacturing and now produces 38% of Indonesian cement. The cement industry has developed within a framework of state protection, and demand has been generated by the state's extensive investments in infrastructure, resource and industrial projects through the development budget. At the heart of Liem's cement interests is P. T. Indocement, owned 45% by the Liem family, 45% by the Djuhar family, 5% by Sudwikatmono and 5% by Risjad. Indocement operates five cement companies.

TABLE 9.5
INVESTMENT AND PRODUCTION OF THE INDOCEMENT
GROUP, 1980

	Capacity (tons p.a.)	Investment (in US$ mill.)
P. T. Distinct Indonesia Cement	1 000 000	$115
P. T. Perkasa Indonesia	2 000 000	$188
P. T. Perkasa Agung Utama	1 500 000	$219
P. T. Perkasa Indah Cement Putih	200 000	$40
P. T. Perkasa Inti Abadi	1 500 000	$268

Source: ICN 166, 26.1.81.

In addition, Indocement has entered a joint venture with the Sahid group (Sukamdani) and the Metro group (Ciputra) to establish a US$290 million cement plant, P. T. Tridaya Manunggal Perkasa.[32] It has also recently taken over 60% of P. T. Semen Madura, one of the former state-owned plants transfered to the private sector.

The movement of the Liem group into the cement industry clearly demonstrates its development beyond a stage where it can be dismissed as either a comprador business group or simply a speculator in politically derived concessions. While Liem's dominance in the cement industry would not have been possible without either political patronage or integration with international capital, at least in the initial stages (Distinct Cement was originally 44% Hong Kong owned), the group is clearly built upon the accumulation and investment of capital and the raising of investment finance on the international finance market. For example, P. T. Tridaya Manunggal Perkasa was established with a US$97 million dollar equity investment by the domestic partners and US$193 million borrowed mainly from international sources. We may assume the structure of investments in the other cement works to be similar.

In the case of the Liem group it would appear that the windfall profits derived from the monopolies secured through its political connections, Waringin, Mega and Bogasari in particular, have formed the basis of the group's capital accumulation. In the case of the cement industry, the relations between capital and state are built less upon personal political favours and more on the general state policies designed to develop a national import-substitution manufacturing sector and a strong domestic capitalist class, including protection, provision of infrastructure, cheap inputs of electricity, and access to factory sites at Cibinong, close to raw materials, markets and highways.

The most recent industrial venture by the Liem group has confirmed its capacity to mobilise large capital resources, to raise finance on the international market and to tackle complex projects. Together with the state-owned Krakatau Steel and the Metropolitan group of Ciputra, it has planned a US$800 million steel rolling mill for which US$218 million is to be borrowed from international banks, US$334 million in export credits from France and Spain (French and Spanish consortiums are to build the mill), US$100 million provided by the state though P. T. Krakatau Steel, US$25 million provided by the state bank BNI 1946, and the remaining US$213 million presumably equity investment by Liem and Metro.[33]

The Liem group is the first private domestic business group to develop the capacity to move into the larger and more complex manufacturing areas such as cement and steel. Previously only the state was able to mobilise the resources for such investments but, true to its stated policies, it is now facilitating the entry of private business groups as they develop their capital base and corporate structure, and as these areas of investment become more profitable.

Property and Construction

The Liem group has demonstrated a similar explosive expansion in the field of property and construction. The list of property and construction holdings in Table 9.4 is self explanatory, but there are a few points worth emphasising. First, the group's property ventures are becoming increasingly large. In addition to the Wisma Metropolitan and the Mandarin Hotel, the group is planning two new large buildings involving investments of US$52 million and US$88 million through P. T. Perwick Agung and P. T. Kabele Asia Nusantara respectively.[34] Second, the Liem property and construction activities further illustrate the capacity of the group to integrate with large property and construction groups in Southeast Asia as well as with influential domestic political and business partners. Liem's partners in Jakarta land and the Metropolitan companies include the Metropolitan group of Ciputra, head of the Jaya group of companies owned by the government of Jakarta, the authority responsible for the zoning of property and the licensing of building projects.

Finance

The earliest venture into banking by the Liem family was the establishment of the Bank Windu Kencana in 1954, followed in 1957 by the Bank Central Asia which was to become the flagship of Liem's financial interests.[35] After 1965 these banks underwent some reorganisation, with the Bank Windu Kencana reappearing as a military-owned bank, with ownership shared by 'foundations' attached to Kostrad, the Jakarta military command, and with a directorate including the Personal Presidential Assistants, Generals Alamsjah and Hoemardani, and the Financial Assistant of Kostrad, General Soerjo.[36] Reportedly the bank is still managed by Liem but it is relatively small. The bank at the core of the Liem group is the Bank Central Asia (BCA), which is now owned 24% by the Liem family, 17.5% by Mochtar Riady, formerly associated with the Panin Bank, and 32% by Sigit and Siti. Being integrated into the largest private industrial and financial network in Indonesia, it has expanded rapidly and is now the largest private, domestically owned bank, with assets of US$277 million and a string of subsidiary interests, including insurance companies and a financial institution (P. T. Multicor) in partnership with foreign interests.

Despite the importance of these financial operations, in comparison with other private domestic banking groups, they are, as Anthony Rowley observed in the *Fareastern Economic Review*, clearly insufficient to support the financial needs of the Liem group. It would appear that the group finances its activities in four ways:

(a) The use of BCA for daily banking needs for flour and cement distribution.

(b) The use of equity funds generated by windfall profits from the flour and cloves monopolies and from the profits of other investments.

(c) The attraction of large-scale credit from international banks for major industrial projects, sometimes in the form of export credit. Contracts for supply and construction, which are the major components of the industrial and resource projects, are usually dependent upon the major foreign tenderers being able to arrange a substantial proportion of the finance.

(d) Informal credit networks linking major overseas Chinese business groups in Southeast Asia. No precise data is available on this, but Bangkok Bank chief executive Boonchu Rojanastien, in an interview with *Insight*, claimed that the Bangkok Bank was able to support ten or fifteen Southeast Asian business tycoons, including Robin Loh of Singapore and Liem Sioe Liong, to build up their empires.[37] However, the traffic was not all one way. In a previous issue, *Insight* reported that: 'The Bangkok Bank's chairman is said

to be indebted to Liem for secretly covering a US$20
million shortfall on foreign exchange dealings some
years ago, since when they have remained very
close.'[38]

The Liem Group's Offshore Interests

Over the past five years the Liem group has expanded its
interests overseas and now ranks as a major regional business
group. It has not chosen to compete internationally with the
capital-intensive industrial investments of established
MNCs, but to compete in trade and finance.[39] Its success in
several fields has been rapid and considerable. The *International Investor* ranked Liem as one of the twelve richest
bankers in the world, and estimated his assets in excess of
US$1 billion.[40]

The offshore corporate structure (Table 9.6) is built
around two pillars, trade and finance. The details of the
formation of the offshore group are well covered in Rowley's
article, but the points that concern us here are the size of the
overseas operation and the reasons for Liem's move offshore. The ultimate holding company of the First Pacific
group is First Pacific Investments, 30% owned by Liem, 30%
by Djuhar Sutanto (his long-time business partner, Liem
Oen Kian), 10% by Anthony Salim (Liem's son — Liem
Fung Seng), 10% by Tedy Djuhar, 10% by Sudwikatmono
and 10% by Risjad. First Pacific Holdings (FPH) and First
Pacific Finance (FPF) were formed from small and ailing
companies and transformed into the vehicles for the building
of an extensive network of enterprises in finance and trade.
FPH was able to make a recent US$113 million rights issue to
fund the acquisition of the California bank, Hibernia, while
FPH has grown from a small quasi-bank with assets of
HK$10 million to a merchant bank and commercial, trade-
finance bank with assets of HK$832 million, and its capital
has been boosted to more than HK$100 million. The two
most recent and notable investments by the First Pacific

TABLE 9.6

OFFSHORE INTERESTS OF THE LIEM GROUP

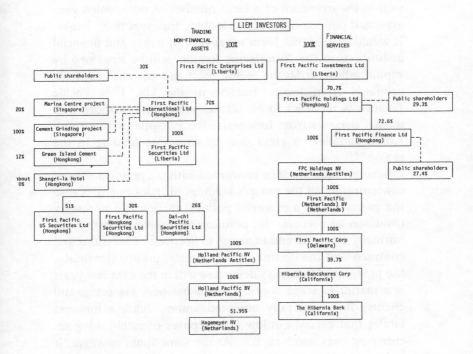

Source: FEER, 7.4.83, p. 46.

group have been the Hibernia Bank and Hagemeyer, involving outlays of US$113.6 million plus an extra US$35 million injection of funds for Hibernia and US$18.6 million for Hagemeyer.[41]

The most obvious point to be made is that the operations of the Liem group in Indonesia have produced sufficient profits for the group to make significant investments in international trade and finance, buying up long-established European and US companies in the process. Why has Liem moved offshore, given the obvious profitability and apparently endless opportunities in Indonesia? A primary reason is that it is now also profitable to operate in finance banking in

the Southeast Asia region, given the rapid emergence of a
substantial capitalist class (largely Chinese) in the region as
well as the existence of a large number of well-heeled generals and politico-bureaucrats looking for investment banks.
It would appear that Liem's 'network of banks and financial
institutions in the Asia-Pacific Region' will be sustained by
capital inflows from the region itself and not necessarily or
primarily from Japan, Europe or the US. First Pacific
Finance is reported to be taking 'substantial offshore (US
dollar) deposits from Indonesia, the Philippines and South
Korea and does a great deal of corporate lending in the
region'.[42]

Second, Liem must be concerned with the political risks of
concentrating all the group's holdings in Indonesia. Because
the patronage of a powerful political faction is a necessary
condition of success, the political demise of a patron has
normally meant an end to access to licences, concessions and
contracts and the decline of the business group. Obviously,
the prospect of Suharto's departure within the next few years
is a matter of some concern to his business associates and
clients. It is generally accepted among Jakarta business
circles that capital outflow for purposes of establishing secure nest eggs is substantial. At the same time, however, it
is important not to overestimate the significance of this in
explaining the Liem group's movement offshore. It is relatively easy for new political leaders to withdraw political
favours from clients of the previous regime and transfer them
to their own business associates when the favours are little
more than trading monopolies, forestry concessions or government contracts. But when the client operates a business
empire which measures its investments (including investments in capital stock) in hundreds of millions of dollars, and
has established extensive and complex financial relationships
with international capital, he is much less easily disposed of.
More important, it is unlikely that Liem could be replaced
without fundamental damage to the coherence of the group
or to its independent corporate elements. A new President

may hesitate to tamper with a business empire which has become a significant component of the Indonesian economy. A more likely scenario upon the retirement of Suharto is the gradual replacement of his family members as shareholders in Liem companies by the family members and political associates of the new President. In this sense the development of the Liem group (and four or five lesser groups) over the past eighteen years represents the beginnings of a fundamental change in the balance of power between a governing class of politico-bureaucrats and a domestic capitalist class.

We must remember, however, that Liem is a Chinese Indonesian capitalist and, as such, is subject to a variety of pressures and resentments from the indigenous community, especially the declining elements of indigenous trading and manufacturing capitalists. The volatility of the race issue has been demonstrated with considerable frequency in the form of anti-Chinese violence, the most recent of which occurred in Central Java in 1980. Although the Liem group appears to have avoided the requirements of the 1974 regulations concerning equity transfer, the uncertainty of Indonesian politics means that Chinese business groups are never sure when the government may feel obliged or inspired to enforce them more strictly.

In the case of Liem, the expansion offshore has not simply been one of money in Swiss or Singapore banks, but a redirection of capital investment and corporate growth outside Indonesia. This is not only a reflection of the increasing maturity of the Liem group as corporate capitalists but reflects the very real pressures placed upon domestic corporate groups to expand into the international arena. Decisions about production, financing and marketing are now most effectively made on an international basis. The Liem group has developed to the point where it is now able to assume a corporate control over its trading activities from collection in Indonesia to distribution in Europe and North America.[43]

The Liem group's offshore holdings may be divided into three areas. One embraces industrial investment projects, such as the Singapore and Hong Kong cement projects, which represent the pursuit of profits through production in foreign markets. This is not a major element because there remains considerable opportunity for this sort of investment, at very high rates of profit, within Indonesia. The central thrust of Liem's move overseas has been trade and finance. Liem has long been involved in international trade, and the purchase of 51% of Hagemeyer, which is already active in exporting Indonesian coffee and other primary products to Europe and US, provides him with an established international corporate trading infrastructure into which he can feed his exporting and importing activities at present handled by a variety of companies. Hagemeyer therefore represents a rationalisation of the Liem international trading interests on an international scale.

The purchase of the Californian bank, Hibernia, also contributes to the rationalisation of the international trading activities of the group. At present the financing of Hagemeyer's and the Liem group's trade with the US is done by US banks, but this will be taken over by Hibernia. Therefore the full range of the US trade, including financing through letters of credit, will be integrated into the Liem empire. Hibernia also handles the US$330 million per year wheat imports to Indonesia destined for Bulog and thence Bogasari, effectively consolidating the wheat/flour sector.[44] In addition to trade financing, Liem's move into international finance has potential for plugging into the large state resource and industrial projects within Indonesia. As mentioned earlier, the financing of these projects has largely been undertaken by international banks and financial institutions. The mobilisation of finance is also closely related to access to the massive contracts for supply and construction which constitute the bulk of the investment. We know that Liem and his son Anthony were actively involved in an attempt to organise international finance for the US$800 million Dumai hydrocracker, backing a consortium of Taiwanese, Spanish and Austrian banks, together with Spanish contractors, all of whom were involved in the financing and construction of Liem's P. T. Perkasa Cement plant. Liem's participation was reportedly at the behest of Suharto himself, who was anxious that the slow progress be expedited, and was to be implemented through a Hong Kong company, Hebrides Investments Ltd., which was to act as a channel for the investment of the consortium.[45] As it turned out, the Indonesian government itself underwrote the cost of the project.

But the point remains that Indonesia's increasing need for international commercial investment finance has created an opportunity for the formation of an Indonesian-owned international finance and banking group. From the point of view of Indonesia's economic planners, the Dumai experience would indicate that such a group is regarded as a valuable instrument in organising international finance for Indonesian resource and manufacturing projects. Minister of Trade Prawiro, and Suharto himself, had strongly supported the Liem-sponsored Dumai consortium.

The Liem Group in the 1980s

As is the case with Soerjadjaja, Liem was not stifled by the regulations of 1974. In a process of 'simplification', as the concentration of corporate capital ownership is cynically referred to within Indonesia, Liem has become the largest capitalist with massive investments in almost all sectors of the economy. This process appears to have accelerated with his reported carving up of the Indonesian cooking oil market with Indra Wijaya, and his successful bid for a 50% share in the milk manufacturer, P. T. Indomilk.[46] He is increasingly able to buy out his foreign partners[47] and independently raise finance on the international market, although joint ventures have played, and continue to play, a crucial role in his investments. His relationship with both the state and the politico-bureaucrats remains excellent. He has benefited from the economic nationalist policies of the late 1970s and, at the same time, continues to derive benefit from the granting of

economic benefices by patrons (the latest of which has been
the granting of monopoly control of lubricants through the
company P. T. Astenia). For the most part Liem's position
and his relationship to Suharto, Kostrad and other centres of
power have not been permissible topics of public debate
since 1974. Ironically it was the President's brother, Probosutejo, who provided the only veiled critique of Liem,
through his now-banned newspaper *Ekuin*, drawing attention to the extent of the Liem group, the low taxes it pays
and, more obliquely, Liem's part in the process of capital
outflow from Indonesia.[48]

Another aspect of Liem's complex relations with Suharto
appears to be the use of his private resources to assist with
state policy objectives. The cold rolling steel mill is an
example of this. It has been government policy to establish a
domestic capacity to produce steel plates, largely to offset an
annual import bill of around $700 million. Given the parlous
state of P. T. Krakatau Steel, already stretched and losing
money, and the limits placed upon state investment by the
declines in oil revenues in the early 1980s, the government
was forced to look to private enterprise. Liem clearly was the
only capitalist with the resources and influence for such a
task and was able to raise $552 million in foreign loans and
arrange for US Steel to become the consultant and manager.
According to Liem, the steel will be dearer but will save
Indonesia $500 million per year in foreign exchange. On the
other hand there seems little prospect that Liem and his
partners, Ciputra and Krakatau Steel, would have volun-
tarily chosen this notoriously unprofitable industry for such a
large investment. It would appear that Liem's access to a
variety of lucrative monopoly and oligopoly positions, and
favourable government intervention in pricing and protection in other sectors, can only be fully understood in the
context of his value and function as an instrument of government policy in sectors normally not commercially
attractive.[49]

Finally, there are signs that Liem is broadening the ownership base of his enterprises. He has announced that 30%–35% of shares in Indocement, an enterprise with reported assets of $2.5 billion, will be gradually sold to the public.[50] In economic terms this will mean an inflow of funds to ease pressure on liquidity caused by high debt-servicing obligations, and in political terms, public ownership of Liem companies will dilute anti-Chinese, anti-*cukong* criticism of the group.

POLITICS AND CHINESE CAPITAL SINCE 1975

Chinese-owned corporate conglomerates have established their dominance in an economic environment which is relatively stable and which provides opportunities to the domestic private investor. Neither the joint venture requirements nor exclusion from state-bank credit imposed in 1974 appears to have caused any major problems, if indeed they have ever been rigorously applied.

Nevertheless, several important questions are posed by the particular political situation of Chinese capital. How secure is Chinese capital and what are the long-term prospects for resisting pressures for various degrees of expropriation? What are the long-term prospects of Chinese capitalists developing the broader dimensions of economic, social and political power normally possessed by a bourgeois class?

Clearly the Chinese continue to be widely resented. At one level, criticism of Chinese capitalists is restricted to those *cukong* who are linked with indigenous political leaders. It is the alliance of politico-bureaucrat, *cukong* and foreign capitalist which comes under attack for its subsumption of the rule of law as well as for its violation of notions of economic justice and balanced economic growth.[51] Despite the increasing political weakness of the urban liberal intelligentsia, this critique continues to play an important role at the ideological level. More immediate and more insidious is the popular resentment of Chinese, which has strong racist overtones in that it tends not to discriminate between different

elements of the Chinese community. Such tensions recently
manifested themselves in widespread anti-Chinese rioting
and looting in Central Java in April and November 1980.
These mass anti-Chinese upsurges can only partly be explained as conflict between declining indigenous capitalists
and Chinese competitors, although the former have always
been prominent participants and no doubt benefit from the
physical destruction of the premises of competing Chinese
retailers. The Chinese are also scapegoats for much broader
political and economic grievances and frustrations which
manifest themselves in racism, nationalism and anti-Chinese
violence. The military, of course, are too powerful to attack,
although there were widespread reports of hostility towards
pribumi officials in the November riots.[52]

Given this background of social resentment, the government is forced to portray itself as not only ruling in the
nationalist interest but in the *pribumi* interest. Consequently
the flow continues of regulations intended to restrict the
operation of Chinese capital and to secure a place for indigenous capital. In 1979 and 1980 regulations were introduced to ensure indigenous participation in government
contracting for supply and construction. Defined as the
'weak economic group', indigenous contractors were given
a monopoly on contracts below Rp50 million and preference for contracts between Rp50 and 100 million under the
Keppres 14 and 14(a) regulations described in earlier chapters. Regulations governing conditions of access to particular
economic sectors require that foreign investment involve the
participation and protection of the 'weak economic group',
particularly in the fields of fisheries, agriculture and forestry.
Participation is not restricted to equity participation but
structural integration as suppliers and contractors.

Nevertheless, the Chinese have managed to cope with
most of these difficulties. The existence of well-developed
networks of credit at both the local and regional level has
meant that they have not been devastated by the reduction of
state-bank credit available to them, from a reported 80% of

credit to private investors in 1969–75 to around 42% of the Rp3 552.4 billion state-bank credit allocated by November 1979.[53]

A second factor in the survival of the Chinese has been their success in integrating with international capital, with indigenous domestic capital and with centres of politico-bureaucrat power, particularly within the military. For the generals and the larger indigenous capitalists, the Chinese have become a vital element in their social and economic dominance, by providing both revenue and corporate and commercial infrastructure. The economic fortunes of the emerging indigenous Indonesian ruling class are firmly inter-twined with those of the Chinese. The resentment of Chinese, therefore, is at its most bitter among the middle and lower reaches of indigenous society in both town and countryside.

Corporate integration between Chinese and indigenous capital is significant. Some of the more important examples of such integration are:

(a) The rescue of Sultan Hamengku Buwono's ailing Bank Dagang Nasional Indonesia by Sjamsul Nursalim's Daya group, which now holds 50% of equity.

(b) The partnerships established between Soedarpo and various Chinese business groups, including a reported venture of Go Swie Kie into Soedarpo's banks, Niaga and Amerta.

(c) The integration of state, Chinese and indigenous capital in P.T. Pembangunan Jaya.

(d) The joint ventures between Ibnu Sutowo and William Soerjadjaja in the early 1970s and the partnership between the state assembler, P.T. Gaya, and the Astra group.

(e) The joint ventures between the Liem group and the Suharto family.

At a more abstract level, the Chinese are protected by their very economic indispensability. Any fundamental social or political assault upon them will, without doubt, have a quite critical impact on the Indonesian economy as a whole. We must of course remember that the major Chinese business groups are not any longer simply traders and fixers whose only asset is their dominance of distribution networks. They are now capitalists whose position and power is based to a significant degree on the ownership of capital.

If anything, the position of the Chinese has been strengthened since the decline in the relative contribution of oil revenues which has forced the government to rely more heavily on the generation of investment finances, general revenues and export earnings by domestic private investment. With 40% of investment for Repelita IV to be generated by domestic private investment, the Chinese capitalists become an even more crucial component of the Indonesian economy and the government placed in an increasingly weak position in terms of restricting their activities. This situation constituted the background for Army Commander General Murdani's statement of 22 March 1984 to members of Kadin that continued use of the terms *pribumi* (indigenous) and non-*pribumi* (effectively, Chinese) presents a challenge to future national unity.[54] Subsequent statements from Kadin (which now includes most of the major Chinese capitalists among its leading members) supported this de-emphasis upon *pribumi* and non-*pribumi*, by stressing the importance of building 'pengusaha nasional' (national businessmen) and solving the problems of small capital.[55] Officially the term *pribumi* has been replaced with Indonesian *asli* (effectively the same), but the term 'golongan lemah' — weak group — now also includes small capitalists who are Indonesian citizens of Chinese descent.[56]

What we are therefore seeing is the building of an economic/political alliance between Chinese and indigenous Indonesians across the top strata of political and social life. It would be incorrect, however, to overestimate the effects of this on the Chinese community. Such security and protection as is being developed is a product of the economic indispensability of Chinese-owned capital. Based on this, the Chinese are able to rely on the goodwill of the major centres of politico-bureaucrat power, but they do not have a political power-base of their own and are not generally accorded a legitimate, public, political role. In addition, we must take into account the internal variety and complexity of the Chinese business community. Political protection is applied most successfully to people like Liem Sioe Liong, but not so consistently and successfully to the masses of Chinese petty capitalists and traders.

For their part, major Chinese business groups have increasingly been extending their corporate assets outside Indonesia. Liem Sioe Liong, Hendra Rahardja, William Soerjadjaja, Go Swie Kie, Yos Soetomo and others have investments in Singapore, Hong Kong and other areas in the region, including Australia. This regional expansion is, at one level, a logical corporate response to the internationalisation of capital. But there are also significant investments in property and manufacture which must be seen in part for purposes of security.

However, such moves in turn feed long-standing doubts about the degree of loyalty Chinese feel towards Indonesia. Chinese investments abroad have aroused critical reaction, with claims that the Chinese are draining profits out of Indonesia without regard to the impact of this capital outflow on the Indonesian economy.[57]

The fragility and vulnerability of the Chinese capitalists is a weakness for the bourgeoisie as a whole in Indonesia, because it means that its leading element, the Chinese, are severely limited in their capacity to provide leadership for the establishment of the political and social dominance of the bourgeoisie as a class, by means, for example, of the establishment of a bourgeois party to challenge the military. Indeed, it is in no small measure a consequence of Chinese domination of the bourgeoisie that the military is able to maintain its political dominance. If the major Chinese capitalists we have considered in this chapter were indigenous, the bourgeoisie in Indonesia would be much more powerful and civilian rule a more immediate proposition.

1. G. Adicondro, 'From Chinatown to Nanyang', *Prisma* 13 (1979).
2. *Tempo*, 9.12.72, p. 46. *Tempo* claimed that these figures were confirmed by the head of the PMDN sub-committee of Bappindo (the Indonesian Development Bank).
3. *Nusantara*, 30.1.73, 10.2.73, 3.1.74.
4. *Tempo*, 9.12.72, pp. 47–8.
5. *Suara Karya*, 27.3.72.
6. *Tempo*, 9.12.72, p. 48.
7. This will be dealt with in Chapter 10.
8. *Tempo*, 9.3.74.
9. Ibid.
10. Soehoed, quoted in *Kompas*, 23.7.74; Silalahi 1974.
11. Wibisono 1981a, pp. 73–4, and 'Antara Mitos dan Faktor', *Prisma* 4 (1981) (hereafter 1981b).
12. Sources include:
BNPT company registrations.
BKPM company investment approval data.
JETRO 1980.
AWSJ, 26.2.80, 24.5.80, 29.5.80, 13.9.80, 25.6.81 (for Sjamsul Nursalim and the BDNI takeover).
J. P. Manguno, 'Tycoon Jailed in Indonesia Tax Fraud', *AWSJ*, 1.10.83 (on Soetomo of the Sumber Mas group).
ICN 100, 24.4.78 (for details of Sumendap group).
M. Habir, 'A Mortgaged Magnate', *FEER 84*, (on Hendra Rahardja and the Harapan group)
ICN 178, 27.7.81 (Harapan Group and Mayer Group)
Sondang P. N., '100 Tokoh Milyarder Indonesia: Apa & Siapa Mereka Itu?' (*Expo* 1 & 2, 4.1.84 and 18.4.84.) This is by far the most comprehensive list of major Indonesian business groups. It confirms and extends information already available through company registrations and other articles and is regarded by businessmen and economic journalists and commentators in Jakarta as being accurate.
'Tempo', *Apa dan Siapa* (Jakarta, 1984).
Details of the early careers of such individuals as Bob Hassan, Go Swie Kie, Yap Swie Kie, Tan Kiong Liep, Jantje Liem and other figures with close ties to the military, Bulog and Pertamina were obtained from sources already cited in Chapters 7 and 8.
Sources used for the Liem Sioe Liong and Astra groups are cited in the case studies later in the chapter.
13. S. Astbury, 'Jakarta's First Contender for International Stardom', *Asian Business* (June 1982), p. 20; *ICN* 80, 27.6.77.
14. *ICN* 80, 27.6.77.

15. The development of government policy on auto imports and content requirements is treated in *ICN* 213, 10.1.83.

16. *ICN* 181, 14.9.83.

17. Astbury 1982, p. 21.

18. J. P. Manguno, 'Indonesia's Astra Breaks Ground in Bonds and Leasing', *AWSJ*, 10.12.81.

19. Ibid.

20. Astbury 1982, pp. 20, 26.

21. *ICN* 213, 10.1.83.

22. *ICN* 181, 14.9.81.

23. ICN 213, 10.1.83.

24. P. N. Sondang, *Expo* 2, 18.1.84.

25. *Insight* (Hong Kong), May 1978; M. Habir and A. Rowley, 'The Extended (Corporate) Family of Liem Sioe Liong', *FEER*, 7.4.83; 'Dulu Rockefeller Kini Taipan Liem', *Tempo*, 2.7.83; 'Pohon Besar Bermilyar Dollar', *Tempo*, 31.3.84.

26. *Kompas*, 29.9.76: interview with Probosutejo.

27. M. Habir and A. Rowley, *FEER*, 7.4.83, p. 51. See Liem's comment to Fikri Jufri that before 1968 '. . . we had only experience', *Tempo*, 31.3.84.

28. *ICN* 213, 10.1.83.

29. *Bangkok Post*, 28.1.71.

30. *ICN*, 24.9.79

31. Ibid.

32. *ICN* 201, 5.7.82.

33. 'Liem & Partner di Krakatau Steel', *Tempo*, 9.7.83.

34. *ICN* 179, 18.8.81.

35. *Insight*, May 1978, p. 13.

36. *BNPT* 74–1968.

37. R. Salamon, 'Chin Sophonpanich, the Bangkok Connection', *Insight*, June 1978, p. 13.

38. *Insight*, May 1978, p. 16.

39. See the comments of A. Salim in *FEER*, 7.4.83, p. 45.

40. Cited in 'Dulu Rockefeller Kini Taipan Liem', *Tempo*, 2.7.83.

41. Rowley, *FEER*, 7.4.83, p. 46.

42. Ibid.

43. See the comments of Liem and his son Anthony in 'Liem Buka Suara: "Orang Banyak Salah Sangka"', *Tempo*, 31.3.84, p. 68.

44. Rowley, *FEER*, 7.4.83, p. 45.

45. J. P. Manguno, 'Doubts Mount on Dumai Oil Project Despite Change in Financing Policy', *AWSJ*, 25.10.80.

46. 'Indonesianisasi Indomilk', *Tempo*, 7.7.84, p. 72.

47. P. T. Perkasa bought out Distinct Cement of Hong Kong in February 1983 (*ICN* 217, 7.3.83).

48. *Ekuin*, 29.1.83 and 28.2.83.

49. The cold rolling steel mill is discussed by Liem Sioe Liong and A. Liem in *Tempo*, 31.3.84, p. 69.

50. *Tempo*, 31.3.84, p. 71.

51. This is the sort of criticism made by students (see 'White Book of the 1978 Students' Struggle', *Indonesia* 25, 1978 and H. Akhmadi, *Breaking the Chains of Oppression of the Indonesian People*, Cornell, 1981). It is also the type of critique made by liberal intellectuals such as Mochtar Lubis.

52. Stories that the riots, for the first time, demonstrated considerable and overt evidence of hostility towards indigenous officials were widely circulated in Jakarta at the time. Non-racial aspects of the riots were also reported by G. Sacerdoti in 'Small Fight with Big Results', *FEER*, 5.12.1980, pp. 10–11.

53. The actual figures for the dispersal of state bank credit for the period 1969–79 as a % of total Rp value of credits are:

Indigenous borrowers	38%
Non-indigenous borrowers	29%
State	32%
Other	1%

Source: Statement by Minister Sumarlin to the DPR quoted in *Kompas*, 1.8.81 and cited in Wibisono, 1981*b*.

54. 'Sebutan Pribumi dan Non pribumi Harus Dihapuskan', *Kompas*, 23.3.84.

55. 'Kadin Bentuk Lagi Wadah Pengembangan Dunia Usaha', *Kompas*, 24.3.84.

56. M. Habir, 'Protecting their Interests', *FEER*, 10.5.84.

57. 'Pelarian Modal ke Luar Bisa Akibatkan Ekonomi Terpukul', *Ekuin*, 28.2.83; *ICN* 178, 27.7.81.

10
Indigenous Capitalists under the New Order

POLITICS AND INDIGENOUS CAPITAL

WHEN the New Order government came to power in 1965, its immediate and urgent concern for the reconstitution of the economy meant a policy which aimed to attract and encourage investors with the largest capital and corporate resources. Neither the technocrats nor the generals were initially committed to special protection for indigenous capitalists. There were several reasons for this. First, a belief on the part of the economic policy-makers that protection and subsidy would be abused or would produce at best a weak, inefficient and dependent capitalist class. As late as 1974 the Minister for Trade, Radius Prawiro, stated that:

Native entrepreneurs will not be helped by providing them with facilities. Attempts will be focused upon eliminating attitudes of dependence on facilities and stressing persistence in specific lines of business.[1]

Second, policy-makers have been strongly influenced by the ideas of theorists from Boeke to McLelland who have argued that business success relates more to cultural than structural factors. At the popular level, management insti-

tutes flourish and the bookshops of Jakarta overflow with the
works of such polemicists as Norman Vincent Peal and Dale
Carnegie. Economic policy-makers also believed that indigenous capitalists could be best served by a general environment of economic growth and large-scale investment in
which technology, skills and opportunities for accumulation
would be spontaneously diffused by international capital.
Those indigenous capitalists who have organised politically
to defend their interests as a class over the past thirty-five
years have been precisely those declining, Muslim-oriented
traders and small-scale manufacturers without the social or
economic power to impose their political will on successive
governments. The more successful indigenous capitalists preferred to consolidate themselves through the existing mechanisms of patronage and joint venture, rather than by
organising publicly in defence of class interests.

In 1966 and 1967 a political front representing elements of
indigenous business, Kapni (Indonesian National Businessmens Action Front), was formed along with other front
organisations to give political support to the new regime and
to press for the dismantling of the Old Order. Early opti-
mism, however, soon faded and Kapni became critical of the
failure of the New Order to support indigenous capital,
publicly claiming that restrictive policies had brought about
the collapse of over 75% of bona fide indigenous businesses,
that the purge of private banks had enabled the Chinese to
take control of the banking sector, that speculation and
manipulation in the allocation of BE certificates had excluded indigenous capital and that the bulk of state-bank
credit was being directed to Chinese. It demanded the aboli-
tion of the Aspri and the participation of indigenous business
in political decision-making.[2]

As the New Order became more firmly entrenched, the
front groups, including Kapni, slipped into obscurity. At the
same time established business associations representing the
declining indigenous traders and manufacturers failed to
recapture even the limited influence spasmodically enjoyed

by similar associations in the 1950s, particularly Kensi.[3] Instead, the political activities of businessmen were consolidated into Kadin (Kamar Dagang dan Industri — Chamber of Trade and Industry), a business association which enjoyed considerable government sponsorship and finance and which became, in effect, the major channel of communication and negotiation between the business community and the state.[4] At the national level Kadin was dominated by businessmen who had emerged from within the state apparatus rather than from the ranks of the Muslim bourgeoisie. Since 1967 its leading figures have included such men as General Isman of Kosgoro (an association of retired military officers); General Sofjar, the head of the Kostrad business group, YDP; Air Marshal Suwoto Sukendar; Probosutejo, the brother of President Suharto; Eddy Kowara; Hashim Ning; and Sukamdani Gitorsardjono — all businessmen with strong links into the state. It is therefore an organisation of the new, politically connected, indigenous capitalists rather than one of the declining, powerless Muslim petty bourgeoisie.

Between 1965 and 1974 the indifference of policy-makers towards indigenous capital became politically untenable as the economic situation of large numbers of indigenous capitalists worsened and resentment against the Chinese and their military patrons became more politically volatile. In the textile industry in particular, the old indigenous producers faced crisis as the industry was reconstructed on the basis of capital intensive, fully integrated mills owned by Japanese and Chinese investors. Indigenous capitalists proved increasingly unable to secure state-bank credit. In 1971 it was reported that, of the forty-nine companies in the textile industry which had received Rp13 billion in credit to that time, only seven were indigenous-owned and these had received only Rp1.7 billion.[5] As of October 1972, 47% of all PMDN projects were Chinese, 15% were joint Chinese/indigenous and 38% indigenous, at least formally, while Ir. Soehoed of BKPM estimated the indigenous share of PMDN investment as a whole to be 26%.[6] By the end of 1972 it was reported that over 80% of state-bank credit had gone to Chinese capitalists, a sum of Rp200 billion.[7]

This continuing crisis of indigenous capital brought increasing public criticism from prominent indigenous business community leaders, including Sutomo; Rachmat Mulyomiseno, who was also Chairman of Parliamentary Commission VII on Banking and Trade; Omar Tusin; J.C. Tambunan; and Sjafruddin Prawiranegara, former Masyumi leader, Cabinet Minister and Governor of the Bank of Indonesia. Their critique had two prongs: that the economic policies of the technocrats surrendered the economy of Indonesia to foreign and Chinese capital, and the use of state power by politico-bureaucrats to underpin economic alliances between certain generals and Chinese businessmen facilitated the consolidation of a new coalition of political and economic power.[8] Their criticisms were expanded in spectacular detail in various newspapers, especially Tengku Hafas' *Nusantara*, a newspaper long associated with right-wing Muslim business interests. *Nusantara*, throughout the early 1970s, provided intricate accounts of the decline of indigenous business and the economic relationships between generals and *cukong*. Before its closure in 1974, Nusantara was developing the rather wild proposition that *cukong* were part of a communist plot to impoverish the nation and seduce indigenous political leaders.[9]

None of the critics operated from a political base of any effectiveness; nevertheless, their views reflected (or exploited) widespread resentment and frustration among the declining indigenous petty bourgeoisie. The potential for political conflict was real, particularly if linked to the already smouldering hostility between fundamentalist Islam and the military. As well, the plight of the indigenous petty capitalists became a *cause célèbre* for middle class critics of the government, as a concrete expression of their arguments about foreign economic dominance, the social dislocation and injustice brought by untrammelled economic growth and the dangers of political corruption.

From 1970 to 1974 protests and demonstrations against economic policy, the domination of foreign and Chinese capital, corruption and the military/*cukong* alliances mounted in intensity. In Bandung in 1973 and Jakarta in 1974 the tension erupted into violence against the Chinese, accompanied, in the case of Jakarta, by attacks on Japanese-owned business premises. The government felt sufficiently concerned to initiate immediate moves to include indigenous capital, in a more systematic way, in the general development of the Indonesian economy. Several steps were taken, the first of which had in fact been commenced as early as 1971:

(a) The establishment of P.T. Askrindo, an institution which would insure credit given by banks to indigenous capital, and P.T. Bahana, an institution to purchase shares in indigenous companies, thereby financing the collateral requirement for loans.

(b) New policies which reserved credit for small-scale indigenous business. In 1973 it was announced that the amount of bank credit to be allocated to loans under Rp100 million was to be raised from 38% to 65%.[10] Following the events of January 1974, the government withdrew state-bank credit to Chinese business and instituted a new system of small credits: KIK (Kredit Investasi Kecil) and KMKP (Kredit Modal Kerja Permanen), providing loans of up to Rp10 million to smaller capitalists with a net worth of less than Rp100 million in industry and construction, and Rp40 million elsewhere and where 75% of the business is owned by indigenous partners. Daroesman reports, however, that by 1980 credits of Rp525.8 billion had reached only 200 000 persons. The average loan was Rp2.8 million ($4 480) for KIK and Rp2.2 million ($3 520) for KMKP. For smaller loans distributed at the local level, the average size of the loan was Rp10 000 ($16).[11] No big capitalist class was going to come out of these programmes, although such loans probably served primarily to defuse tension among petty capitalists.

(c) Moves to ensure the integration of indigenous, Chinese and foreign capital. The first statement indicating this intention was made in March 1972 when President Suharto told a conference of educators that the government planned to buy 50%–60% of the shares of Chinese companies and transfer them to indigenous investors.[12]

This objective was never put into effect, but as we have seen in Chapter 5, following the 1974 riots new regulations were introduced requiring all PMA joint ventures to include national partners, whose equity was to be increased to 51% within ten years. At the same time, all national companies were to have indigenous partners, whose equity was to be increased to 51% within ten years.

It is not clear exactly what effect these moves have had upon the economic condition of the bulk of indigenous capitalists, although it is likely that many have enjoyed greater access to credit and benefited from the huge sums poured into the countryside in the 1970s through Inpres, Banpres and other schemes, despite claims that the bulk of these find their way into the hands of Chinese business.[13] It is probable that indigenous capital investment at these levels has moved from areas such as textiles into service industries and transport and that the new indigenous capitalists are plugged increasingly into Golkar and military patronage networks, a process begun in the late 1950s. In other words, it is likely that the old Muslim petty bourgeoisie is being replaced by a more 'abangan' petty bourgeoisie, to use Geertz's categories. However, substantial research is yet to be carried out on the development of indigenous capitalism at this level.

MAJOR INDIGENOUS BUSINESS GROUPS:
THE SURVIVORS OF THE 1950s AND 1960s

The major indigenous capitalists of the New Order may be
divided into three main categories:

- (a) The survivors of the Benteng and Guided Economy
      periods.
- (b) Politico-bureaucrats of the New Order establishing
      private business groups.
- (c) New capitalists who have emerged with the patronage
      of the new centres of politico-bureaucratic power.

Emerging from either the trading bourgeoisie or from within
the bureaucratic strata itself, the indigenous capitalists of the
Benteng and Guided Economy eras built up their enterprises
in a period plagued with inflation and general economic
decline but where access to the normal means of doing
business — credit, licences and contracts — were to be
secured only within a maze of political in-fighting and
caprice. As we have seen, domestic business was hard hit in
the Sukarno period by inflation, lack of imports and decaying
infrastructure, as well as the more general effects of balance
of payment crises. With the exception of those able to send
money overseas — and these were usually Chinese — domestic private business concerns entered the New Order period with few liquid resources and their capital tied up in
plant. In the tight credit regime of the late 1960s they found
difficulty in making new investments. To make matters worse,
existing investments were ineligible for PMDN benefits,
forcing them to operate at a disadvantage with new investors,
foreign or Chinese, who enjoyed tax concessions and could
import raw materials and machinery at a lower price.

Perhaps the most dramatic blow was the collapse of old
political patrons. New patrons, particularly the military, came
to power complete with established business relationships,
almost exclusively with Chinese capitalists who proceeded

to take the lion's share of economic concessions available in
the early New Order period: BE import credit, Bulog distributorships, forestry concessions, import licences and state-
bank credit.

For several indigenous capitalists, particularly those close
to Sukarno, the political changes brought disaster. The assets
of the three largest indigenous importer/exporters, Aslam,
Markam and Bram Tambunan, were confiscated. Aslam and
Markam were jailed and Tambunan remained in Holland.
Interestingly, Markam was to reappear with a road construction company in Aceh in 1977, claiming that his re-emerg-
ence in business was due to help from Golkar.[14]

Most of the surviving indigenous capitalists had been
involved in the import and distribution of automobiles and
machinery, often as sole agents. These agencies immediately
came under pressure, not only from the new power holders
looking for lucrative concessions but also from the new
foreign manufacturers anxious to ensure contracts for supply
and adequate service and back-up. Two of the largest sole
agencies, those of Mercedes and Volkswagen, owned by
Suwarma and Panggabean, were quickly acquired by the
military companies, Berdikari and YDP.

Existing indigenous agents found themselves at a disadvantage, with assembly plants in need of new investment and
with sole agencies importing cars increasingly unable to
compete with the new Japanese products. Fritz Eman's
Udatin group, for example, with a production capacity of
6 500, assembled only 498 vehicles in 1976. Only 13.6% of
Hashim Ning's ISC production capacity of 10 000 vehicles
was used in 1976 for the declining Dodge and Fiat makes.
P.T. DAF assembled only ten trucks, 1% of its capacity,
while P.T. Masayu, with a capacity for assembling 2 500
vehicles, did not produce a single car. By comparison, Ibnu
Sutowo's Mitsubishi assembly plant (Krama Yudha) and
Soerjadjaja's Astra group (Toyota) worked at 90% and 88%
of capacity respectively.[15]

Of the most prominent agency holders, Agoes Dasaad was

the major casualty. His automobile sole agency, P.T. Daha (Fiat), which he owned together with Hashim Ning, dropped out of the top five in 1975 and quickly declined thereafter. Dasaad's Westinghouse and Kaiser Aluminium agencies were lost, as was the important Lockheed agency. Lockheed had decided that Dasaad was without sufficient influence to be of further use, especially in view of the Indonesian Air Force's decision to establish its own company to deal with commissions on contracts.[16] The loss of these lucrative agencies was a crucial blow to the Dasaad group, which found itself increasingly unable to make new investments to maintain its industrial ventures, notably the formerly prominent Kancil Mas textile factory. According to Agus Dasaad's son Eddy, the rump of the old trading and textile interests were in such difficulties that the most important remaining asset was now a 20% share in a South Sumatran timber-venture with Singaporean partners.[17] It is not clear whether the Dasaad group retains control of the equity it formerly held in P.T. Pembangunan Jaya or in P.T. Daha.

P.T. Masayu also encountered difficulties after 1965, and by 1976, as mentioned, its assembly plant was without work. Masayu has survived by securing joint venture partnerships with British and Dutch firms in cable manufacture, diesel engine installation and servicing, and installation of sugar factories. Significantly, the military company P.T. Tri Usaha Bhakti and the Bank of Indonesia are also domestic partners in two of these ventures.[18] Recently, Masayu's assembly plant has begun assembling Isuzu vehicles in association with the state-owned P.T. Pantja Motor, a military-dominated company which is the Isuzu sole agent.[19] Clearly, Masayu is acceptable to elements within the state and the military. However, survival cannot be totally attributed to personal influence or contacts. As a legacy of the new joint venture requirements, indigenous companies able to operate in the engineering field with some reputation for reliability and efficiency are at a premium.

Hashim Ning is probably the most interesting and versatile

of the old sole agent assemblers. He entered the New Order period well entrenched in automobiles, trade, property and construction and well connected to a wide variety of political figures in the military. He has had to share his stakes in the automobile industry with new forces, notably Ibnu Sutowo who is now a partner in the Chrysler sole agent, P.T. Jakarta Motors, and who also bought a majority share and assumed the President Directorship of the Chrysler/Fiat assembler, ISC. But Ning has expanded well beyond automobiles, and his business interests now consist of a constellation of joint venture partnerships in hotels, electronics import and assembly, construction, brewing and tourism. His partners include prominent indigenous and Chinese capitalists, among them Panglaykim, the Soedarpo group, Bakrie, Masayu and, of course, Ibnu Sutowo.[20]

Other indigenous investors in the sole agency business have generally experienced decline through limited capital resources, old plant, unfashionable products and limited political access. These include Kusmuljono, Fritz Eman (Holden), and Garuda Diesel. One exception to this is the Wahab Affan group, which moved out of trade and shipping into the lucrative Nissan agency. In 1964, even before the New Order came to power, Affan had been restructuring his business interests. By 1973 he had entirely divested himself of his shipping companies, realising that other fields were more lucrative than the increasingly competitive shipping industry.[21] After 1965 Affan reportedly secured the patronage of elements within the military, particularly Alamsjah and Hoemardani, and with their backing purchased Bouraq Airlines. By far his most significant move, however, was the acquisition of the sole agency for the import of Nissan cars (P.T. Indokaya), the only major Japanese producer not yet in Indonesia. Between 1979 and 1980, however, Affan was forced out of the Nissan agency, and the process of his decline offers several important insights into the nature of the sole agency arrangements, and the general relations between the state and various elements of capital, both foreign and domestic.

In 1979 Marubeni (the Japanese conglomerate controlling the export of Nissan components) stopped the supply of CKD (completely knocked down) components, on the grounds that Indokaya was unable to repay more than $15 million in loans and that it had mismanaged the operations of Nissan in Indonesia, resulting in poor Datsun sales *vis-à-vis* its major rivals, Toyota and Mitsubishi. Consequently, Marubeni demanded that the Affan shareholding be reduced to 10% and new Indonesian owners be brought in. An incentive for government support in this dispute was Marubeni's offer to invest in a $200 million spare parts venture. Indokaya counter-charged that the poor performance was largely the consequence of ineptitude on Nissan's part and that the motivating factor behind Nissan's action was Indokaya's move into steel pressing with the establishment of P.T. Indopres.[22] Such a move threatened Marubeni's vertical control of the production process. The government was faced with several dilemmas. It was anxious to force Japanese car-makers to invest in more upstream production, including engine and parts manufacture, but Indokaya's investment intiative would potentially give domestic capital much more autonomy from the Japanese conglomerates and a much greater independent capacity for control in the auto industry. In the interests of future industrial plans in which Japanese participation played a major role, the Minister for Industry, Ir. Soehoed, backed Nissan. But the issue was politically complicated. Indokaya's struggle with Nissan and the government brought to the surface pro-*pribumi* and economic nationalist sentiments. The conflict coincided with the growing strength of indigenous business groups and their increased political influence through Kadin. One of the groups which made a bid for Indokaya after the Affans had been persuaded to accept a reduced role in ownership (by Alamsjah) was P.T. Yuddhistira, a company owned by a consortium of leading indigenous businessmen: Affan, Hashim Ning, Probosutejo, Fritz Eman (of the Holden assemblers and sole agents, P.T. Udatin) and Jukardi Odang.[23] Of particular significance here was the role of Probosutejo, the President's brother. As we will see, Probosutejo's business empire grew out of politico-bureaucratic power and was forged in joint ventures with Chinese business groups, but in political terms he has become increasingly a militant protagonist of indigenous capital.

The Affan decline raises a few other interesting considerations. First, just as Nissan's alarm over the steel press was a real factor, it is clear that Nissan required a local agent larger and more efficient than Indokaya if it was to compete with Sutowo's Krama Yudha (Mitsubishi) or Soerjadjaja's Astra (Toyota), both of which were big, efficient and well connected. At the same time, it cannot be ruled out that powerful politico-bureaucrat forces had been angling to move in on a lucrative concession held by a politically defenceless business group. Alamsjah had long since ceased to be a patron of significance and the two new contenders for Indokaya were P.T. Garuda Mataram (YDP and Liem Bian Koen) and P.T. Wahana, a company owned by a retired military officers' association, Perabri, under the leadership of General Sukadi, also a chairman of Golkar, which was ultimately successful in its bid.

Several indigenous capitalists emerged from trading relationships with foreign companies in the pre-1965 period in which they acted as sole importers, and in many cases, distributors of foreign products, to become joint venture partners in import-substitution manufacturing. After 1965 it became more attractive for the foreign companies to manufacture within Indonesia because of the incentives provided by the new PMA Laws and the booming domestic markets in the first decade of the New Order. As a result, local trading partners were taken into the industry as joint venture partners, although they continued to retain their importing and distribution function. As we have seen in an earlier chapter, most domestic joint venture partners were Chinese. If indigenous, they were politically influential. But in a few cases the foreign partner preferred to remain with an indigenous partner of long standing rather than plunge into the capricious world of generals and *cukong*. After the new joint

venture regulations of 1974, the position of indigenous businessmen with proven track records was strengthened immeas-
urably, as foreign investors were forced to look around a
fairly bare cupboard for potential indigenous partners. Their
position became further entrenched with the requirement
that all domestic distribution functions be undertaken by
national companies.

Among the most prominent indigenous traders who have
become joint venture partners in manufacture are: Harlan
Bekti, Nahar Zahiruddin Tanjung, Machdi, Eddy Kowara
and Mrs Zainal Abidin. Their origins are remarkably similar,
indicating the long-term effectiveness of political patronage
in the early stages of capital accumulation, during the revolutionary period and under Benteng.

Harlan Bekti came from a family of minor officials and
began business during the revolution as an importer. He was
associated with Kowara in the early years of the trading
company, Teknik Umum, and later obtained Benteng licences and credits. Machdi also came from a West Java
family of minor officials, training as a pharmacist in the
pre-war period and becoming involved as an importer of
medical supplies for the revolutionary forces between 1945
and 1949. By 1949 he owned two dispensaries, which were to
expand to nine by 1959. In that year he also established a
factory which was in reality an assembly plant, packaging and
distributing imported ingredients.[24] A third indigenous capitalist from West Java is Eddy Kowara, who founded, with
Ali Achmad, the trading company Teknik Umum in 1940.
During the period of Japanese occupation, Kowara worked
as an official in the Japanese administration in the management of an oil company. After the departure of the Japanese,
Kowara became manager of this now apparently state-owned
enterprise (Perusahaan Tambang Minyak Republik Indonesia). It would appear that Kowara was able to obtain
contracts for his own private company, Teknik Umum, to
provide electrical and machinery installations for the oil
company he managed. In 1950 he received from Moh. Hatta

a letter to BNI for Rp10 000 to capitalise Teknik Umum (approximately US$1.575 million in today's terms) and, in his own words, 'received' a big project from Sultan Hamengku Buwono.[25] Zainal Abidin, a West Sumatran, was, together with Hashim Ning, a personal assistant to Hatta in the revolutionary period. Aided by Benteng facilities, the Abidins, both trained pharmacists, established dispensaries and a pharmaceutical import firm. Nahar Zahiruddin Tanjung's Marison group had its origins in trade in the interwar years but also expanded in the 1950s with Benteng facilities.

In the mid-1960s these small, struggling importers were faced with a developing import-substitution manufacturing sector which threatened to supplant the import of commodities. Their limited capital resources and limited access to credit meant that they were able to move into manufacture and benefit from state subsidy and protection only by integration with foreign corporations. Harlan Bekti's group now comprises minor shareholdings in textile mills, a steel pipe manufacturing plant and an engineering plant, while Machdi's interests now include shareholdings in pharmaceuticals, steel founding and textiles.[26] Kowara's Teknik Umum is now a major contractor for supply and installation of electrical equipment but the group has also expanded, as a joint venture partner, into the manufacture of spare parts, high tensile steel bars and cables, cattle farming, vegetable oils and general construction contracting. He is also sole agent for Massey Ferguson.[27] The Abidins now operate as partners in several large pharmaceutical and cosmetic companies.[28] Finally, Nahar Zahiruddin Tanjung's group, Marison, became a partner of the Australian Dairy Corporation in the production of milk and ice cream (Indomilk) and later expanded into manufacture of machinery for sugar mills as well as retaining its distribution function for Indomilk.[29] Most recently it has become a partner of Liem Sioe Liong both in Indomilk and in a cooking oil venture.

Other indigenous capitalists involved in both trade and

manufacture before 1965 faced the choice of competing in the ISI sector with inadequate capital resources or integrating with foreign capital. These included Th.M. Gobel, an electrical manufacturer whose growth since 1965 has been in association with the Matsushita group involving joint ventures in the manufacture of televisions, radios and air conditioners, batteries and tractors and, completely outside the manufacturing industry, in a forestry concession.[30] Ir. Aminuddin, an ardent economic nationalist, also became convinced that expansion, and indeed survival, was only possible through the joint venture, despite his success in securing Rp1.5 billion for the expansion of his textile mill in 1970. In 1974 he entered his first joint venture, with a Taiwanese company in ship building and repair.[31] The long-established co-operative, GKBI, moved away from importing cambrics for its members in the small-scale batik production sector into large-scale manufacture of textiles in partnership with the government and Japanese companies.[32] Even the former giant amongst domestic textile manufacturers, the Tamin group, found itself forced to try and halt the gathering decline of its textile interests by entering joint venture arrangements.[33]

Among the whole range of surviving indigenous capitalists the pattern is similar: joint ventures in manufacture and resource exploitation combined with smaller, fully domestic investments in hotels, property and trade. Some of the major indigenous groups I have not covered include T.D. Pardede (fishing and cold storage, hotels), Sjamsoeddin Daeng Mangawing (steel and engineering), Haji Sulchan (fishing and cold storage). [34]

One of the more significant survivors has been Soedarpo Sastrosatomo. As outlined in earlier chapters, his group emerged in the 1950s under the patronage of major PSI-associated figures, notably Sultan Hamengku Buwono. These links have shown quite remarkable resilience, surviving well into the New Order period. Close associations remain with the Sultan, the Bank of Indonesia and other former PSI business groups, including Indomarin and Wibowo. However, the Soedarpo group is probably the strongest surviving indigenous business group because of its corporate structure and capital base.

Soedarpo's group is based in shipping, an industry protected from foreign competition and capital participation and therefore one in which there has been considerable development through conglomeration of domestic companies: indigenous, Chinese and state-owned. Soedarpo's shipping companies now encompass deep-sea liners, log carriers, barges and container ships, while the group intersects with those of such prominent figures as Joginder Singh, Siradjudin Baso, Jarry Sumendap, Adil Nurimba and Julius Tahija. Integration with domestic capitalist groups extends beyond shipping into finance, where P.T. Private Development Finance Company of Indonesia is an outstanding example of conglomeration at the domestic level, including as shareholders the government of Indonesia and major Chinese and indigenous business groups.

A crucial element of the Soedarpo interests is the integration of industrial, commercial and finance capital. Soedarpo has substantial interests in two banks: Bank Niaga, which is the third largest Indonesian foreign-exchange bank, with assets of Rp78 billion; and Bank Amerta, one of the largest non-foreign exchange private banks, with assets of Rp19 billion. In both cases, the banks were founded in the 1950s in partnership with the Bank of Indonesia, which still retains its shareholding although a major partner is now Julius Tahija, former Caltex President Director. With two large banks at the centre of the group and the major state bank as partner, Soedarpo possessed the capacity for internal financing, an option not available to other domestic capitalists. There have been recent, unconfirmed reports that Go Swie Kie has bought into both of the Soedarpo banks.

A final group to be considered is that of Sultan Hamengku Buwono, which falls between the categories of surviving groups and politico-bureaucrat groups to be considered later

TABLE 10.1
THE SOEDARPO GROUP

Company	Interests
Soedarpo Corp.	Holding company and trade
Ista Shipping Agency	
P.T. Panurjawan	Inter-island shipping — with Julius Tahija and Idham
P. T. Samudra Indonesia	International shipping — with Sumendap, Sutan Han Saibi and others
P.T. Bhaita	Tug and barges — with Wibowo and Indomarin
P.T. Pahoka	Log carrying — with Japanese partners
P.T. Indonesia National Bulk Carriers	Bulk carrying — with various Chinese partners including Adil Nurimba
P.T. Bank Amerta	Bank
P.T. Bank Niaga	Foreign exchange bank — Soedarpo, Julius Tahija and Bank of Indonesia
P.T. PDFC	Financial institution — with P.T. TUB, Bank of Indonesia, Panin Bank, P.T. Gading Mas and others

Source: various BNPT (see Robison 1977 for details); Financial Directory of Indonesia, 1980; Expo 2, Year 2, 18.1.84.

in the chapter. His business activities first came to light in 1952 when, together with Dr. Sumitro, the Sultan was the subject of a parliamentary motion of no-confidence alleging illegal allocation of government order for the import of vehicles and armaments to three companies associated with the PSI. But the Sultan also owned companies personally, and his private business group was to expand significantly after 1965. Unlike other capitalists from the 1950s and 1960s, the Sultan has held power within the New Order, first as a Minister and then as Vice-President. This must be taken into account when considering the factors which underly his business activities.

The Sultan's business group falls into two major categories. One is a series of shareholdings in companies owned partly by the CITA group of Teuku Daud and the Putera group of Djamzu Papan. CITA is an interesting indigenous group which had its origins in 1947 when the Army established the Central Trading Company (CTC) in West Sumatra to resume supplies for the revolution. Teuku Daud, then a

TABLE 10.2
THE SULTAN HAMENGKU BUWONO GROUP

Company	Sector	Shareholders
P. T. Molino Pramuka	Holding co.	Sultan HB & Scouting movement
P. T. Asia Indo Tobacco	Tobacco & cigarettes	P. T. Molino Pramuka, *Singapore*
P. T. Urecon	Property	Teuku Daud, Moh. Suleiman & Ir. Tirtajaya
P. T. Urecon Utama	Property	Teuku Daud, Moh. Suleiman, Ir. Tirtajaya & BRM Kasworo
P. T. BASF	Tapes	P. T. Urecon, Teddy Chandrajaya
P. T. Taylor Woodrow	Contracting	P. T. Urecon Utama, *UK*
P. T. Universal Realty	Property	P. T. Urecon Utama, *Singapore*
P. T. Chandra Jaya	Fishing	P. T. Urecon Utama
P. T. Nusantour Duta	Holding	Sultan HB, Sri Budojo
P. T. Duta Merlin	Hotel	P. T. Nusantour Duta, P. T. Duta Indo Jaya, *HK*
P. T. Wavin Duta Jaya	PVC pipes	P. T. Nusantour Duta, P. T. Pembangunan Jaya, *Holland*
P. T. Eastern Polymer	Textiles	P. T. Nusantour Duta, *HK*
P. T. Jogjatex	Textiles	BRM Kasworo & other investors
P. T. Bank Dagang Nasional Indonesia (after 1981)		P. T. Nusantour Duta & P. T. Nusantour Duta Jaya (Sultan HB), P. T. Daya Patoya & P. T. Daya Madya (Sjamsul Nursalim)

Source: BNPT (see Robison 1977, App. B for details); *AWSJ,* 25.6.81 for details of P. T. Bank Dagang NI; *BKPM* investment approvals, 30.12.72.

lieutenant-colonel, was one of the directors. In 1949, CTC was reformed as the basis for development of national business at the urging of Hatta, taking over the assets of the Dutch Trading Company, HVD. Plans were made to expand its activities into industry, mining and estates.[35] It was in the early 1950s that CTC became associated with the Sultan, Dr. Sumitro and the PSI, the driving forces behind the establishment of national, state-owned companies.

After 1958, CTC became Panca Niaga but remained under the control of the same Acehnese Army officers originally associated with CTC, who maintained a reputation for efficiency in a period when most state corporations were being plundered by their military managers. During the 1960s the old CTC directors, under the leadership of Teuku Daud, began to move into private enterprise, establishing a trading company, a crumb rubber factory and a construction company. A major component, however, is now property development, and it is this component which is the basis of the partnership between the Sultan (through his son, BRM Kasworo), Daud, Petrus Tirtajaya and Teddy Chandrajaya of the giant Putera group of Semarang, which has extensive interests in cardboard manufacture, cold storage and fishing. This three-way partnership also owns a prawn fishing venture and a sole agency for the import and assembly of BASF tapes, and has constructed a luxury housing development in Jakarta. Independent of this, BRM Kasworo has a 10% share in a Rp1 000 million Jogjakarta textile mill with several Chinese partners.

A second element hinges around the Duta company, a major holding of which is the Bank Dagang Nasional Indonesia (BDNI), a foreign-exchange bank established in the 1950s and owned 95% by the Sultan. In 1978 it was revealed that the BDNI had defaulted on debts of close to $30 million. This disaster was largely attributable to attempts by two of its executives, including former PSI figure Paulus Wibowo, to save two foundering steel companies, P.T. Irosteel and P.T. Baja Utama (both owned by Wibowo). After a three-year struggle, BDNI accepted a rescue operation by the Chinese businessman Sjamsul Nursalim, whose extensive business interests did not include a foreign-exchange bank. His only chance of obtaining such a licence was to purchase a bank which already held one. With a $15 million loan from the French bank, Société Générale, Nursalim secured 50% ownership through his Daya group of companies.[36] Several interesting features emerge from this. First, the Sultan was unable to raise the necessary finance to maintain ownership of his foreign-exchange bank. Second, the refinancing of the BDNI meant that major Chinese interests secured yet another foreign-exchange bank and that foreign banks are playing an increasing role as financiers and managers of private domestic Indonesian banks.[37] This is not to say that the Sultan has been squeezed totally out. He still controls 47% of BDNI, and Nursalim is reported as saying that a further Rp6 billion will be injected into BDNI to make it the largest private foreign-exchange bank — half of this coming from the Sultan's group.[38]

MAJOR INDIGENOUS BUSINESS GROUPS: POLITICO-BUREAUCRATS AS CAPITALISTS

In post-colonial Indonesia the major indigenous capitalists have emerged not from the struggling indigenous trading and manufacturing sector but from within the state apparatus itself.

Until 1965 state power was used by the politico-bureaucrats to accumulate personal wealth and to secure the political position of the parties or military units in which their base of power was located. It was not, however, used extensively as the basis for private capital accumulation. Certainly, companies owned by the military and by political parties were important in this period, and many state and party officials entered business on their own behalf, but few attained any degree of significance in the world of domestic corporate capital.

Under the New Order, this has changed. The largest set of indigenous business interests is that of the Suharto family, and until the mid-1970s the Sutowo family and associates represented the second major pillar of indigenous capital. The long-term significance of these business groups and others like them depends on whether they prove to be the core of a domestic capitalist class. Will the major indigenous capitalists of the twenty-first century trace their origins back to the free-wheeling generals and officials of the 1970s and 1980s who used political muscle to accumulate capital? Will the Suhartos and Sutowos of the 1970s and 1980s be Indonesia's Rockefellers and Morgans of the 1980s? Will the dual role of politico-bureaucrats as capitalists bring the existing contradictions in the relationships between state and capital to a crisis point? These questions will be looked at later in the chapter; in the meantime it is necessary to look at the way in which the Suharto and Sutowo groups have developed and the structure they have taken.

The Suharto (Cendana) Group

Members of the Suharto family who are, or have been, corporate shareholders include:

> Ibu Siti Hartinah Suharto (Mrs Suharto)
> Probosutejo (brother of the President)
> Sudwikatmono (step-brother of the President)
> Benny Jonosiswono (brother of Mrs Suharto)
> Bernard Ibnu Hardoyo (brother of Mrs Suharto)
> Soemoharmanto (now deceased, father of Mrs Suharto)
> N. Siti Hardijanti (daughter)
> Sigit Harjoyudanto (son)
> Bambang Triatmotjo (son)
> Indra Kowara (son-in-law)

This group most clearly illustrates the integration of politico-bureaucrat power with capital, both international and Chinese. In fact the Suharto group has almost exclusively developed as a vast collection of minority shareholdings in the major Chinese corporate groups. There are four distinct segments of the Suharto group:

(a) The Suharto family and the Charitable Foundations (Yayasans) — Yayasan Harapan Kita, Yayasan Kartika Chandra, Yayasan Trikora.
(b) The Suharto/Liem Sioe Liong group.
(c) Miscellaneous Suharto family enterprises.
(d) Probosutejo enterprises.

TABLE 10.3
THE SUHARTO FAMILY BUSINESS INTERESTS

Company	Sector	Shareholders
YAYASANS		
Yayasan Harapan Kita	Holding co.	Mrs Suharto, Mrs Sutowo
Yayasan Kartika Jaya	Holding co.	Persatuan Isteri Tentara
P.T. Kartika Chandra Hotel	Hotel	Yayasan Kartika Chandra & Sukamdani Gitarsarjono
P.T. Pacitakan Batas Gunung	Printing	Yayasan Kartika Chandra & various military officers
P.T. Hanurata	Forestry	Yayasan HK & Yayasan Trikora
P.T. Kahala	Forestry	P.T. Hanurata & HK
SUHARTO/LIEM SIOE LIONG GROUP		
P.T. Waringin Kencana	Trade & crumb	Sudwikatmono 5% (President/Director)
P.T. Arimono	Trade	Sudwikatmono 25%
P.T. Bogasari	Flour milling	Sudwikatmono 4% (President/Director)
P.T. Bank Central Asia	Foreign exchange	Sigit 16%, Siti 16%
P.T. Indocement	Cement manufacture	Sudwikatmono 5% (President/Director)
P.T. Distinct Cement	" "	
P.T. Perkasa Cement	" "	
P.T. Perkasa Agung Utama	" "	
P.T. Perkasa Indah Putih	" "	
P.T. Perkasa Inti Abadi	" "	
MISCELLANEOUS		
P.T. Gunung Ngadeg Jaya	Trade	Soemoharmanto) Bernard Ibnu Hardoyo) 50%
P.T. Kabelmetal	Cable manufacture	P.T. Gunung Ngadeg Jaya & *W. Germany*
P.T. Pasopati	Holding co.	Bernard Ibnu Hardoyo, Bob Hasan
P.T. Semen Nusantara	Cement manufacture	P.T. Gunung Ngadeg Jaya & *Japan*
P.T. Rejo Sari Bumi	Agricultural estates	Probosutejo, Siti, Sigit
P.T. Indonesia Japan Tobacco	Cigarettes	Benny Jonosiswono, *Japan*
P.T. Bayu Air	Air cargo charter	Sigit
P.T. Subentra	Construction	Sudwikatmono, Mukmin Ali (Panin Bank)
P.T. Subentra Multi Petrokimia	Construction	P.T. Subentra
P.T. Metropolitan Inter-Asia Dev.		Panin Bank, P.T. Subentra

TABLE 10.3
THE SUHARTO FAMILY BUSINESS INTERESTS

Company	Sector	Shareholders
PROBOSUTEJO		
P.T. Mercu Buana	Clove import monopoly	Probosutejo 20%
P.T. Plastic Universal	Plastics	Probosutejo 12.5%
P.T. Sri Teguh Kurnia		Probosutejo 30%
P.T. Buana Estate	Property	Probosutejo 45%
P. T. Mercu Buana Contractors	Contracting	Probosutejo 40%
P.T. Kondang Kautaman		Probosutejo 50%
P.T. Cipendawa	Poultry	Probosutejo 50%, *Taiwan*
Bank Ramayana		Probosutejo 7%, with Ong Seng Keng & other Chinese shareholders
P.T. Bank Jakarta		
P.T. Bank Sumber Ekonomi Asia		
P.T. Mercu Buana Chemicals	Chemicals	Probosutejo 30% Agus Nursalim 50%
P.T. Kedaung Subur	Glass manuf.	Probosutejo 35% Agus Nursalim & P.T. Kedaung 65%
P.T. Multifrance Motor	Renault sole agency	Probosutejo 25% P.T. Multivest 75%
P.T. Garmak	Sole agent & assembler of Chevrolet/LUV	
P.T. Sagitarius Sari	Auto components	

Sources: *BNPT* (see Robison 1977, App. B. for details); *BN Anggaran Dasar* 5, 1970; *ICN* 165 (1981), 209 (1982), 213 (1983); *AWSJ*, 20.9.82; *Financial Directory of Indonesia* (Jakarta, 1980); other sources cited in the following case studies.

THE YAYASANS

There is a difficulty in distinguishing between companies owned by politico-bureaucrats on behalf of political institutions and those where capital is owned and invested on their own private behalf. Probably there is no clear delineation of these facets in any one firm. Yayasans Harapan Kita, Kartika Jaya and Trikora have members of the Suharto family as shareholders. The degree to which they function as charitable institutions, as sources of funds for the military or for patronage, or as the private investment of the Suharto family, is a matter of conjecture. They receive funds both from direct investments and from other companies which specifically set aside a portion of their profits. Such companies include P.T. Karana Line and P.T. Bogasari, companies in which the major shares are held by Bob Hasan and Liem Sioe Liong.[39] Direct investments by the Yayasans include a hotel, a logging company and a printing firm.

THE SUHARTO/LIEM GROUP

The largest element of the Suharto family's corporate investments is that constituted in equity holdings in the Liem Sioe Liong group. Through Sudwikatmono, the Suharto family holds 5% shares in the giant Tiga Roda cement group, 4% in the Bogasari flour milling company and at least 5% in Waringin Kencana, the trading and rubber milling firm. Sigit and Siti hold 32% of the Bank Central Asia, the largest private foreign-exchange bank. Sudwikatmono is also President Director of Waringin, Indocement and Bogasari.

The growth of this group, as outlined in the previous chapter, has been assisted by favourable political decisions. Waringin rose to prominence in the late 1960s, able to virtually ignore export quota restrictions and to delay the repayment of substantial government credits. It also enjoyed a near monopoly as importer and supplier of parts to P.N. Timah, the state tin mining corporation allegedly controlled by appointees of General Soerjo.[40] The Commission of Four on Corruption singled out Waringin as a company requiring urgent investigation. As detailed in Chapter 7, P.T. Bogasari has held a *de facto* monopoly on flour milling in Indonesia since the state logistics agency, Bulog, forced the competing mill out of the market.

MISCELLANEOUS SUHARTO FAMILY ENTERPRISES

The largest of these is P.T. Gunung Ngadeg Jaya, a trading company which has become a shareholder in large cable manu-

facturing and cement ventures with initial investments of
Rp1 058 million and Rp20 billion respectively. The Suharto
family's holding in P.T. Pasopati through Bernard Ibnu
Hardoyo is the mechanism for entry into the extensive busi-
ness empire of Bob Hasan outlined in the previous chapter.
P.T. Subentra is a joint venture between Sudwikatmono and
Mukmin Ali of Panin Bank, whose subsidiary P.T. Subentra
Multi Petrokimia recently secured a $2 million construction
contract in South Sumatra. The most interesting company is
Sigit's P.T. Bayu Air, which does little air freighting on its
own account but reportedly receives a 5% levy on all air
cargo flown in and out of Indonesia, enforced by the Air
Communications Director General.[41] Sigit himself is a shad-
owy figure whose name appears on few company records
but who is reputed to play a major role in business. Persistent
claims by the business community include the secret transfer
of shares in state corporations to Sigit and his involvement in
the sale of spot oil.

Recently, a son, Bambang Triatmotjo, and a son-in-law,
Indra Kowara, secured a lease agreement from Pertamina
for two tankers to ship liquid natural gas to Korea. Through
their companies P.T. Samudra Petrindo Asia and P.T. Fast
Marine Service, Triatmodjo and Kowara have secured
brokerage rights for a deal worth $130 million for each ship,
amortised over twenty years. To secure the leasing agreement for the ships, in which they also hold shares, they were
involved in a long struggle with another Suharto son, Sigit
Harjoyudanto, who was reportedly lobbying Pertamina to
commission Korean shipyards to build at least one tanker.[42]
Although it has long been alleged that the Suharto family has
played the role of intermediary, at an informal level, in
leasing, purchasing and contracting deals between capital
and the state, this is the first movement by the family to
institutionalise this role within a corporate structure.

PROBOSUTEJO

Originally a schoolteacher, Probosutejo began his business career in 1953 with P.T. Orici, a company owned by a Chinese businessman with whom he later established P.T. Setiabudi Murni in Medan.[43] In the Guided Economy period he became involved with P.T. Irian Bhakti, which held a monopoly on the Irian Jaya trade between 1963 and 1965 under Kostrad sponsorship. After 1965 his company, P.T. Mercu Buana, was granted one of two licences to import cloves into Indonesia, and so began his movement into the realms of big business. Several of Probosutejo's companies are partnerships with other indigenous shareholders, probably from Solo. These include Mercu Buana, Mercu Buana Contractors, and Buana Estate. His large poultry interest, P.T. Cipendawa, is a joint venture with Taiwan investors. For the most part, however, Probosutejo's business interests are shareholdings in a variety of the major Chinese business groups, in chemical and glass manufacture with Agus Nursalim, in the Kostrad-associated Bank Ramayana with Arief Husni, and in the automobile industry with the Astra group.

As a political figure, Probosutejo is an interesting crystallisation of the contradictions which exist within the structure of the capitalist class in Indonesia. While his rise has been clearly reliant upon political influence, he has been loud in trumpeting the virtues of the entrepreneurial spirit. Similarly, while his business ventures have been inextricably linked with the major Chinese business groups, he has taken a fairly militant *'pribumi'* stand and has been critical of the influence of major Chinese capitalists and the outflow of Chinese-owned capital. Many of these sentiments were publicised through his newspaper, *Ekuin*, which was eventually closed by his brother, the President.[44]

One aspect of the structure of the Suharto business group is its integration with Chinese and foreign-owned capital, constituting a concrete terminal for common interest between capital and indigenous politico-bureaucrat power. At another level, the creation of a substantial base of capital ownership has meant that the Suharto family's economic position has shifted from a total reliance on the exercise of power towards capital accumulation. The Suhartos are now both politico-bureaucrat and capitalist.

Yet critics within the business community cast doubts upon the long-term prospects of survival for the Suhartos as capitalists. One argument is that they will be progressively expropriated by the new power-holders after Suharto leaves office. Much depends upon the nature of the transfer of power. If it is bitter and violent like the 1965 experience, then we may indeed see the wholesale expropriation of the Suharto wealth. If, as is more likely, the transfer is benign and carried out within the political and ideological structures established under Suharto, then it will be difficult for the family's assets, with the probable exception of some of the more blatant monopolies, to be touched. Capital assets are much more difficult to expropriate than trading monopolies or forestry concessions. Another mitigating factor is the very interest of the capitalist class, in Indonesia as elsewhere, to sanctify private property and, to an increasing degree, to regularise the process of accumulation within a legal and predictable framework. Despite the fact that arbitrary political action has been a central feature in the establishment of business groups, this is likely to become less acceptable as the capitalist class entrenches itself.

Nevertheless the Suharto group faces some real problems. Unlike the Liems, the Astra group, Soedarpo or even Sutowo, the Suharto group does not integrate ownership of capital with ownership and management of a corporation. Whereas in advanced capitalist economies owners of capital may invest in a well-established capital market, Indonesians who simply have a lot of money must buy into family-based companies or international corporations. In the case of foreign corporations, access to equity by domestic investors is enforced by legislation, so foreign partners do not take domestic partners because they need their capital. The most valuable commodities to be offered by a local partner are experience, knowledge of the local market or political influence. After Suharto's retirement, the inevitable decline of the family's political influence will make them increasingly unattractive as partners, with the result that unless the Suhartos establish an independent corporate base for their capital they will find it difficult to maintain their present position.

The Sutowo Group

Between 1967 and 1975 Ibnu Sutowo, the President Director of the state-owned oil company Pertamina, built the largest private indigenous business group in Indonesia. The group was involved in a wide range of investments including manufacture, auto assembly, trade, logging, banking, property and shipbuilding and was enmeshed in a network of joint ventures with several of the largest business groups in Indonesia and the Southeast Asian region. It illustrates the crucial role of the state in capital accumulation in general and the development of indigenous business groups in particular. The boundaries between Sutowo's public and private business empires were often blurred; his partners and clients in private business included employees, contractors and business partners of Pertamina. The structure of the Sutowo group also illustrates the importance of import-substitution manufacture, and the integration between politico-bureaucrat power and Chinese and, to a lesser degree, indigenous private capital.

That part of the Sutowo group fully owned by members of the Sutowo family is relatively small. It includes a logging company, an architectural firm and, most notably, the Bank Pasifik, the smallest of the eleven foreign-exchange banks, with assets of Rp42 billion.[45]

Outside the wholly-owned family companies, the first level or inner core of the Sutowo group is constituted by partnerships with the South Sumatran businessman, Moh. Joesoef (sometimes known as Joesoef Gading), and with Sjarnubi

Said. Joesoef is generally considered to be the man who ran the Sutowo business interests, at least until the early 1970s. Sjarnubi Said was Director of Maintenance for Pertamina until 1976, one of several Pertamina employees who were private capitalists in their own right. If we look closely at these 'core companies' it becomes evident that few operate without either foreign or Chinese partners, or both.

The largest component of the Sutowo group in the mid-1970s consisted of a series of joint ventures with the Astra group, mainly in property and construction through the joint holding company, P. T. Indophing, but also in manufacture and auto assembly and import. These ventures are substantial and include some of the largest domestic companies, the most ambitious of which was a Rp4.5 billion mini steel mill. Perhaps the most interesting element of the Sutowo group is its relationship with the Hong Kong and Singapore businessmen Robin Loh and Tong Djoe. Robin Loh headed a large ship-building and manufacturing group in Singapore, but had long maintained close links with Indonesia, where he had lived to the age of eighteen. In the late 1960s he became Pertamina's main supplier of pipes and equipment, and received large contracts for tanker deals, ship repairs and the building of infrastructure.[46] Although there is only one private joint venture between Loh and Sutowo — a cattle ranch — informed sources claim a much more important role for Loh in Sutowo's business group; for example, in establishing the Adiguna shipyard for Ibnu's son Ponco. Tong Djoe was a former Palembang shipper who moved his operations to Singapore and established the Tunas group of companies. In 1964, Tunas of Hong Kong sold Permina (the precursor of Pertamina) five small motor ships. By 1966, Tunas owned three tankers, a small feeder tanker and a tug, all of which were on charter to Pertamina. By the late 1960s, Tunas' Handara shipyard in Hong Kong was supplying Pertamina with tugs and barges. Together with Loh's Ednasa groups, Tong Djoe was Pertamina's major Southeast Asian supplier.[47] But Tong Djoe's relationships

TABLE 10.4
THE SUTOWO BUSINESS GROUP AT ITS HEIGHT IN 1975

Company	Sector	Shareholders
AUTO ASSEMBLY IMPORT & DISTRIBUTION		
P.T. Krama Yudha Tiga Berlian	Mitsubishi sole agency)	with Sjarnubi Said and Mitsubishi
P.T. Krama Yudha Mitsubishi	Mitsubishi assemblers)	
P.T. Inter Astra Motors	Daihatsu sole agency	with Sjarnubi Said, Moh. Joeseof and the Astra group
P.T. German Motors	VW and Mercedes assembly	P.T. Indophing and *West Germany*
P.T. Star Motors	Mercedes sole agency	P.T. Gading Mas and *West Germany*
P.T. Jakarta Motors	G.M. sole agency	with Bakrie, Hashim Ning and Abdul Mutalib
P.T. ISC	G.M. assembler	with Hashim Ning?
P.T. Superior	Auto components	P.T. Jakarta Motors
PROPERTY & CONSTRUCTION		
P.T. Masari Karya		with Sjarnubi Said
P.T. Indobuildco		P.T. Indophing and Sjarnubi Said
P.T. Indonesialand		P.T. Indobuildco and Astra
P.T. Town and City		P.T. Indophing and Multivest
P.T. Marineland		P.T. Gading Mas and Astra
P.T. John Holland		Ibnu Sutowo and *Australia*
P.T. Tongkangmas		P.T. Masari Karja and Tunas group
MANUFACTURE & SHIPBUILDING		
P.T. Adiguna	Shipyard	P.T. Indophing and Ponco Nugro Susilo

P.T. Paksaguna	Shipyard	P.T. Adiguna and *Japan*
P.T. Tunas	Shipyard	P.T. Adiguna and Tunas group
P.T. Dewi Arimbi	Aluminium extrusion	with Moh. Joesoef and *Singapore*
P.T. Intalan	Aluminium extrusion	P.T. Indophing and P.T. Sempurna
P.T. Karimum	Granite	P.T. Indophing and *UK*
P.T. Surya	Engineering	P.T. Gading Mas and Astra
FINANCE		
P.T. Bank Pasifik	Foreign-exchange bank	Sutowo family
P.T. PDFC	Finance institution	P.T. Gading Mas, Bank of Indonesia
		Panin Bank, P.T. Tri Usaha Bhakti, Soedarpo
FORESTRY		
P.T. Sarana Buana Handana		with Bob Hasan
P.T. Alas		with Bob Hasan
P.T. Benuaran		Sutowo family
MISCELLANEOUS		
P.T. Handara Graha	Architecture	Udaya Hadibroto and Ponco Nugro Susilo
P.T. Nugra Santana		Sutowo family
P.T. Gading Mas Tobacco		P.T. Gading Mas
P.T. Dharma Bhakti Pelita		Sutowo family, General Yunus, Tony Ardi
P.T. Indonesia Petroleum		Sutowo family with P.T. Dharma Bhakti Pelita
P.T. Tunas companies	Travel, insurance, trade, hotel	with Tunas group

Notes: P.T. Indophing is a holding company in which the shareholders are Ibiu Sutowo, Moh. Joesoef and the Astra group.
P.T. Gading Mas is a holding company in which shares are held by the Sutowo family and Moh. Joesoef associates.
The Tunas group is associated with Tong Djoe.
Sources: From *BNPT* (see Robison 1977 for details) and other sources cited in the following analysis of the Sutowo group.

with Pertamina were complemented by substantial private business partnerships with Sutowo, including a small shipyard, travel, insurance and engineering companies and the proposed P. T. Tongkangmas, a multi-billion rupiah international hotel to have been built on the oil terminal island of Batam.

Sutowo's private business network also extends into the ranks of the very powerful. P. T. Sarana Buana Handana is a partnership with the Diponegoro/Kostrad *cukong* Bob Hasan and General Subroto Kusmarjo, while P. T. Alas is a large paper milling venture which includes Sutowo's son Ponco, Bob Hasan, Japanese partners and, reportedly, members of the Suharto family. As mentioned earlier, the auto industry was subject to a major reshuffle in the late 1960s. Sutowo was the main beneficiary of this reshuffle and the subsequent move of the Japanese into the market. His first move was into the G. M. sole agency (Jakarta Motors) and assembler (ISC), where he now operates in partnership with its former owners, Hashim Ning and other indigenous capitalists. He then moved into the Mercedes and VW sole agency/assemblers (P. T. German Motors and P. T. Star Motors), which had passed from the old order businessmen, Suwarma and Panggabean, to P. T. Berdikari and then to Sutowo. However the big prize was the Mitsubishi sole agency and assembler, Krama Yudha, a partnership with Sjarnubi Said. Together with Astra's Toyota group, Krama Yudha dominates the auto industry.[48] To this Sutowo has added P.T. Inter Astra Motors, the Daihatsu sole agent — a partnership with Astra, as is German Motors.

Other areas of investment include property, hotels, shipyards, engineering and aluminium extrusion — all sectors where domestic capital enjoyed increasingly heavy protection under the joint venture and DSP legislation, and which, in the case of manufacturing, relied heavily on access to government contracts for supply.

The significance of politico-bureaucrat power in the formation of indigenous capital is illustrated not only by Sutowo's own private business group but by a number of indigenous capitalists who grew up around the Sutowo/Pertamina complex. Moh. Joesoef's textile firm, Sempurna, developed with Pertamina contracts in the 1960s, and in the early 1970s became a partner in a massive Rp62 billion artificial fibre complex with Pertamina and the Japanese Teijin petrochemical company. But the most interesting indigenous capitalists who emerged around Pertamina were a group of young, rich businessmen from prominent families associated with Hipmi (Young Businessmens Association of Indonesia). The foremost of these was Siswono Judo Husodo, the son of the former deputy governor of Jakarta Dr. Suwondo, and an engineering graduate of ITB Bandung. Others included former student leader, Fahmi Idris; Sutowo's own son, Ponco Nugro Susilo; Suryadharma Tahir, the son of General Tahir; Guntur Sukarno, son of the former President; and Teuku Sjahrul, the son of Jusuf Muda Dalam.

A clear insight into the process of establishing corporate groups under the New Order came from a series of interviews conducted by the writer with several Hipmi members. According to the informants, the power and resources to launch indigenous Indonesians into business on a competitive basis was in the hands of no more than half a dozen individuals, including the President and one or two of his closest advisers (probably Moertopo and Hoemardani), the Governor of Jakarta, and the President Director of Pertamina. With these few men rested the power to give contracts for supply and construction, directorships, and even to provide finance. The Palace was not seen as a source of patronage, because it was closed to those outside the immediate Suharto family, associates from the royal families in Solo, Kostrad and certain Chinese clients. In any case, the Palace group were not considered to be interested in the creation of a genuine indigenous capitalist class or even in becoming capitalists themselves, as was Sutowo, but in obtaining a 'cut' from Chinese-owned groups. Military enterprises were similarly closed. Even the Chinese Astra group, it was claimed, employed more indigenous executive staff than the Palace, or the military who relied entirely on Chinese. It was also alleged that P.T. Pembangunan Jaya no longer offered opportunities to indigenous capitalists now that it was 'under the control' of the Chinese director, Ciputra.

The Hipmi business men interviewed were quite open about the importance of political patronage to private capital accumulation, but argued that it could be used constructively, together with general economic policy, as a tool in nurturing an indigenous capitalist class. They were quite hostile to those political power-holders who directed their patronage to Chinese rather than indigenous clients. Sutowo was admired because he was prepared to back young indigenous capitalists and because he was seen to have a genuine concern for the development of an indigenous capitalist class.

Since the Pertamina crisis there has been some opportunity to identify the Pertamina contractors and the relationships between Pertamina and private capitalists, because their situation became public in the course of the government rescue operation mounted when Pertamina proved unable to meet debts and fulfil contract obligations. In a major article in *Tempo*,[49] it was suggested that contractors were selected before tenders were called and official contract prices exaggerated both to the advantage of 'speculators' within Pertamina and the contractors. Siswono was identified as a major contractor with several projects totalling, in Siswono's words, 'thousands of millions of rupiahs'. Contract payments were cut by 50% after scrutiny by a government-appointed review team under Sumarlin. The state oil company had not only been supplying contracts but opportunities for accumulation — virtually state-funded injections of potential investment finance to private business groups. Apart from Siswono, other clients to be affected were Fahmi Idris, the former student leader and President Director of P. T. Krama Yudha, whose company P. T. Kwarta Daya had contracted to build Pertamina flats; and Taufiq Bahauddin and Maryadi Darmawan, former student leaders, whose company P. T. Enmitra had the contract to build the hospital at Cilacap.

How devastating was the Pertamina crisis to Sutowo and the Pertamina clients? We have seen in an earlier chapter how the military company, Propelat, a major Pertamina contractor, was severely hit by the sudden loss of contracts. Robin Loh was estimated to have lost 25% of his fortune in the Pertamina débâcle.[50] William Soerjadjaja claimed that he made substantial losses on the property investments and on the mini steel mill.[51] The extent of the impact upon the young Hipmi capitalists is not clear. It is likely that some were not affected because their participation did not involve actual capital investment. As the *Tempo* article pointed out, although the contractors received the contract and a proportion of the contract price to proceed with the initial work, much of the construction was done by sub-contractors who were required to finance themselves. In other words, they performed a role similar to the Benteng 'briefcase' entrepreneurs. Because such contractors would have no capital invested, or interest payments on loans due, the cuts had no direct effect on capital and could be passed on to the sub-contractors.

For the indigenous contractors favoured by Pertamina who did have capital and industry, the set-backs of 1975 and 1976 were not as devastating as they might have been, because of the boom in construction that followed oil price rises and the exponential growth of the development budget in the late 1970s and early 1980s. Construction contracts once again flowed freely, and larger domestic contractors able to undertake projects in excess of Rp1 billion were in short supply. Private indigenous contractors, including Siswono's P. T. Bangun Cipta Sarana, operated in consortiums, together with state companies and often with foreign contractors, on multi-billion dollar projects. Siswono estimates his corporate assets to have risen from Rp33 billion in 1979 to Rp48 billion in 1980, and the component generated by construction to have risen from Rp21 billion to Rp39 billion.[52] He recently received a large loan from the state bank, BNI 1946, and won Middle East contracts in excess of Rp1 billion.[53] In the case of Siswono at least, the opportunities for 'primitive' or politically generated accumulation presented by Pertamina constituted a launching pad for the development of a substantial indigenous capitalist group.

What of Sutowo himself? Can private bureaucrat-capitalists survive the diminution of their own political power and lessened control over the allocation of state contracts? Some elements of his group declined in the period after 1976, particularly his property ventures. Struggles between shareholders for control of companies have begun to occur, including disputes between Sutowo and Moh. Joesoef over P. T. Indobuildco and between Sutowo and Sjarnubi Said over Krama Yudha.[54] Recent reports indicate that Sutowo has taken full ownership of the Hilton Hotel in return for ceding Krama Yudha to Said and Star Motors to Moh. Joesoef. Bank Pasifik has lost ground to other private foreign-exchange banks, its relative decline being attributed to fewer oil company deposits following Sutowo's loss of control over Pertamina.[55] It is, however, unclear whether companies within the Sutowo group, such as P. T. Intalan or P. T. Adiguna, have found their positions as Pertamina suppliers fundamentally affected by Sutowo's fall.

FROM POLITICO-BUREAUCRAT TO CAPITALIST

We also see under the New Order a trend for generals and officials to go into business upon retirement. The most important of these have been Ali Sadikin, the former mayor of Jakarta (construction and property), and General Sumitro (forestry and pharmaceuticals).[56] This trend indicates another dimension of the importance of the state to the development of a capitalist class. It gives officials the opportunity to accumulate finance, develop contacts and secure concessions as a base for corporate, capitalist activity after departure from office.

Three other business groups whose roots stretch back into the Sukarno era may be included in this category: the Poleko group, the Kosgoro group and the Konsultasi Pembangunan group.

The Poleko Group

Poleko is another group for which it is difficult to unravel the roles of private and state capital. P. T. Poleko was established in 1958 as a trading company owned by Sulawesi shareholders, among whom the Baramuli family was most prominent.[57] Until the late 1960s the Poleko group remained a small outer-island trader, but from the early 1970s it expanded rapidly. A major recapitalisation programme was undertaken, including an injection of Rp500 million into Poleko and Rp2 108 million into P. T. Poleko Sulinda, a sack and bag factory. But the major developments have been the entry of Poleko into several very large joint ventures with Japanese companies. These include 51% of a Rp680 million textile mill (P. T. Pacific Textiles), 16% of a $87.3 million synthetic fibre mill (P. T. Indonesia Toray Synthetics), and a 40% share of a $4.8 million joint venture in chemicals.[58]

Although the Poleko shares are held by the Baramuli family, the group is closely associated with the Department of the Interior. These links are apparent in the career of the leading figure in the group, General Arnold Baramuli. Between 1956 and 1962, Baramuli rose from Attorney in Makassar to Governor of North Sulawesi. From 1962 to 1965 he appears to have fallen from favour and was without official post, but in 1965 when General Sumarno became Minister of the Interior, Baramuli was given the post of co-ordinator of the regional enterprises confiscated from the Dutch in 1958 and handed over to the Department of Interior. Control of these enterprises confirmed Baramuli's reputation as the 'financial' general of that Department — an equivalent to generals like Sofjar, Soerjo and Hoemardani.

Between 1966 and 1969, while General Basuki Rachmat

was Minister for the Interior, Baramuli was promoted to Head of the Economic and Finance Branch of the Department, a position he retained after General Amir Machmud became Minister in 1969. It is not clear whether the Poleko group is operated by Baramuli on behalf of the Department of Interior, or is a genuinely private business group, or an amalgam of the two. Neither is it clear how many of the Poleko companies are the former state-owned companies which came under Baramuli's direct jurisdiction in 1965. Whatever the case, Poleko is a business group whose rise was closely associated with the Department of Interior and whose main shareholder was the Department's Financial Chief.

Kosgoro

Kosgoro is the business group of the Indonesian Veterans Organisation which operates with the expressed intention of raising finance for welfare purposes. Its directors are men of considerable political influence, particularly General Isman and General Martono, former Vice Chairman of Golkar. Long-established contacts with Japanese business are balanced domestically with contacts throughout the government through veterans' associations and through the former student army organisation, TRIP. While the early activities of Kosgoro were confined to importing and the operation of night clubs, its recent development has been taken in corn farming and property. In the corn farming venture, Kosgoro has contributed $735 000 of the total investment of $6.5 million for its 49% equity,[59] while the Kosgoro Building involves an investment of approximately $38 million in which Kosgoro's equity is 10%.[60]

The Konsultasi Pembangunan Group

Another interesting group, Konsultasi Pembangunan, is owned by former Army officers involved in the PRRI/

Permesta rebellions of the late 1950s, the most important of whom are Nicolas Sumual, Barlian, Daeng Edward Mogo, Bing Latumahina, Maludin Simbolon and Achmad Husein. The sudden emergence of these officers from prison in 1965 to business prominence indicates that they had access to considerable resources as well as political support. The patronage of the New Order was apparent when, in 1966, most of these officers appeared as executive members of the Army-sponsored trade union, Soksi, under the chairmanship of Colonel Suhardiman, Indonesia's most powerful military entrepreneur of the time.[61] In the breakup of the forestry concessions of the late 1960s, Konsultasi secured no less than three concessions, one of which is among the largest in Indonesia, another indication of the favour of the state.[62] The rise of Konsultasi also suggests that at least some of the funds raised by the military in the outer islands through smuggling operations in the 1950s and 1960s may have been channelled into investments.

The Konsultasi Pembangunan group was focused initially around forestry, construction and small-scale shipping, but, in common with Poleko and Kosgoro, it has moved strongly into joint ventures in construction, bulk log carrying and even hotels.[63]

MISCELLANEOUS NEW ORDER CLIENT GROUPS

Since 1965, several major indigenous business groups have emerged under the ownership of capitalists who are not holders of political power. The most important of these are shown in Table 10.5.

The Sahid Group

Sukamdani has been in business since the early 1950s, operating small trading and printing firms and pharmaceutical dispensaries. From the late 1960s his business group was

TABLE 10.5

NON-ESTABLISHMENT BUSINESS GROUPS

Group	Sector	Major Shareholders
Bangun Cipta Sarana	Property & construction	Siswono Judo Husodo
Sahid	Hotels, property, construction and cement	Sukamdani Gitorsardjono
	Property, aluminuim extrusion	Sucipto Amidharmo
Mahkota	Property, construction, hotels, chemicals	Widodo Sukarno
Adiguna	(See Sutowo group)	Ponco Nugro Susilo

transformed with great rapidity. His hotel, Sahid Jaya, was established with Rp1 billion investment in 1973, and he began negotiations in 1974 with Swiss interests to build a Rp 18 billion cement plant in which Sukamdani was to hold a 75% equity share holding. This latter project did not come to fruition until 1982 in the form of a fully domestic partnership between the Sahid group, Liem's Indocement group and the Metropolitan group associated with Ciputra. By this time the cost was US$290 million of which US$97 million was to be put up by the shareholders.[64] Sukamdani's sudden rise to national prominence owes much to his remarkable access to extremely large amounts of equity capital. It is generally claimed within the Jakarta business community that Sukamdani is the conduit for the investment of finance raised by Mrs Suharto.[65] While no documentary evidence has been presented to support these allegations, Sukamdani certainly has several business relationships with the Suharto family, including a 17% shareholding in the Kartika Chandra hotel,[66] a directorship of Mrs Suharto's miniature Indonesia project, and a partnership with the Suharto family in P. T. Tridaya Cement through their holdings in Indocement. Other investments by the Sahid group include construction (P. T. New Sahid Builders) and timber (P. T. Sahid Timber). He also holds the Pusri (state fertiliser company) distributorship for Central Java.[67]

Others

Of the other groups, Siswono and Ponco Nugro Susilo have been dealt with earlier. Both the Mahkota group and Sucipto's group are expanding and diversified. Mahkota in particular has extensive holdings in property, construction, tourism and manufacture, integrating with foreign and Chinese capital as well as with former PSI-associated indigenous capitalists and the military.[68] Sucipto's business interests were, until the late 1960s, confined to the old life assurance company, Bumiputera 1912, of which he was a director.[69] Since then he has expanded into property and manufacture with both Chinese and foreign partners.

THE POLITICAL SIGNIFICANCE OF INDIGENOUS PRIVATE CAPITAL

In the eighteen years of New Order rule which have now elapsed, it is clear that a significant number of large indigenous business groups and indigenous capitalists have emerged or had their existing positions expanded and consolidated. While still far less important than state-owned, foreign or Chinese capital, indigenous capital has moved into a variety of fields, including manufacture, forestry, hotels and tourism, shipping and finance. Its representatives are not simply dealers in political concessions but owners of capital. What political significance flows from this? Have these developments produced any substantial political organisation of indigenous capital which can serve to secure its ascendancy over rival groups?

In contrast to the declining elements of the indigenous capitalist class, the major indigenous capitalists have not been prominent in confronting foreign and Chinese capital. Indeed, their emergence under the New Order has been achieved by integrating with them in joint ventures, construction consortiums, distribution and management arrangements. Such integration has been built upon public legislation which guaranteed the entry of indigenous capital into joint ventures and restricted the entry of foreign and Chinese capital into specific fields of investment. It has also been constructed upon access to political influence involving preferential access to finance, licences and contracts for individual firms, which in turn has made these firms more attractive to foreign investors looking for indigenous partners. Consequently, there is little incentive for major indigenous capitalists to agitate for political power as a class when the military rule so effectively in their interests. At the same time there is no reason whatever for the major indigenous capitalists to put any real venom into campaigns against foreign or Chinese capital while they are guaranteed a stake in the growth of these groups.

What then is the political task which confronts the major indigenous capitalist? Primarily it is to secure a guaranteed position in the conglomerate of capitalist factions operating in Indonesia. Given the increasing internationalisation of capital, the prospect of an autonomous and independent indigenous capitalist class, dominating ownership of capital and investment decisions, becomes increasingly irrelevant. Instead, its future is as a more or less developed component of complex international corporate and financial structures. Its task is a continuous process of bargaining and negotiating to fix its relationships with Chinese and international capital. Given the relative weakness of the indigenous corporate and capital base, this process must be a political one.

At another level, the major indigenous capitalists have an important role to play in the developing general relations between state and capital. Although their capital and corporate base is weak in relative terms, it nevertheless exists and constitutes their social interest at least in part. In common with international and Chinese elements of the capitalist class, such issues as interest rates, the price of labour, government fiscal policy, access to the market and corporate competition are now essential to their survival. Their significance as a component of the capitalist class is not the extent of their ownership of capital but their potential to act politically and publicly on behalf of capital against the immediate interests of the state and its officials who may see revenue collection, long-term planning and control of the terminals of state economic power as more important than short-term problems of accumulation.

The focal point for attempts by the larger bourgeoisie to gain a more formal and influential role in the process of decision-making has been Kadin. Long regarded as a club for well-connected businessmen, a clearing house for concessions and an agency of the government, it is now being suggested that Kadin be given a more central role in policy-making.

In a recent newspaper interview,[70] Eddy Kowara compared relationships between state and business in Indonesia unfavourably with those in India, noting with approval that, in the latter case, the big twelve companies control the government. He contented that the only business forum in Indonesia, Kadin, was just a receiving platform — a debating house. It should have a legal constitutional basis rather than being dependent upon the energies and influence of its leaders, and relations beween Kadin and the government must become a partnership or there would be (unspecified) repercussions.

Kowara was, in effect, arguing for a constitutionally guaranteed place for private business within the existing political and economic framework. There are no implications of a bourgeois challenge to military power, but rather a reshuffling of the existing corporatist structures to institutionalise the position of capital. Similar arguments have also been put forward by Hashim Ning and Sukamdani Gitorsardjono.[71] Arguing that the interests of national capital should be mediated by Kadin, Ning and Sukamdani criticise the government's neglect of the private sector and argue that Kadin possesses the knowledge and skills to provide valuable inputs into government policy. Sukamdani even suggests Kadin participation in closed sessions of the cabinet.

What are the prospects for a greater political role for Kadin? On the one hand there remains the tendency for businessmen to solve problems on an individual basis through political contacts rather than through corporate action in defence of general class interests. There is also the problem that Kadin, historically an organisation of indigenous capital, has not yet sufficiently integrated with foreign and Chinese capital, the dominant elements of the capitalist class in Indonesia.

On the other hand, there has been a significant change in its leadership. Early leaders, including General Sofjar and Air Marshal Suwoto Sukendar, reflected the dominance of the politico-bureaucrat over business activity. The more recent leaders, Kowara, Sukamdani and Ning, represent well-connected capitalists with significant bases. Many of the major Chinese businessmen are now members and there is increasing corporate integration between major indigenous and Chinese capitalists.

It is clear that the prospects for the development of a civilian base of power within the new order lies not with the urban intelligentsia, as it did in the 1950s and 1960s, but with the larger indigenous capitalists. Together with Golkar, Kadin represents the logical place to begin a devolution of power designed to broaden the political base of the regime without threatening the structure of the social order over which it presides. The major politico-bureaucrat families themselves now span and embody the interests of state official, politico-bureaucrat and private capitalist, consequently embracing all the contradictions and linkages inherent in these relationships. The extent to which these different interests and functions will be reflected in a future division of political institutions will depend upon the development of the contradictions. Certainly the statements of Kowara, Ning and Sukamdani suggest that these are already at a high level on such issues as official corruption, efficiency of administration, licensing of exporters, and quality of long-term planning and consultation. Since the oil price crisis of 1982/83, we must add to these the issues of taxation, tariff protection, investment credit, and government subsidy of import-substitution manufacture. Not only do these issues increase the tension between the state and capital, but they also mean that the problems of individual capitalists are less amenable to solution on the basis of private political arrangements and require more concerted action on the basis of general class interest.

1. *Suara Karya*, 5.4.74 (*USPRT*).

2. See Kapni statements in *Pelopor Baru*, 20.4.68; *Angkatan '66*, 12.4.67; *Operasi*, 22.11.67; *Revolusimi*, 17.10.67; *Angkatan Baru*, 25.1.68

3. Forum Swasta Nasional under the chairmanship of Ir. Aminuddin attempted to secure state recognition as the 'official' association of business, but his request was rejected by the government (*Harian Kami*, 24.12.68). Other associations which declined in this period were Omar Tusin's Kensi and KKNI (Konfederasi Karyawan Nasional Indonesia).

4. See the section on Kadin and its relations with the state in Robison 1977, pp. 422–8.

5. 'Kredit PMDN-Antara Koneksi dan Investasi', *Tempo*, 9.12.72.

6. *Tempo*, 9.12.72; *Kompas*, 23.2.74.

7. Unpublished Bappenas document, *Perkiraan Kebutuhan Daha Untuk Menunjang Program Peningkatan Usaha Pribumi dalam PMA dan PMDN* (Jakarta, 1973).

8. See statements by these businessmen in the article 'Yang digunting dan yang Terbanting', *Tempo*, 24.9.74 as well as Sutomo's statements in *FEER*, 7.5.73. Sjafruddin Prawiranegara's extensive criticisms of economic policy, corruption, foreign capital dominance and *cukong*ism may be found in *Angkatan Bersendjata*, 28.6.68; *Budaya Jaya*, Nov. 1969; *Kompas*, 27.5.69; *Harian Kami*, 3.8.70; *Abadi*, 6.8.70. The author also conducted interviews with Sjafruddin, Tambunan, Tusin, Sutomo and Mulyomiseno.

9. *Nusantara*, 7.1.71 drew attention to the relationships between General Soerjo and various *cukong*, particularly Ong Seng Keng, with whom it was alleged Soerjo had been associated from his days as head of military finance. Other prominent *cukong*, Cokrosaputro, Robby Tjajadi, Go Swie Kie and Liem Sioe Liong, as well as the companies Coopa, Mega, Mantrust, Bogasari and Astra are dealt with in issues of 24.9.70, 8.9.72, 10.2.73 and 9.2.73. On the *cukong* as communists, see the issue of 15.2.71. On state bank credit to the *cukong* as communists, see the issue of 15.2.71. On state bank credit to the *cukong*, see issues of 24.9.70, 13.11.72, 30.1.73 and 9.2.73.

10. *Business News*, 13.4.73.

11. Daroesman 1981, pp. 17–18.

12. *Pedoman, Suara Karya, Proklamasi*, 29.3.72.

13. The most interesting public claim that Inpres was being channelled to

Chinese capitalists came from Sutanto, Vice-Chairman of Parliamentary Commission VI, in *Berita Buana*, 4.9.76.

14. *Sinar Harapan*, 13.4.77.

15. *ICN* 89, 7.11.77.

16. Boulton 1978, pp. 122–3.

17. Interviews with Eddy Dasaad.

18. P.T. Perkins Diesel (*Tempo*, 3.2.73) and a company involved in the installation of sugar factories which is a joint venture with a Dutch company and the Bank of Indonesia (*BKPM*, 28.2.74).

19. *ICN* 202, 19.7.82.

20. Ning's interests include:
P.T. Indonesia Service Co. (GM Sole agent/assembler)
P.T. Daha Motors (Fiat)
P.T. Jakarta Motors (GM Distributors) *BNPT* 295–1973
P.T. Pembangunan Jaya (Construction) *BNPT* 189–1964
P.T. Industria (electrical assembly) *BNPT* 22–1967
P.T. Mohtex (trading) *BNPT* 20–1971
P.T. Guiness Brewery *BNPT* 43–1974 and *BKPM*, 23.4.73
P.T. Kemang Raya Hotel
P.T. Pembangunan Pertama Construction.
For further details see Robison 1977, Appendix B, p. 5, and *Suara Karya*, 22.6.74. The latest company is P.T. Nidera, a $19.7 million property development office building in partnership with Dutch investors, and P.T. Dersco, a Chinese company (*ICN* 210, 15.11.82).

21. Dick 1977, Chapter 6.

22. The Indokaya/Nissan dispute is treated in *Tempo*, 27.9.80 and 13.6.81; *AWSJ* 2.4.81, 6.9.80, 1.10.80, 11.10.80 and 17.10.80.

23. I. Chalmers, Third World State: Epicentre or Epiphenomenon? (The Motor Vehicle Industry in Indonesia) (Sydney, August 1983).

24. Material obtained in interviews with Bekti and Machdi – 5.3.74, 15.3.74 and 29.10.74.

25. Interview with Kowara in *Eksekutif*, August 1981, pp. 9–19.

26. For details of the corporate structure of these groups see Robison 1977, Appendix B, pp. xiii and ix.

27. *Eksekutif*, August 1981.

28. The major Abidin companies are P.T. Shailendra Arya, P.T. Abdi and P.T. Tunggal which are associated in four major joint ventures with German cosmetics and pharmaceutical companies each with initial approved share capital of over Rp100 million. See: *BNPT* 21–1968, 22–1970, 302–1970, 221–1971 and 345–1973.

29. *BNPT* 7–1968, *BNPT* 369–1972, *BKPM* 6.2.74. The sugar refinery is a substantial venture with an approved investment of Rp15 650 (*BKPM* 6.2.74). Interview with Nahar Zahiruddin Tanjung, 5.3.74.

30. Details of the Gobel group are given in *ICN* 133, 10 September 1979. The major company, P.T. National Gobel, has an issued capital of $2 400 000 of which Gobel's equity is $960 000. The forestry company, P.T. Arrow M. Gobel, is the second largest of the group with an issued capital of $2 568 407. We may assume loan capital of at least the total issued capital if normal patterns of investment prevail.

31. Interview with Aminuddin, 21.3.74; *Tempo*, 9.12.72.

32. The major GKBI mills are P.T. Prima-Texco: authorized capital Rp2 800 million — GKBI 26.6%, Japan 73.3% (*BKPM* 26.2.71); P.T. Primissimo: authorized capital Rp1 230 million — Dept. Textile Industry 60%, GKBI 40% (*BNPT* 209–1972).

33. P.T. Daralon Textiles, *BNPT* 138–1973.

34. For details see Robison 1977, Appendix A.

35. E. D. Hawkins, *Case Studies of Indonesian Business Firms* (Jogjakarta, 1959).

36. The Bank Dagang Nasional Indonesia crisis is treated in: *AWSJ*, 26.2.80, 24.5.80, 13.9.80, 12.11.80, 25.6.81.

37. The two largest FE banks, BCA and Panin, are predominantly Chinese owned. Of the indigenous-owned banks, only Soedarpo's Niaga is amongst the top group, with Sutowo's Bank Pasifik the smallest and Berdikari's Bank Dharma Ekonomi the third smallest (*ICN* 203, 9.8.82, p. 11).

38. *AWSJ*, 25.6.81.

39. See the sections of *BNPT* headed 'Pembagian Keuntungan' (division of profits) in P.T. Hanurata — *BNPT* 148–1967 and 320–1973; P.T. Karana — *BNPT* 44–1968; P. T. Bogasari — *BNPT* 258–1970.

40. Reports of the Commission of Four, *Sinar Harapan*, 18–23 July, 1970; Crouch 1975, p. 624; *Nusantara*, 8.1.70.

41. H. McDonald, *Suharto's Indonesia* (Blackburn, 1980), pp. 233–4.

42. J. P. Manguno, 'Suharto Relatives to Provide Tankers to Ship LNG to Korea', *AWSJ*, 12.9.83.

43. *Kompas*, 29.9.76.

44. For example, see *Ekuin*, 29.1.83 and 28.2.83 and the articles 'Dengan Jaminan Nama Liem, Matsushita Semakin Berani Melangkah' (With the Liem name as a guarantee Matsushita is making increasingly bold strides) and 'Pelarian Modal Ke Luar Bisa Akibatkan Ekonomi Terpukul' (Outflow of Capital can Damage the Economy).

45. *ICN* 203, 9.8.82, p. 11.

46. *Indonesia Raya*, 3.12.69; *Insight,* March 1978, p. 11.

47. Dick 1977, Chapter Six.

48. Of the 146 000 commercial vehicles produced between 1979 and 1981, Mitsubishi (Krama Yudha) accounted for 65 000 and Toyota (Astra) for 40 000 giving them 72% of the market. Of 31 000 passenger cars produced in the same period, Toyota comprised 12 000 (40%) and Mitsubishi 6 000 (20%). The Astra/Sutowo joint venture produces another 6 000 Daihatsus (another 20%). (*ICN* 202, 19.7.82).

49. 'Suara Kontractor', *Tempo*, 22.11.75.

50. *Insight*, March 1978, p. 11.

51. S. Astbury, 'Jakarta's first contender for International Stardom', *Asian Business*, June 1982, p. 21.

52. 'Masa Panen Kontrakter Besar', *Eksekutif,* August 1981.

53. *ICN* 182, 1981.

54. 'Sengketa Lain Ibnu Sutowo', *Tempo*, 21.1.83; 'Sengketa Dua Sahabat', *Tempo*, 18.6.83.

55. *ICN* 203, 9.8.83, p. 16.

56. Sumitro's interests include P.T. Rigunas, which is a 300 000 ha. forestry concession in Irian Jaya; P.T. Tjakra Sudarma, a manufacturer and supplier of weapons to the military; and P.T. Riasima Abadi which manufactures pharmaceuticals ('Trio Jaminan di Cicadas', *Tempo*, 2.1.82, pp. 67–8). Sadikin's major interest is the construction company P.T. Arcalina.

57. *BNPT* 760–1960.

58. For details, see Robison 1977, pp. 308–9; and details of P.T. Arjuna Utama Kimia in JETRO 1981, pp. 9, 29.

59. JETRO 1981, p. 41.

60. *BKPM* 4.2.74.

61. *Sinar Harapan*, 11.1.68.

62. *BNPT* 26–1970, *BNPT* 28–1974 and *BKPM* 26.10.71. The largest is P.T. Taliabu Luna which was established with Japanese partners in 1974 with an authorised capital of Rp2 000 million in which Konsultasi has an 11% shareholding.

63. P.T. Sarinitokyu Hotel, authorised capital $29.5 million of which Konsultasi Pembangunan has a 2.22% share (JETRO 1981, p. 54); P.T. Cahaya Bulk Log Carrying (*BKPM* 21.5.71), and P.T. Kadi Construction (*BNPT* 536–1972).

64. *ICN* 201, 1982.

65. President Suharto called together the proprietors of newspapers who had printed such allegations and requested apologies from them (*Merdeka*, 22.1.74).

66. *BNPT* 87–1970.

67. Details are in Robison 1977, Appendix A, p. xix.

68. For details of the Mahkota group, see *ICN* 209, 1.11.82; and Robison 1977, Appendix A, p. xxiv.

69. The Bumiputera 1912 group is detailed in *ICN* 210, 15.11.82.

70. *Eksekutif*, August 1980, pp. 9–19.

71. 'Pemerintah Belum Sepenuh Hati Mau Bekerjasama dergan Kadin Indonesia', *Kompas*, 9.9.83; 'Hasyim Ning: Kadin Bisa Meringankan Beban Pemerintah', *Kompas*, 14.5.82.

PART IV
New Directions

11
Oil Prices, the World Bank and Capital in the 1980s

WITH the collapse of Dutch colonial rule in the 1940s and the subsequent decline of the export enclave economy in the 1950s, Indonesia entered a period in which no domestic class exercised political or economic dominance in any cohesive form. By the end of the 1970s, however, a substantial domestic capitalist class had been established. It was, however, fractured by internal tensions and conflicts and had not established political authority over the state apparatus.

International capital is the key element in the conglomerate that is the capitalist class in Indonesia, constituting the most important source of direct investment in oil and gas and in the more technologically complex industrial projects as well as being the major source of finance capital. Its re-entry into the Indonesian economy was a necessary condition for the reconstitution of capitalism in the mid-1960s, providing the bulk of investment and expertise as well as acting as a *de facto* political financier of the New Order. However, the period between the late 1960s and the early 1980s was one in which the domestic element of the capitalist class significantly expanded its capital and corporate base, partly through integration with international capital and partly under the protection and subsidy of the state. There emerged pressures to restrict the operations of international capital, in order to make way for developing domestic capitalists, and to force international capital to play a much more structured role in assisting this development.

The state played its key role in the development of the capitalist class, not only providing the political conditions for capital accumulation, including the political repression of labour and the subsidisation of food and fuel prices, but actively investing in infrastructure and production. At another level it was active in resolving the conflicts internal to the class alliance, intervening decisively on behalf of domestic capital in the mid- and late 1970s. However, the very fragmentation of the capitalist class enabled the state to play a relatively autonomous role in its relations with capital. The relative weakness of indigenous elements within the capitalist class meant that no powerful bourgeois party emerged to challenge the formal hegemony exercised over the state apparatus by military and, to a lesser extent, civilian politico-bureaucrats, whose political power grew out of the state apparatus itself. In this separation of political and economic power, the capitalist class, particularly international capital, financed the state and the centres of politico-bureaucrat power which exercised hegemony over it, through formal revenues (oil taxes) and informal funding. The relationships between state, politico-bureaucrat and capital and were further complicated by the bonds between individual politico-bureaucrats and capitalists, not to mention the fact that an increasing number of politico-bureaucrats were themselves also capitalists.

In the early 1980s, however, the complex relationships between capital and state faced their most fundamental challenge since 1965, largely as a consequence of a decline in oil prices. This induced:

(a) An increasing challenge by international capital to force an integration of the Indonesian economy with the global capitalist economy. This implied not only opening the doors to international capital investment but a restructuring of the Indonesian economy on the basis of 'comparative advantage' and 'allocative efficiency'. The major threat here was to that group of domestic capitalists who had benefited most from state protection in the ISI strategy.

(b) A relative decline in the state's capacity to underwrite and finance the development of a domestic capitalist class, through provision of infrastructure and direct investments in major projects. This implied a greater role for private domestic capital in investment and the generation of state revenues.

(c) A relative decline in the state's capacity to subsidise and protect the weaker, generally indigenous, elements of domestic capital. The implication here is that the more powerful, generally Chinese, elements of domestic capital obtained greater opportunities to accumulate free of political restraint.

(d) Increasing pressures to regularise the state apparatus and the relationship between state and capital. On the one hand the needs of capital to maximise accumulation, and the state's needs for a strong non-oil revenue base were conflicting with the needs of politico-bureaucrats for sources of finance to underpin their political and economic dominance. The major threat here was to the autonomy of the politico-bureaucrats.

ECONOMIC STRATEGY AND THE DECLINE OF THE OIL MARKET

In the early 1980s we begin to see a slowing down of the state-led drive to achieve an integrated, national, industrial capitalist economy. At the heart of the state's faltering capacity to maintain this drive has been the decline in its oil income, which had constituted the basis of the huge investments in infrastructure and industrial and resource projects.

The importance of oil to the Indonesian economy in the

1970s and early 1980s cannot be over-estimated. Foreign earnings from oil and gas between 1978/79 and 1981/82 leapt 157%, from $7.4 billion to $19.0 billion. At the same time, government revenues derived from oil and gas sector taxes rose 271%, from Rp2 309 billion in 1978/79 to Rp8 575 billion in 1981/82. Oil and gas constituted 65% of foreign-exchange earnings in 1978/79, rising to 81.9% in 1981/82, while taxes from the oil and gas sector constituted 53% of government domestic revenue in 1978/79, rising to 70% in 1981/82.[1]

Taxes and foreign earnings from oil and gas constituted the basis of the government's capacity to finance industrial resource and infrastructure projects through direct investment or the raising of foreign loans. The oil dollars enabled the government to press ahead with its industrialisation plans, to introduce stricter requirements on the entry of foreign capital, and to absorb the decline in direct foreign investment of the late 1970s and criticism of its economic nationalist policies from the IBRD and other sources.

However, in 1982 the Indonesian economy began to encounter severe difficulties. Oil and gas export earnings for 1982/83, originally estimated at $21.4 billion, were revised in October to $17.2 billion, representing a decline in anticipated earnings of 9.5%. Even this estimate did not take into account an eventual price drop of $5 per barrel and continuing declines in production, so the shortfall is likely to be greater. Nor did non-oil export earnings provide any consolation for the Indonesian government. In the three years since the rise of 55% following devaluation in 1978, the value of non-oil exports declined 9.7%, 25% and an estimated 12%.[2] These declines resulted from falls in commodity prices due to the world recession, increased domestic consumption and a fall in log exports due to the government attempt to replace these with exports of processed wood.

Naturally, such declines were reflected in the budget. Domestic revenues from oil and gas in 1982/83 are estimated to fall 18%, from Rp8 575 billion to Rp7 000 billion, after an initial estimate of a rise of 6.4% to Rp9 122 billion, and will probably decline further. Non-oil domestic revenues were expected to rise from Rp3 699 billion to Rp4 635 billion, a rise of 25%, but recent estimates put the likely revenues somewhere between Rp3 000 billion and Rp3 900 billion, a decline of 11% or a rise of 5% on the previous year. All this means a projected revenue shortfall for 1982/83 of between Rp2 900–3 800 billion, or 34–44% of the Rp8 600 billion development budget. Gray estimates a total revenue shortfall for 1982/83–1985/86 of Rp10.6 trillion, representing 43% of direct government investment, 25% of total public sector investment, and 28% of projected development budget expenditure over the four year period.[3]

When the decline in export revenues began, the Indonesian government was confident of riding out the period of difficulty on the cushion of large foreign exchange reserves without having to reduce the domestic industrialisation programme. Current account surpluses of $2.2 billion and $2.1 billion were produced in 1979/80 and 1980/81. As late as January 1982, Indonesia held $10 billion in net foreign exchange reserves, earning $1.5 billion interest. However, the situation began to deteriorate rapidly. The current account deficit for 1982/83 was expected to be at least $6.7 billion and foreign reserves were expected to drop to approximately $3.0 billion, a decline of $7.7 billion over twelve months.[4]

The problem is not a temporary one. Despite signs of recovery in 1983/84, it cannot be expected that the oil will assume its former prominence as an export earner once the oil glut subsides and the international recession eases. Arndt estimates that crude oil production will grow by 3.5% p.a. to about 680 million barrels in 1985 and then level off to reach 700 million barrels in 1990. At the same time domestic consumption is expected to rise at a rate of 12% p.a., reaching 500 million barrels in 1990, leaving only 200 million for export.[5]

The World Bank Report of 1981 saw a bleak future for Indonesia's balance of payments in the 1980s. Although predicting a surplus in current accounts by 1985/86, this is

TABLE 11.1
SHARES OF GROSS INVESTMENT IN GDP

	1975	1980	1985	1990
Public	7.4	10.0	14.8	14.3
Central Government	5.0	6.8	9.4	9.3
Public Enterprises	2.4	3.2	5.4	5.0
Private[a]	10.5	11.6	12.4	13.3
Total	17.9	21.6	27.2	27.6

[a] Includes public enterprises such as Pertamina. This means of course that the categories in the table underestimate the public sector investment.

Source: Gray 1982, p. 5.

expected to have turned into a deficit of between $7.5 billion and $11.5 billion in 1990/91.[6] Even these figures now seem optimistic because they assumed rises in the real world market price of oil and gas at 3% p.a. and substantial increases in non-oil exports. Instead, by 1983 oil prices had fallen from $34 to $29 per barrel and there had been substantial declines in the value of non-oil exports and the world market prices for such commodities as rubber, timber, copper, coffee and palm oil.[7]

The immediate prospect presented by the oil crisis is a decline in central government revenues, which had risen from 12% of GDP in 1969/70 to 25% in 1981/82, sustained largely by the explosion in oil revenues from 26% of non-aid revenue in 1970/71 to almost 70% in 1981/82. The most serious threat posed by the state's fiscal crisis is a reduction in government investment. A World Bank Staff Report of 3 May 1982 argued that a 16% annual increase of public investment would be required to maintain GDP growth at 7.5% for the period to 1986.[8] Some idea of the relative importance of government investment is given in Table 11:1.

It is now clear that the 16% growth in public investment, and therefore a general GDP growth rate of 7.5%, cannot be maintained. The task for the government has become one of maintaining gross domestic investment in the face of fiscal crisis and growing foreign debt.

THE WORLD BANK REPORT

The World Bank Report on Indonesia[9] published in 1981 was important because it offered a comprehensive critique of the Indonesian development strategy at a time when the fiscal difficulties flowing from the oil market crisis were first becoming apparent. The pressures on revenues and export earnings which began to pile up made it difficult for the Indonesian government to resist many of the readjustments urged by the World Bank.

Underpinning the World Bank critique are the notions of comparative advantage and allocative efficiency embodied in the general free-trade, free-market approach to problems of economic development. These are in turn associated with strategies of export-oriented industrial development which use the South Korean and Taiwanese experiences as practical models for development. In the case of Indonesia, the Report argued that the structural approach to development planning, together with the accompanying state regulation of investment and intervention in the economy, produced distortions which inhibited not only economic growth but the proclaimed social objectives: the generation of a domestic (and in particular an indigenous) bourgeoisie and redistribution of wealth. It claimed that protection subsidy and regulation, especially the development of a large import-substitution industrial sector, resulted in inefficient production and has benefited a relatively small and well-connected group of industrialists for whom mobilisation of political resources has constituted a more important skill than expertise in investment and production. Restrictions on trade, investment and credit operate in favour of the owners of capital stock against the rural economy, while consumers and workers bear the burden of an inefficient and protected domestic entrepreneurial class in the form of lower wages, higher prices and ineffective allocation of investment funds.

The following specific policy recommendations were made by the Bank:

(a) A movement away from reliance upon oil taxes through a more effective mobilisation of domestic resources, including:

  (i) A sustained programme of developing non-oil domestic taxation.

  (ii) Improved efficiency in the domestic capital-market and banking sector, specifically the removal of fixed ceilings and preferences in credit policy. This would necessitate ending preferential access to credit for indigenous investors, the bulk of whom would not be considered acceptable credit risks in the banking sector in capitalist economies.

  (iii) Phasing-out of budget subsidies which totalled Rp3.4 billion in 1981/82, representing 15% of the total budget and 4.2% of GDP, redirecting these funds to areas of productive investment.

(b) The dismantling of the DSP restrictions on investment to allow the market to determine allocative efficiency. This would involve a shift from import-substitution manufacture into sectors which could be internationally competitive, and the removal of restrictions on investment based upon ownership. A crucial consequence of such a change in policy would be the removal of existing structural constraints on foreign and domestic Chinese investment in favour of investment by state and indigenous private investment.

(c) Improvement of the legal and administrative infrastructure for economic activity to provide efficient, predictable and rational procedures to replace the present capricious and cumbersome system.

(d) Deregulation of the economy to eliminate the complex and costly procedures which deter investment, consume inordinate time and energy and breed corruption.

THE REACTION OF THE INDONESIAN GOVERNMENT

In moving to address the state's balance of payments and fiscal crises, the Indonesian government had a variety of possible courses of action available.[10] Initially it sought to take those measures which would not fundamentally affect the strategy of integrated national industrial development. However, as the difficulties have compounded it has been forced closer to a point where it is making fundamental concessions, in the areas summarised below.

Increased Aid and Borrowing

Both the IBRD and IGGI have shown themselves anxious to provide borrowing packages to enable Indonesia to ride out the crisis. In 1982/83 international loans totalled just under $5 billion and IGGI voted a record $2.2 billion for the 1983/84 fiscal year.[11] The World Bank's 1983 report on Indonesia estimated that the country would need to obtain $4.5 billion per year from 1984/85 to 1986/87 to cover foreign exchange needs, of which $3.4 would come in the form of IGGI and commercial overseas loans. Foreign aid as a percentage of total government receipts will rise from 12.7% in 1980/81 to 21.5% in 1984/85.[12] While foreign loans appear attractive as a way of avoiding unpleasant elements of structural change, they also hold real dangers. Total foreign debt stands at around $27 billion and, after years of surplus, a $7.3 billion current account deficit in 1982/83 is expected to decline to a $4.7 billion deficit in 1988/89. Debt service ratio is predicted to rise from 23% in 1983 to an estimated 28% in 1985 before declining again.[13] While the prospect of being caught in a debt trap as consuming as those of Brazil, Argentina or Mexico is remote, Indonesia's reliance on loans makes it increasingly susceptible to pressures from the World Bank for structural adjustment.

Increasing Non-Oil Exports

For some years the Indonesian government has been attempting to increase non-oil export earnings, especially in the manufacturing sector. Priorities set out in the DSP offer tax and other incentives to investments which would increase foreign exchange earnings. In 1978 a devaluation of 33.6% was made to increase the competitiveness of Indonesian exports. Its effectiveness was short lived and by 1981 the rupiah was back to within 4% of its pre-devaluation level, prompting a second, 27.6% devaluation in April 1983.[14] In early 1982 an export investment package was introduced, providing low interest rates for export credits. Finally, a counter purchase scheme required foreign firms which obtained domestic government contracts in excess of Rp500 million to purchase and export from Indonesia goods to the value of the machinery and raw materials imported.[15]

The results, however, have been disappointing. Manufacturing exports had reached only 6.5% of total exports in 1983.[16] Although there are recent signs of an upturn in general non-oil exports, including manufactures, due to improved commodity prices and the recent devaluation, non-oil exports have not performed well enough over the past decade to give any assurance that they can be relied upon to solve the balance of payments and foreign debt problems. Total non-oil exports declined from US$6 171 million in 1979/80 to US$3 574 million in 1982/83.[17] The reasons are not merely related to foreign exchange regimes and fluctuating commodity prices but to problems of production and productivity. This particularly affects manufacture where, despite the low wages, unit costs of labour are high and the industry as a whole has been developed as an import-substitution exercise designed to meet domestic market needs. Increasing productivity and efficiency appears to be the key, and yet even foreign investors have generally resisted the move into such higher value-added, export-oriented sectors as plywood, paper and pulp, although metal processing has been attractive because of its use of cheap local energy. While foreign investors demand the opening of the Indonesian economy, it would appear that their investment preferences remain in the ISI sector or more labour-intensive, low value-added export industries.

Increasing Domestic Non-Oil Revenues

Because of the substantial revenues available from oil company taxes over the last decade, littel attention has been paid to developing non-oil taxes as a revenue base. Corporate tax has notoriously been a matter for negotiation between assessor and company officials. In 1982 income tax constituted only 2.3% of government revenues, and non-oil corporate tax, 10.6%. However, tax reforms which have come into force at the beginning of 1984 aimed to broaden the domestic tax base by introducing value-added tax (VAT), and by reforming corporate and income tax.[18] If successful, these moves will make tax a serious cost to domestic capitalists for the first time. More importantly, effective taxation will provide incentives for the capitalist class to establish more formal, institutional controls over disbursement of revenues and the framing of budgets. It will also require regularisation of procedures and accountability of officials. The fiscal crisis of the state has therefore generated a contradiction between the revenue requirements of the 'state' and those of its officials as appropriators of the state apparatus. Finally, the new taxes have not been popular with capital investors. President Suharto was forced to delay the VAT proposal in 1984 and modify his tough stance on tax holidays and capital whitening in the face of continuing decline in PMDN and PMA investment.[19]

Cuts in Budget Expenditure

The government has chosen to make its first cuts in the area of subsidies to petrol and oil products, and foodstuffs — an

area of expenditure which has long been the target of criticism by free-market economists. In the 1982/83 budget, the oil
subsidy was reduced from Rp1510 billion to Rp924 billion and
food subsidies were reduced from Rp310 billion to Rp188
billion, allowing planned development expenditures to rise
by 35% while routine expenditures fell by 7%.[20] In taking
this step the government had to balance the fiscal gains
against some potentially difficult political consequences.
Rises in energy costs (petrol rose 60% in early 1982) not only
hit the subsidised and protected import-substitution manufacturers but resulted in higher prices for domestic goods,
which can only exacerbate declining demand due to the
general effects of the recession. The Jakarta press in 1983
carried accounts of production cutbacks, including some in
that most sensitive barometer of the market: the *kretek*
cigarette industry. At the same time, the upward movement
of prices places pressure on wages, an area of concern for the
government which is anxious to maintain strict control of
labour, for political reasons, and constraints on wages, to
attract export-oriented foreign investment into the manufacturing sector. Already the early 1980s have seen an upsurge
in industrial unrest which is bound to be exacerbated by
these price rises. Nevertheless, the government appears determined to continue this course and planned to totally
eliminate food subsidies by the end of 1984.

An obvious target for expenditure cuts, and one urged by
the IBRD, were the large industrial and resource projects.
However, throughout 1981 and 1982, both the Industry
Minister Soehoed, one of the main architects of industrialisation, and President Suharto himself were stressing the need
to press on with the projects in the face of approaching fiscal
crisis.[21]

By 1983, the pressure to make cuts in project investment
had become irresistable, and in May 1983, Economic Coordi-
nation Minister Ali Wardhana (who had just replaced Widjojo) announced that forty-eight capital-intensive projects
with a value of more than US$20 billion were to be post-

poned, rephased, cancelled or financed by non-government sources.[22] The cuts represent a setback to the policy of economic development based upon capital-intensive industrial projects. They imply a downturn in the booming construction and supply industries, affecting both international and domestic capitalists and the politically connected 'fixers' who are involved in the arrangement of many of these deals.[23]

Mobilisation of Domestic Savings

The World Bank has long argued that the potential for private domestic capital accumulation has been inhibited by regulation of interest rates and imposition of credit ceilings. In June 1983, these controls were either removed or relaxed. However, a weakening of the investment climate due to the recession has led to a strong surge in deposits and a declining demand for credit, thereby delaying the intended effect of the reforms: to create new sources of domestic capital.

FROM STATE-LED NATIONAL INDUSTRIALISATION TO 'ALLOCATIVE EFFICIENCY' WITHIN AN INTERNATIONAL ECONOMY

The notions of 'allocative efficiency' and 'comparative advantage' reflect at the ideological level what constitutes at the concrete level the logic of capital accumulation by international corporations operating on a global scale. From the point of view of the international firm this means the freedom to locate elements of the production process according to criteria determined within the firm itself: mainly profitability and access to markets. From both international capital and the free-market ideologues, there is pressure upon a vulnerable Indonesian government to change from an inward-oriented industrial strategy to an outward-looking strategy which seeks to integrate Indonesia into the New International Division of Labour and to make investment decisions on the basis of efficiency and comparative advantage. The IBRD economists have pressed for a reassessment of the industrialisation programme, arguing that the protection and subsidy of industries which produce real negative value-added merely diverts investment capital from industries which may be internationally competitive. For example, while conceding that such industries as fertilisers, cement and mineral processing may be economically viable, Gray claims that domestic assembly of automobiles and manufacture of engines is not. If these industries were abandoned in favour of import of fully manufactured cars, the savings could be used both to pay the displaced workers and invest in more competitive and efficient industries.[24] The general point is that a highly subsidised and protected economy focused on import-substitution industrialisation involves not only large state expenditures which Indonesia can no longer afford but creates an inefficient and uncompetitive manufacturing sector unable to constitute an alternative source of export earnings.

It is not only the World Bank but international corporate interests which are urging deregulation and reform. Apart from lifting protective barriers and ending the negative DSP lists, they have called for deregulation of licensing procedures, an end to corrupt practices and increases in the efficiency of the bureaucracy.[25] Given the sharp downturn in foreign investment between 1975 and 1980 and the increased importance of foreign sources of investment finance since the decline in oil revenues commenced, the state is in a much weaker bargaining position with both the IBRD and private foreign corporate capital.

While the Jakarta government has responded with efforts to simplify regulations and attempts to woo foreign investors back[26], they have been less willing to dispense with the goals of national integrated industrialisation. President Suharto's 16 August speech of 1983 stressed the concept of national resilience which, if it means anything in economic terms, means that the government does not intend Indonesia to become a fragment of an international economy whose internal structure is determined by international capital.

Although recognising the need to move more forcefully into export-oriented industrialisation, the government did not accept free-market arguments. The move into EOI is clearly intended to be achieved within planned development of backwards and forwards linkages. For example, the move into plywood production was motivated not by comparative advantage but higher value-added production in the forestry industry. Retaining log production for export would have been the path to follow if allocative efficiency was sought. Export earnings from plywood have not yet made up for lost export earnings from raw logs.[27]

Negative lists in the DSP continue to grow. The support of Widjojo and Wardhana for the free-market IBRD line is counteracted by a strong economic nationalist approach by Research and Technology Minister Habibie and Junior Minister of Domestic Production, Ginanjar Kartasasmita, who has the support of the powerful State Secretary, Soedharmono.[28] Habibie's commitment to the manufacture of high technology as a long-term development strategy flies directly in the face of notions of EOI and comparative advantage. The President has clearly supported these projects with enthusiasm, particularly the Nurtanio aircraft manufacturing project.[29] The State Secretariat, now in charge of domestic procurement, remains committed to preference for domestic goods. Policies of tariff protection remain largely intact and the World Bank estimated in 1984 that consumer subsidies for domestic current producers remained high ($156.8 million; of which for steel billets $74.8 million, televisions $43.6m, and synthetic yarn $24.6m).[30] In his 1983 budget speech, Suharto introduced further controls on non-essential imports.[31]

Demands for a free-trade, free-market approach represent not only a disagreement over economic strategy but a major challenge to the existing structure of political and economic

388 THE RISE OF CAPITAL

power in capitalist Indonesia, threatening to alter radically the balance of ownership and control between different elements of the bourgeoisie in Indonesia. They also threaten the formal and informal political and economic relationships which have made possible the emergence of the major domestic business groups.

The major problem is the existence of large domestic business groups of military bureaucrats and private capitalists now firmly entrenched in the import-substitution sector in auto assembly, textiles, cement, steel and heavy engineering, metal fabrication, and pharmaceuticals. Their continued existence has been based upon government intervention involving protection, subsidy, contracts, direct investment and mediation of integration with foreign capital. Promises of long-term, abstract benefits, which the IBRD economists suggest will flow from a freeing of the market, are no consolation to those groups which have attained their present position precisely through the imposition of political constraints upon the market. If, indeed, these ISI capitalists were induced to take a giant leap of faith in the generative properties of comparative advantage, there is no guarantee that it would be they who would constitute the promised new capitalist class emerging as a consequence of the removal of regulatory constraints. Their position would no longer be guaranteed if international investors were not required to take local partners or appoint local distributors and contractors or to stay out of such sectors as logging and trade. If allocative efficiency becomes the guiding force of economic planning, their large investments, locked into an uncompetitive ISI sector, may well evaporate.

We have, therefore, a complex set of contradictions. Indonesia's attempt to create an integrated industrial economy is in contradiction with structural developments in the international division of labour. The Indonesian state, besieged by fiscal crisis, is increasingly unable to finance this development and therefore to resist pressures for an increased degree of integration into the structures of international capitalism. As international capital and international finance become more essential and necessary components in the generation of economic growth in the wake of decline in oil revenue, fundamental structural change will become increasingly irresistable.

In concert with this, there has emerged a domestic capitalist class, sustained by political intervention in the economy, and constituting an integration of politico-bureaucrat power and private domestic capital (largely Chinese). In the context of the state's diminished capacity to finance long-term, inward-looking industrial strategies, involving expensive capital-intensive projects, and to protect and subsidise the ISI sector, there arises a contradiction between the immediate interests of this emerging coalition and continuing development of Indonesian capitalism.

READJUSTMENTS IN THE STRUCTURE OF DOMESTIC CAPITAL

Because of the decrease in oil income the state has been forced to transfer to the private sector a much greater role in capital accumulation and investment than hitherto projected. The government expects private capital investment to provide Rp67.5 trillion of the Rp145.2 trillion total investment required for Repelita IV.[32] Such a transfer of emphasis cannot be achieved simply by fiat, since there were good structural reasons for the original dominance of state capital. Nevertheless, the fiscal squeeze on the state promises a new phase in the development of domestic capital in Indonesia.

The state has taken several moves to assist the private capitalists to undertake some of these major investment responsibilities. Deregulating interest rates and eliminating credit ceilings for domestic commercial banks was designed to release domestic finance capital. State projects have also been transferred to private investors. The state has allowed private participation in the Cilegon cold rolling steel mill. Four cement plants at various stages of construction have been offered to the private sector and several state-owned agricultural projects are to be offered to private purchasers.[33]

However, the fiscal difficulties of the state and its consequent need to rely more heavily on private domestic capital also has implications for the internal structure of the domestic capitalist class. Over the past decade, the state has provided smaller and weaker elements of capital through special credit arrangements and through protective policies. Its capacity to continue these programmes is now diminished. More importantly, these weaker, generally *pribumi*, elements of domestic capital are unable to undertake the sort of investment the state is now seeking from the private sector. The only domestic, private corporate groups with the capacity to make the necessary investments and with the necessary corporate structures are the larger, mainly Chinese-owned, groups discussed in Chapter 9 — Liem Sioe Liong, Astra, Roda Mas, Berkat, Harapan and a few others. The state's need to rely even more heavily on these groups is resulting in an acceleration of the already advanced process of concentration of domestic, largely Chinese, corporate wealth. It is Liem Sioe Liong who has been the first to benefit from the transfer, taking over cement projects and investing in the Cilegon steel mill. As a result, it has become necessary for the state to attempt to overcome the divisions between Chinese and indigenous elements of the domestic capitalist class to encourage Chinese capitalists in particular to keep their money in Indonesia. Appeals by General Murdani for an end to categories of *pribumi* and non-*pribumi*, and the endorsement of these moves by Kadin (discussed in Chapter 9) are an indication of its concern.[34] Clearly, if there is to be a significant domestic capitalist class it must be one in which the Chinese play the dominant part. However, it is the very dominance of the Chinese which, at the same time as giving the domestic capitalist class its economic strength, implies important political limits.

RELATIONSHIPS BETWEEN STATE AND CAPITAL: REGULARISATION AND CORRUPTION

Among the more persistent complaints of the World Bank Report, and of international business and free-market economists, has been the degree of corruption in Indonesia. Corruption constitutes a sizeable leakage of funds which may potentially be more constructively invested. At the same time it imposes substantial costs and frustrations on investors, particularly in strategic departments such as Customs and the BKPM itself, where 'charges' of up to 20% of projected investment have reportedly been made for investment licences.[35] Corruption also constitutes a major obstacle to an effective tax-gathering service, an indispensible feature of any attempt to increase domestic non-oil revenues.

To end corruption is, however, not simply a case of introducing legislation or undertaking eradication programmes, because the phenomenon of corruption goes deep into the very nature of power in Indonesia. It is perhaps useful here to look at two of Weber's categories of bureaucratic authority. On the one hand, rational, legal authority is that in which both the official and the process of decision-making are constrained by the operation of formal rules and regulations. The official carries out tasks defined by the terms of his or her appointment and exercises powers inherent in the office. In the patrimonial form of bureaucratic authority, bureaucratic office and its attendant powers are appropriated by the official.[36] Both of these dimensions exist in the Indonesian political system. The persistence of the patrimonial form is explained by observers such as Anderson and Willner[37] as the persistence of traditional cultural values. This may be so, but the question must be asked: why have such cultural values persisted? The answer is that in a relative vacuum of class-based political power, the officials, in particular the military, have been able to appropriate freely the apparatus of the state. Given the limitations upon foreign and Chinese bourgeoisie directly exercising public power and

the failure of domestic political parties, few political constraints are placed upon the ruling politico-bureaucrats.

Appropriated state power has been manifested in many
ways. Simple bribery is the most simple form, or, in the case
of the military, extortion, protection rackets, forced purchase of crops at special prices, smuggling or large-scale
appropriation of the funds of state corporations. But appropriated state power has also constituted the basis upon which
the alliance between the politico-bureaucrats and capital has
been established. Whereas in Western, industrial capitalist
societies the relationship between state and capital is one in
which public policy creates the general conditions for capital
accumulation and normally does not discriminate between
firms, in the Indonesian situation the relationship between
state and capital is also exercised on the basis of specific and
personal relationships between individual capitalists and individual politico-bureaucrats. The latter are able to appropriate the power to allocate licences for import, credit,
forestry concessions, construction and supply contracts; and
the emergence of domestic business groups in the post-
Independence period has been largely based upon their
ability to gain access to these appropriated concessions.

The question of corruption has been a major political issue
in Indonesia since 1949 and a major focus of broader anti-
government movements. For the urban middle classes, especially the intelligentsia, the appropriation of state power
by the officials of the state is seen as one of the pillars upon
which arbitrary and authoritarian forms of rule have been
constructed. Periodic campaigns by students and Muslim
groups, publicising the extra-legal use of state power by state
officials, often directed at specific members of the ruling
groups[38], have been damaging to the legitimacy of the New
Order, which had itself used the corruption issue to discredit
the former Sukarno regime and to establish itself as 'clean'
and technocratic. Such charges have clearly had an effect
upon the New Order, which has mounted several, albeit
unsuccessful, campaigns against corruption.[39]

All the evidence points to corruption being as prevalent in Indonesia in the 1980s as it has been in previous decades. The head of the Financial Audit Board, Umar Wirahadiku-suma, publicly admitted in 1981 that no departments are clear of corruption, while the vice-president, Adam Malik, spoke of corruption reaching epidemic proportions.[40] A *Tempo* survey in the same year found that many respondents (43.8%) considered corruption to be the greatest threat to the nation — many more, for example, than those who most feared the return of the PKI (21.6%).[41]

In the booming construction industry, Emil Salim claimed that:

If corruption and deviation in the Department of Public Works can be overcome, this will mean that a large part of state finance can be made safe because Public Works absorbs more of the Development Budget than any other department. [Rp761 billion][42]

There is little point in further cataloguing the obvious. Certainly, international capital is convinced that corruption is a major problem for investors — a concern spelt out both by the American Chamber of Commerce Report of 1981 and the World Bank Report itself.

Is corruption a permanent feature of Indonesian capitalism and an obstacle to its corporate development? Previous political campaigns against corruption had little more than moral force. However, a new set of factors has been intro-duced into the conflict. The fiscal difficulties of the state and the need to boost non-oil export earnings mean that the state itself must weigh the financial needs of its officials against the revenue needs of the state and the needs of corporations to realise their huge capital investments.

If we look back to Weber, he argues that the transformation from patrimonial to legal and rational forms of bureaucratic authority in Europe was enforced by an emerging bour-geoisie because the development of industrial capitalism could not proceed without laws and policies which provided a predictable and rational infrastructure for the accumulation of capital.[43] This is precisely what international capital, the World Bank and the free-market economists are demanding in Indonesia. However, they have to contend not only with the fact that the very power of the politico-bureaucrats is predicated upon their capacity to appropriate office and to command benefices, but also with the fact that the leading elements of the domestic bourgeoisie rely upon privileged access to licences, concessions, credit and contracts achieved through special relationships with the politico-bureaucrat appropriators. Indeed, many of the leading bourgeoisie are at the same time major power-holders.

We can only expect the domestic bourgeoisie to move against the appropriation of state power by its officials when patronage relationships become a fetter on the accumulation process. There are already circumstantial indications that these developments may be coming into play. For example, when political patrons lose power it has been normal for economic clients to decline with them. Businessmen who criticise the government or whose connection becomes politically unacceptable may find access to credit, contracts and licences denied. General Yoga Sudama, the head of Bakin, openly declared this as official policy.[44] This may have been bearable when all that was at stake was a trading or logging licence. However, when the stakes involve extensive industrial holdings with huge borrowings and the bulk of assets in the form of capital stock, the prospect of a change of political power becomes more worrying and the pressures to establish a more predictable, 'rational' and publicly accountable system more urgent. Having already established a capital base, albeit through the mechanisms of patronage, the capitalist must now consider whether the best prospects for the future development of the firm lie in the normal processes of accumulation rather than windfalls obtained through access to a patrimonial bureaucracy and its attendant risks.

Therefore the challenge to patrimonialism in Indonesia as elsewhere relates ultimately to the strength of capitalist revolution and the transformation of capital from merchant to industrial and finances, from family to corporate based.

CONCLUSION

What is important about the oil price crisis is that it constitutes a watershed in the nature of relationships between state, politico-bureaucrats and domestic capital. The capacity of the state to underpin the development of domestic capital by its investment projects, by protection and subsidy has been diminished. The state is being forced to rely more heavily on private domestic capital as a source of investment and revenue. It is also dealing, in the 1980s, with a domestic capitalist class of much greater substance than it was in 1965. The major elements of this class in Indonesia can no longer be regarded as comprador, dependent upon foreign capital. Indeed, the complex integration of capital on a global scale makes the question irrelevant. Domestic Indonesian business groups have developed significant corporate and capital bases in both industry and banking and have themselves expanded internationally. The state had intervened decisively on their behalf in conflicts with international capital, ensuring that, for many, the joint venture has assisted accumulation, experience, management and technical expertise as well as corporate development.

Nor can we say that the domestic capitalist class is simply a pariah class, dependent upon and limited by arbitrary political intervention in the commercial sphere by officials of a patrimonial state. It is true that the development of the major dometic business groups was predicated upon state intervention, but the leading capitalist clients have now developed independent capital bases. While they still need access to monopolies, contracts and concessions as individual firms, the state on the other hand needs their capacity as a class to provide investment finance and the corporate framework for production, a need heightened by the recent oil crisis.

There are important indications that the domestic capitalist class is expanding its influence within the existing authoritarian state structure. Kadin is becoming more vocal and its membership more influential and there is a likelihood that prominent domestic capitalists will play an increasing role in Golkar. Most leading politico-bureaucrat families are now also capital owners and embody the competing interests of capital accumulation and the needs of politico-bureaucrats to appropriate the state apparatus. The penetration of the capitalist class into the state apparatus therefore invades and subsumes the very heart of military and politico-bureaucrat power. As a consequence, the demands of capital are impressed more insistently and immediately upon the power-holders. This, however, does not imply bourgeois democracy or bourgeois reformism. The political circumstances of the rise of capital in Indonesia are far different from those which produced these phenomena in Europe a century earlier. No bourgeois party is likely to emerge with any success in Indonesia's immediate future. Whether a party of a corporatist type will be created by the regime to give a broader political base to their rule or not, the fact is that the state is already being more effectively harnessed to the needs of capital accumulation. This holds implications for politico-bureaucrat hegemony and the attendant arbitrary, inefficient and personal aspects of this rule. It suggests a regularisation of the state apparatus, and South Korea and Singapore suggest themselves as much more likely models of a future capitalist state in Indonesia than does Europe or North America.

1. Gray 1982, Table 8, p. 21; A. Nasution, 'The Indonesian Economy: Problems of Adjustment to Global Recession and Lower Oil Prices', *Indonesian Quarterly* 12, 2 (1984), Table 5, p. 23.

2. Gray 1982, pp. 8, 9, 13; Nasution 1984, Table 5, p. 23.

3. Gray 1982, pp. 13, 18.

4. Ibid., pp. 21, 25; Dick 1982, p. 20.

5. H. Arndt, 'Survey of Recent Developments', *BIES* 17, 3 (1981), p. 12.

6. Ibid.

7. Ibid., pp. 14, 16.

8. World Bank, *Indonesia: Financial Resources & Human Development in the Eighties* (Jakarta, 1982), p. 23, cited in Gray 1982, p. 3.

9. The following analysis of the World Bank Report refers to the Report itself (IBRD 1981) and commentaries on the Report, including: J. P. Manguno, 'World Bank Tells Jakarta to Alter Economy', *AWSJ*, 28.4.81 and 'Indonesia Urged to Relax Investment Laws', *AWSJ*, 5.5.81; G. Sacerdoti, 'Overdraft of Inefficiency', *FEER*, 29.5.81.

10. 'Sulit dan Makin Sulit Tahun Depan', *Tempo*, 27.11.82 is one of the most interesting sources for government and business response to the developing fiscal and export earning difficulties. It includes interviews with, and reports of statements by, various ministers, economic commentators and businessmen (including Wardhana, Subroto, Sumitro, Wijoyo and the businessmen, Gobel and Idham). The article concentrates on fiscal responses – taxation, import and export levels, budget subsidies.

11. P. McCawley, 'Survey of Recent Developments', *BIES* 19, 1 (1983), p. 9.; E. Lachica, 'US to Help Indonesia Win $2 Billion in Aid this Year', *AWSJ*, 6.6.83.

12. S. Awanohara, 'Jakarta at a Jog', *FEER*, 17.5.84, p. 97. Official 1984/85 budget figures cited in P.R. Silalahi, 'Perekonomian Indonesia dalam Repelita IV', *Perspectif Repelita IV* (Jakarta, 1984).

13. Arndt 1983, p. 17; Awanohara, 17.5.84, p. 97.

14. Gray 1982, pp. 26–31.

15. *ICN* 191, 8.2.82 and 203, 9.8.82; S. Awanohara, 'Aiding & Abetting', *FEER*, 19.4.84, pp. 56–7. Foreign capital has been less than happy about the counter purchase schemes, although, as *Asian Business* has pointed out, there were $246 million worth of commitments to May 1983. Clearly the $4.5 billion in contracts offered by Indonesia was an incentive for cooperation (S. Astbury, 'Diminishing Oil Revenues Plague Suharto's Budgetary Projections', *Asian Business*, May 1983, p. 71).

16. H. Hill, 'Survey of Recent Developments', *BIES* 20, 2 (1984), Table 4, p. 10. See also Arndt 1983, p. 19.

17. Nasution 1984, p. 19, In 1982/83, non-oil exports amounted to $3 894 million compared with $14 744 million for oil and LNG. This was about 20% of the total. An upturn began in mid-1983, with plywood exports in particular looking promising at $272 million by August (P. Rosendale, 'Survey of Recent Developments', *BIES* 20, 1, 1984, p. 7). Textile exports, after reaching $122.5 million in 1979, had crawled to $175 million in 1982 (*FEER*, 18.8.83, p. 45). Official projections expected non-oil exports to reach 35.4% of the total by 1988/89 (Rosendale 1984, citing *Repelita IV*, Vol. 1, Tables 5–7).

18. B. Glassburner and M. Poffenberger, 'Survey of Recent Developments', *BIES* 19, 3 (1983), pp. 12–15.

19. S. Awanohara, 'Whitening the Red Tape', *FEER*, 27.9.84. p. 136.

20. Dick 1982, pp. 8–10.

21. S. Awanohara, 'Tomorrow is Postponed', *FEER*, 26.5.83 (see statements of both Suharto and Soehoed cited on p. 83).

22. Nasution 1984, p. 18. See also S. Awanohara, 'Projects Rephasing', *FEER*, 18.8.83, p. 51; J. P. Manguno, 'Suharto Order May Ice $40 million in projects', *AWSJ*, 23.5.83.

23. See Professor Sumitro's warning of 'dark forces' applying pressure for the resumption of these projects, in the *Jakarta Post* editorial of 25.6.84.

24. Gray 1982, pp. 36–51. This is the approach taken by the BIES in general and by the World Bank. Of course it may be that Indonesia at the moment has no comparative advantage in anything other than oil, raw materials and certain agricultural products.

25. The most comprehensive critique was the Report of the American Chamber of Commerce in Indonesia, summarised in Manguno, *AWSJ*, 23.10.81.

26. See the extensive feature on Indonesia prepared by BKPM for *AWSJ*, 18.8.81, pp. 7–19, including a foreword by Suhartoyo, Chairman of BKPM.

27. Arndt 1983, pp. 19–22. The combined value of log and plywood production declined from $1 489 million in 1980/81 to $795 in 1983/84 (M. Habir, 'Waterlogged Timber', *FEER*, 6.9.84, p. 113).

28. S. Awanohara and M. Habir, 'Overview', *FEER*, 18.8.83, pp. 39–41 and Glassburner and Poffenberger 1983, pp. 18–20.

29. Habibie's views are explained at length in Prof. Dr. Ing B.J. Habibie, *Beberapa Pemikiran Tentang Strategi Transformasi Industri Suatu Negara Sedang Berkembang* (Bonn, 1983).

30. World Bank Report of 1984 cited in M. Habir, 'Some things are the other way around here', *FEER*, 27.9.84, p. 110.

31. Suharto Government Statement on the Draft State Budget for 1983–84 to the House of the People's Representatives, Republic of Indonesia, 6.1.83, pp. 18, 19.

32. *AWSJ*, 17.1.84; '"Pri", "Non Pri", dan Investasi Rp. 67.5 trillion', *Tempo*, 31.3.84; 'Mendorong Swasta ke Mana?', *Tempo*, 25.2.84, pp. 68–9.

33. M. Habir, 'Stripping in Public', *FEER*, 23.6.83, p. 84; *Tempo*, 25.2.84.

34. See Minister Ali Wardhana's statement in *Tempo*, 25.2.84.

35. These allegations were made in the World Bank Report itself.

36. M. Weber. *The Theory of Social and Economic Organisation* (New York, 1974). See Sections 111 (ii and iii) on the definitions of legal and traditional authority.

37. Anderson 1972; A. R. Willner, 'The Neo Traditional Accommodation to Political Independence: the Case of Indonesia', in J. McAlister (ed.) *Southeast Asia: the Politics of National Integration* (New York, 1973).

38. For an overview, see Robison 1977, pp. 353–70. For specific student critiques of corruption, see 'White Book of the 1978 Students Struggle', *Indonesia* 25 (1978), pp. 151-82; Akhmadi 1981.

39. In the late 1960s the TPK (Team Pemberantas Korupsi) operated without distinction. The recommendations of the Presidential Commission of Four on Corruption were ignored. Admiral Sudomo's anti corruption-task force, Ostib, began with a fanfare but is now regarded with considerable cynicism. Apart from my overview (1977), some articles which give an

insight into the corruption issue are: 'Korupsi: Terasa Ada, Terkatakan Tidak', *Ekspres*, 26.7.70; 'Be Careful About Corruption', *Tempo*, 19.6.76 (*USPRT*); 'Korupsi-Mana Ada Yang Bersih', *Tempo*, 31.10.81; 'Malik-Korupsi Sudah Epidemik', *Sinar Harapan*, 2.11.81.

40. *Sinar Harapan*, 2.11.81.

41. *Tempo*, 31.10.81.

42. Ibid. The same article reported that the Director General of Public Works had designed a form which asked contractors to say whether they have given 'commissions'. So far all have been returned empty. When asked to comment, Hashim Ning of Kadin said that, 'It is now too early to be as honest as this. It is just utopia, unless we want to stop being businessmen'.

43. Weber 1974, p. 357.

44. *FEER*, 27.6.80, p. 26.

Select Bibliography

1. NEWSPAPERS, SPECIALISED JOURNALS AND BUSINESS MAGAZINES REFERRED TO IN THE PERIOD OF STUDY

A. NON-INDONESIAN PUBLICATIONS

Fareastern Economic Review
Asian Wall Street Journal
Asian Business

B. JAKARTA NEWSPAPERS AND WEEKLY JOURNALS

Nusantara (closed 1974)
Sinar Harapan
Kompas
Tempo
Business News
Indonesian Commercial Newsletter (ICN)
Eksekutif

The United States Embassy Translations of the Jakarta Press were also used, particularly for the period 1965–73. These covered a wide range of newspapers apart from those cited above. Where these translations have been quoted, such use has been indicated by: *USPRT* .

2. OFFICIAL PUBLICATIONS

Address of State by the President of the Republic of Indonesia before the House of People's Representatives on the Occasion of the ( ) Independence Day, August 17th. (1973–1983). Jakarta: Department of Information.

Government Statement on the Draft State Budget for (1973/1974 – 1984/1989) to the House of Peoples Representatives Delivered by the President of the Republic of Indonesia. Jakarta: Department of Information.
Republic of Indonesia. *Berita Negara-Tambahan Perseroan Terbatas*. Jakarta, 1965–76.
BKPM (Badan Kordinasi Penanaman Modal). *Perkembangan Penanaman Modal Bulan . . .* (Monthly Reports of Capital Investment). 1974–1976.
Republic of Indonesia. *Act No. 1, Foreign Capital Investment (Berita Negara*, 1, 1976).
Republic of Indonesia. *Act No. 6, 1968, Domestic Capital Investment (Berita Negara*, 33, 1968).
Habibie, B. J. (Menteri Negara Riset dan Teknologi). *Beberapa Pemikiran Tentang Strategi Transformasi Industri Suatu Negara Sedang Berkembang*. Pidato disampaikan Bonn, 14 June 1983.

3. BOOKS, ARTICLES, REPORTS AND PROCEEDINGS OF CONFERENCES AND SEMINARS

Achmad, S. The Dynamics of the Nationalisation of Dutch Owned Enterprises in Indonesia. Ph.D. thesis, Indiana University, 1963.
Adicondro, G. 'From Chinatown to Nanyang'. *Prisma* 13 (1979).
Akhmadi, Heri. *Breaking the Chains of Oppression of the Indonesian People*. Translation Series, 59. Ithaca, Cornell Modern Indonesia Project, 1981.
Allison, J. M. 'Indonesia: Year of the Pragmatists'. *Asian Survey* 9,2 (1969).
Anderson, B. R. O'G. 'The Idea of Power in Javanese Culture'. In C. Holt (ed.), *Culture and Politics in Indonesia*. Ithaca: Cornell University Press, 1972.
———. 'Last Days of Indonesia's Suharto? '*Southeast Asia Chronicle* 63 (1978).
———. 'Old State, New Society: Indonesia's New Order in Comparative Historical Perspective'. *Journal of Asian Studies* 42, 3 (1983).
———. Nationalism and the State in Modern Indonesia. Paper presented to the Japanese Political Science Association Round Table Conference on National Interest and Political Leadership. Tokyo, March-April 1982.
———, and Kahin, A., (eds). *Interpreting Indonesian Politics: Thirteen Contributions to the Debate*. Interim Report Series, 62. Ithaca, Cornell, Modern Indonesia Project, 1982.
Anspach, R. 'Indonesia'. In F. Golay, R. Anspach, R. Pfanner and E. Ayal, (eds), *Underdevelopment and Economic Nationalism in Southeast Asia*. Ithaca, Cornell University Press, 1969.
———. The Problem of a Plural Economy and its Effects on Indonesia's Economic Structure. Ph.D. thesis, University of California, Berkely, 1963. Ann Arbor, University Microfilms, 1980.
Arief, S. *Who's Who in Indonesian Business*. Jakarta: Sritua Arief Ass., 1975.
———, and Sasono, A. *Indonesia: Dependency and Underdevelopment*. Kuala Lumpur: META, 1980.
Arifin, M. 'Which Road Must be Taken'. *Ekspres* 18, 26 January 1974 (*USPRT*).
———. *Fakta Analisa Lengkap dan Latar Belakang: Peristiwa 15 Januari*. Jakarta: Publishing House, 1974.

Arndt, H. W. 'Economic Disorder and the Task Ahead'. In T. K. Tan (ed.), 1967.
———. 'P.T. Krakatau Steel'. *BIES* 11, 2 (1975a).
———. 'Survey of Recent Developments' *BIES* 11, 2 (1975b).
———. 'Survey of Recent Developments' *BIES* 17, 3 (1981).
———. 'Survey of Recent Developments' *BIES* 19, 2 (1983).
Arun, A., Booth, A., Sundrum, R. 'Labour Absorption in Indonesian Agriculture' *BIES* 17, 1 (1981).
Astbury, S. 'Foreign Investors Reassess Indonesia: the Party's Over'. *Asian Business* (February 1982).
———. 'Jakarta's First Contender for International Stardom'. *Asian Business* (June 1982).
Block, F. 'Beyond Relative Autonomy: State Managers as Historical Subjects'. *Socialist Register* (1980).
Boediono. 'Economic Recession and the Industrial Structure'. *Prisma* 27 (March 1983).
Boeke, J. H. *Economics and Economic Policy of Dual Societies*. Haarlem: H. D. Tjeeuk Willink, 1951.
Booth, A. and McCawley, P. (eds). *The Indonesian Economy During the Soeharto Era*. Kuala Lumpur: Oxford University Press, 1981.
———, 'The Indonesian Economy Since the Mid-Sixties'. In A. Booth and P. McCawley (eds), 1981.
Boulton, D. *The Lockheed Papers*. London: Jonathan Cape, 1978.
Bratanata, Slamet, Praktet Demokrasi Dalam Peralihan. Paper given to a meeting of PBC Siliwangi, Cipayung, 10–12 April 1970.
———. *Menundjang Perekonomian Pribumi*. Jakarta: unpublished mimeo, 1972.
———. *Mengenal Bebrapa Tantangan Kita*. Jakarta: Lembaga Studi Pembangunan, 1978.
Brenner, R. 'The Origins of Capitalist Development: A Critique of Neo-Smithian Marxism'. *New Left Review* 104 (1977).
Castles, L. 'Socialism and Private Business: The Latest Phase'. *BIES* 1, 1 (1965).
———. 'The Fate of the Private Enterpreneur'. In T. K. Tan (ed.), *Sukarno's Guided Indonesia*. Brisbane: Jacaranda, 1967. (1967a)
———. *Religion, Politics and Economic Behaviour in Java: the Kudus Cigarette Industry*. Cultural Report Series No. 15. New Haven: Yale University Centre for Southeast Asian Studies, 1967.
———. *Bureaucracy and Society in Indonesia*. Unpublished discussion paper, Australian National University, 1974.
Centre for Strategic and International Studies. *Seminar Strategi Pembinaan Pengusaha Nasional, 29–31 Mai, 1975 di Jakarta*. Jakarta: 1975.
Chalmers, I. Third World State: Epicentre or Epiphenomenon? (The Indonesian Motor Vehicle Industry). Paper delivered to the Conference of the Australian Political Science Association, Sydney, August 1983.
Collier, W. 'Tebasan System, High Yielding Varieties and Rural Change'. *Prisma* 1 (1975).
———. 'Food Problems, Unemployment and the Green Revolution in Java'. *Prisma* 9 (1978).
Crouch, H. *The Indonesian Army in Politics*. PH.D. thesis, Monash University, 1975.
———. 'Generals and Business in Indonesia'. *Pacific Affairs* 48, 4 (1975/76).
———. *The Army and Politics in Indonesia*. Ithaca: Cornell University Press, 1978.

Daroesman, R. 'Survey of Recent Developments'. *BIES* 17, 2 (1981).

Diah, B.M. 'Why Does the World Isolate Us?'. *Merdeka*, 13, 14, 15 January 1976 (*USPRT*).

Dick, H. The Indonesian Interisland Shipping Industry. Ph.D. thesis, Australian National University, 1977.

_____. 'Survey of Recent Developments.' *BIES* 18, 1 (1982).

Dobbin, C. 'Economic Change in Minangkabau as a Factor in the Rise of the Padri Movement, 1784–1830'. *Indonesia* 23 (1977).

Economic Research Bureau of the University of Gadjah Mada. 'The Batik Industry in Central Java'. *Ekonomi dan Keuangan* 11, 7 (1958).

Embassy of the Republic of Indonesia in the United States of America and the American Indonesian Chamber of Commerce, Inc. (ERI [USA] & AICC). *Seminar on New Opportunities*. New York, 24 and 25 September 1975.

Fakultas Ekonomi Universitas Indonesia. *Five Papers on Indonesian Economic Development*. Jakarta: 1970.

Feith, H. *The Indonesian Elections of 1955*. Interim Report Series. Ithaca: Cornell Modern Indonesia Project, 1957.

_____. *The Decline of Constitutional Democracy in Indonesia*. Ithaca, Cornell University Press, 1962.

_____. 'The Dynamics of Guided Democracy'. In R. McVey (ed.), 1963.

_____. The Politics of Economic Decline'. In T. K. Tan (ed.), 1967.

_____. 'Suharto's Search for a Political Format'. *Indonesia* 6 (1968). .

_____. 'Political Control, Class Formation and Legitimacy'. *Kabar Seberang* 2 (1977).

_____. The Indonesian Student Movement of 1977–78. Mimeo, Monash University, 1978.

_____. 'Repressive Developmentalist Regimes in Asia'. *Prisma* 19 (1980).

_____ and Castles, L. (eds). *Indonesian Political Thinking: 1945–65*. Ithaca: Cornell University Press, 1970.

Franke, R. 'Limited Good and Cargo Cult in Indonesian Economic Development'. *JCA* 2, 4 (1972).

Frobel, F. et al. 'The New International Division of Labour'. *Social Science Information* 17, 1 (1978).

_____. 'The Current Development of the World Economy'. *Review* 5, 4, (1982).

Furnivall, J. *Netherlands India: A Study of Plural Economy*. Cambridge: Cambridge University Press, 1944.

Geertz, C. *The Development of the Javanese Economy: A Socio-Cultural Approach*. Cambridge, Mass.: Centre for International Studies, M.I.T., 1956.

_____. *Peddlers & Princes: Social Development and Economic Change in Two Indonesian Towns*. Chicago: University of Chicago Press, 1963.

_____. *The Social History of an Indonesian Town*. Greenwood, Conn., 1975 (reprint of Boston: M.I.T. Press, 1965).

_____. *Agricultural Involution: The Process of Ecological Change in Indonesia*. Berkeley: University of California Press, 1976.

Gibson, J. 'Foreign Enterprise and Production Sharing'. In T. K. Tan (ed.), 1967.

Glassburner, B. (ed.). *The Economy of Indonesia: Selected Readings*. Ithaca: Cornell University Press, 1971.

_____. 'Economic Policy-Making in Indonesia, 1950–1957'. In B. Glassburner (ed.), 1971. (1971*a*)

————. 'Indonesian Economic Policy after Sukarno'. In B. Glassburner (ed.), 1971. (1971b)

————. 'Indonesia's New Economic Policy and its Sociopolitical Implications'. In K. D. Jackson and W. Pye (eds), 1978.

————. 'Political Economy and the Suharto Regime'. BIES 14, 3 (1978).

———— and M. Poffenberger. 'Survey of Recent Developments'. BIES 19, 3 (1983).

Gray, C. 'Survey of Recent Developments'. BIES 18, 3 (1982).

Grenville, S. 'Commercial Banks and Money Creation', BIES 13, 1 (1977).

————. 'Monetary Policy and the Formal Financial Sector'. In A. Booth and P. McCawley (eds), 1981.

Halim, B. 'Industrial Expansion in Indonesia During the Five Year Plan'. Indonesia (Jakarta) 7 (1971).

Hambali, S. 'Semen: Profil Industri Yang Menguntungkan'. Eksekutif (May 1981).

Hawkins, E. Case Studies of Indonesian Business Firms. Jogjakarta: Gaja Mada University, 1959.

Hill, H. 'Survey of Recent Developments'. BIES 20, 2 (1984).

Hinkson, J. 'Rural Development and Class Contradiction in Java'. JCA 5, 3 (1975).

Hoemardani, Soedjono. 'The Decline of National Companies'. Kompas 3 December 1973.

————. 'Indonesia-Japan Relations in the Future'. Suara Karya, 23, 24 and 26 January 1974 (USPRT).

Husken, F. 'Landlords, Sharecroppers and Agricultural Labourers: Changing Labour Relations in Rural Java'. JCA 9, 2 (1979).

Indonesia Research and Development Co. Financial Directory of Indonesia. Jakarta, 1980.

Institute of Developing Economies. Japanese Direct Investment in Indonesia. Joint Research Program Series, No. 9. Tokyo, 1978.

IBRD. World Bank Report, 1980. Annex 5, Indonesia: Selected Issues of Industrial Developments and Trade Strategy: Direct Foreign Investment in Indonesia. 1981.

———— Indonesia: Policies and Prospects for Economic Growth and Transformation. East Asia and Pacific Regional office, 26 April 1984.

Jackson, K. D. and Pye, Lucian (eds). Political Power and Communication in Indonesia. Berkeley: University of California Press, 1978.

————. 'Bureaucratic Polity: A Theoretical Framework for the Analysis of Power and Communications in Indonesia'. In Jackson and Pye (eds), 1978.

Jessop, R. 'Recent Theories of the Capitalist State'. Cambridge Journal of Economics 1 (1977).

JETRO (Japan External Trade Research Organisation). List of Japanese Investment Projects in Indonesia. Jakarta, 1981.

Joedono, S. B. 'Partisipasi Pengusaha Nasional Ekonomi Lemah'. In Mangkusuwondo, Suhadi., Joedono S. B., Kuntjoro Jakti, Dorojatun (eds), Prospek Perekonomian Indonesia. Jakarta: LPEM, Fakultas Ekonomi Universitas Indonesia, 1973.

Kahin, G. Nationalism and Revolution in Indonesia. Ithaca: Cornell University Press, 1952.

Kamar Dagang dan Industri dan CSIS. Seminar Strategi Pembinaan Pengusaha Swasta Nasional, 29–31 Mei, 1975. Jakarta: CSIS, 1975.

Kamar Dagang dan Industri. *Hasil Lengkap: Diskusi Peranan Pengusaha Nasional Dalama Pembangunan Ekonomi Untuk Mewujudkan Kesatuan Bangsa*. Jakarta, 11 and 12 June 1975.

Kwik, Kian Gie. 'Indonesianisasi Perusahaan Asing atau Multinasionalisasi Karyawan Indonesia'. *Kompas*, 18 January 1974.

──────. 'Foreign Capital and Economic Domination'. *Indonesian Quarterly*, April 1975.

──────. 'Non-Pribumi, Dominasi Ekonomi dan Keadilan Sosial'. *Kompas*, 23 June 1978.

Lane, M. 'Voices of Dissent in Indonesia'. *Arena* 61 (1982).

Lev, D. *The Transition to Guided Democracy: Indonesian Politics, 1957–59*. Monograph Series, Modern Indonesia Project. Ithaca: Cornell University, 1966.

Levine, D. 'History and Social Structure in the Study of Contemporary Indonesia'. *Indonesia* 7 (1969).

Leys, C. 'Underdevelopment and Dependency: Critical Notes'. *JCA* 7, 1 (1977).

Lubis, T. M. 'Pleidoi Bagi Pengusaha Non-Pribumi'. *Prisma* 4 (1981).

────── and Abdullah, F. *Langit Masih Mendung: Laporan Keadaan Hak-Hak Asasi Manusia de Indonesia 1980*. Jakarta: Lembaga Bantuan Hukum, 1981.

Luckham, R. 'Militarism: Class, Force and International Conflict'. *Institute of Development Studies Bulletin* (Sussex University) 9, 1 (1977).

McCawley, P. 'Some Consequences of the Pertamina Crisis in Indonesia'. *Journal of Southeast Asian Studies* 9, 1 (1978).

──────.*Industrialization in Indonesia*. Occasional Paper No. 13. Canberra: Development Studies Centre, Australian National University, 1979.

──────. 'The Growth of the Industrial Sector'. In A. Booth and P. McCawley (eds), 1981.

──────. 'Survey of Recent Developments'. *BIES* 19, 1 (1983).

McDonald, H. *Suharto's Indonesia*. Blackburn: Fontana, 1980.

MacDougall, J. A. 'Patterns of Military Control in the Indonesian Higher Central Bureaucracy'. *Indonesia* 33 (1982).

Mackie, J. A. C. 'The Political Economy of Guided Democracy'. *Australian Outlook* 13 (1959).

──────. 'The Commission of Four Report on Corruption'. *BIES* 6, 3 (1970).

──────. 'The Indonesian Economy, 1950–1963'. In B. Glassburner (ed.), 1971.

────── (ed.). *The Chinese in Indonesia: Five Essays*. Melbourne: Nelson, 1976.

──────. 'Anti-Chinese Outbreaks in Indonesia'. In J. A. C. Mackie (ed.), 1976.

McVey, R. (ed.). *Indonesia*. New Haven: H.R.A.F., 1963.

──────. 'The Post-Revolutionary Transformation of the Indonesian Army' (Parts I & II). *Indonesia* 11 (1971) and 13 (1972).

──────. 'The Beamtenstaat in Indonesia'. In B. Anderson and A. Kahn (eds.), 1982.

Marwadi, H. A. Chalid. *Pemandangan Umum Fraksi Persatuan Pembangunan atas Pidato Pertanggungjawaban Presiden Mandataris MPR*. Jakarta, 15 March 1978.

Moertopo, A. *The Acceleration and Modernization of 25 Years' Development*. Jakarta: CSIS, 1973.

————. *Strategi Politik Nasional.* Jakarta: CSIS, 1974.

Mortimer, R., 'Class, Social Cleavage and Indonesian Communism'. *Indonesia* 8 (1969).

———— (ed.). *Showcase State: the Illusion of Indonesia's Accelerated Modernisation.* Sydney: Angus & Robertson, 1973.

————. 'Indonesia: Growth or Development'. In R. Mortimer (ed.), 1973.

Nasution, Anwar. 'The Indonesian Economy: Problems of Adjustment to Global Recession and Lower Oil Prices'. *Indonesian Quarterly* 12, 2 (1984).

Nishihara, M. *The Japanese and Sukarno's Indonesia.* Honolulu: University of Hawaii Press, 1967.

Nitisastro, Wijoyo (ed.). *Masalah-masalah Ekonomi dan Faktor-faktor Ipolsos.* Jakarta: LEKNAS, 1965.

———— 'Persoalan-Persoalan Ekonomis Teknis dan Ekonomis Politis Dalam Menanggulangi Masalah-Masalah Ekonomi'. In W. Nitisastro (ed.), 1965.

Oey Hong, Lee (ed.). *Indonesia after the 1971 Elections.* Hull Monographs on Southeast Asia. London: Oxford University Press, 1974.

O'Malley, W. Indonesia in the Great Depression: A Study of East Sumatra and Jogjakarta in the 1930s. Ph.D. thesis, Cornell University, 1977.

Onghokham. The Residency of Madiun: Priyayi and Peasant in the Nineteenth Century. Ph.D. thesis, Yale University, 1975; Ann Arbor, University Microfilms, 1978.

Paauw, D. 'From Colonial to Guided Economy'. In R. McVey (ed.), 1963.

Palmer I. *The Indonesian Economy Since 1965.* London: Cass, 1978.

———— and Castles, L. 'The Textile Industry'. *BIES* 2 (1965).

Panglaykim, J. *An Indonesian Experience, Its State Trading Corporations.* Jakarta: Fakultas Ekonomi, Universitas Indonesia, 1967.

————. 'Marketing Organisation in Transition'. *BIES* 9 (1968).

————. 'Economic Development, Multinational Corporation and National Integrated Units'. In *The World of Strategy and the Foreign Policy of Nations.* Jakarta: CSIS, 1973.

————. 'Struktur Domestik dalam Interdependensi Ekonomi Dunia'. *Analisa Masalah-masalah Internasional* 2, 12 (1973).

————. *Persoalan Masa Kini: Perusahaan Multinasional.* Jakarta: CSIS, 1974.

————. 'Organisasi Bisnis dalam Rangka Pembangunan Ekonomi di Asia Tenggara'. In J. Panglaykim, 1974.

————. *Indonesia's Economic and Business Relations with ASEAN and Japan.* Jakarta: CSIS, 1977.

———— and Thomas, K. 'The Five Year Plan'. *BIES* 5, 2 (1969).

Pauker, G. 'Indonesia: The Age of Reason?'. *Asian Survey* 13, 2 (1968).

Polomka, P. *Indonesia Since Sukarno.* Melbourne: Pelican, 1971.

Probosutedjo. Pengarahan Bapak Probosutedjo Dalam Temu Wicara Tanggal 19 April 1984. Unpublished address, Jakarta, 1984.

Ransome, D. 'The Berkeley Mafia and the Indonesian Massacre'. *Ramparts* 9 (1970).

Rice, R. and Hill, H. 'Survey of Recent Developments'. *BIES* 13, 2 (1977).

Rieffel, A. and Wirjasaputra, A. 'Military Enterprises'. *BIES* 7, 2 (1972).

Robinson, W. 'Imperialism, Dependency and Peripheral Industrialisation: the Case of Japan in Indonesia'. In R. Robison and R. Higgott (eds), *Southeast Asia: Essays in the Political Economy of Structural Change.* London: Routledge, 1985.

Robison, R. Capitalism and the Bureaucratic State in Indonesia'. Ph.D. thesis, Sydney University, 1977.
———. 'Towards a Class Analysis of the Indonesian Military Bureaucratic State'. *Indonesia* 25 (1978).
———. 'Culture, Politics, and Economy in the Political History of the New order'. *Indonesia* 31 (1981).
———. 'The Transformation of the State in Indonesia'. *Bulletin of Concerned Asian Scholars* 14, 1 (1982).
Rocamora, J. Nationalism in Search of an Ideology: the Indonesian Nationalist Party, 1946–65. Ph.D. thesis, Cornell University, 1974.
Roeder, O. G. *Who's Who in Indonesia*. Jakarta: Guning Agung, 1970.
Rosendale, P. 'Survey of Recent Developments'. *BIES* 20, 1 (1984).
Rudner, M. 'The Indonesian Military and Economic Policy'. *Modern Asian Studies* 10, 2 (1976).
Sadli, M. 'Structural and Operational Aspects of Public (especially industrial) Enterprises in Indonesia'. *Ekonomi dan Keuangan* 13, 5/6 (1960).
———. 'Indonesian Economic Development'. *Conference Board Record* 6 (1969).
———. 'Development Policies for the Private Sector'. In Fakultas Ekonomi Universitas Indonesia, 1970.
———. 'Boeke's Theory of Dualistic Economies'. In B. Glassburner (ed.), 1971.
Salim, E. 'Masalah Ekonomi yang Timbul (Atan Ada) Sekitar Coup G305'. In W. Nitisastro, 1965.
———. 'Kearah Demokrasi Ekonomi'. *Indonesia* (Jakarta) 5 (1970).
———. *Tulisan-tulisan*. Jakarta: Bappenas, 1971.
Sarbini, S. 'Non Economic Aspects of Development'. In Fakultas Ekonomi Universitas Indonesia, 1970.
———. 'Some Notes on the Perspectives of Long Range Development Planning in Indonesia'. *Indonesia* (Jakarta) 22 (1973).
Schmitt, H. 'Foreign Capital and Social Conflict in Indonesia'. *Economic Development and Cultural Change* 10, 3 (1962).
———. 'Post-Colonial Politics: A Suggested Interpretation of the Indonesian Experience'. *The Australian Journal of Politics and History* 9, 2 (1963).
Schrieke, B. *Indonesian Sociological Studies*, Parts I and II. The Hague: van Hoeve, 1966 and 1957.
Short, K. *Australian Manufacturing Companies in Indonesia: A Case Study*. Research Monograph No. 7, Transnational Corporations Research Project. Sydney: University of Sydney, 1977.
Silalahi, P. 'Perimbangan Modal Swasta Nasional di Indonesia'. *Analisa Masalah-Masalah Internasional* 3, 5 (1974).
———. 'Perekonomian Indonesia dalam Repelita IV'. *Perspectif Repelita IV*. Jakarta: CSIS, 1984.
Sitsen, P. *Industrial Development of the Netherlands Indies*. New York: Council of the Institute of Pacific Relations, 1942.
Soehoed, A. R. 'Manufacturing in Indonesia'. *BIES* 8 (1967).
———. 'Commodities and Viable Economic Sectors - A Possible Basis for Development Planning'. *Indonesian Quarterly* 5, 1 (1977).
———. Japan and the Development of the Indonesian Manufacturing Sector. Paper given at the Seminar on Industrialisation in the Framework of National Development. Jakarta: CSIS, 1981.

————. 'Industrial Development During Repelita III'. *Indonesian Quarterly* 10, 4 (1982).

Soesastro, H. 'Repelita IV: Ekonomi Politik Target Pertumbuhan Lima Persen'. *Perspectif Repelita IV*. Jakarta: CSIS, 1984.

Sondang, P.N. '100 Tokoh Milyarder Indonesia: Apa dan Siapa Mereka Itu?. *Expo* 1 and 2 (4.1.84, 18.1.84).

Student Council of the Institute of Technology, Bandung. 'White Book of the 1978 Students' Struggle'. *Indonesia* 25 (1978).

Sudjatmoko. International Relations in a New Era - Japan and the Economic Development of Asia. Paper presented to an Academic Symposium, Sophia University, Tokyo, October 1973.

Suhartono, R. B. 'Industrial Development in Indonesia'. *Indonesian Quarterly* 8, 1 (1980).

Suhartoyo. Penanaman Modal dan Industrialisasi. Paper given at Seminar on Industrialisation in the Framework of National Development. Jakarta: CSIS, 1981.

Sutowo, Ibnu. 'Saya Tidak Pernah Berfikir Ingin Jadi Dirut Seumur Hidup'. *Tempo*, 17.1.76.

Sutter, J. *Indonesianisasi: Politics in a Changing Economy, 1940–1955*. Data Paper No. 36 (4 Vols.) Ithaca: Department of Fareastern Studies, Cornell University, 1959.

Tan, T. K. (ed.). *Sukarno's Guided Indonesia*. Brisbane: Jacaranda, 1967.

————. 'Sukarnian Economics'. In T. K. Tan (ed.), 1967.

Thee, Kian Wie. 'Japanese and American Direct Investment in Indonesian Manufacturing Compared', *Ekonomi dan Keuangan Indonesia* 32, 1 (1984).

————. *Regulating Foreign Investment in Indonesian Manufacturing*. (forthcoming).

Thomas, K. and Panglaykim, J. 'The New Order and the Economy'. *Indonesia* (Cornell) 3 (1967).

————. *Indonesia – the Effects of Past Policies and President Suharto's Plans for the Future*. Melbourne: CEDA, 1973.

Trimberger, K. 'A Theory of Elite Revolutions'. *Studies in Comparative International Development* 7, 3 (1972).

Tsurumi, Y. 'Japanese Investments in Indonesia: Ownership, Technology Transfer, and Political Conflict'. In G. Papanek (ed.), *The Indonesian Economy*. New York: Praeger, 1980.

United States Economic Survey Team to Indonesia. *Indonesia: Perspective and Proposals for United States Economic Aid*. New Haven: Southeast Asian Studies Centre, Yale University, 1963.

van Dijk, C. 'The Hariman Siregar Trial'. *Review of Indonesian and Malay Affairs* 9, 1 (1975).

van der Kroef, J. 'Indonesian's Economic Future'. *Pacific Affairs* 32, 1 (1959).

van Leur, J. C. *Indonesian Trade and Society: Essays in Indonesian Social and Economic History*. The Hague: van Hoeve, 1956.

van Niel, R. *The Emergence of the Modern Indonesian Elite*. The Hague, van Hoeve, 1960.

Ward, K. 'Indonesia's Modernisation: Ideology and Practice'. In Mortimer (ed.), 1973.

————. *The 1971 Election in Indonesia: An East Java Case Study*. Monash Papers on Southeast Asia, No. 2. Melbourne: Centre of Southeast Asian Studies, Monash University, 1974.

Wertheim, W. *Indonesian Society in Transition: A Study of Social Change.* 2nd rev. ed. The Hague: van Hoeve, 1959.

Wibisono, C. 'Saham "Pri" dan "Non-Pri"'. *Tempo*, 14.3.81. (1981*a*)

_____. 'Antara Mitos dan Faktor'. *Prisma* 4 (1981*b*).

Wijaya, F. (et al). 'Growth, Capital Formation and Sources of Funding'. *Prisma* 14 (September 1979).

Index

354, 360; and loan capital, 276; production sharing, 79–80; removal of controls on private, 137; Spanish, 305, 312; Swiss, 362; United States, 8–9, 156–8, 295, 312
Investment priority scales (DSP), 184–6, 188, 273, 354, 382, 386, 387
Ippilo, P.T., 284
Irda, P.T., 270 n.25
Irian Bhakti, P.T., 348
Iron, 126, 221. See also Steel
Irosteel, P.T., 341
Irrigation, 141
ISC, P.T., 90, 330, 332, 352, 354
Iskaq Tjokrohadisoerjo, 44, 45, 49
Isman (General), 325, 360

JAKARTA, government of 55, 90, 262, 306, 386; Governor of, 355
Jakarta Motors, P.T., 332, 352, 354
Jauw Tjong Kie, 287
Japanese: attacks on business premises of, 327; Prime Minister's visit (1974), 164–5. See also Investment
Jassin (General), 269 n.12
Jatiluhur dam project, 277
Jaya Bhakti, P.T., 96, 252
Jaya group, 298, 300
Joesoef, Moh. (Joesoef Gading), 290, 292, 350–1, 352–3, 355, 358
Joint ventures, 144, 187, 297, 324, 337, 350, 395; with Chinese, 191, 272 ff, 334, 339; and domestic capitalist class, 191–7; and indigenous capital, 334–42, 363–4; with Japanese, 187, 264, 279, 293–4, 337, 339, 359, 370 n.62; with military, 251–68; and regulations, 167, 169, 183, 188–91, 315, 331, 349–50, 354, 363–4
Jonosiswono, Benny, 343–4
Jukardi Odang, 333

KAISER ALUMINIUM agency, 53, 331
Karana Line, P.T., 260, 279, 346
Karim, Abdul, 49
Kabele Asia Nusantara, P.T., 299, 306
Kadin (Chamber of Commerce), 61, 225, 252, 263, 318, 325, 333, 365–6, 390, 396
Kancil Mas., P.T., 93, 331

Kang Ho (Sukanto, T.), 283
Kang King Tat. See Soetomo, Yos
Kapni (Indonesian National Businessmen Action Front), 324
Karkam, P.T., 91
Kartasasmita, Ginanjar, 387
Kartika Ratna, 240–1
Karya Sakti Utama, P.T., 281, 290
Kasworo, BRM, 340, 341
Kayaba, P.T., 290, 294
Kayumas, P.T., 261
Kedaung Subur, P.T., 285
Kensi (All-Indonesian National Economic Congress), 60–1, 86, 325, 367
Klochner Industries Anlagen, 240
KNIP (National Advisory Committee), 54, 61
Kodak franchise, 289, 291
Kodam, 97, 259, 265
Kodim, 97, 259, 265
Kolognas, 229
Kompas, 244
Konsultasi Pembangunan group, 359, 360–1
Kopkamtib, 164
Korea, South, 310, 347; as model, 379, 396
Kosgoro, 325; Building, 360; group, 359, 360
Kostrad, 97, 227, 229, 232, 250, 259, 301, 302, 303, 306, 314, 348, 355; business group, 262–3, 325
KOTI, 69
Kowara, Eddy, 51, 325, 335–6, 365, 366
Kowara, Indra, 343, 347
Krakatau Steel, P.T., 152, 153, 181, 219, 223, 237, 238, 240, 243, 284, 305, 314
Krakatau Cold Rolling Mill, P.T., 223, 300, 301
Krama Yudha, P.T., 330, 334, 354, 355, 358, 369 n.48
Kretek industry, 23, 26, 28, 35 n.65, 57, 58, 85, 144, 282, 285, 296, 302, 384. See also Cloves
Krupp agency, 54
Kusmuljono, R.M., 51, 54, 55, 90, 332
Kussarjono, 54
Kwarta Daya, P.T., 356
Kwee Hian Long, 240

424INDEX

Tan Tjoe Hing. *See* Hendra Rahardja
Tapes, 340, 341
Tarumatex, P.T., 303
Taxation, 125, 367; concessions, 186, 329; corporate, 383; incentives, 225–6, 382
Tax farming, 19–20, 26
Tea, 51, 99 n.15
Technocrats, 127 n.6; economic policies of, 39, 110–11, 122, 132–47, 156–8, 186, 243–5, 258, 326. *See also* Bappenas. CSIS
Teijin petrochemical company, 355
Teknik Umum, P.T., 335–6
Tekstil, P.T., 93
Telecommunications, 152, 218, 283
Telkom, P.T., 218, 242
Textiles: exports, 147, 397 n.17; foreign investment in, 164, 166, 170, 200, 325, 359; imports, 8, 21–2, 52, 58–9, 82, 100 n.37, 185; and indigenous capital, 331, 336, 337, 340, 341, 359; and ISI, 141, 143–4, 185, 289, 388; and petrochemicals, 221; production, 24–5, 28, 53, 57, 82–3, 85, 88, 89, 93, 114, 126, 140, 142, 179, 222, 225, 279, 280, 282, 283, 287, 297, 298, 303, 328; and state, 40–1, 43–4
Thahir, Haji, 240–1, 243
Thahir, Ibrahim, 241
Thahir, M., 298
Tiga Roda, P.T., 346
Timah, P.N., 217, 227, 228, 241, 242, 236
Timber, 79, 177, 179, 221, 279, 280, 286, 331, 362, 378, 382. *See also* Forestry; Logging; Paper
Tin, 8, 10, 79, 99 n.15, 217, 298, 346
Tirtajaya, Petrus, Ir., 340, 341
Tirtoadisoerjo, Raden Mas, 28
Tirtomuljono, Bambang, 241, 298, 301
Tirtosudiro, Achmad (General), 229, 231, 252
Titiheru, 89
Tjai Ko Tjiang (Th. D. Rachmat), 285
Tjan, Harry, 107, 157, 158
Tjia Hong Tiong, 282
Tjia Kian Liong. *See* Soerjadjaja, William

Tjokroaminoto, Omar Said, 28
Tjokrosaputra, 287
Tobacco, 9, 10, 32 n.15, 99 n.15, 340
Tokyo Senpaku Kaisha, 67 n.40, 93
Tong Djoe, 351, 354
Tongkangmas, P.T., 352, 354
Topik, 157
Tourism, 142, 200, 332, 363
Towage, 254, 266
Town & City, P.T., 291, 292, 352
Tractors, 337. *See also* Heavy equipment
Trade, 40, 185, 200, 213, 220, 273, 278, 279, 291, 298, 301, 308, 312, 332, 337, 341, 344, 346, 350, 353, 361; Department of, 47
Trakindo Utama, P. T., 269 n.7
Transport, 28, 184, 213, 273, 328; bus, 42; trucking, 261. *See also* Air; Shipping
Travel companies, 353, 354
Triatmotjo, Bambang, 343, 347
Tridaya Cement, P.T., 362
Tridaya Manunggal Perkasa, P.T., 300, 304–5
TRIP (student army organisation), 360
Tri Usaha Bhakti, P.T., 252, 259, 261–2, 331, 353
TUB, P.T., 261, 262, 339
Tunas, P.T., 351, 352
Tusin Omar, 51, 83, 89, 286, 367 n.3
Tyres, 9, 90, 279, 287, 298

UDATIN, P.T., 289, 330, 333
Umar Wirahadikusuma (General), 393
United States: Economic Survey Team, 74; State Department, 134. *See also* Investment
University of Indonesia, Cibulan Discussion Group, 163
Unrest: industrial, 384; social, 124, 125, 166, 168
Usindo, P.N., 40, 73

VALUE-ADDED, 143, 144, 177, 179, 200, 382–3
Velodome, N.V., 55
Veterans Affairs, Department of, 83
Veterans' associations, 360

Wahana, P. T., 334
Wahana Bhakti Utama, P.T., 261
Wanandi, Sofjan. *See* Liem Bian
 Koen
Wardhana, Ali, 127 n.6, 384, 387
Wardley-Summa, P.T., 291, 295
Warehousing, 93, 254, 261, 266
Waringin, P.T., 298, 301, 302, 305
Waringin, Kencana, P.T., 298, 301,
 344, 346
Wasesa Line, P.T., 260, 279
Waskita Karya, P.T., 227
Weapons, 370 n.56
Weaving, 23, 144. *See also* Textiles
Weber, Max, 391, 393–4
Welfare, social, 141
Westinghouse agency, 53, 89, 289,
 331
West Java Contracting and Engi-
 neering, P.T., 264
Weyerhauser corporation, 188, 262,
 270 n.25
Wheat, 231, 233. *See also* Flour
Wholesaling, 26
Wibowo, Paulus, 338, 339, 341
Widjojo Nitisastro, 127 n.6, 384,
 387
Wijaya, Endang (Yap Eng Kui),
 228
Wijaya, Indra, 284–5, 313

Wilopo (Prime Minister), 39, 54, 65
 n.4
Wirontono (Mr), 233
Wisma Kartika, P.T., 265
Wisma Metropolitan, P.T., 298, 306
World Bank, 138, 217, 385, 394;
 Reports, 126, 377–81, 391. *See*
 also IBRD

Yamaha Indonesia Motor, P.T.,
 281
Yance Lim (Yani Haryanto), 283
Yap Swie Kie (Sutopo Jananto), 279
Yap Tek Ciang. *See* Hartono, Mul-
 yono
Yayasan: Dharma Putra (YDP),
 232, 252, 259, 262, 302, 325, 330,
 334; Harapan Kita, 232, 343, 344,
 345; Kartika Chandra, 343, 344;
 Kartika Jaya, 260, 344, 345; Kar-
 tika Siliwangi, 264; Kopra (Copra
 Foundation), 43, 62; Marhaen,
 48; Persediaan, Perindustrian, 49;
 Trikora, 262, 343, 345
Yuddhistira, P.T., 333
Yunus (General), 353

Zachri, Achmad, 274
Zahiruddin, Usman, 51
Zoro Corporation, P.T., 50